SO FAR FROM HOME

SO FAR
FROM HOME

RUSSIANS IN EARLY CALIFORNIA

EDITED BY GLENN J. FARRIS

Heyday, Berkeley, California
Santa Clara University, Santa Clara, California

This California Legacy book was published by Heyday and Santa Clara University.

© 2012 by Glenn J. Farris

Library of Congress Cataloging-in-Publication Data
So far from home : Russians in early California / edited by Glenn J. Farris.
    p. cm.
"California Legacy book."
Includes bibliographical references and index.
ISBN 978-1-59714-184-0 (pbk. : alk. paper)
1. Fort Ross (Calif.)--History--Sources. 2. Russians--California--Fort Ross--History--Sources. I. Farris, Glenn J.
F864.S6425 2012
305.891'71079418--dc23
                              2012018987

Church photo: "Orthodox Church at Fort Ross," July 31, 2010, Fort Ross Celebration of Russian America. Photo by Franco Folini. This file is licensed under the Creative Commons Attribution-Share Alike 2.0 Generic license. Map image: "Section of Coast of Northwest America from Fort Ross to Point Great Bodega [Tomales Point]," 1817 (corrected 1819). Original in the State Naval Archive, St. Petersburg, Russia.
Cover Design: Rebecca LeGates
Interior Design/Typesetting: Leigh Mclellan Design
Printing and Binding: Worzalla, Stevens Point, WI

So Far from Home was published by Heyday and Santa Clara University. Orders, inquiries, and correspondence should be addressed to:

Heyday
P.O. Box 9145, Berkeley, CA 94709
(510) 549-3564, Fax (510) 549-1889
www.heydaybooks.com

10 9 8 7 6 5 4 3 2 1

CONTENTS

INTRODUCTION   *1*

1

HIGH ANXIETY ABOUT RUSSIANS IN THE
NORTH PACIFIC AND SPAIN'S STIMULUS TO
SETTLE ALTA CALIFORNIA, CA. 1768–1769   *7*

Junta held at San Blas to plan the occupation of
Monterey Bay (May 16, 1768)   *9*

2

SEA OTTER POACHING BY YANKEE SHIPMASTERS
USING RUSSIANS AND ALASKAN NATIVES,
STARTING IN 1803   *11*

3

VISIT BY REZANOV IN 1806 TO OBTAIN
SUPPLIES FOR ALASKA: THE START OF A
SERIES OF RUSSIAN VISITS TO CALIFORNIA   *17*

Report from Rezanov to Rumiantsev concerning trade
and other relations between Russian America, Spanish
California, and Hawaii (June 17, 1806)   *20*

Langsdorff on the Rezanov–Argüello romance (1806)   *25*

Langsdorff's narrative of Rezanov's voyage
to Nueva California (1806)   *28*

Fr. Señán's reaction to Rezanov's visit (1806)   *41*

Follow-up letter from Rumiantsev to Stroganov
suggesting the value of mutual trade between
California and Russian America (April 20, 1808)   *42*

4

THE RUSSIAN AMERICAN COMPANY
MOVES INTO CALIFORNIA   *45*

Directions from Baranov to Kuskov as to his expedition
to California (October 14, 1808)   *48*

Report by Kuskov to Baranov of his expedition to
"New Albion" (October 5/17, 1809)   *58*

Report from Luis Argüello to Governor Arrillaga
(February 16, 1809)   *61*

5

TARAKANOV AND CHIEFS IÓLLO AND VALLÍ:ÉLA
AND THE NEGOTIATIONS FOR FORT ROSS   *63*

6

CONSTRUCTION AND EARLY YEARS
OF FORT ROSS, 1812–1815   *75*

Fort Ross in its first year under Kuskov (post 1831)   *76*

Luis Argüello's report to Governor Arrillaga of
Lieutenant Moraga's visit to Fort Ross (September 7, 1812)   *78*

Report of Gabriel Moraga and Gervasio Argüello's visit to
Fort Ross (1814)   *80*

Kuskov's response to Governor Arrillaga's letter about
the status of Fort Ross (1814) — 82

Equipment and supplies sent to Fort Ross (1812–1815) — 84

7

TRADE WITH CALIFORNIA BY THE RUSSIAN
AMERICAN COMPANY, PARTICULARLY KHLEBNIKOV — 87

Letters from Fr. Gil y Taboada to Khlebnikov (1825–1831) — 90

Khlebnikov's journal (July 18/29, 1824) — 96

8

STORY OF THE BRIGANTINE *LYDIA/IL'MENA* — 97

Letter to Kuskov from Khlebnikov from the site of the
wreck of the *Il'mena* (1820) — 101

9

RUSSIAN ROUND-THE-WORLD ADVENTURERS
VISIT CALIFORNIA, 1822–1824 — 103

Schabelski describes a visit of the Russian warship *Apollon*
to California (1822–1823) — 106

Zavalishin's account of a visit to California aboard
the *Kreiser* (1823–1824) — 114

The Russian-built "Kanaka Hotel," from *Two Years Before
the Mast,* by Richard Henry Dana, Jr. (1840) — 123

10

RUSSIAN AND KODIAK DESERTERS,
CAPTIVES, AND MARTYRS: BOLCOFF,
EGOROV, AND ST. PETER THE ALEUT — 125

11

TRIPS UP THE RUSSIAN (SLAVIANKA) RIVER

(1820 AND 1833)   *139*

Khlebnikov on the Russian River (July 20/31, 1820)   *140*

Wrangell on the Russian River (September 1833)   *141*

12

BOTANISTS ON RUSSIAN EXPEDITIONS TO

CALIFORNIA IN 1816 AND 1824   *145*

Alice Eastwood on the botanical collections of Chamisso

and Eschscholtz in California (1944)   *146*

The collections of Eschscholtz (1826)   *148*

Excerpts from Chamisso's journal (1816)   *150*

Fauna named by or for Russians (1984)   *152*

13

THE TRANSFORMATION OF FORT ROSS'S

PRIMARY FUNCTION FROM FUR HUNTING

TO AGRICULTURE AND LIGHT INDUSTRY   *153*

Governor Wrangell's report concerning a visit to Fort Ross (1833)   *156*

Kostromitinov's report to the headquarters of the Russian

American Company (July 31/August 10, 1833)   *168*

Chernykh and the Scottish thresher at Fort Ross (1836–1841)   *171*

Chernykh's report on agriculture in California (1841)   *175*

14

RUSSIAN INTERACTION WITH THE

NEIGHBORING INDIANS   *183*

Kostromitinov's observations on the Indians of

Upper California (1839)   *186*

Kashaya accounts of life at Fort Ross (1964)   *197*

15

FOREIGN VISITORS TO BODEGA BAY AND FORT ROSS   *211*

Canonigo Fernández de San Vicente, accompanied by
Fr. Payeras (1822)   *213*

Auguste Bernard Duhaut-Cilly (1828)   *218*

John Work, Michel Laframboise, and the Hudson's Bay
Company Brigade (1833)   *226*

Kashaya versions of the Hudson's Bay Company Brigade
at Fort Ross (1833)   *229*

Cyrille Pierre-Théodore Laplace's visit to Bodega Bay and
Fort Ross (1839)   *235*

Eugene Duflot de Mofras's travels on the Pacific Coast (1841)   *268*

16

THE RUSSIANS LEAVE FORT ROSS   *281*

A report on the economics of Fort Ross and the decision
to sell (1842)   *284*

Inventories of sale for Fort Ross, Bodega Bay, and
neighboring ranchos (1841)   *286*

Il'ya Gavrilovich Voznesenskii, Russian naturalist and
ethnographer (1840–1841)   *293*

Sandels's description of a visit to post-Russian Fort Ross (1843)   *296*

17

RUSSIAN REDISCOVERY OF FORT ROSS   *301*

Trip to Fort Ross by Bishop Nikolai (March 2/14, 1897)   *303*

18

THE ENDURING ROMANCE OF FORT ROSS   *309*

Excerpt from "Natalie Ivanhoff" (1902)   *311*

19

STORY OF THE "KODIAK BELL"

AT MISSION SAN FERNANDO REY   *315*

A Mysterious Bell (1927)   *317*

20

FORT ROSS IN THE COLD WAR, 1950–1951   *321*

EPILOGUE   *325*

Acknowledgments   *331*

Notes   *333*

Glossary   *345*

References Cited   *347*

Index   *359*

About the Author   *369*

INTRODUCTION

"THE RUSSIANS ARE COMING, THE RUSSIANS ARE COMING!" Although this clarion call to arms is now most associated with the eponymous 1966 movie starring Alan Arkin as Russian submarine lieutenant Rozanov, it underscored the intense level of anxiety that stemmed from the Western world's Cold War fears of Soviet Russian imperialism. However, this worry about Russian invaders was not new to America. Two centuries before the film and the political atmosphere that inspired it, the Spanish Empire of the 1760s was so concerned about the security of its Pacific coast territory known as "California" that it put into action the long delayed exploration and colonization of Upper (Alta) California, finally completing the settlement of northern New Spain begun by Francisco Vásquez de Coronado in 1540.

Before this final settlement and for several centuries after the Spanish conquest of the New World, the Pacific Ocean was effectively a Spanish lake. For the most part, the rich Manila galleons could cruise between the Mexican Pacific port of Acapulco and Spanish-controlled Manila, in the Philippines, without need of the convoys required to accompany Spanish treasure fleets across the Atlantic. (Of course, there was an occasional burp, like the unwelcome incursion of England's Sir Francis Drake in 1579, however, this was something of an aberration. Although Drake left his mark on the land in assigning the name "Nova Albion" to the portion of the Pacific coast north of the Spanish possessions, more than two centuries passed before the English actively sought to colonize parts of the west coast of America.) When Spaniard Sebastían de Vizcaíno was sent to map the Pacific coast in 1602 and 1603, his mission was particularly to scout out support bases for the returning Manila galleons, which usually made landfall around Cape Mendocino and then sailed south along the coast, returning to Acapulco.

Although the Spanish Empire was in major control of the South Pacific Ocean (often referred to as "the Southern Ocean"), the North Pacific was left to the Russians, who had pushed across the vast stretches of Siberia in search of fur-bearing animals. Arriving at the Pacific shores of Russia, they then set out in small boats to explore the Aleutian Islands. The Russian tsar Peter I sent Danish explorer Vitus Bering and Russian Aleksei Chirikov to search out sea routes that might link ports in northern Russia with the Pacific. On the heels of their second expedition, in 1741, during which Alaska was "discovered," the Russian fur hunters spread across the newly named Bering Strait and established themselves in the islands adjacent to the Alaskan mainland. Kodiak Island was a principal base and became the first administrative capital of Alaska, although it was eclipsed by the port of New Archangel (Sitka) after 1804.

On January 23, 1768, Spain's King Charles III sent to the Viceroy of Mexico, Carlos Francisco de Croix, an order warning of Russian movements into the North Pacific. Acting on this directive, on May 16, 1768, Visitador General Joseph de Gálvez convened a council (*junta*) at the Pacific naval base of San Blas. Members organized a joint overland and naval expedition starting from Lower (Baja) California, the goal of which was to rediscover the bay of Monterey first identified by Vizcaíno some 166 years earlier, and to establish there a military and ecclesiastical base to provide support for the Manila galleons arriving on the coast. It was also meant to create a military presence (i.e., to fend off other nations who might want to claim California) and to develop a civilian population based on Christianized natives as well as colonists from New Spain. Unlike other areas of the New World that had been claimed by the Spanish, there was initially little or no expectation that wealth would be gained from this land in the form of gold and silver. On the other hand, the Spanish did come to realize that another form of wealth, "soft gold," was available on the coast in the form of valuable sea otter pelts. These pelts were especially prized because they were one of the few trade items sought by the Chinese, and trade with China was particularly important because of Spain's need for their quicksilver (mercury) to extract precious minerals from the ore mined in

New Spain. Knowing that the Russians were similarly focused on these furs inspired a specific anxiety in the Spanish authorities.

Therefore, in 1769, the Gaspar de Portolá expedition set north from Loreto, in Baja California, and by May of that year it had arrived at the bay of San Diego, where the first Catholic mission in Alta California was established. In the course of the next year, two overland expeditions were made up the coast of California to the bay christened Monterey. At both ports—San Diego and Monterey—naval ships made rendezvouses with the soldiers, establishing a basis of resupply for the mounted explorers. Whereas various offshore islands and a limited number of locations on the coast had been visited on several occasions since explorer Juan Rodriguez Cabrillo's voyages in 1542, the overland expedition of 1769–1770 would guarantee contact with many of the native peoples that inhabited the country. Fr. Junípero Serra and Fr. Juan Crespí applied themselves to scouting out promising locations for mission establishments, usually based on where the Indians were most concentrated.

The story of the development of the chain of missions up and down California has been told many times elsewhere; suffice it to say, the focus of the enterprise shifted from defense against the Russian interlopers when said bogeymen failed to appear. In fact, it was not until another third of a century had passed that, in 1803, a Russian face was seen in California, and that was in the form of two Russian American Company employees sailing on an American ship (the *O'Cain*) who were acting as the overseers to a contingent of forty Alaskan native men hired to hunt sea mammals, particularly sea otter and fur seals.

The Russian American Company had been granted an official monopoly on the fur trade in the Russian possessions in the North Pacific in 1799 but lacked enough ships of their own to mount expeditions to California. Another three years passed before any Russian official visited the shores of California; it wasn't until 1806 that Count Nikolai Rezanov sailed aboard the *Juno* into San Francisco Bay. It is amusing to read the account of the anxious Spanish military authorities racing up and down the beaches near the Presidio of San Francisco trying to suss out these potentially threatening foreigners, and finally having the visitors identify themselves as Russians. "¡*Vienen los Rusos!*" This might have been the cry uttered by the Spanish sentry, but it was Count Rezanov, not Lieutenant Rosanov, who was the source of the excitement.

The Russian American Company relied on contracts with American ships to provide transport to California for several more years, but in 1808, the RAC chief manager, Alexander Baranov, sent his trusted lieutenant, Ivan Kuskov, to seek out a base for hunting and agricultural production in the portion of California north of the Spanish settlements in the San Francisco Bay Area. Although his first establishment was at Bodega Bay, Kuskov subsequently decided to move up the coast to a better-protected location, which he called Fort Ross. In 1812 the stockade and a number of key buildings were constructed, and this became the headquarters of Russian California for the next thirty years. The colony was composed of Russian *promyshlenniki* (frontiersmen), Aleuts,[1] Creoles,[2] and some of the local Bodega Miwok and Kashaya Pomo Indians. As the importance of the post shifted from sea mammal hunting to agricultural production meant to support the Alaskan colonies, there was increased interaction with the local Indian peoples, whose labor was needed to tend and reap the crops being grown. The Russians' influence on local Indians included intermarriage and cultural impacts including the acquisition of a number of Russian words into the Kashaya Pomo language.

The inability of the Spanish and later Mexican authorities to oust the Russians meant that the Fort Ross establishment was often considered an insult to the Spanish/Mexican claim to California. In contrast, traders sent from Sitka/New Archangel by the Russian American Company—the most notable of whom was an agent named Kirill Khlebnikov—were widely welcomed by the Spanish and Mexican ecclesiastical and civil authorities in California. The merchants were seen as bringing much-needed supplies, whereas the *settlers* at Fort Ross posed the threat of having established a foothold on the land. In addition, visits by a number of Russian naval ships, and other vesssels seeking a sort of R&R from their picket duty in the North Atlantic, meant a considerable demand for provisions in the Spanish and Mexican settlements, which brought needed cash and goods into California pockets as well as foreign economic support for the local government. Another element brought by Russian ships were naturalists, who collected and studied the plant and animal life of the area, and named several new species. (The California poppy, now the state flower, was dubbed *Eschscholzia californica*, named after the botanist Johann Friedrich von Eschscholtz by his fellow naturalist Adelbert von Chamisso, both of whom came to California on a Russian ship.)

Given the circumstances, the Russians were doing well in California, but as the hunting prospects died down and agricultural endeavors started to cost more than they were worth, the Russians eventually abandoned Fort Ross, selling the properties to Swiss immigrant John Sutter in 1841. With that, the Russians had vacated their stronghold in California.

Although it has been more than two hundred years since the Russians first came to California, certain Russian place names have endured, particularly Fort Ross and the Russian River (Anglicized from the Russian name Slavianka). Driving north along Highway 1 from San Francisco to Fort Ross, one passes both the Muniz Ranch, named for a Russian overseer, and Russian Gulch. Other Russian locations, such as Moscow and Sebastopol, found in the Russian River drainage, are products of later historical events.

The romantic image of the Russian tenure in what became the Golden State has resonated with the Russian people right up to the current time. This has been true both for the people of Russia as well as for the sizable number of Russian immigrants in the United States. The historic importance of Fort Ross led to its eventual ownership by the State of California, which now preserves it as a State Historic Park. Fort Ross has also achieved national recognition as a National Historic Landmark. Efforts to reconstruct a number of the key buildings from the Russian era have generated wonderful cooperative efforts among researchers of this period of history, as well as presented the public with an exotically beautiful historical park that has endeared itself to generations of visitors. The momentous two hundredth anniversary of the founding of Fort Ross, in 2012, has inspired increased interest in the fort and the history it represents. It has stimulated additional research into the archives of Mexico, Spain, and Russia to complement the documentary record already available in California, Alaska, and in the U.S. National Archives. Translations of recent finds from Russian archives will be printed here for the first time to accompany many documents assembled from a variety of published sources that are not readily available to the average reader. Presentation of these documents will hopefully broaden and balance the history of Russians in California by showing how they saw the California mission and military establishments and how they were, in turn, seen by the Spanish and Mexican Californios. The ever increasing nature of this intense interest in and excitement about the subject could not come at a better time considering the backdrop of California's economic downturn, which has threatened Fort Ross State Historic Park.

In the following pages I will present an assortment of documents related to various aspects of the interaction between Russians and the Spanish, Mexican, and Indian populations in California. I will focus on the story of the Russian American Company and the people involved in its actions to exploit the resources of the state. Of course, there have been innumerable Russian immigrants to California, including religious and political dissenters fleeing from persecution of first the tsarist government and subsequently the Soviet authorities; their stories must be sought in other sources. My goal is to add to the reader's appreciation of the Russians and their Native Alaskan employees who came to California at the behest of the Russian American Company in the age of imperial expansion and the ferment of exploration that took place in the first half of the nineteenth century.

NOTES ON THE TEXT

In order to clarify some of the peculiarities found in the text of this volume, a few notes are in order. First, there are two different typefaces, used to differentiate the documentary material from my introductions and commentary. Second, since the Russians at that time were still using the older Julian calendar as opposed to the Gregorian calendar adopted in the West, many dates will be noted with the old and new divided by a slash. Although the dates differed by twelve days in the early nineteenth century, the effect of the International Date Line meant that in California the Gregorian dates were only eleven days ahead. Thus, July 2 in the Julian calendar was July 13 under the Gregorian system. Third, editorial comments added to historical sources in this volume will appear in brackets after the abbreviation "ed." All other bracketed notes are from the authors or editors referenced in the source note at the end of each piece and expanded in the References Cited section at the back of the book. Fourth, the style (i.e., italics, spelling, punctuation) of the reprinted historical documents in the book will reflect those of the original sources listed at the end of each piece. Finally, for some of the pieces that I had previously published elsewhere, I have taken the liberty to update/edit them in this version, which will explain slight differences from the originals.

Glenn J. Farris
Davis, California

1

HIGH ANXIETY ABOUT RUSSIANS IN THE NORTH PACIFIC AND SPAIN'S STIMULUS TO SETTLE ALTA CALIFORNIA, CA. 1768–1769

AMONG THE EUROPEAN POWERS, it was Spain that first settled California, beginning in 1769. Given the fact that Spaniards had first explored the California coast in 1542, however, the two-hundred-year gap demonstrates how little concern they had about foreign nations becoming active in the area. Only when reports started to circulate that the Russians were moving into the North Pacific (i.e., Alaska) did the Spanish galvanize efforts toward actual settlement in the area (versus simply exploration). The coincidence of this action in 1768 with the recent expulsion of the Jesuits from the Spanish Empire the year before resulted in the missionary influence in Alta California being led by the Franciscan order of Catholics, with Fr. Junípero Serra in the lead. (Curiously enough, the image held by non-Spaniards of the Catholic missionary work in New Spain often led them to refer to the California priests as Jesuits, probably due to the negative political overtones of the name at the time; the Jesuits were seen as the more militant and intellectual of the two orders, as compared to the followers of St. Francis, who were considered more amenable to advancing the royal aspirations of King Charles III of Spain.)

Although Acapulco was an active commercial seaport on the Pacific and had been since the sixteenth century, the Spanish authorities decided it was necessary to develop a naval base closer to the Californias in order to oversee the new frontier colonies. They chose a place called San Blas.

San Blas, on the Pacific coast of Mexico, was originally established in 1531 but only gained prominence in 1768, when a contingent of troops and their families under the command of Manuel Rivera (a.k.a. Ribero) arrived to develop a naval base. In this same year, a meeting of various Spanish officials was held there on May 16, 1768, to relay a royal order to undertake a land and sea expedition to relocate the harbor of Monterey and there establish a "presidio and settlement at that place…against any attempts by the Russians or any northern nation" (Watson and Temple 1934: 20–22). It was this crucial gathering that both established San Blas as the principal port from which supply ships left for California and decided the details of the expedition that would shape the future of Alta California and place a clear Spanish imprint on the land.

JUNTA HELD AT SAN BLAS TO PLAN THE
OCCUPATION OF MONTEREY BAY (MAY 16, 1768)

Don Joseph de Gálvez.
From Watson and Temple (1934).

Marquès Carlos Francisco de Croix.
Courtesy of Bicentenario México,
bicentenario.gob.mx.

In the harbor and new settlement of San Blas of the Kingdom of Nueva Galicia on the coast of the South Sea on the sixteenth day of May of the year 1768, the Most Illustrious Señor Don Joseph de Gálvez, of His Majesty's Supreme Council of the Indies, Quartermaster General of the Army, Visitador General of the Tribunals and of the Royal Treasury of these Kingdoms, empowered with fullest authority by the Most Excellent Señor Marqués de Croix, Viceroy, Governor and Captain General of this Nueva España, summoned to his quarters in the government buildings, the Engineer, Don Míguel Costansó; the Comandante of the Navy & this Harbor, Don Manuel Ribero Cordero; Don Antonio Fabeau de Quesada, Professor of Mathematics, and experienced in the Navigation of these Seas and those of the Philippine Islands; and Don Vícente Vila, Pilot of the Royal Armada of His Majesty on the Atlantic Ocean, and designated as Chief Pilot of the vessels that ply this Pacific Ocean.

A Royal Order of His Majesty sent by His Excellency the Marqués de Grimaldi, of the Council & First Secretary of State, under date of the twenty-third of January of this year to the Most Excellent Señor, Marqués de Croix,

Viceroy of this Kingdom, having been read to them, which imparting definite knowledge of the attempts which the Russians have made to facilitate
their communication with this America, warned His Excellency to dispatch
instructions and orders to the Governor of California to observe from there
the designs of that nation and to frustrate them as far as possible; and the
Junta was also informed of the official letter & order of His Majesty, a copy
of which His Excellency the Viceroy had passed on to the Señor Visitador
General so that, being fully acquainted with it and putting into practice the
former plans of occupancy with a Presidio at Puerto de Monterrey, situated
on the Great Ocean, on the west coast of California, he might adopt those
measures he deems most expedient in order to explore by land and by sea so
important a harbor, sending an engineer so that, having taken exact observations and having made a map of the harbor, the useful project of establishing
ourselves at that place may be accomplished.

[…]

At the same time it was also agreed that it would be most important
to undertake an entry or search by land, at the proper seasons, from the
missions to the north of California, so that both expeditions might unite at
the same harbor of Monterrey, and by means of the observations made by
one and the other they might acquire once and for all complete knowledge
and in this wise aid greatly the founding of a presidio and settlement at
that place which is truly the most advantageous for protecting the entire
west coast of California and the other coasts of the southern part of this
continent, against any attempts by the Russians or any northern nation.

[…]

Thus it was decided and His Illustriousness signed with the others who
were present at this Junta and conference.

[Signatures of] Joseph de Gálvez, Miguel Costansó, Antonio
Fabeau Quesada, Manuel Ribero Cordero, Vizente Vila.

Source: "Junta Held at San Blas by the Visitador General Joseph de Gálvez, May 16, 1768,
at which the plan to occupy the Puerto de Monterrey by expeditions by land and sea was
formulated in accordance with the Royal Order of his Majesty, Don Carlos III, January 23,
1768," in Watson and Temple 1934: 20–22.

※ 2 ※

SEA OTTER POACHING BY YANKEE SHIPMASTERS

USING RUSSIANS AND ALASKAN NATIVES,

STARTING IN 1803

Drawing of Aleut hunters made on the Billings-Sarychev expedition of 1790–1792.
From Gavril Sarychev's *Atlas of the Northern Part of the Pacific Ocean*, 1826.
Courtesy of the Rasmuson Library, University of Alaska, Fairbanks.

ALTHOUGH IT WAS FEAR of a Russian incursion from the North Pacific that stimulated Spain's exploration and settlement of the land called Alta or Upper California, the Russians themselves were slow to make an appearance there. Even then, it was not to seize territory but to exploit the valuable trade in fur-bearing animals that had earlier impelled the Russians across the vast expanses of Siberia and then across the Bering Strait to Alaska.

The Russians were not the only ones who appreciated the value of sea otter pelts, however. Pelts were among the few trade goods (along with silver coins and bullion) that the Spanish and other Europeans could use to entice the Chinese, who had ready supplies of mercury, which was crucial to the extraction of silver from ore in the mines of the Spanish empire. The Spanish were aware of the availability of furs from the native tribes of the northwest shores, and they also realized that abalone shells, so prevalent on the California coast, were also highly desired trade items. In the 1790s, the Spanish viceroy, the Conde de Revillagigedo, enacted numerous regulations to limit foreign traders from the California market, however these edicts were frequently flouted by surreptitious smuggling that was undertaken by American merchant ships in particular.

Traders from New England, often referred to collectively as "Boston men," were especially avid for access to the sea otter pelts that sold at a premium in the Chinese market port of Canton during the first decades of the nineteenth century. Historian James Gibson notes that the sale price in Canton for otter skins fluctuated between twenty and thirty dollars apiece during the period of 1801 to 1810 (Gibson 1992: 58–59). However, trading with the local California inhabitants for sea otter pelts was rendered difficult (although not impossible) by the restrictions on trade maintained by the Spanish government. In order to circumvent this and develop an even more efficient way to hunt sea otter, various American sea captains hit on the idea of contracting with the Russian American Company, which used Alaskan native hunters in their *baidarkas* (kayaks) to more successfully hunt sea mammals. In 1803, Captain Joseph O'Cain sailed to Kodiak and struck a bargain with the Russian American Company chief manager in Alaska, Alexander Baranov, to take with him to California forty hunters and twenty *baidarkas*. He then sailed down to San Diego and hunted off the Baja California coast until March of the following year, returning to Kodiak with a generous haul of otter skins. Since the Spanish lacked vessels in the area capable of patrolling the coast, O'Cain and his Alaskan hunters could act with impunity, especially on the offshore islands. Most of these *baidarkas* had two cockpits, although occasionally there would be one with three, to allow for a passenger, usually a Russian overseer, or *baidarshchik*. Accompanying this expedition were two Russians, named Afanasii Shvetsov and Timofei Tarakanov (Pierce 1990: 469, 497–499), who were placed in charge of the Alaskan hunters. They should be considered the first Russians to come to California.

By December 1803, the *O'Cain* had arrived off the coast of San Diego, but upon being rebuffed by the Spanish authorities in a request to land, it continued south into Lower California to the bay of San Quintín. There, Captain O'Cain pleaded hardship of the sea, saying that he needed to land and refit his ship after a long voyage. Permission was given by Captain José Manuel Ruiz, commandant of the Presidio of San Diego. O'Cain's initial request to stay for three days was drawn out to last three months.

The main limitations faced by these hunting expeditions were the availability of fresh water, provisions for feeding the ships' crews and sizable numbers of Alaskan native hunters and, on occasion, materials needed to repair the ships. The need for fresh water was paramount and certainly the most basic requirement, and the Spanish soldiers, in defense of their land, learned to stake out potential watering spots where the Alaskans in their *baidarkas* might put in to seek water. Alaskan natives were sometimes captured during such ambushes, from San Pedro (near Los Angeles) up to San Francisco Bay. O'Cain himself was confronted by a Spanish military contingent led by Corporal Juan Maria Osuna, who was himself captured but finally released by Captain O'Cain. By this time the *O'Cain* had obtained 1,100 sea otter pelts by hunting (and another 700 through trading with various people on the California coast) and the captain decided it was time to leave the area. In the course of this hunt, Spanish presidio commandant José Ruiz claim that all the sea otter from Mission Rosario to Mission Santo Domingo (an area basically covering the northern part of Baja California) were wiped out (Ogden 1941: 46–47).

Upon his return to Alaska, the success of the voyage inclined Baranov toward further contract arrangements. More ships were sent out from Boston in 1805, and in 1806, young Jonathan Winship arranged for the *O'Cain* to once again hunt sea otter on the California coast. The Russian in charge this time was named Sysoi Slobodchikov. This expedition took aboard more than one hundred Kodiak otter hunters and fifty *baidarkas*. In addition, there were twelve Alaskan women brought along to support the hunters in domestic duties. Winship cleverly distributed the Kodiaks on various islands along the California coast and left them to do their hunting while he meanwhile sheltered at the Bahía de San Quintín. Departing from the area after a five-month stay, he picked up the various hunting teams and made his way back to Alaska with a nice haul of seal and otter skins worth about sixty thousand dollars.

The *Peacock*, commanded by Oliver Kimball (O'Cain's brother-in-law), picked up another group of Alaskan natives after concluding a contract with Baranov in October 1806. The Russian in charge on this occasion was Timofei Tarakanov,[1] who had previously come to California on the *O'Cain* with Shvetsov in 1803. Since the Spanish were cottoning on to what the Americans were doing and were now less willing to buy the sad tales of their needing safe harbor

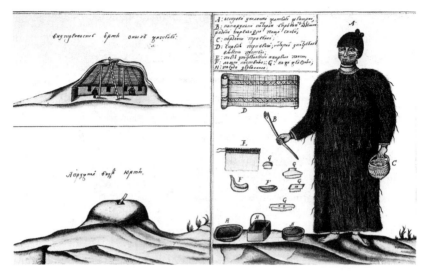

An Aleut woman and objects of daily life, by M. D. Levashov, ca. 1760s.
Russian State Archives of the Navy. Photo by Chris Arend.

in Spanish ports to mend their ships, Kimball decided to stay away from the occupied Spanish areas and set up a base instead at Bodega Bay, in Northern California, in 1807. It was probably during this visit that Tarakanov made an agreement with the local Indian chiefs for permission to occupy this part of the coast.[2] The story of this transaction was obtained from two Bodega Miwok natives at Mission San Rafael in 1819 by Fr. Mariano Payeras. In their narrative, the Indians used the name "Talacani," which was their closest approximation to Tarakanov (Farris 1993b: 7–9; 1998: 2–12).

In 1808 and 1809 George Washington Eayrs, captain of the *Mercury,* brought down more Alaskan natives. (His contract with Baranov has recently been published in Russian [Istomin et al. 2005: 177–183].) A couple of years earlier, in 1806 and 1807, the *Mercury* had sailed along the California coast from Port San Luis (the port for Mission San Luis Obispo) down to various ports in northern Baja California, under the command of Captain William Heath Davis, Sr., who successfully traded with various local people for a total of 2,848 otter skins that had been hunted by the Spanish and Indians. The account book of the *Mercury* shows payments of up to ten dollars for a prime sea otter pelt.[3] When the *Mercury* returned to the Pacific coast, Captain Eayrs decided to contract with the Russians rather than purchase the skins from the local people, and made several successful hunting trips. Ultimately, the ship was captured by the Spanish in 1813.[4]

In 1808 and 1809 a Russian ship, the *Kadiak,* carried Ivan Aleksandrovich Kuskov and a crew of 40 Russians, along with 130 Unalaska and Kodiak natives and 30 native Alaskan women, to explore the coast north of San Francisco and scout out a location to develop a base in "New Albion." Along the way they stopped to hunt at Trinidad Bay in Northern California and then came down to Bodega Bay, where they set up their base. After approximately eight months they returned to Sitka/New Archangel with a cargo of 2,350 sea otter skins.

Kuskov returned to Bodega Bay in 1811 on the *Chirikov.* The ship also visited the Farallon Islands, off the coast of San Francisco, and when it departed for Sitka was loaded with 1,238 sea otter skins as well as a cargo of sea lion meat. The Russians subsequently set up an *artel*[5] on the Farallones to harvest and process sea lions and fur seals. Sea lion meat was much revered by the Alaskan native people and periodically a *baidara* (a large umiak-like open skin boat, much bigger than a *baidarka*) was dispatched from the mainland Russian settlement to procure thousands of pounds of this meat for local consumption. In addition, the hides of the sea lions were needed to keep the skin boats in repair, since the warmer waters of California were harder on the skin boats than the frigid waters of the North Pacific.

The major Yankee interest in the sea otter trade seems to have tapered off as both prices and numbers of otters declined, in about the winter of 1812–1813. The capture of the *Mercury* in 1813 also likely had an impact (Miller 2001). It appears, however, that the Russians continued to be willing to take a stab at hunting on their own while living on the islands. In 1814 Baranov sent down a ship named the *Il'mena* (formerly known as the *Lydia,* but renamed when purchased by the Russian American Company). This was the first "Russian" ship that ventured south of the Farallones into Southern California. It deposited contingents of Alaskan hunters at various Channel Islands, near Santa Barbara and Los Angeles.

One of the Russians in charge of the otter hunters on this trip was named Yakov Babin. It appears that the Alaskan hunters under his command got into altercations with (and possibly even committed a massacre of) native California Indians on at least one of the Channel Islands (probably San Nicolas), resulting in the death of a number of Indians (Istomin et al. 2005). Yakov Babin was subsequently taken to Fort Ross and interrogated there by Ivan Kuskov about his role in the event. The renowned story of the "lone woman of San Nicolas Island" wherein a woman remained on the island of that name after the rest of the people had been taken to the mainland, may well be related to this event (Farris 2007: 24–25). Mystery surrounds the one woman who survived on the island until she was taken in 1853 to Mission Santa Barbara, where she soon after died and was buried. Although believed to be a native Californian woman, descriptions of her dress and tools suggest the possibility that she might have been one of the Alaskan native women. (One popular retelling is Scott O'Dell's young adult novel *Island of the Blue Dolphins*.)

Source: Farris 2007: 20–33. Reprinted by permission of Glenn J. Farris.

3

VISIT BY REZANOV IN 1806
TO OBTAIN SUPPLIES FOR ALASKA:
THE START OF A SERIES OF RUSSIAN
VISITS TO CALIFORNIA

COUNT NIKOLAI PETROVICH REZANOV, chamberlain to the tsar, son-in-law of Grigori Shelikov,[1] and a founder of the Russian American Company, visited Russian America in 1805 and found the colony at Sitka/New Archangel on the verge of starvation. Desperate to resupply the settlement, he directed his ship, the *Juno,* south to California, where he landed at San Francisco on April 8, 1806. There, he engaged in talks of trade for food with the comman-dant of the presidio, José Dario Argüello. Interestingly, the Russian visit was expected: the Californians had been informed by the authorities in New Spain that Rezanov would be arriving and directed that he should be accorded all courtesy. In addition to dealing with Comandante Argüello, Rezanov was visited by the governor of California, José Joaquin de Arrillaga, who came up from Monterey for the meeting. Although a number of historians have suggested that Arrillaga was antagonistic toward Rezanov and any interaction with the Russians, in fact he had received orders from higher Spanish authorities to welcome him should he arrive in California. Rezanov was quite impressed with the efficiency of Spanish communications between Europe and the New World, which had provided such timely news to Governor Arrillaga.

The count sought to enhance the relationship between the Russians and California by romancing Argüello's daughter, María Concepción, as described in both romantic and practical detail by Dr. Georg H. von Langsdorff, a surgeon aboard the *Juno*, in a document that follows. This story has been told many times, so in the selection included here I have sought to place my emphasis on Rezanov's report of his conversations with Governor Arrillaga, which were very illuminating indeed.

Rezanov succeeded in obtaining a cargo of much-needed wheat to carry back up to Sitka, however, he himself died in 1807 on his trip across Siberia, returning to St. Petersburg, a turn of events that made all the more valuable the lengthy reports he had prepared for authorities in Russia prior to leaving Sitka. It is evident that the California officials—not only civil but ecclesiastic—were quite thrilled by the possibilities of this new trade, as evidenced by a letter from Fr. José Señan (reprinted here) written quite soon after Rezanov's visit, in which the priest outlines the advantages of such an arrangement.

In addition to opening trade to help support the Alaskan colonies, the *Juno*'s visit resulted in two invaluable records: drawings by Langsdorff of scenes at the missions, including dances of the Indians, and also an intensive survey of the San Francisco Bay by the captain of the *Juno*, Lieutenant Nikolai Aleksandrovich Khvostov. In all, this early visit to California involved far more than the romantic tale of Rezanov and Concepción Argüello that has so captured the popular mind. For ethnographers and historians of the Indians in the missions—especially Missions San Francisco de Asís and San José—the observations and drawings as well as artifacts that were brought back to Russia from this visit are the true golden nuggets from California.

It is interesting that the visit of the *Juno* occurred very soon after the California missions were hit by a devastating epidemic of measles. Curiously, the Russians hardly noted this event, except in a brief mention by Langsdorff, who wrote that it slowed down the loading of supplies aboard the *Juno*. This omission is especially peculiar since Langsdorff was acting as the ship's doctor.

Following the visit of Count Rezanov, the Foreign Minister, Count Rumi-antsev, sent a letter to Russia's representative to the court of Spain in 1808 outlining the advantages of trade between the Russian colonies in the North Pacific and the Spanish province of California. Thereafter, the Russians did trade with California, especially after the outbreak of the Mexican revolution in 1810, which drastically cut down the number of Spanish ships coming to California. In addition, various Russian naval ships, mostly on round-the-world voyages of discovery, stopped in the ports of San Francisco and Monterey in the following years.

Nikolai Rezanov, Chamberlain to the Tsar. From the State Historical Museum, Moscow. Courtesy of the Fort Ross Interpretive Association.

REPORT FROM REZANOV TO RUMIANTSEV
CONCERNING TRADE AND OTHER RELATIONS
BETWEEN RUSSIAN AMERICA, SPANISH CALIFORNIA,
AND HAWAII (JUNE 17, 1806)

Gracious Sir, Count Nikolai Petrovich [ed: Rumiantsev].

From my latest dispatches to Your Excellency and to the Main Administration of the Company, you are well aware of the desperate situation in which I found the Russian American territories. You know of the famine which we experienced all last winter. People barely managed to stay alive on the provisions we bought along with the ship *Juno*. You also know about the illnesses and the miserable condition which affected the entire region, as well as the resoluteness with which I made a voyage to New California, putting out to sea with an inexperienced and scurvy-ridden crew and risking everything to save the region or die. Now, with the help of God, I have carried out this arduous voyage and I am pleased to submit to Your Excellency this report concerning the initial ventures of the Russians in that land.

[Rezanov then relates the particulars of their voyage down the Pacific coast to California. The passengers and crew were subjected to scurvy as well as difficulties with heavy winds that prevented them from exploring the Columbia River. Arriving in San Francisco Bay, Rezanov was first greeted by the acting commandant of the Presidio, Luis Antonio Argüello, who was standing in for his father, Don José Argüello. Later, not only did the older Argüello arrive but the governor of California, Don José Arrillaga, traveled up from Monterey to meet with Rezanov, despite the considerable pain he suffered from a severely injured leg. Conversations between Rezanov and Arrillaga illuminate the status of affairs, and it is apparent that Arrillaga was very disturbed by the way his government was handling the interaction of California with outsiders, but he was too loyal an old soldier to overtly go against orders.]

"I am very grateful that you have come," he [ed: Arrillaga] told me one day. "It has given me an opportunity to resume my repeated reports concerning the necessity of trade, which never received proper attention because this place is so remote. Sometimes I would become bitter when my friends reported unfavorable responses from the ministers [who would say], 'This cursed land of California! It is nothing but trouble and expense!' Did they think I was responsible for the unprofitability of the establishment?"

"Tell me," I asked. "How much does it cost to maintain it per year?"

"At least half a million piasters."

"And what revenue does it produce?"

"Not a single reál."

"But did you not once tell me about a tithe on grain?"

"That is collected only from the invalided [ed: retired] veterans, and even that is set aside for the benefit of the mission in case they have a crop failure. That is why they have sentries on guard at their warehouses. In a word, the King maintains the garrisons, naval vessels and missions, and also provides funds for the construction and beautification of the churches, because his principle goal is to propagate the faith, and keep the people happy. As a true defender of the faith he bestows all his privileges on religion."

As I listened to this outburst I could hardly refrain from laughing.

"This is very commendable, and salutary for the soul," I said piously, "but unfortunately we see so much moral corruption that there are already entire nations who do not profess the goal of true beatitude and who are so deluded that they seek temporal pleasures rather than eternal salvation. The noble intentions of your heart and the fervor of your prayers are powerless to protect your religion, or even yourselves, from such outcasts of the human race."

"You are right," he replied, "and I have several times requested that our military forces be increased, but when your presence in the north involved such a limited number of men, our peoples' fears were calmed and my requests evoked only promises. However, at the present time the boldness of the Bostonians has awakened us. This year the authorities have promised to send me a naval frigate to put a stop to the vessels of the American states which are constantly smuggling along our coast and carrying on illicit trade. But this is a relatively minor problem. Sometimes they [ed: the Bostonians] leave ten or fifteen men among us who are hardened criminals, and because our garrison is so small this creates a very bad situation here and corrupts our morals. They even put women ashore. They try in every possible way to settle here among us permanently.

"Some time ago I spoke of the Bostonian, Captain O'Cain," the Governor told me one time. "In 1803 he brought 40 [native] islanders from Unalaska with their baidarkas, and they hunted sea otters all winter long. We do not know where he concealed himself. I will be much obliged if you will repeat this story, which I perhaps should report to the Viceroy."

Here I feel I must inform Your Excellency about this situation. Captain O'Cain came to Kodiak aboard a ship of the same name. He contracted with Baranov for 40 baidarkas to hunt sea otters on an equal share basis on a new island he had discovered. He promised that if he happened to anchor in a place where he could provision, he would allow the prikash-chik [ed: administrator] to purchase supplies for the [Russian American] Company. He was not to participate in this transaction. When he obtained the [Kodiak] people he went directly to California and put them ashore. Whether he deceived Baranov, or whether Baranov was to have profited from this fraud, I leave it to Your Excellency to decide. I will only add that at the time [Baranov's people] were starving to death and their lives were saved by several barrels of flour which O'Cain brought.

At the present time a similar contract has been negotiated with [John D']Wolf, to which I could not object. Having bought his ship I did the same thing, without any censure and in a large way. However, I gave the Spanish the following account of this matter.

"I am very glad that you have reminded me of this incident," I said. "The Bostonians harm us more than they do you. They put people ashore in your territory, but they abduct them from ours. In addition to carrying on trade in our waters, this scoundrel of whom you are speaking seized a departing hunting group of our American natives from Kodiak, 40 men and their families. The next year young Captain [ed: Henry] Barber, the same kind of knave, returned 26 of them to Kodiak, saying he had paid ransom for them in the Queen Charlotte Islands and that he would not hand them over to us unless we paid him 10,000 rubles. We had to do this out of humanity, but we still do not know what O'Cain did with the others.

"The ones who were returned testified that they had been in various places on different vessels, but which vessels, and where, we could not ascertain because they themselves did not know. I venture to assure you that this and other such things the Bostonians have done have taught us to be more careful. We are now also taking measures to disassociate ourselves from these intruders. However, because of the many straits in our waters, we do not have the necessary means to do this."

"I can tell you," he said, "that I have drawn up orders which should probably drive them away. I have ordered mounted patrols to ride along the coast. As soon as they sight a ship on the horizon, from their height on horseback, they are to report to the nearest presidio. They are not to lose sight of the ship's course, and as soon as it puts a boat ashore, I am confident it will be seized."

And in fact, about five days later the Governor showed me a notice he had received from the port of San Diego reporting that an Anglo-American brigantine, *Peacock,* 108 tons, 6 cannon, 4 falconets, Captain Oliver Kimball, had approached the coast and landed a boat with four men; the boat was captured but the ship managed to escape. The navigator, Bostonian Thomas Kilvain,[2] second quartermaster Jean Pierre from Bordeaux, and two sailors were captured. They testified that they had left Boston in September of 1805; they reached the Sandwich islands on February 2 [ed: 1806]; only fourteen of the crew were left; their cargo was arms and various items which they were taking to the Russian American possessions to exchange for furs; and they had put ashore only to take on fresh supplies. The following day a letter to the navigator was found on shore; in the letter the ship's captain assured the navigator that he would sail along the coast for several days and that he should try to escape. But the men [from the ship's boat] were shackled and taken to San Blas."

[In a fascinating aside indicating how *au courant* Governor Arrillaga was to affairs in Europe, Rezanov reports the following:]

I asked the governor how often he received news from Europe.

"Officially I received reports once a month aboard a special packetboat that brings them in from Cadiz, but commercial vessels bring news more often. Also, in addition to the usual monthly courier, special messengers bring urgent news to all the important places."

I envied this system and thought how ill-served our possessions are in this regard in this unfamiliar new world. As a result of expanding our trade, we might receive news twice a year.

"But in wartime if your packetboat were to be seized by the enemy," I asked, "would not your dispatches fall into their hands?"

"No, never," he replied. "The dispatch box is always fastened to a heavy lead weight and in case of attack it is thrown overboard. The same news will be brought with the next vessel, because in wartime dispatches and letters as well are sent in duplicate and even in triplicate. If you should wish to write to Europe," he added, "you may be certain your letters will reach their destination safely."

I accepted his offer and sent a report to His Imperial Majesty, a copy of which, together with my letter to the Viceroy, I have the honor of including here for your Excellency.

Source: "A Confidential Report from Nikolai P. Rezanov to Minister of Commerce Nikolai P. Rumiantsev, concerning trade and other relations between Russian America, Spanish California, and Hawaii," in Dmytryshyn et al. 1989: 112, 135–138, 139–140.

LANGSDORFF ON THE
REZANOV–ARGÜELLO ROMANCE (1806)

The romance between Count Nikolai Rezanov and Concepción Argüello has touched hearts both in California and in Russia. The depth of this latter attachment was made clear to me on a visit in 1988 by noted Russian historian Svetlana Fedorova, who asked me to help her track down Concepción's final resting place in Benicia, California. We arrived at the Catholic cemetery shortly before it was due to close for the day and finally found what we were looking for. I photographed Dr. Fedorova next to a bas relief that was erected by the Native Sons of the Golden West and also next to a picture of the simple gravestone dedicated to "Sister Domenica Argüello" upon her death in 1857. In the following selection, I've isolated the portions of Langsdorff's narrative of the Rezanov voyage

Russian historian Svetlana G. Fedorova in 1988, standing by the monument
to Concepción Argüello erected by the Native Sons of the Golden West.

Photo by Glenn J. Farris.

Gravestone of Concepción Argüello, Benicia Catholic Cemetery, California.
Photo by Glenn J. Farris.

that specifically concern the Rezanov-Argüello romance. Langsdorff's account
is reproduced more fully in the document following this one.

...We were received in the most hospitable manner by Señora Argüello,
esposa of the comandante permanente [ed: Don José Darío Argüello, who
was absent at the time], and her family.

[...]

Their simple, natural cordiality captivated us to such a degree that we
forthwith desired to become acquainted with each individual member of the
family, and to learn the name of each one, having at once formed a strong
attachment for them, and becoming interested in their personal welfare.

The Señora Argüello was the mother of fifteen children, and of these
thirteen were living at this time. Some of the sons were absent upon military
duty, and the others were at home. Of the grown-up unmarried daughters,
the Doña Concepción most particularly interested us. She was distinguished
for her vivacity and cheerfulness, her love-inspiring and brilliant eyes and

exceedingly beautiful teeth, her expressive and pleasing features, shapeliness of figure, and for a thousand other charms, besides an artless natural demeanor. Beauties of her kind one may find, though but seldom, only in Italy, Portugal, and Spain.

[...]

Our intimate association daily with the Argüello family, the music and dancing, the sports, aroused in the mind of Rezanov some new and important speculations. These led to the formation of a plan of a very different nature from the original scheme for the establishment of commercial relations.

The bright sparkling eyes of Doña Concepción had made upon him a deep impression, and pierced his inmost soul. He conceived the idea that through a marriage with the daughter of the comandante of the Presidio de San Francisco a close bond would be formed for future business intercourse between the Russian American Company and the provincia of Nueva California. He had therefore decided to *sacrifice* [ed: emphasis mine] himself, by wedding Doña Concepción, to the welfare of his country, and to bind in friendly alliance both Spain and Russia.

The first obstacle in the way to such a union was the difference between the religions of the parties. But to a philosophic head like that of Rezanov this was by no means insurmountable. The gobernador, however, called his attention to the critical political situation in Europe, and the well-known suspicious nature of the Spanish government, and gave him little hope of support in his trade speculations.

Rezanov thereupon assured the gobernador that immediately on his return to Saint Petersburg he himself, as an ambassador extraordinary from the imperial Russian court, would go to Madrid so that every possible misunderstanding between the two courts would be obviated. Thereafter, he would sail from some Spanish port to Vera Cruz and Mexico, and finally come on to San Francisco to claim his bride and settle all commercial matters. It will be perceived from this that Rezanov was no less daring in forming his projects for the binding of the two nations, than quick in laying the foundation for the means of carrying them out.

Source: Langsdorff 1927 [1814].

LANGSDORFF'S NARRATIVE OF
REZANOV'S VOYAGE TO NUEVA CALIFORNIA (1806)

Georg von Langsdorff. From Langdorff's *Narrative of the
Rezanov Voyage to Nueva California in 1806* (1927).

Indians at Mission San Jose preparing for a dance. Drawing by Georg
von Langsdorff. Courtesy of The Bancroft Library, University of California, Berkeley.

California Indian artifacts. Drawing by Georg von Langsdorff.
Courtesy of The Bancroft Library, University of California, Berkeley.

Hardly had we arrived at our destination on the morning of March 28, 1806, o.s., April 8, N.s., after a voyage of thirty-two days, when fifteen horsemen came out of the fort [El Fuerte de San Joaquín de] San Francisco, and advanced at full gallop to the shore near our place of anchorage. They demanded, by calls and signs, that we send a boat ashore, and manifested much impatience while we lowered one, and Lieutenant Davidov and myself went therein to the shore.

Here we were received by a Franciscan padre and several military officers, when a fine-looking young don, not otherwise distinguished from the others but by a singular garb, was presented to us as the comandante of the establishment. Over his uniform he wore a sort of mantle of striped woolen cloth, which resembled very much the coverlet of a bed, with a slit in the middle, through which his head passed, the longer part covering the breast and back, the narrower part the shoulders. He, as well as the other officers, wore peculiarly embroidered boots, of a particular make, with unusually large spurs. Most of them also had wide, full cloaks. As neither Lieutenant Davidov nor myself understood Spanish, the conversation was carried on in Latin, between me and the Franciscan padre [ed: Fr. Antonio Uria of Mission San José], this being the only medium by which either one could make himself intelligible to the other.

The first inquiry made was as to who we were and whence we came. The reply was, that our ship belonged to a Russian voyage of discovery, and that the commander thereof, His Excellency the Count Rezanov, was on board; that our intention had been to go to Monterey, as the seat of government, but that we were delayed by contrary winds, and that, owing to insufficiency of provisions, we had been under the necessity of putting into this port, as the nearest we could make. We therefore solicited the comandante's permission to purchase the needed supplies, and to make necessary repairs to our ship.

The reply was made, that a long time had elapsed since the comandante had received information as to our expedition, which was accompanied with an order from the Spanish king, that if the ships put into this port they were to be received in the most amicable manner and provided with everything needed; hence all kinds of supplies that the country and the season afforded were entirely at our service. It was also called to our attention that the advices received further stated that when the expedition sailed from Kronstadt it was composed of two ships, the Nadeschda and the Neva, the former under the command of Captain Krusenstern, and the latter under Captain Lisiansky, and they asked what had caused so great a change, as that the Chamberlain Rezanov (whose name they seemed to be familiar with) had now come with only one ship, and that one neither of the two mentioned, and under the command of different officers.

To this we replied, that the original ships of the expedition were, from various causes, compelled to return to Europe from Kamchatka, and that his Majesty the Czar of Russia had ordered the Count Rezanov to proceed with the ship Juno, under the command of Lieutenants Khvostov and Davidov, for the purpose of examining the establishments of the Russian American Company in the Aleutian Islands and the northwest coast of America, from whence we had come to this harbor. This answer seemed to be satisfactory to them. They promised all necessary assistance, and entreated that Rezanov come ashore, saying they would remain and wait for him and conduct him to the residence of the comandante at the Presidio. Upon this we at once returned to the ship with this gratifying invitation. Being joined by the chamberlain and Lieutenant Khvostov, we went to the Presidio, as each military establishment in California is called.

On our way to the Presidio we were told that the comandante permanente, Don José Darío Argüello, was absent, and that his son, the Alférez Don Luis Antonio, with whom we were then conversing, was comandante temporal until the return of his father. In a little more than a quarter of an hour we were at the Presidio, and here we were received in the most hospitable manner by Señora Argüello, esposa of the comandante permanente, and her family.[3]

The whole establishment of [the Presidio de] San Francisco externally has the look of a German farmstead. Its low one-story buildings surround a somewhat long quadrangular court. The house of the comandante is small and mean. A whitewashed room, half of the floor of which was covered with straw matting, had but little furniture, and that of an inferior quality. The furnished half served as a reception-room. The welcome over, refreshments were served, and we were invited to partake later of as good a dinner as their kitchen and larder would provide. It was not long before dinner was ready and once again, after long privation, we enjoyed an excellent repast, and to our great surprise, the poor quality of the house-furniture considered, in a rich service of silver tableware. This precious Mexican metal can be found in even the most remote Spanish possessions. Mutual esteem and harmony glowed without diminution in the conduct of this kindly family, who knew scarcely any other diversions or pleasures than those resulting from family joys and domestic happiness.

Their simple, natural cordiality captivated us to such a degree that we forthwith desired to become acquainted with each individual member of the family, and to learn the name of each one, having at once formed a strong attachment for them, and becoming interested in their personal welfare.

The Señora Argüello was the mother of fifteen children, and of these thirteen were living at this time. Some of the sons were absent upon military duty, and the others were at home. Of the grown-up unmarried daughters, the Doña Concepción most particularly interested us. She was distinguished for her vivacity and cheerfulness, her love-inspiring and brilliant eyes and exceedingly beautiful teeth, her expressive and pleasing features, shapeliness of figure, and for a thousand other charms, besides an artless natural demeanor. Beauties of her kind one may find, though but seldom, only in Italy, Portugal, and Spain.

Don Luis Argüello, the son and substitute of the comandante permanente, imparted to us the news that England had declared war against Spain, and told us that when they had first seen our vessel that morning, she was supposed to be English, and an enemy. He now expressed his gratification that he was mistaken.

In the afternoon he dispatched a courier to the gobernador at Monterey, announcing our arrival and requesting further instructions in regard to us. Count Rezanov also sent a few lines by the courier.

Besides Padre José Antonio Uría, who received us this morning at the shore, we were introduced also to Padre Martín Landaeta, and from both we received an invitation to visit Misión San Francisco de Asis the following day. This is an ecclesiastical establishment, lying a short German mile eastward from the Presidio. We returned to the ship in the evening, much delighted with the day passed.

On arriving we received the pleasing report that the comandante of the Presidio had sent far more supplies than our debilitated promyshleniki could consume in several days. Among the supplies were four large, fat oxen, two sheep, onions and garlic, lettuce and cabbage, as well as several other kinds of vegetables.

At eight o'clock on the morning of the 29th [ed: April 8] the saddle-horses were waiting for us at the shore, as agreed upon, to carry us to the Misión, and Padre Uría himself had come to conduct us. The Count Rezanov, Lieutenants Khvostov and Davidov, and myself, were in this pleasure-party. As we had to pass the Presidio on our way, we called there, just to bid good morning to the Argüello family, and were served with chocolate, after which we rode onward to the Misión. The road thither is through loose sand, and is not good for either walking or riding. The surroundings are mostly bare, and the hills, covered in places with low shrubs, afford but little of anything interesting. Birds were almost the only things that attracted our attention, and I saw several kinds unknown to me. There were also a few rabbits and hares.

In about three quarters of an hour we arrived at the Misión. Padre Martín Landaeta, whom we had seen at the Presidio yesterday, received our party at the door with a third religioso, the Padre Ramón Abella, to whom we were presented, and we were tendered a hearty welcome and conducted at once to the church, where a short prayer was offered. We were shown all that was deemed worthy of our attention in the chapel and sacristy; but these were merely ecclesiastical paraphernalia. Our cicerone, Padre Uría, who, generally speaking, seemed to be a man of sound and accurate judgment upon most matters, understanding that I was a naturalist, took me by the hand when we were in the chapel and forced upon my attention a painting representing the Agave Americana, Linn., from the middle of which, instead of a flower-stalk, rose a holy virgin, by whom, as he assured me, many extraordinary miracles were wrought. His story was related with such an air of belief and certainty that, through an assumed appearance of courtesy and admiration of this phenomenon, I thus expressed my envy of the painter who had witnessed it with his own eyes.

Shortly after this we were taken to the residence of the religiosos, which had several spacious apartments. Refreshments of several kinds were served, and afterwards we were shown the other buildings of the establishment, with everything appertaining thereto worthy of notice.

The name "misión" indicates an ecclesiastical establishment having for its object the propagation of the doctrines of the Roman Catholic church. In the misiones founded in the peninsula of Antigua California, as well as those in Nueva California, there are commonly two or three padres, who are protected in their holy work by the presidios, that is to say, the military government of the country. The padres in Nueva California are all frailes of the Franciscan order. Each of these frailes, before he comes from Spain to this part of the world for the purpose of Christianizing the benighted natives, must enter into an engagement to remain here ten years, upon the expiration of which it is optional with him whether he shall remain or not. On his voyage hither, as well as on his return if he should so decide, he is maintained solely by the Spanish government, and has nothing to think of but his Bible and prayer-book. None of these misioneros can acquire any property, so that it is impossible for one of them even to entertain the idea of enriching himself. Everything that the frailes can save or gain goes into the chest of the misiones. Hence, in case of their return to their native country, they are as poor as when they left it.

The number of misioneros brought every year from Europe to Vera Cruz is supposed to amount to three hundred. Each has an allowance of four hundred piasters annually, which is devoted to his own needs, and those of the community to which he belongs. Payment is not made in money, but in necessary or useful articles, —manufactured goods for clothing, household utensils, and the like. They are sent to them by the Franciscan College [of San Fernando], in Mexico, on which all the misiones in Nueva California are dependent, and are placed on board government vessels at San Blas, a port on the northwest coast of Mexico (latitude 21°30'N.). Among the principal goods are, linen and woolen cloth, wine, brandy, sugar, chocolate and cocoa, iron tools, wax tapers for church service, kitchen utensils, agricultural implements, etc.

In the provincia of Nueva California, extending from San Francisco (latitude 37°55'N.) to San Diego (latitude 32°9'N.), there are at the present time nineteen misiones, each of which has from six hundred to a thousand neófitos. Protection for the misiones is afforded by, if I am not mistaken, six [four: San Francisco, Monterey, Santa Bárbara, and San Diego] presidios, but all told, there are not more than from two hundred to three hundred cavalry.

The Misión Santa Clara de Asís, lying between San Francisco and Monterey, is, with regard to its fine situation, fertility of soil, population, and extent of buildings and grounds, considered the largest and richest mission.

All the misiones have cattle in great numbers, and an abundance of other productions necessary to the support of man, and the padres, in general, conduct themselves with such prudence, kindness, paternal care, and justice, in their attitude toward the neófitos, that tranquility, happiness, obedience, and unanimity are the natural results of their methods. Corporal punishment commonly follows disobedience. The padres have recourse to the presidios only on very extraordinary occasions, as, for instance, when expeditions are sent out in pursuit of prospective converts, or when couriers carrying communications require protection, or as a precaution against sudden attacks.

The number of soldiers being so small, and their services so slight, it does not seem worth while to maintain an establishment for them. The Presidio de San Francisco has not more than forty, and it has three misiones under its protection. These are, San Francisco (same name as the Presidio), Santa Clara, and San José, the last named being established but a few years ago [1797]. There are seldom more than from three to five soldiers at any time at any misión, but this seemingly small number has hitherto been always found sufficient to keep the Indians under proper restraint. I was assured by a person worthy of credit that the Spanish cortes does not spend less than a million piastres annually for the support of the misiones, and their military establishments, in the two Californias, and that, too, without deriving any advantage from them, other than the spreading of Christianity in these provinces of Nueva España.

Each of the frailes has several horses for his own use, and when one starts out on an expedition for finding prospective neófitos, he is always escorted by one or more soldiers, who precede him on the way. At such times the soldiers commonly throw over their breast and shoulders a deerskin mantle, which is intended as a protection against the arrows of the Indians, these being incapable of piercing leather. This mantle is worn on other occasions, also, as on dress parade, and when approaching a presidio or misión. By a royal command, it is not permissible for the misioneros to go any distance without military protection. As they carry only the Bible and the cross as their personal protection, a military escort accompanies them at such times.

This information was imparted while we were enjoying our breakfast, after which we were taken around to see whatever was worthy of notice.

Behind the residence of the frailes there is a large courtyard, inclosed by houses. Here live the Indian women of the Misión, who are employed, under the immediate supervision of the padres, in useful occupations, such as cleaning and combing wool, spinning, weaving, etc. Their principal business is the manufacture of a woolen cloth and blankets for the Indians' own use. The wool of the sheep here is very fine and of superior quality, but the tools and looms are of a crude make. As the misioneros are the sole instructors of these people, who themselves know very little about such matters, scarcely even understanding the fulling, the cloth is far from the perfection that might be achieved.

All the girls and women are closely guarded in separate houses, as though under lock and key, and kept at work. They are but seldom permitted to go out in the day, and never at night. As soon, however, as a girl marries, she is free, and, with her husband, lives in one of the Indian villages belonging to the Misión. These villages are called "las rancherías." Through such arrangements or precautions the misioneros hope to bind the neófitos to the misión, and spread their faith with more ease and security. About a hundred paces from the buildings properly called the Misión, lies one of these Indian villages or barracks. It consists of eight long rows of houses, where each family lives separate and apart from the others. The Indian neófitos here are about twelve hundred in number.

The principal food of the Indians is a thick soup, composed of meat, vegetables, and pulse. Because of the scarcity of fish here, or the want of proper means of catching them, the misioneros obtained a special dispensation from the pope allowing the eating of meat on fast-days. The food is apportioned three times a day,—morning, noon, and evening,—in large ladlefuls. At mealtimes a big bell is rung and each family sends a vessel to the kitchen, and is served as many measures as there are members. I was present once at the time the soup was served, and it appeared incomprehensible to me how any one could consume so much nourishing food three times a day. According to what we were told by our cicerone, from forty to fifty oxen are killed every week for the community. Besides this, meal, bread, Indian corn, pease, beans, and other kinds of pulse, are distributed in abundance, without any regular or stated allowance.

After satisfying our curiosity at the ranchería, we inspected several other serviceable institutions for the promotion of production and economy in the establishment. There was a building for melting tallow, and another for making soap; there were workshops for locksmiths and blacksmiths, and for cabinet-makers and carpenters; there were houses for the storage of tallow, soap, butter, salt, wool, and ox-hides (these being articles of exportation), with storerooms for corn, pease, beans, and other kinds of pulse.

When one considers that in this way two or three misionero padres take upon themselves such a sort of voluntary exile from their country, only to spread Christianity, and to civilize a wild and uncultivated race of men, to teach them husbandry and various useful arts, cherishing and instructing them as if they were their own children, providing them with dwellings, food, and clothing, with everything else necessary for their subsistence, and maintaining the utmost order and regularity of conduct, —when all these particulars, I say, are considered, one cannot sufficiently admire the zeal and activity that carry them through labors so arduous, nor forbear to wish the most complete success to their undertaking.

Meanwhile we were called to dinner, and were served with a very appetizing soup seasoned with herbs and vegetables of different kinds, roast fowl, leg of mutton, different kinds of vegetable dressed in different ways, salad, pastry, preserved fruits, and many fine sorts of food dishes prepared with milk. All these were things to which our palates had been so long strangers, that we were not a little pleased with them. The wine offered us had been brought from the peninsula of Antigua California, and was of but an ordinary quality. Soon after dinner we were served with tea of poor quality, and chocolate of superexcellence.

Thereafter we were shown the kitchen-garden, but it did not equal our expectations. There was very little fruit, and that of inferior quality. Most of the beds were overgrown with weeds. Of fine vegetables and herbs there were few. Northwest winds, which prevail on this coast, and a soil dry and sandy by nature, are insurmountable obstacles to horticulture. The only vegetables that grow well in the gardens are asparagus, cabbage, several kinds of lettuce, onions, and potatoes. In outlying fields, more sheltered from the winds, pease, beans, corn, and other pulse, are cultivated, and thrive fairly well. Corn is here less productive than it is in some other parts of Nueva California. Notwithstanding this, the Spanish government thought it necessary to establish a misión in the neighborhood of such an excellent port as that of San Francisco, with a presidio for its protection. Both establishments are in a flourishing condition, principally on account of the great number of cattle bred.

In order to convey a more accurate idea of the fertility of the soil, with which the padres found fault when compared with that of other misiones, I subjoin the comparative quantities of seed sown and the crops produced for four successive years, as given me by Padre Martín Landaeta.

Grains &c.	1802		1803		1804*		1805	
	Seed	Crop	Seed	Crop	Seed	Crop	Seed	Crop
	Fanegas**	Fanegas	Fanegas	Fanegas	Fanegas	Fanegas	Fanegas	Fanegas
Wheat	233	2322	201	1457	229	938	173	2622
Barley	108	1289	122	1720	143	826	195	2414
Pease	12	525	11	509	9	344	8	330
Habas	6	132	7	214	8	206	8	294
Frijoles	2	10	1	60	2	30	3	40
Maize	1	20	2	60	1	156	1.5	100

*In 1804 most of the seed dried in the ground, because of extreme drought.
**A fanega is about a hundredweight.

Although we acquired but a slight knowledge of the Indians of this Misión on this day, yet I will combine here all that I learned concerning them with my observations during our entire stay.

The neófitos of the Misión San Francisco are the original inhabitants of these and the neighboring parts. A few come from the mouth of a large river that flows into the northernmost part of the harbor, and some from the neighborhood of Port Bodega, which lies to the north of San Francisco. All these are divided into tribes, under the names of Estero, Tuiban, and Tabin. Some other tribes, who live more inland, to the eastward of these, and who were formerly in continual warfare with them, called themselves Tscholban and Tamkan.

The former are nomadic, with no fixed abode. Their food consists partly of fish, sea-dogs, shellfish, and other sea-foods, partly of animals killed in the chase, and partly of seeds, herbs, and roots. The last mentioned are considered the greatest dainties.

Their habitations are small round huts of straw, cone-shaped, erected at any stopping-place. These huts are burned upon their leaving, and the hut in which a person dies is also given to the flames. Both sexes go almost naked, wearing merely a girdle tied around the waist. Only in the coldest days of winter do they throw over their bodies a covering of deerskin, or the skin of the sea-otter. They also make for themselves garments of the feathers of several kinds of water-fowl, particularly ducks and geese. These they bind closely together in a string-like fashion, which strings are afterwards joined tight, making a dress of a feather-fur appearance. Both sides are alike, and it is so warm that it would be an excellent protection against the cold of even a more northerly clime. Sea-otter skins are also cut by them in small strips, and these they twist together and join in the same manner as with the feathers, both sides alike. These coverings are worn principally by the women, and but very rarely by the males.

[Langsdorff goes on describing the physical appearance of the Indians in not particularly flattering terms.]

Their weapons consist of the bow and arrow, and as these contribute essentially to the acquisition of many of the necessaries of life, their construction seems a principal object of their skill and industry. The shape of the bow is pleasing in appearance. It is made of wood, is from three to four and a half feet long, neatly constructed, and drawn together very ingeniously with tendons of the deer. By this means the wood is kept in place securely, and the bow has such elasticity that very little strength and dexterity are required to draw the arrow. Both the bow and the arrow are very neatly made, and the arrows are pointed with vitrified lava, or obsidian, which is inserted in the shaft and bound with tendons. The Spaniards, on their first encounters in the country, had reason to remember with sorrow the skill of the Indians in the use of this weapon.

Among the articles in use in their habitations I saw baskets made of the bark of trees. These were so ingeniously woven, compact, and impervious to water, that they are used as drinking-vessels, food-dishes, and even as roasting-pans. Corn and pulse are put in them, and the Indians, by turning them quickly and dexterously over a slow charcoal fire, get every grain thoroughly browned without the basket being scorched in the least. Many of these baskets, or vessels, are ornamented with the scarlet feathers of the Oriolus phoeniceous, or with the black crest-feathers of the California partridge (Tetraonis cristati), or with shells and corals.

Source: Langsdorff 1927 [1814].

FR. SEÑÁN'S REACTION
TO REZANOV'S VISIT (1806)

Apparently missionaries throughout California were heartened by news of the Rezanov visit and negotiations. Following is a letter Fr. José Señán (1962: 18) at Mission San Buenaventura wrote to the procurator of his College of San Fernando in Mexico City, Fr. José Viñals, on June 6, 1806.

For the welfare of the missions and their inhabitants I shall be glad when open and free commerce is established with this Province, for then the poor settlers and residents will be able to use the proceeds of their meager harvest to clothe themselves and to procure iron farming implements and other necessities, all of which are sorely lacking...

M. Rezanov, a Russian general [ed: sic], whose frigate put in at San Francisco brought away great quantities of grain, tallow, and lard for the Russian establishments in the north. It is said that he was more than pleased with the hospitality and assistance he received. When he returns to St. Petersburg he intends to beg the Emperor's authorization to go to the court at Madrid as Ambassador Extraordinary. Then he will press for reciprocal trade between their settlements and ours. He expects his proposals to be approved, and if they are, this Province will benefit greatly.

Source: Señán 1962: 18.

FOLLOW-UP LETTER FROM RUMIANTSEV TO STROGANOV SUGGESTING THE VALUE OF MUTUAL TRADE BETWEEN CALIFORNIA AND RUSSIAN AMERICA (APRIL 20, 1808)

Further remarks on the perceived value of mutual trade were included in a letter from Russian Foreign Minister Nikolai Petrovich Rumiantsev to Grigori Stroganov, the tsar's minister plenipotentiary to Spain, who resided in Madrid.

St. Petersburg, 20 April 1808

The late Chamberlain Rezanov, who was charged by the tsar emperor to inspect the North American Russian colonies, after having reached them and thoroughly investigated the immediate needs of this new territory and sought the most likely means to meet the needs of Kamchatka and Eastern Siberia, decided to sail to California, where he hoped to achieve the object of his plans.[…]

From a communication of Chamberlain Rezanov with the Californian governor in Monterey it is evident that the governor himself affirmed the necessity of trade with the Russians, purportedly their nearest neighbors in America, and for this reason he then agreed to represent to his superior, the Mexican [New Spain] viceroy, during Rezanov's stay there several of the provinces constituting California entreated the governor to allow them to inaugurate trade with Russia.

The striving of California's residents for the opening of trade with Russia is based upon the following circumstances:

California abounds in horned cattle [cattle, sheep, and goats] and horses, which are scattered in innumerable herds even as far as the Columbia River [ed: sic]. The Spanish government in order to prevent damage to grainlands from these livestock have determined the killing each year of 10 to 30 thousand head. By contrast, the Okhotsk-Kamchatka territory has a great need of cattle.

California abounds in many grains and, not having the means for marketing them, is forced annually to abandon more than 300 thousand puds [ed: 10,800,000 pounds—this hardly seems credible]; by contrast, our American settlements must obtain grain more than 3,000 verstas overland through Siberia, from which it costs the [Russian-American] Company itself about 15 rub[les] per pud, and that taken to Kamchatka by the state for the local soldiery costs more than 10 rub[les] per pud.

California has an extreme shortage of cloth of every kind and iron; Russia, on the other hand, abounds in these articles.

Given such mutual needs and the mutual means of satisfying them with equal benefit to both sides, the tsar emperor enjoys Y[our] Ex[cellen]cy to solicit the Spanish ministry for permission to send no more than two Russian ships to enter the ports of California—San Francisco, Monterey, and San Diego—provided that our other ships do not arrive before the departure of these first two ships; in return our side proposes that with respect to California's need of cloth and iron, H[is] I[mperial] M[ajes]ty is ready to permit local [Californian] ships to enter not only the ports of Russian America but also those of Kamchatka itself and thereby open trading relations useful to both sides. I suggest only two ships each time our ships enter California [ports] so as to better dispose the Spanish government with a moderate request; however, when Y[our] Ex[cellenc]y has succeeded in obtaining such permission for a larger number of our ships, then this will be even more advantageous for our trade.

Source: Kalani 2011: 38. Reprinted by permission of James R. Gibson and the Fort Ross Interpretive Association.

4

THE RUSSIAN AMERICAN COMPANY
MOVES INTO CALIFORNIA

AFTER FIVE YEARS (1803–1808) of using American ships to hunt for sea mammal furs along the California shore, the Russian American Company's chief manager, Alexander Baranov, decided to establish a permanent Russian presence on what is now the Oregon and Northern California coasts. He sent out two expeditions: one under the command of Nikolai Bulygin, sailing on the *St. Nikolai* and destined for the coast of today's Washington State, and the other under the command of Ivan Kuskov, sailing on the *Kadiak* for California. The *St. Nikolai* and its passengers suffered a shipwreck on the shores of the Olympic Peninsula near Destruction Island, between La Push and Gray's Harbor. The exploration party, made up of Russians and Alaskans, was soon taken captive by the local Indians and held for almost two years before being ransomed by American sea captain Thomas Brown in 1810. A key individual on the *Nikolai* voyage was Timofei Tarakanov, who had been involved in a number of other expeditions under American sea captains to California coastal waters. His account of the wreck of the *St. Nikolai* and the imprisonment of its party was later obtained by Captain Vasilii Golovnin (Owens and Donnelly 1985).

The second expedition, led by Kuskov, set out for the California coast and was unaware of the disaster that had befallen the *St. Nikolai*; Kuskov had expected to make rendezvous with Bulygin and Tarakanov, but they never showed up. After briefly exploring Trinidad Bay on his way south, Kuskov headed for Bodega Bay, as directed by Baranov based on descriptions he had received from Tarakanov from the latter's visit there on the *Peacock* in 1807. Kuskov and his party landed at Bodega Bay in December of 1808 and settled in for a stay of five months, until May of 1809.

Kuskov had with him an experienced Russian *promyshlennik* named Sysoi Slobodchikov, who had acquitted himself well on several previous expeditions farther south in California. In particular, Slobodchikov had been ordered to take a party of hunters north from Bodega Bay to seek out another large bay reputed to have many sea otters. Although it is uncertain which bay this might have been, the only major bay north of Bodega was Humboldt Bay, more than 200 miles to the north. If it was indeed Humboldt Bay, it is interesting that the native people of Bodega Bay were aware of the other settlement so far to the north. As it happened, Slobodchikov's party of hunters was not particularly successful in either finding sea otters along the rough coast around Point Mendocino or in their attempts to trade with local people. The hunting in the area of Bodega Bay and within San Francisco Bay was fairly profitable, however, because after about five months Kuskov was able to return to Sitka/New Archangel with 2,765 pelts of sea otters and fur seals.

The forays into San Francisco Bay alerted the Spanish authorities to the presence of the Russians and led to reports on the situation from the commandant of the Presidio of San Francisco, Luis Argüello, to the governor of California, José Arrillaga. In one report Argüello noted that the Kodiak hunters had apparently managed to enter San Francisco Bay by paddling down to Point Bonita (just outside the Golden Gate on the Marin Headlands) and then portaging their kayaks overland to Huymenes (Richardson) Bay before paddling up into San Francisco Bay itself. Argüello's report also mentions several desertions of Anglo-American sailors during the months spent at Bodega Bay—first of four sailors and later of four Kodiak native hunters—and he describes how some of them sought asylum with the Spanish authorities. Presumably, life at Bodega Bay left something to be desired and some sailors and Kodiak natives believed they would be better off joining the Californios in settlements that would not be subject to the strict conditions of the Russian American Company.

Over the next year there were several reports of Alaskan natives or Russians either deserting or being captured by the Spanish. The Spanish authorities undertook the care and feeding of these individuals but carefully toted up the costs, to be presented to the Russian officials for reimbursement at a later date; by their calculation, it cost 1½ reals per day to house, feed, and clothe these people. Of course, California was regularly the recipient of deserting sailors from many other ships that landed in its ports, and generally speaking the inhabitants were willing to integrate these individuals into the population of the province, which was generally having a hard time attracting settlers from the motherland (either Spain or New Spain).

DIRECTIONS FROM BARANOV TO KUSKOV AS TO HIS
EXPEDITION TO CALIFORNIA (OCTOBER 14, 1808)

Russian American Company chief manager in Sitka/New Archangel, Alexander Baranov, provided detailed instructions to his lieutenant, Ivan Kuskov, regarding his mission to explore the coast of California and to establish an appropriate permanent location from which to hunt sea mammals. As seen in the following selection, Baranov relied very much on the experiences of Timofei Tarakanov, who had visited Bodega Bay in 1807 on a hunting expedition with American captain Oliver Kimball.

Alexander Baranov, chief manager of the Russian American Company. Painting by Mikhail Tikhanov. From the State History Museum, Moscow.

Courtesy of the Fort Ross Interpretive Association.

Ivan Alexandrovich Kuskov. From the Totma Regional History Museum.
Courtesy of the Fort Ross Interpretive Association.

October 14, 1808

My dear Ivan Aleksandrovich:

Because of the present unsatisfactory progress of our hunting efforts on
Kodiak and in this area, and the substantial diminution of common assets
because of various unforeseen expenditures, we are compelled to seek sources
of revenue in regions other than those which have been assigned to us in
order to improve and enlarge our fur trade and other activities. This will
benefit our current shareholders whose interests are inseparable from the
benefits of the entire Company, and the future goals of the Empire.

I have invoked God's assistance in this endeavor and have adopted what
I consider to be a good plan to dispatch a hunting party to the coast of the
American New Albion with the Company vessels *Mirt Kadiak* and *Nikolai*.
These ships and their commanding officers, navigators of the 14th rank, are
to protect the hunting party as well as to survey and describe the entire coast
from the strait of Juan de Fuca to California, with complete accuracy plac-
ing on the charts plans of important sites such as harbors, bays and straits

where there might be suitable anchorage, provided they have the means to carry out this assignment. The experience of previous groups of our men aboard foreign vessels, in regard to the undisputed profits of that region, gives considerable hope, because in a very short time a number of small groups have discovered and attained substantial trade possibilities. For this reason a small vessel, the *Nikolai,* has already been sent there under the command of [Nikolai I.] Bulygin on September [date missing] of this year with instructions to make a full description of these shores and to discover harbors, bays, straits and islands with anchorages for large vessels. Enclosed are copies of the instruction I gave Bulygin and the ship's supercargo, [Timofei] Tarakanov. Since the importance of this matter requires very sound and careful attention to the selection of sites for settlements and enterprises and to the problems of supply, as well as great care and patriotic zeal in regards to all the details of the venture, I felt I should go there personally, first aboard the *Aleksandr* and then aboard *Neva,* from Kodiak. Unfortunately, various unforeseen circumstances have prevented me from doing this, including the following:

1. I am waiting for Captain O'Cain to come from Sanak, because I am the only one who can resolve the important question of the Company's capital.

2. I am also waiting for the naval frigate from St. Petersburg, which was to have arrived here long ago with official instructions for me from the Main Administration of the [Russian] American Company. This is just as important as the above.

3. The ship *Neva* remains idle here, under the supervision of local authorities, awaiting instructions to be brought by the same frigate or via Okhotsk on a transport vessel, which will inform us whether trade with the Chinese is permitted in Canton. *Neva* is to be sent there as the primary destination for her voyage. This lack of information is now preventing me from making decisions, and for that reason I cannot leave this port, since the burden of issuing instructions and administering the region still falls on me alone. This may be incompatible with my poor health and advanced years, but I am determined to use whatever strength and years I have left to do everything in my power to work for the benefit of this country. I challenge Your Excellency to distinguish yourself through this illustrious deed as proof of your loyal devotion which you owe to our generous Monarch and to our Fatherland. You have a duty as a subject of the Empire to do

this, and even more because you have been granted great favor by being elevated from a middle level to a high level staff position.

Although I trust your good judgment and many years of experience in organizing successful hunting and commercial profit ventures, and providing for the men entrusted to your command, nevertheless I do feel I must advise you of my views pertaining to hunting, trading and politics in regard to that region.

1. From the instructions I have mentioned, for navigator Bulygin, who is being dispatched aboard the brig *Nikolai,* you already know that his first rendezvous is set for the coast of Albion in the port or bay of Gray's Harbor, located in 47° northern latitude and 236° 3' longitude from London. You are to proceed there directly with the vessel *Mirt Kadiak,* and if you find him there or if you receive information about him as per his instructions, then depending on local circumstances, weigh the potential of the hunt there and remain for some time to give the hunting party an opportunity to gain experience in this area.

If the results are unsatisfactory, leave the place and proceed south to Trinidad Bay located in 41° 3' northern latitude and 236° 6' longitude from the London meridian, which is the place designated for the second rendezvous with Bulygin. You are to stop there without fail. Do not enter the Columbia River; I foresee no need for this, for it is far above the channel located on Vancouver's maps. It is possible Bulygin will anchor there to make his observations. The mouth of the Columbia River and the channel are surrounded by many sandy reefs and banks, and therefore the entry is dangerous for large vessels. There are many [native] people living along the shores and it is possible the American Bostonians have already supplied them with firearms. Their goal is to settle and establish a colony there, as you know. For that reason it is doubtful whether our hunters should be put to work there, even if marine animals are seen. Indeed it is doubtful that there are furbearing animals in the river there, except for river beavers and mountain animals. I wish you a safe arrival at Trinidad Bay.

2. Whether or not you meet Bulygin there, or receive news of him, make all preparations to hunt there. First, send Slobodchikov to a bay which is not more than 20 miles south along the coast and learn from him whether Bulygin is there. If he is not, and has not been there, explore and make

careful measurements of the entrance and the interior of the bay, and if the entry seems suitable and your ship *Mirt Kadiak* can enter, immediately move your ship there for safe anchorage, because the Trinidad roadstead is not safe. Then give instructions for hunting in various locations.

The experience of the hunting group led by Tarakanov is very encouraging because there, where Kimball anchored, and also near Bodega and Drake's bays, a goodly number of animals were sighted, and although the hunting party was small, it nevertheless was very successful. For that reason it would be appropriate to establish a main camp there, selecting one of three sites: in Slobodchikov Bay, or where Kimball anchored, or Bodega Bay, if it is possible for ships to enter there.

Periodically send promyshlenniks to Trinidad and farther south to hunt, gain knowledge of the area and of the people who live there, especially in those places where the brig *Nikolai* may not have the chance or opportunity to go. However, at the present time it is not necessary to build large structures there while the whole coast from San Francisco harbor in California to the Strait of Juan de Fuca remains completely unsurveyed and we do not have formal permission from our government to occupy and settle there. However, at the most suitable place you are to build a fortress with proper living quarters for secure temporary housing for yourself and your men.

Do not dissipate your energies on things not absolutely necessary. Your only objective is to hunt and determine where all the most advantageous places are along the coast of Albion. For this reason if there should be danger from the natives, you are to employ more Russians on hunting expeditions. However, you must strictly prohibit even the slightest exploitation of the local natives either by Russians or by members of the hunting groups; they must not be either insulted or abused. You personally and your subordinates must make every effort to win their friendship and affection. You must not use fear because of the superiority of your firearms, which these people do not possess. Rather, seek to attract them through kind gestures based on humanity, and occasional appropriate gifts to win them over. Do not neglect any opportunity to gain future benefits.

Even in their natural weaknesses, their predilection for theft and deceit, you should pardon minor transgressions due to animal thoughtlessness which circumscribes their comprehension and morals. However, even while you forgive minor transgressions, let them know your displeasure, and little by little teach them to understand the difference between good and bad, and to see how they bring destruction upon themselves through harmful and evil deeds. When you become better acquainted with them try to secure from them, by purchase if necessary, two or three young lads from among their prisoners. When you have clothed them decently, teach them the Russian language. As soon as they can understand the words for things, in your free time write down useful vocabularies so that in the future you can use them as interpreters. Also, you may gain some understanding about the meaning of basic concepts.

You are strictly to forbid anyone from accepting even the most trivial item from them as a gift; not even a bit of food is to be accepted. Pay a little something for everything, using our goods and trinkets which they may desire. Entertain their respected leaders and give them food to eat every time they visit, if you have enough food to do this. In short, teach them to view all Russians and partovshchiks as benevolent friends who pose no danger to them. Obviously, you should on these and all other occasions take all precautions necessary for your safety.

3. According to Tarakanov, Bodega Bay, up to now, more than any other known place along that coast, offers the best prospects for hunting, because with the incoming tides a multitude of sea otters enter the bay to feed; the bay is narrow, has a sandy spit with a clay bottom, and remains calm in all storms. It probably has plenty of shellfish, which is the principal food of the sea otter.

The entrance to the bay is very narrow and well suited to the use of nets for trapping. If the high and low tides are similar to those of the Yakutat Bay, one can anchor farther off the mouth of the bay and send the hunting party to the interior of the bay to drive the sea otters out into the net. Near the mouth the sea otters are so abundant that in one hour [Tarakanov] while sitting quietly onshore, was able to kill five with his gun. It is always possible, even if there are breakers at the entrance to the bay, to enter it [by portaging] across the spit, as well as from Drake's Bay, from where there is a portage of less than two versts according to Tarakanov. The interior of the bay is possibly quite similar to San Francisco Bay; the northernmost Spanish fortress, with the same name, is at the entry to the bay. It would be useful for future political considerations to explore the area between those two bays very cautiously, so as not to give the Spanish the slightest reason for suspecting our intention to hunt in such close proximity. For that purpose you should dispatch a group of your most dependable and unassuming men. Although they should be properly armed as a precautionary measure, they should be strictly ordered that at no time during their expedition are they to fire at a single animal or bird, unless a member of the expedition is in great danger.

You should definitely appoint Tarakanov to head the hunting party unless it is possible to detach one of the leaders from the vessels, someone who could fulfill this assignment more faithfully, that is, to use the compass to chart the isthmus in the narrowest place between these bays, especially the location of San Francisco Bay, where the route to Bodega begins and ends. Describe this with annotations indicating the distance from the river fort. But if by some unforeseen chance this should arouse the curiosity of the Spaniards from the fort, order the group to return at once. Likewise, if it is impossible to send a navigator to do this, and it is left to Tarakanov to carry out this assignment, in that case you are personally to move temporarily to Bodega and Drake's bays, proceed north either to the harbor where Kimball anchored, or to Slobodchikov or Trinidad bays where our vessels are to be anchored at that time. This procedure is especially important to follow if any naval vessel is sighted at the Spanish fortress. If there is no naval vessel, anticipate no danger because the Spaniards have no rowboats there.

4. While you and your ships or detachments are near the Columbia River, determine whether there are any American Bostonian vessels there, and whether their government is trying to establish colonial settlements there. If this is the case and if you happen to encounter [Bostonians] or explorers from other European nations, or Spaniards themselves, if you have an opportunity to enter into conversation with them, do not embark on any negotiations concerning the allocation of occupation rights in local places. You are only to say that the Russians have the same right as other nationals to hunt marine animals and seek profits along all coasts and islands, from the port of New Arkhangel south to California, where other nations have not established claims in accordance with natural law. This does not apply to places already occupied by other enlightened powers. Tell them you are sailing with a group of promyshlenniks from place to place, where it is

profitable solely to hunt.

5. If by some chance you should have an opportunity to negotiate or discuss matters with the Commandant of the above-mentioned Spanish fort of San Francisco, [Don] Luis, the son of the former Commandant, Señor Aksenii [sic: Argüello] with whom our late representative, His Excellency Nikolai Petrovich Rezanov in 1806 had a gratifying meeting and friendship, and to whom the beautiful daughter of the latter and the sister of the former, Concepcion, became engaged, you should first inform them of the death of Rezanov in accordance with the letter given to Shvetsov, a copy of which has been given to you. Then send fitting gifts from among the things you have taken with you and ask their kind permission for our hunting parties to operate in the oft mentioned bay of San Francisco. At the first opportunity promise to pay one piaster's worth of any of our goods they wish for each large sea otter, except for a *koslok* [half grown] or *medvedka* [young, suckling]. Also suggest that you have a list and samples of such goods. For these goods you will ask to receive the same value in food supplies which the deceased general [Rezanov] received, at the same asking prices, but more flour, if the prices are lower than those quoted to the general. Do not hesitate to bargain, even if they ask twice as much as the going price for wheat.

You are fully aware of other aspects of the situation: what is available, what the prices are, and what we need most. But above all you are to try, if you have a chance, to establish future mutually advantageous, amicable trade and hunting relations, so we can freely supply them with our goods in exchange for their products. Do not make sea otters an item of trade, nor take them at any price, until such time as you make the Spanish more inclined to allow our hunting parties to hunt without interference along the coast of California in places where there are most animals and where hunting is more desirable. For this, offer to pay them a specified amount each year, or an amount for every 1,000 pelts, counting only the *bobrs* [adult males] and *matkas* [adult females], [and secure for us] permission to obtain provisions freely through voluntary trade with church missionaries.

6. After wintering on the coast of Albion, early in the spring, around March, when you ascertain that it is safe to settle in inhabited places and that you may hunt with profit, but no longer need one of the ships for

protection, it would be a good idea to send it with a small group of men farther south to search for islands off the Coast of California, islands which have not been located on maps, and to explore the island of Guadeloupe which is located at some distance off the mainland at 29° 17' northern latitude and [missing] degrees longitude from the London meridian. This detachment should ascertain whether there may be potential for profitable hunting of sea otters or fur seals on that island or others similar to it which are located at some distance from the mainland.

However, this sailing and searching should be undertaken with the greatest caution because of the danger from Spanish royal vessels and French privateers who may be in those waters looking for the English, although this is not anticipated. Nevertheless we have long been unaware of European developments, so order your men to avoid contact as much as possible.

7. If the Benevolent Peacemaker gives you bountiful success in your hunting by May or June of 1809, but you believe there may be still greater profits to be made by leaving a group of Russians and hunting parties behind in a secure position in those or in other newly discovered places, and if you personally decide to stay there, and then if these hunting opportunities and dangers come to an end, you should decide about our future course of action and when to return there with the entire party of hunters and with the vessels. Finally, if you should feel it advisable, send back a small vessel, bringing part of the furs and news about everything that has happened up until then. I entrust that decision to your good judgment, in the hope that you will not let any opportunity slip by which might secure profits for the Company, for our public and for the Fatherland.

If you chance to encounter the American Bostonian Captain [George W.] Ayers [ed: Eayrs] in those waters, negotiate with him. I made a special contract with him on Kodiak regarding hunting and provisioning from California. He has been assigned 26 baidarkas, under the command of Shvetsov, with my nephew as his assistant. If necessary, draw up an agreement in conformity with the contract, a copy of which is being sent to you, but with new terms if there is an opportunity anywhere for joint hunting. Make your plans, taking into consideration local prospects for success. Try in every possible way to move him away from the coast of Albion, even if you do make a joint agreement, so that neither [the Bostonians] nor other foreigners will discern our directions and intentions.

9. [ed: sic, no 8 in the text] In the detachment of this expedition which is entrusted to you, be as humane as you possibly can and have the greatest regard for all peoples, Russian and Aleut, who make up the hunting party. If it is within your power, anticipate all necessities, potential shortages, and physical exhaustion which may enervate the men. Show special compassion toward the sick and spare no effort to restore them to health and to their previous strength. This concern, along with precautions for safety, must be your prime consideration in new settlements. For that purpose ten *vedros* [ed: 27 gallons] of rum and one barrel of molasses have been provided for you.

In conclusion, I recommend that you not forget that orderly habits among all enlightened people require that you keep a daily journal of events which may happen from the time of your departure from here. In particular, you should not omit from this journal any noteworthy information deserving attention, even if it is heard from native inhabitants of the area. Remember also to inquire around Bodega and Trinidad whether it is true, as the California missionaries told the general [Rezanov], that cattle and horses are already widely spread out along the coast of New Albion. You and your people should try to learn whether it is possible that detachments will be sent farther inland from the coast, especially to little known places where pasture lands suitable for grazing livestock and for shelter may be found.

I am also appending a copy of the instructions I gave to navigator Petrov regarding the orders for his first voyage.

Written October 14, 1808 in the American port of New Arkhangel.
Administrator, Collegiate Councilor
Cavalier Aleksandr Baranov

Source: Dmytryshyn et al. 1989: 165–174.

REPORT BY KUSKOV TO BARANOV OF HIS EXPEDITION
TO "NEW ALBION" (OCTOBER 5/17, 1809)

Following his exploration trip to "New Albion"—a name that lingered from the time of Francis Drake's visit in 1579 and cast into question Spanish ownership of the coast of California north of San Francisco Bay—Ivan Kuskov wrote a report to his boss, Alexander Baranov.

New Archangel, October 5/17, 1809

With reference to Your Honor's instructions of October 14 last year, 1808, regarding our departure from the port of New Archangel, I was ordered and assigned a first rendezvous with the ship *Nikolai* (sent out earlier from New Archangel and piloted by the navigator Mr. Bulygin) at the port of Gray's Harbor, 47° North Latitude and 263° 3' West Longitude (from Greenwich). Following this route, we encountered obstacles occasioned by continuously contrary and strong winds when we approached the above-mentioned destination. We sailed about for a while and finally were forced to leave. We headed toward Trinidad Bay, where I hoped to join the above-mentioned ship *Nikolai,* and arrived there on the 28th of November.

[…]

After leaving the Trinidad roadstead on December 7, we reached Bodega on December 15 in good shape. After selecting a place to stay, we found the best harbor to be Tuliatelivy Bay, named after the natives that lived there, where the American, Captain [Oliver] Kimball, had earlier visited [on the brig *Peacock,* in 1806–1807—translator's note, SW]. Since we were ready to hunt, we made attempts to do so in various places nearby. But at the very beginning we had little success, due to the small number of sea otter, and then stormy weather hampered us.

But circumstances required that we stay. First, the rigging and sails needed to be changed, and other ship repairs were necessary. After these repairs were made, we needed to communicate with the commandant of San

Francisco, the Spanish fort, and, if permitted, proceed to this port for trade and to request permission to hunt in San Francisco Bay. In case, however, permission should be denied, and the *Nikolai* not arrive, we would proceed southward where a group under our agent Slobodchikov had earlier been.

Secondly, we had to wait for some time, of course, for the ship *Nikolai*. But since the repair and the equipping of our ship went quite slowly, we were delayed until May of this year, 1809. In the meantime, four sailors deserted—first in late December, and then from time to time others threatened to as well. Since we could not rely on many of them, we were therefore forced to give up both our [anticipated] negotiations with the commandant at the Spanish presidio of San Francisco and our voyage southward. I could not confidently leave the ship, for they [the deserters] might possibly fall into the hands of enemies cruising in these waters (as explained later on).

We accepted the plan of going to Trinidad Bay and leaving a hunting party of Kodiak and Fox Islanders there on shore, under the direction of Slobodchikov and his assistants. Although we could not expect much success from hunting, at least this group would remain trustworthy in the future. But when we were all set, two baidarkas of these Kodiak hunters followed the deserters' example.

I feared that we might meet similar misfortunes on our voyage through unknown places and harbors and that many of the crew might seek to desert and leave the rest of us in bad straits, thus delaying the voyage. So I sent out a group under Slobodchikov's command to hunt northward along the coast. We learned [from the local people that lived] at Tuliatelivy Bay that there was, as it were, a large bay to the north with sea otter.

Buoyed by hopes of reaching it, our hunting party near Cape Mendocino proceeded at great risk along this shoreline, with its rocks, cliffs, and heavy surf, but there was nothing to hunt. Nor was there much success in acquiring furs through trade.

The entire party twice attempted to search for our deserters: at Bodega Bay, around Trinidad Bay, and inside the northern arm of San Francisco Bay, where one might roam all over, and where we undertook most of our fur-hunting activities. In all, we took in 1,866 adult and yearling sea otter pelts, 476 young-pup pelts, and 423 fur seals. Meanwhile, the time we spent on the shores of New Albion was prolonged until the middle of last August.

Concerning all that occurred throughout this period, I have the honor of presenting you the following herewith: a daily log-book and records of the crew (both male and female), who came along on board the *Myrtle-Kodiak,* and of various instances of death or desertion.

Humbly yours,

Commerce Councilor [Ivan A. Kuskov]

Source: Kuskov 1980.

REPORT FROM LUIS ARGÜELLO TO
GOVERNOR ARRILLAGA (FEBRUARY 16, 1809)

1809 February 16 San Francisco.

Luis Argüello, Commandant,
to Governor Arrillaga regarding the Russians

On the 14th day of the current month two Anglo-Americans presented themselves, among the Christian Indians that had come from the other shore of the port, saying that they had deserted a Russian frigate anchored at the Port of Bodega. These were, without a doubt, the two that three days ago (having heard and seen a rifle shot from the guard of the forecastle) gave me a report and I then went to the said port and reconnoitering the opposite cost, we saw two figures going in that small bay, and its result was their coming with the said Indians passing by, and according to the explanation of one of them, he was one of the four that Russian General Mr. Nicolas Rezanov held as prisoners exiled from the island adjacent to the presidio during his stay at this port. The certain thing is, Sir, that they present themselves to us everywhere, since I just received a report from the corporal of the military escort of Mission San José in which they tell me, "Yesterday around 12:15 three armed subjects presented themselves at the house of the fathers, said to be Russians who, having taken some refreshment in the kitchen, I brought to this guardhouse where they are kept deposited until orders are received regarding this matter." For this reason on this date I am sending an order to the corporal so that he may bring them to this presidio.

For this reason I called the above stated persons that came with the Indians of this mission, and again asking them questions: I gained from them that the frigate is named *Kadyak* and that its [ed: passengers were] commander Goosebfh [Kuskov], 40 Russians, and 150 Indians including 20 women, from Onalaska [Unalaska], Coiak [Kodiak], and other places. Also, these subjects have said that those who were fishing [ed: sic, hunting sea otters] inside the bay with canoes had retired, not from the port, since having disembarked in the cove of Huymenes [Richardson Bay], on another part of the port, they carried their canoes and went to the hills until arriving at Bonetes Point [Point Bonita, outside the Golden Gate] where they again embarked to continue their route.

This is confirmed by the same Indians (that, even though they saw them and there would be some 50 of them) who were walking around; to which is added the great amount of commerce, that I am persuaded that the said Russians or Americans have been with these natives, because these have brought some of their effects, such as jackets, shirts, and some small cloths.

Nevertheless, in that these days the air has been very clear, nothing has been reported or seen at a distance from the curve of Point Bonita to that of Point Reyes, and the entire coast seems good; and I am keeping a close lookout and giving reports of the results to Your Lordship.

Today the Indian from Onalaska [Unalaska] left this presidio as Your Lordship has directed me to do.

Source: Document 3 in Mathes 2008. Reprinted by permission of the Fort Ross Interpretive Association.

❧ 5 ❧

TARAKANOV AND CHIEFS IÓLLO AND VALLÍ:ÉLA
AND THE NEGOTIATIONS FOR FORT ROSS

TIMOFEI TARAKANOV[1], one of the first Russians to visit California, was a trusted and effective "field man" for the Russian American Company. Baranov assigned him to lead hunting parties and provide critical reports of his finds that would help the Russians develop a program of exploiting the sea mammal resources of California. These facts aside, traditional histories have not given Tarakanov his due, and one story that did acknowledge his contributions turned out to be forgery on the part of one of Hubert Howe Bancroft's hired historians, Ivan Petrov,[2] who concocted a fictional character he named Vasilii Tarakanov. Fortunately, the real Tarakanov, Timofei, was mentioned in enough accounts and contexts that we can piece together a fair amount of his story, including the intriguing reference to him in a description obtained from two Indians from Bodega Bay. (The people living around Bodega Bay have been called the "Bodega Miwok" by anthropological linguists who consider the group's language a dialect of Marin Miwok.) In this account, Tarakanov was the prime actor in Russian negotiations for land in the vicinity of Bodega Bay, north of Spanish occupied lands, although historians have generally followed Bancroft's lead in giving Ivan Kuskov the credit.

The two Bodega Miwok Indians, then residents of Mission San Rafael, told the story of this transaction to Fr. Mariano Payeras sometime between 1819

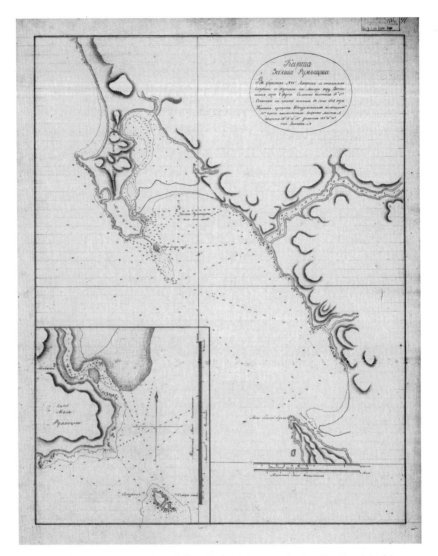

Chart of Rumiantsev Bay by Kislakovsky (1818). From the Russian Naval Archive, St. Petersburg. Courtesy of the Fort Ross Interpretive Association.

and 1822. The account has been put forth by Hubert Howe Bancroft (1886: ii, 297) as a key point in the Russian claims to Fort Ross and Bodega Bay:

The native chiefs were made friends by the distribution of petty gifts, and there is not much doubt that they made, either now

[1811] or the next year, some kind of a formal cession of territory to the newcomers. The price paid, according to the statement of the natives in later years, as Payeras tells us, was three blankets, three pairs of breeches, two axes, three hoes, and some beads. Always more or less hostile to the Spaniards and to their brethren under Spanish rule [ed: i.e., Christian Indian neophytes], the natives were indeed glad to have the strangers come as allies and protectors. In later disputes the Russians dwelt upon this cession as one of the strongest elements in their title—so expedient has it always been found in the New World to affirm the natives' right of ownership where the soil could be bought for a song, and to deny it when forcible possession must be taken.

Further information on the negotiations and who acted on the part of the Russians comes more directly from Fr. Mariano Payeras, once the Father President of the Missions of California. About six months before his death (in the spring of 1823), he made a visit to Fort Ross in the company of Canonigo Agustin Fernandez de San Vicente, the representative of the new (and short-lived) imperial government of Mexico. The *diario* written by Fr. Payeras following the trip is a lively and informative description of Fort Ross in late 1822, when Karl Schmidt was the commandant. As an addendum to the *diario,* Fr. Payeras penned a short item called *Notas para el Diario* (MSBAL Doc 1842), which is found in the Mission Santa Barbara Archive-Library. This document provides a brief description of the purchase of Fort Ross and the "rental" of Bodega Bay by the Russians early in their stay. The information was said by Payeras to have been provided by two Indian neophytes of Mission San Rafael named Vicente and Rufino. These two men were Bodega Miwok people from the village across the bay from the Russian harbor settlement of Port Rumiantsev (Bodega Bay).

The Christians of San Rafael, Vicente and Rufino of the Estero of San Juan Francisco Regis [Tomales Bay] opposite Bodega, say that it is true that the commander of a Russian ship named Talacani first came and stopped at Ross, and bought that place from its chief, Pánac:úccux, giving him in payment three blankets, three pair of trousers, beads, two hatchets, and three hoes. Afterwards he went down to La Bodega and bought it from its chief, Ióllo (he is already dead and his son Vallí:éla is now chief) for an Italian-style cape [capingon], a coat, trousers, shirts, arms, three hatchets, five hoes, sugar, three files, and beads. This was not purchased, but rather it was like giving permission, and so the Indians would give them help. It is said that they did buy Ross, but only Ross, not the neighboring places. (Payeras 1995: 335)

The identity of "Talacani" was a mystery for many years. It was difficult to determine if it was meant to be the name of the ship or the ship's captain, although either supposition led nowhere because the ship that Ivan Kuskov arrived on was called the *Chirikov*. On the other hand, we know that Timofei Tarakanov had been at Bodega Bay with Captain Oliver Kimball in 1807. When Kuskov arrived in 1811 he joined up with a party of Aleut hunters being led by Timofei Tarakanov (Pierce 1990: 497–499), and when the names and details of Tarakanov and Talacani are compared, it is evident that they refer to the same person. The replacement of the "r" in Tarakanov by an "l" to make Talacani

Notes by Fr. Payeras of an interview with Indians at Mission San Rafael regarding the Russian "Talacani" at Bodega Bay. Courtesy of the Mission Santa Barbara Archive-Library.

is seen in other consonant replacements found in the Bodega Bay Miwok language (see Callaghan 1970: 71 for an example of the Spanish word *interprete* becoming *télpite* in Bodega Miwok).

The notion of a lower-level official doing the negotiating for properties in California rather than the leader, Ivan Kuskov, may seem odd at first, however, it makes more sense when one considers that Timofei Tarakanov had had extensive experience dealing with Indians (Owens 1990; Owens and Donnelly 1985: 39–65) and may have even learned some of the Miwok language in the months he had spent hunting sea otter in the area of Bodega Bay (Dmytryshyn et al. 1989: 169–170) prior to Kuskov's first trip to the California coast in 1809. The Bodega Miwok Indians quite reasonably would have considered Tarakanov to be the leader of the Russians if he were acting as spokesman in these dealings. Other instances, particularly in Oregon and Hawaii (Owens and Donnelly 1985: 34, 84), also underscore Timofei Tarakanov's leadership skills, particularly in difficult situations.

But when exactly did Tarakanov enact these negotiations with the Bodega Miwok? Historical evidence puts him in California in 1806–1807 and 1810–1811. Tarakanov did not accompany Kuskov on the 1808–1809 trip to California because he was attached to the ill-fated exploration of the Oregon country aboard the *St. Nikolai* (Owens and Donnelly 1985), whose members were captured by local Indians. Tarakanov was only ransomed and returned to Sitka/New Archangel in 1810. Shortly after his repatriation to the Russian American Company's Alaska headquarters, however, he was once again assigned to lead a flotilla of *baidarkas* to hunt along the California coast. Sailing on the *Isabella* sometime in June 1810, he arrived in California waters off the Farallones by July 8/20, 1810, and in November was at Drake's Bay. At the end of February 1811, with the arrival of Kuskov to Bodega Bay, a party of *baidarkas* was sent to San Francisco Bay, where it located Tarakanov with his forty-eight *baidarkas*. He then is believed to have stayed in California through the summer of 1811 before going back to Sitka. Tarakanov may have negotiated with the Indians in 1811, but then perhaps it *would be* odd that Kuskov did not have more direct involvement.

The information that Tarakanov provided to Baranov for the latter's instructions to Kuskov in 1808 was derived from Tarakanov's previous visit, in 1806–1807. On October 25, 1806, Baranov made a deal with the American sea captain Oliver Kimball to take twelve *baidarkas* onboard his ship, the *Peacock,* to hunt along the California coast, beginning at Trinidad Harbor. Timofei Tarakanov was put in charge of the *baidarkas,* with the instructions that they were not to approach any Spanish settlements. The group of otter hunters led by Tarakanov made Bodega Bay the base for their otter hunting in the area north of San Francisco (Owens 1990: 139). At that time the Spanish had not yet extended their presence northward beyond San Francisco Bay. After a successful voyage, Kimball returned to Sitka on August 3, 1807 (Pierce 1990: 497–498).

The historical record (Pierce 1990: 497–499) is not clear on whether Tarakanov made his dealings with the Bodega Miwok chief, Ióllo, during the 1810–1811 visit or on the earlier trip in 1807, but the later date is obviously correct for the following reason: Fr. Payeras's account states that Tarakanov negotiated for the site of Fort Ross, as well as for the assistance of local Indians, and since by all accounts the Russians did not even investigate Fort Ross until the 1811 trip by Kuskov, during which the Indian site of Métini (the Kashaya Pomo name for the area of Fort Ross) was identified as a likely location for a fort, Tarakanov could not have engaged in negotiations for Fort Ross before that date.

The price paid for Fort Ross (according to Payeras, "three blankets, three pair of trousers, beads, two hatchets, and three hoes") has always seemed a ridiculously small amount to pay for Fort Ross. A revised image of the transaction perhaps helps explain the discrepancy: the payment came not from Ivan Kuskov, fresh off the ship *Chirikov* from Sitka/New Archangel, but rather from Timofei Tarakanov, a *promyshlennik* who was traveling light as the head of a fleet of small *baidarkas;* very likely, the items offered to the Indians were the few things Tarakanov could readily scrape together for the transaction.

It is intriguing to note that there were two separate exchanges: one with the Kashaya Pomo chief at Fort Ross, Pánac:úccux, for an actual transfer of possession of property, and one with Ióllo, chief of the Bodega Miwok, that specified only that a use permit was obtained for the land adjacent to Bodega Bay. (In the previous excerpt, according to Payeras and his informants, only the area of Fort Ross was actually acquired.

Here is an additional record of this Russian-Indian land-use agreement, in an account by Captain Vasilii Golovnin from a visit in 1818 (1979: 163):

According to established usage, the Russians had an absolute right to settle on this coast, whereas the Spanish want to drive them out on the basis of unfounded and trifling claims. The Russians established their settlement with the voluntary agreement and permission of the native inhabitants of this country [ed: California], a people who do not recognize the rule of the Spanish and are in constant warfare with them. These people gave permission to select a place and settle on their shores for a specific sum given to them in various goods.[3] The friendly relations of these people with the Russians, which continue to this day, clearly prove that the Russians did not seize this land by force. Singly or in pairs, Russian *promyshlenniks* go hunting for wild goats [ed: sic, mule deer] in the woods, frequently spend the night with the Indians, and return safely without being injured or accosted by them. In contrast, the Spaniards do not dare appear in small numbers or unarmed for fear of being killed. These Indians willingly give their daughters in marriage to the Russians and the Aleuts, and there are many Indian wives in Fort Ross. This establishes not only friendly but family ties.

Chiefs Ióllo and Vallí:éla appear in a variety of contexts in historical documents, and using those we can begin to piece together a fuller portrait of the ongoing relationship between the Bodega Miwok tribes and various Russian visitors and settlers. The account provided by Mission San Rafael neophytes Vicente and Rufino identifies the chief of the village near Bodega as Ióllo at the time of the transaction, but by 1822 (when their record was made), he had died and his son Vallí:éla had succeeded him. This latter chief, identified as "Valenila" by Vasilii Golovnin (1979: 165) in 1818, is undoubtedly the same person. Golovnin reports his interaction with the Bodega Miwok chief in the following excerpt.

The chief of the people living next to Port Rumiantsev came to see me when my sloop was anchored there. He brought gifts consisting of various parts of their regalia, arrows, and household items, and asked to be taken under Russian protection. An Aleut who had lived over a year among these people acted as interpreter. This chief, called Valenila, definitely wanted more Russians to settle among them in order to protect them from Spanish oppression. He begged me for a Russian flag, explaining that he wanted to raise it as a sign of friendship and peace whenever Russian ships should appear

Captain Vasilii Mikhailovich Golovnin, commander of the *Kamchatka*. From the Central Naval Museum, St. Petersburg. Courtesy of the Fort Ross Interpretive Association.

near the shore. In view of all this, it would be contrary to justice and reason to assert that the Russians occupied land belonging to someone else and settled on the shores of New Albion without having any right to do so.

Another, more jaundiced, description of the chief comes from Fedor Lütke, also aboard the *Kamchatka* in 1818 (Dmytryshyn et al. 1989: 275–276):

There is no evidence that they [ed: the Indians of Bodega Bay] revere God, and in general it seems that not only do they have no understanding of God, but that they never even wonder how and for what purpose they and everything else around them were created. Nevertheless there was one among them who called himself their leader, and whom our people by custom refer to as a *toion*. But we could not determine how extensive his power is over all the others. We did not even see any exterior indications of respect shown him by the others, and he would not have looked any different from the others if some of our people had not given him two shirts the day before, both of which he wasted no time in putting on. It appears that this position is hereditary, because his father was also a toion.

In a separate account of Golovnin's visit (Matiushkin 1971: 66–70) we learn more of Vallí:éla.

The very day we weighed anchor the Indian chief sought to pay us a visit. He came out to us in a longboat, wearing two shirts (given as a present to him for some service) and a garland of intertwined grasses. Looking over our ship, he was impressed by its size. Although our captain [ed: Golovnin] gave him some axes, knives, etc., most important of all for him was a Russian military flag, which he was told to raise as soon as he saw a ship like ours. On such occasions he was promised valuable gifts from our fellow countrymen. This Indian, Valennoela, who visited us, is not an elder of the settlement here, but because of the chief's illness, he was chosen by his comrades on account of his bravery.

Upon the arrival of Golovnin's ship the *Kamchatka* on September 21/October 2, 1818, one of Golovnin's lieutenants, Fyodor F. Matiushkin, says he went ashore at Bodega Bay and walked along the shoreline.

About a mile beyond the anchorage I saw a puff of smoke from behind a small promontory. I climbed it and saw a band of New Albion nomads. They all looked at me, but since I was aware of their peace-loving nature and special affection toward Russians, I approached them boldly and soon noticed our painter in their midst. Surrounded by savages, he laughed and played with them, while drawing their pictures. Most of all, he amused them when they saw some one of them on paper. Mikhail Tikhonovich drew many of them just for pleasure, and from these he made two paintings. One represents their chief, lying in a hut of branches and

Tikhanov drawing of Bodega Miwok Indians in various activities. The *Kamchatka* can be seen through the opening in the tule hut. From the Scientific Research Museum, Russian Academy of Fine Arts. Courtesy of the Fort Ross Interpretive Association.

reeds, at the point of death. His wife is in tears, and several men surround his bed. One of them, with a bunch of feathers, seems to be acting both as a physician (for he is pulling straps across the sick man's stomach) [ed: this interpretation is questionable] and as a priest, telling the sick man's fortune. The other painting shows a woman cooking food. (Matiushkin 1971)

The painter referred to was Mikhail Tikhonovich Tikhanov, who made several drawings of the people in the vicinity of Bodega Bay. One of these portrays the inside of a tule hut in which a ritual ceremony is underway. Matiushkin identifies the individual shown lying on his back as none other than the old chief, Ióllo. Given the sad look on the face of the woman by his head (possibly his wife) and her short, disheveled hair, this painting is likely a remarkable rendering of the scene closely following his death. (California Indian women commonly cut their hair short during mourning.) Two men shown in the drawing seem to be making some form of offering, the one wearing the hairnet and hairpin holding a plume of feathers and strings of black, white, and yellow cylindrical beads.

In terms of subsequent comments on the chief at Bodega Bay, on October 3/14, 1822, Russian American Company agent Kirill Khlebnikov (1990: 96) noted in his journal that while at Bodega Bay, "in the afternoon we crossed the mountains to visit the Indian inhabitants but they had all gone into the forest to gather acorns for the winter. The chief of the Indians here, Valenil, lives in the fort." This statement seems rather strange—why would the chief of the Bodega people be living up in Fort Ross? did Khlebnikov actually mean *inside* the stockade or just nearby?—and I wonder about a mistranslation.

Vallí:éla appears again in the historical record in a lengthy report by Lieutenant Mariano Vallejo (2000) of his visit to Fort Ross and Bodega Bay in late April and early May of 1833. At Bodega Bay, Vallejo encountered the chief of the Indian village across the bay from the Russian port establishment. He gives the name of the chief as Gualinela.[4] The following passage implies a stark contrast between Indian-Spanish interactions and Indian-Russian interactions.

There are no fortifications at the port of Bodega. The only people living there are an Indian chief and his people whose rancheria is called Tiutuye. It currently consists of 43 men and women. His task is to protect the buildings the Russians have constructed. They are not bothered on their rancheria by the Russians. On the contrary, Gualinela, which is the name of the chief of this rancheria, informed me that a few days before I arrived at this place, 200 armed men, both gentiles and Christian Indians from Mission San Rafael had been there to see for themselves if any troops had passed through that area. A mission Indian from San Rafael named Toribio assured them of this, telling them that they would be killed or taken to San Francisco. A "great captain of soldiers" (this is the name they give their leaders) was in charge of the troops who would do this and the Indians should prepare themselves to fight or see which side to take. In saying these things, Toribio managed to scare the gentiles as well as the Christians who had fled from various missions. They immediately told him that a large number of Indians had gathered together and were armed and ready to die or not allow themselves to be taken to other lands by the soldiers as they always were doing.

In September 1817, the Russian American Company deemed it advisable to reaffirm the accord with the Fort Ross Kashaya Pomo by entering into an agreement. This was done by Leontii Hagemeister, a Russian naval officer soon to replace Alexander Baranov as the governor of Russian America in Sitka/New Archangel. In this agreement, Hagemeister gave the chiefs medals inscribed with the monogram of Tsar Alexander I; the reverse said "Allies of Russia." The chiefs were told to be sure to wear the medals when they came to visit Fort Ross.

This agreement has been cited on numerous occasions as an indication of how differently the local Indians were approached by the Russians as compared to by the Spanish. The Russians were willing to consider that the Indians had rights to the land they wished to use, whereas the Spanish simply considered it their entitlement to claim and take over any lands despite the fact that another people lived upon them and considered the land their own. The contrast between these attitudes may well have been due to the fact that the Russians were a merchant company with no plans for broad colonization but simply a desire to trade with the local people and to employ them as needed in laboring around Fort Ross or Bodega Bay. Whenever the legitimacy of their presence on the land was questioned, the Russians were quick to reference their agreements with the Indians.

Source: Parts of this section were published in the *Fort Ross Interpretive Association Newsletter* (Farris 1993b).

6

CONSTRUCTION AND EARLY YEARS
OF FORT ROSS, 1812–1815

REALIZING HOW EXPOSED HIS PEOPLE WERE to attacks by sea at Bodega Bay, Ivan Kuskov sought to find a better location for a permanent Russian settlement. Exploring the lands north of the area, he decided on a cove about eleven miles north of the mouth of the Russian River; it had a good beach, a freshwater creek, plenty of wood for building, and a nice bench of land suitable for constructing a fort and planting fields. The creation of Fort Ross in 1812 was the official beginning of the Russian American Company's establishing a genuine presence in California, in the form of both a colony and a formal protective structure—the Fort Ross stockade—located on a spot that was hard to approach by land and could be readily defended from the sea. Kuskov and his men constructed the fort rapidly; they started soon after the arrival of the schooner *Chirikov,* on March 15/26, 1812, and were ready to dedicate it by August 30 on the Russian calendar (September 10), to coincide with the name day of the tsar.

The Russians' establishment at Bodega Bay, by contrast, was not armed with cannons or any fortified protection, and it was the construction of Fort Ross as a permanent base that significantly alarmed the Spanish authorities. It was not long before they sent emissaries to scout out the new facilities. Kuskov received these officers cordially, but gently rebuffed any demands that the new fort be abandoned.

FORT ROSS IN ITS FIRST YEAR
UNDER KUSKOV (POST 1831)

On the basis of this Imperial consent, Mr. Baranov appointed Commerce Counsellor Kumov [ed: Kuskov] the head of this settlement, having chosen 40 of the best Russian men and 80 Aleuts and furnished them with goods, supplies, materials, and everything that was necessary for only the initial establishment. To take men and things one of the best vessels in the colonies at that time, the schooner *Chirikov*, was detailed under the command of the skilled navigator Mr. Benzeman. He left Sitka in February 1812 and on March 15 safely reached Bodega Bay, where he anchored. Immediately after arriving Mr. [Kuskov] undertook an examination of the site for settlement. Prikazchik [ed: Sysoi] Slobodchikov and the student of navigation Kondakov [Kadnikov?] with 10 of our Aleuts were sent on foot [to the area] between Bodega and the Slavanaya [ed: also Slavyanka/Slavianka or Russian] River. Upon examination no place proved suitable for a settlement, and so Mr. [Kuskov] decided to found a colony 15 verstas [ed: 10 miles] past the [Slavyanka] on a small bay.

After having chosen this site for a settlement, Mr. Kuskov transferred all of his men and the vessel from Bodega Bay to this cove. The goods and the rest [of the cargo] in the vessel were unloaded, and the vessel itself was pulled ashore. The men erected several tents for housing and, taking every possible precaution against the savages by mounting guards and patrolling at night, immediately afterwards they were occupied in preparing timber for the construction of a fort and dwellings. Despite the fact that there was timber very near by, it cost the men much effort to haul it to the site for want of any livestock then. The Russians and some of the Aleuts were engaged in felling and building and the others in hauling trees from the forest, and by the end of August they had already succeeded in enclosing the fort's site area with smooth [hewn or planed] upright logs, and 2 two-story bastions on opposing corners in which the men established their initial quarters. They designated 30 August [September 10, N.S.] 1812 as the day to raise the flag over the fort, and for this they implanted a spar from the topmast in the

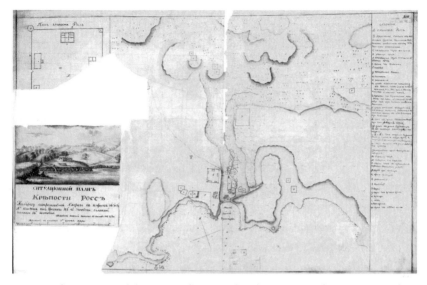

Map of Fort Ross and the surrounding area dated 1817. From the Russian Naval
Archives, St. Petersburg. Courtesy of the Fort Ross Interpretive Association.

ground in the center of it. After the usual prayer reading, they raised the flag
with the firing of cannon and rifles.

Work during the founding was devoted solely to construction, and in
the course of the year—besides the fort—they made communal barracks,
a cookhouse, a blacksmithy, a locksmithy, and a shed [*balagan*] for goods
inside the fort, and outside a bathhouse [*banya*] and a barn [*skotnik*] with
a corral [*prigon*].

Source: Anonymous. "A Historical Note about the Organization of the Russian-American
Company Settlement Subsequently Called Ross," in Kalani 2011: 265–267. Reprinted by
permission of James R. Gibson and the Fort Ross Interpretive Association.

LUIS ARGÜELLO'S REPORT TO GOVERNOR ARRILLAGA
OF LIEUTENANT MORAGA'S VISIT TO FORT ROSS
(SEPTEMBER 7, 1812)

1812 September 7 San Francisco

Through the Indians that come and go to the other shore of the port [ed: of San Francisco] I found out that a ship had gone aground a little above the port of Bodega, as I reported to Your Lordship previously; and, although I later found out from the same Indians that the aforementioned ship had been repaired and had left, I ordered Lieutenant don Gabriel Moraga to go and investigate and verify the truth from close at hand, and he did this; and having left this presidio and passed through the port on the 25th of last October, the said lieutenant with four soldiers returned on the 1st of the current month notifying me that he had found the ship aground some eight leagues, more or less, above the said Port of Bodega, not of large size, but rather a small schooner or brigantine whose crew was made up of some 80 men; everything is there, and its commandant is named Coscof [Kuskov]; all are Russians [ed: sic] from Onalaska [Unalaska] or Kamchatka, they have no interpreter, and for this reason I could not find out so much; and, according to what they explained through great effort, it had been five months since they arrived there with their ship, being lost because of taking on a lot of water, and currently they are in great need of provisions.

According to what the said lieutenant stated, they are establishing themselves because they are fortifying and building houses since they already have the square enclosed, similar to a high wall, and although it is of wood it is sufficiently strong and thick, and all of the square would be of some 150 varas, with 3½ to 4 varas in height, with two opposed towers or bulwarks, one of which faces the sea, and the other to the field [ed: land], sufficiently elevated and with artillery, although I did not see the caliber of it; and inside the said square they are constructing housing that is well built, and accordingly it demonstrates as stated that they plan to establish themselves there. Finally, I omit saying to Your Lordship the rest, since the same Lieutenant don Gabriel Moraga will inform Your Lordship verbally of all of the rest that he noted, since on this date he is going to where Your Lordship is located; I will only conclude by saying to Your Lordship that the mentioned Commandant Coscof [Kuskov] demonstrated good manners to the said lieutenant and his troops, receiving them with great gratitude.

Source: Document 10 of Mathes 2008: 61. Reprinted by permission of the Fort Ross Interpretive Association.

REPORT OF GABRIEL MORAGA AND

GERVASIO ARGÜELLO'S VISIT TO FORT ROSS (1814)

San Francisco, July 30, 1814

Regarding Fort Ross

He [Moraga[1]] thinks that there are no less than 40 Westernized people in the fort—there is a great number of Kodiaks—their arms are long, large caliber muskets and sabers.

It has been 2 years, more or less, since it was established. From any part of it all directions can be observed and anyone who goes from here, before coming down from the mountains, is seen by the sentinel since he must then come down through a large draw [Fort Ross Creek] where the Russians have vegetable gardens, a hangar [large covered area], and another little house so close to the sea that the water almost reached the said covered area, only a few varas were lacking for the large waves to reach it.

The fort is all of very strong wood, in the form of a square; on entering a tower with little embrasures that is said to have cannons is seen at the left corner: at the opposite corner is another of the same shape, the number of embrasures of the 2 towers is about 26, seen from the outside since they do not permit anyone entry to them. "At the other two corners they have the same; but then it is seen that they have nothing [i.e., no armament]."

[Ed: This paragraph is my new translation.] Within the square is an attractive roofed construction with partitions—the lower part is used as a barracks; the upper as a storehouse. In another [building] the artisans work— a large house in which live the commandant [Kuskov] and the pilot—in very good condition—filled with windows—on a lower floor is the wine storehouse (almacen de caldos); other things can be kept upstairs.

The covered area in the draw he considered to be a sort of supply area or equipment storage since in it they had the rigging and other things for ships. The latter, he thinks, had gone to Sitka to take grain and pelts.

There were also some boats and kayaks of sea lion skin.

"If the need were to arise to attack them, it would be necessary to find a trail to enter into combat with them where they have their log dragging routes and think it out well, because to my thinking it is not as hand over hand [ed: i.e., not so easy], and further these are very astute people as shown by the factories that they have built in such a short time and the differences that are found from one day to the next."

Between the beach and the fort on the same mesa to the North there is another walled square (the inside was not seen) with a house; they say that the cattle, there are already some 30 head, and the horses are kept there.

At night there is a sentinel at the house of Commandant Coscoff [Kuskov].

Source: Document 18 in Mathes 2008: 21–22. Reprinted by permission of the Fort Ross Interpretive Association.

KUSKOV'S RESPONSE TO GOVERNOR ARRILLAGA'S LETTER
ABOUT THE STATUS OF FORT ROSS (1814)

In response to the reports reproduced in the previous section (pages 78 and 80), Governor Arrillaga wrote a letter to Kuskov demanding that the Russians desist from establishing a base at Fort Ross.

In the following letter, Kuskov explains to Governor Arrillaga why he was unable to comply with the governor's demand, saying that his inability to read or understand Spanish stood in his way; we can't know whether this was true or simply artful dissembling to buy time. Kuskov goes on to show his goodwill by bestowing on the governor a tent that some Russian group had left in San Francisco Bay.

Finally, Kuskov brings up the subject of Kodiak natives who had been seized by the Spanish in 1813, asking that they be returned.

Your Excellency
Gracious Sir

Your Excellency's letter from the Port of Monterey, forwarded by your officer Mr. [ed: Lieutenant Gabriel] Moraga I had the honor to receive on the 16/22 [ed: sic] day of April, 1814, but its contents have remained unknown to me for the reason that I neither read nor write Spanish. Though your officer, the above-mentioned Mr. Moraga, endeavored to make me understand the object of your Excellency's communication, his explanations were hardly sufficiently clear as we had no interpreter to justify me in taking official action on the premises.

I have been informed by Mr. Moraga that Your Excellency have in your possession a tent which has been left behind through the carelessness of some of our men in the Port of San Francisco. I take the liberty of making Your Excellency a present of the same as I intended to do so before I received your communication and had made arrangements to have it forwarded to you by the Comandante Don Luis Argüello.

With regard to the Kodiak men now at the Port of San Francisco I have more than once asked the Commandante to intercede with Your Excellency for their return to us and once received an encouraging reply, but later a refusal followed, saying that Your Excellency directly, in the name of the Honorable Russian-American Company, under special protection, of His Majesty the Emperor of all the Russias that the above-mentioned inhabitants of Kodiak be returned to us. It appears that they have done no wrong, but were only compelled to save themselves from the surf in the bay at the Port of San Francisco, where they were captured. Of the natives of Kodiak who visited that place during last year, 1813, two men and two women were also detained without the least cause. I was informed by the above-mentioned officer Mr. Moraga and by Don Gervasio [ed: Argüello] that Your Excellency had given orders to the Commandante of the port of San Francisco [ed: Luis Argüello] to return these Kodiak men to us, but whether this is true or not, time will show.

With the greatest respect I ask Your Excellency's permission to call myself

Your Excellency's faithful servant
Commercial Councillor Ivan Kuskoff [Kuskov]
June 9th/20th, 1814.

Source: Document 16 in Mathes 2008: 68. Reprinted by permission of the Fort Ross Interpretive Association.

EQUIPMENT AND SUPPLIES
SENT TO FORT ROSS (1812–1815)

The following list of items sent to stock Fort Ross in its early years provides some intriguing details about the establishment. The large number of locks (762) gives the impression that fear of theft was a major concern. Musical instruments, including an organ, suggest a more laid-back side to life in the settlement. There is mention of a sizable quantity of pewterware (dishes, plates, and teapots), but no indication of any ceramic tableware. Looking at the list as a whole, it is sometimes hard to determine what supplies were for domestic use as opposed to trade with either the Indians or Spanish Californians; the 15 cannons were almost certainly for the fort, but the 162 mirrors may well have been trade goods.

The following have been forwarded to Mr. Commerce Councillor Kuskov from the New Archangel Office during the Years 1812 through 1815 (according to six accountings):

	rubles	kopeks
60 barrels of powder	4,746	
42 poods, 19 lbs. [ca. 1,530 lbs.] of powder	40	50
	4,786	50
guns of various calibers:		
10 bronze cannon	2,674	
15 iron cannon	4,100	
221 rifles } 20 sabers }	5,219	
22 pistols	130	
	5,349	
various military materials:		
gunlocks and flints, powder cartridges and horns, grape-shot, wicks, swords, spears [ed: pikes?], etc. at	3,702	88.2

	rubles	kopeks
scales and various weights	1,071	97
nails of various sizes	705	72
various domestic items:		
chimney flues, door accessories, glass and tableware	2,766	56
762 door locks and hanging locks—iron and bronze	2,359	40
162 mirrors of various sizes	769	62
tools: for carpentry, joinery, barrel-making, metalworking and blacksmithing	7,727	6.2
mathematical and navigational instruments:		
one telescope	25	
one sextant	100	
one octant	35	
three jacks	450	
two bronze bells (130 lbs.)	188	
71 small bells	117	
137 iron and pewter spoons	588	10
musical instruments: one organ	300	
various agricultural implements:		
spades, shovels, scythes, sickles, ploughshares, etc.	1,909	22.5
clothing and footwear:		
jackets, trousers, vests, overcoats, boots, shoes, etc.	8,012	7.5
three linen tents	7	25
glassware:		
bottles, glasses, wine-glasses, decanters, and half-liters at	324	93.2
pewterware: teapots, dishes, and plates	171	
casks and barrels—oak and fir	1,955	70
24 different irons	118	50
36 iron-heaters		
12 pieces of cloth—for flags at 25 rubles at 48 rubles	453	

	rubles	kopeks
one flag	40	
one pennant	15	
20 church icons	49	45
29 dozen silk, worsted, and cotton stockings	1,534	80
161 hats: knitted, downy, and felt	1,195	45

Source: "Account of the Capital Goods for the New Settlement of Ross, Copied at the Main Administration [in St. Petersburg] from Information Received from the New Archangel Office [Sitka], December 1815." Extract from unspecified Russian American Company papers sent by Svetlana Fyodorova to Mike Tucker, Department of Parks and Recreation, Sacramento; dated Moscow, April 11, 1980. Translated by Stephen Watrous. Reprinted by permission of Stephen Watrous.

7

TRADE WITH CALIFORNIA BY THE RUSSIAN AMERICAN COMPANY, PARTICULARLY KHLEBNIKOV

THE MAJORITY OF SPANISH-RUSSIAN TRADE was focused on the purchase of wheat and other grains. This set the Russians apart from most of the other (primarily American) merchants who came to the coast who were interested in the hides and tallow available in California. The demand for bread grains, including wheat, rye, and barley, was of special importance to the Russians, and they also traded for legumes as well as fruits and vegetables that might be transported easily to Alaska. Salt was also a central part of this trade relationship.

During the period of Spanish control of California (1769 to 1821), trade with foreign ships was officially discouraged, although the local authorities often condoned it in times of need. Foreigners were particularly able to exploit the gap created by disruption of shipping to and from Spain due in part to the wars raging in Europe and, by 1810, the beginnings of the independence movement. Government payments to troops in California were generally not forthcoming, a circumstance that made them rely even more on what they could obtain from the missions and from local authorities taking advantage of ships from other nations. Although merchant ships were particularly lucrative to tap for customs duties, income and supplies were also extracted from the sizable number of whalers who put in to the coast of California for rest and refitting, as well as Russian warships that were engaged either in round-the-world expeditions or in naval exercises, such as picket duty in the North Pacific during the summer months.

Following the success of the Mexican War of Independence in 1821, California became more open to foreign enterprises, and many traders found it an opportune moment to settle in California and open businesses offices. In time, the products they offered, as well as their prices, competed with Russian inventories. Russian trade remained viable, however, due to their interest in the niche market for grains, as well as the strong personal connections developed by the Russian American Company's chief agent, Kirill Khlebnikov. In addition to carrying general goods (cloth, tools, building supplies, etc.), Khlebnikov tailored his services by getting to know his customers and their particular desires. A trove of letters from various California correspondents to Khlebnikov, held in the State Archives of the Perm Region, in Russia, provide insight into these personal relationships. Writing in 1851, Californio writer Antonio María Osio (1996: 70) also gives us a touching comment on the interaction between Khlebnikov and the Californios:

> The Russian-American Company already had begun its trade, which benefited those engaged in agriculture. Each December two or three ships would come down from the settlements which they had on both sides of the Bering Strait and load up with wheat. Don Kiril Khlebnikov, the agent in charge of this operation, gained the respect of every inhabitant of California by his gentlemanly behavior. In conducting his business, he never experienced any problems or had any disagreements with anyone, since he always acted clearly and honorably. To assure himself of a regular supply of wheat, he offered to pay three pesos silver per *fanega* every year, even though he knew from various people in the country that, depending on the harvest, the wheat was not worth more than one peso or twelve reales per *fanega*. He also would bring very fine goods from Europe and Asia, including fabrics of superior quality and beauty which were ordered by the Reverend Fathers of the missions for vestments and church ornaments.

In contrast, some American and British traders went a step further than the Russians to permanently establish themselves on California soil by marrying local *hijas del pais* (daughters of the land). One of these men, William Hartnell, was enterprising enough to align himself with the Russians and carry on business in the local market on behalf of the Russian American Company. He even obtained a Russian dictionary to help out in this regard, and it appears that in about 1833, when Khlebnikov returned to Russia, Hartnell took on a more active role on his behalf.

LETTERS FROM FR. GIL Y TABOADA TO KHLEBNIKOV

(1825–1831)

Kirill Khlebnikov dealt with many Californians, but the largest collection of letters sent to him from a single individual (found in the State Archives of the Perm Region) are from Fr. Luís Gonzaga Gil y Taboada. Most of the letters were sent from Mission Santa Cruz, with the final one coming from Fr. Gil's last posting, at Mission San Luis Obispo. The letters show a long-time relationship in which Fr. Gil had come to appreciate very much the periodic visits made by Khlebnikov. There are several mentions of José Bolcoff (a.k.a. Osip Volkov), the Russian Creole who lived in Villa Branciforte, adjacent to Mission Santa Cruz, and often acted as an interpreter or go-between for missionaries dealing with the Russians.

Of course, Fr. Gil makes many references to items he wished to receive from the Russians. One of the most intriguing was a snuff box with the image of Tsar Alexander I; it is touching to see Fr. Gil's effort to write out the tsar's name in Cyrillic. Other items of interest are the mission's purchase of bells from the Russian American Company, and a mention of wagon parts.

Section of the letter from Fr. Luis Gil to Kiril Khlebnikov requesting
a snuff box with the image of Tsar Alexander I. Perm Archive, Russia.
Document courtesy of James Gibson.

Fr. Gil also complained about his delicate health on several occasions, once asking Khlebnikov to arrange to have a ship's doctor come see him. (Interestingly, Fr. Gil himself was often involved in caring for the sick in several of the missions where he was assigned [La Purísima, San Rafael, and Santa Cruz]. Fr. Vicente Sarría of Mission Carmel noted that Fr. Gil was accomplished at caesarean deliveries, although this usually meant the extraction of a baby from a dead or dying mother in order to baptize it into the Catholic religion.)

Following is a selection of the letters sent by Fr. Gil to his friend and business associate Kirill Khlebnikov between the years 1824 and 1831. (Unfortunately, there are a number of hard-to-read passages in some of the letters, which explains the numerous brackets used in this reprinting.)

Viva Jesus, Mary and Joseph
Sr. Don Cirilo Clebnicoff [Khlebnikov]

My dear Sir who commands my first attention,

My main reason for writing concerns the bell that weighs 26 puds and 17 [funts] which equals 31 arrobas, 17 [libras], 5 [onzas] in Spanish measure.[1]

As to other things like beeswax, there has also been a discrepancy. I will see you tomorrow, God willing, we will talk, but without fail, I will expect you.

Joseph[2] took with him a list of various items that I would like to order and others that I request you to give me.

I hope that you are well and that you will come as soon as possible so that I can give you an abrazo [hug] and in the meantime I remain your attentive servant who kisses your hand.

Fr. Luis Gil [rubric]
Sta Cruz   November 12, 1825.[3]

Sr. Don Cirilo Clebnicoff
Santa Cruz,   November 28, 1825

My favored Sir,

The accounting [bill] accompanies this [letter] to you in the knowledge that [ed: it] has been counted and weighed with great care.

Now I wish for you to send me a quintal (100 pounds) of talc, a bell if it is like that which Joseph Bolcoff has and 2 arrobas of beeswax. I am seeking from you a piece of *sayasaya nacar* [pearl Chinese silk⁴], and if you have a coffee pot of tin plate or brass, please send it to me. And when you come here, you will receive the money that remains.

I am sending you 5 dozen tongues, 18 cheeses, 4 arrobas of flour, a [bor??] of [ya brugui?], and the seeds that you ordered. Please excuse the small things and take the grandness of my affections. Please answer me using a small Spanish primer which you can learn from.

I desire that the occasions will arise to express my sincere professions of my affection as one who kisses your hand.

Fr. Luis Gil [rubric]

Viva Jesus, Mary and Joseph
Sr. Don Cirilo Clebnicoff   Sta Cruz, December 4, 1825

My Honorable Sir,

I have received the thick wagon-shaft, two coffee-pots, and a bushel and a half of [St.] Petersburg sugar. In all, I give you the just payments and would like to make a present to you as you merit the deepest of my affections and remembrances.

I am returning the tissue [with gold and silver threads] because I don't want them at 12 pesos, since you told me they would be only 7½ pesos. Also, I am returning the taffeta because I wanted the scarlet color.

It is added to the account against [English merchant William] Hartnell. Bolcoff delivered to you 8 ounces of gold and 4 pesos, 1 real of silver in seeking to settle the accounts.

If you give me the red brocade at 7 pesos, send me 10 varas; and if the bell you gave me at 30 pesos per quintal [100 pounds], I will also take. And [ed: if] the money you received from Fr. Thomas is in San Francisco then send it there.

I ask you to exchange this pipe for one of yours; and if you have a snuff box with an image of Emperor Alexander [ed: his name is written in Cyrillic], I would appreciate it very much.

Snuff box with image of Tsar Alexander I, similar to the one requested by Fr. Luis Gil in a letter to Kiril Khlebnikov. Photo courtesy of Leibshtandart Antiques, Moscow, Russia, and the Fort Ross Interpretive Association.

Also, I would like from you a little of the sailcloth and some needles for sewing the sailcloth.

When will you send the still? And lastly, I seek with all good sentiments for you to come and give me an embrace, but perhaps you will not return to see us.

You know that in the meantime as long as you live I send best wishes for a long life and an offering to please you, then I trust in the Lord to whom I commend best wishes in your future.

I seek in the greatest consideration to say to you that I am your attentive servant who kisses your hand.

Fr. Luís Gil [rubric]

P.D. The only papers of "Merica" [America?] that I have, go [to you]; and request of you to send them then, and soon to Bolcoff.

🌸 🌸

Viva Jesus, Mary & Joseph
Sr. Don Cirilo Clebnicoff   Santa Cruz, November 4, 1827

My esteemed friend and honorable sir,

Your welcome arrival in Monterey pleases me. I hope that you won't leave without seeing me. I cannot go [there] because I am not well. If you can bring the noted surgeon which Bolcoff had for me, I would appreciate it. I have requested him from the English frigate, but do not know if he will come.

If you bring brocades, braid and beeswax, please keep the best for this church.

I would like for Jacob to repair the clocks.

The first bell that I bought from you is not working because it is badly cracked.[5]

Tell me when you can come and when I can see you in which I can serve as the least of your servants who kisses your hand.

Fr. Luis Gil [rubric]

P.D. Did you bring the organ that you told me about?

Viva Jesus, Mary and Joseph
Sr. Don Cirilo Clebnicoff

My dearest and much appreciated friend,

I was very sensible that you did not permit the sea which must give us an embrace; patience.

I send you that which was requested from me with Bolcoff;

2 Bags hazel nuts	12 [piastres]. 0 [reales]
3 arrobas [75.9 pounds] cheese	9".
3 dozen tongues	7". 4 reales
	27. 4

I am also sending to you presently a crate of pears.

Also, we are sorry not to see the Sr. Captain and his wife[6]; and Bolcoff and his wife[7] also hope to see them, and we remain disappointed. We salute them and yourself with affection and [ed: you] are commended by your unchanging friend who kisses your hand.

Fr. Luis Gil [rubric]
December 10, 1828

P.D. Could you send me beeswax or sugar or that which you will, and tell me if you will send Jacob[8] to repair my chronometer.

Viva Jesus, Mary and Joseph

Don Cirilo Clebnicoff   Santa Cruz, November 25, 1829

My esteemed friend,

In answer to your query I say that I happily celebrate your arrival and that of the other men.

You have arrived in a sad period of which the lack of water in the past year has resulted in a lack of harvests in various missions and settlements and also this year it appears to be the same. In short, Bolcoff told you that which he had heard.

The expressions which manifest my gratitude to the memory of me cannot be contained and with no mention of my Doña Prudenciana.[9] If you go to the ship, please give my regards to that lady.

I still suffer from my ulcer and bad stomach. I wish that I could get you to come so I could give you a hug [*abrazo*] from your friend who kisses your hand.

Fr. Luis Gil [rubric]

My very dear friend, Don Cirilo,

I learned with pleasure of your happy arrival and that you enjoy good health. I send you the general accounting for the tobacco and the pipe that you sent me. I request of you that if you can bring superfine tea, you can sell me two pounds, and also of good black tea. And I ask you to put the amount in my name to Don Estevan Munras or I will pay for it by Don David,[10] as you wish.

If you wish to come, I will give you 100 fanegas of wheat in exchange for things for the church.

Please give my regards to all my Russian friends and I wish you the best from your friend who kisses your hand.

Fr. Luis Gil [rubric]

San Luis Obispo

November 14, 1831

To Don Cirilo Clebnicoff

Monte-Rey

Source: Kalani 2011: 270–289. This selection translated by Glenn J. Farris.

Reprinted by permission of Glenn J. Farris and the Fort Ross Interpretive Association.

KHLEBNIKOV'S JOURNAL (JULY 18/29, 1824)

The following contains a list of items Khlebnikov bought from the Santa Cruz Mission for the Russian American Company.

🦋 🦋

The padre refused outright to take cash, asking instead to be paid with goods needed at the mission. But the main reason he did not want to accept cash was that the government, in need of funds, was collecting money from all the missions. Hence, he ordered the following goods on the basis of our above-mentioned debt [ed: for 3,096 piasters, 4 reals]:

From goods requested last year:

1 bell weighing about 5 puds [ed: 180 pounds]
1 coffee mill
1 quintal of wax table-candles
4 quintals of local candles
1 quintal of large candles with ornaments
brocade for chasuble
1 quintal of mica
1 barometer
1 quintal of three-inch nails
1 dozen locks for chests
1 dozen small English scissors
1 Nativity statue

To which he added the following:

1 dozen medium-sized and large padlocks
1 dozen round containers of wax
3 large candlesticks
12 small lanterns
scarlet velvet
1 paired-oared boat about 20 feet in length for fishing

Source: Khlebnikov 1990. Reprinted by permission of the University of Alaska Press.

8

STORY OF THE BRIGANTINE
LYDIA/IL'MENA

WHEREAS IT WAS the swift little skin *baidarkas* that were the key to hunting sea otters, the great supporting role in the fur trade was the ocean sailing ships that first transported the Kodiaks and their skin boats to the hunting grounds, and then took the valuable furs to the market at Canton, China. Many of these ships were initially American ships that were then sold to the Russian American Company at its Pacific headquarters in New Archangel (and before that at Kodiak). One intriguing example of this transfer is the story of the brigantine out of Boston that was originally named the *Lydia*.

This ship was said to have been built in the East Indies of teak wood and was acquired by New England commercial interests. The earliest mention of the *Lydia* that I have come across is from 1804, when the brig, owned by Theodore Lyman and Associated, cleared Boston in August bound for the Northwest coast. The brig was captained by Samuel Hill. When it visited Nootka, it came across the two survivors of the ship *Boston*. One of these men, John Hewitt, managed to get a message to Captain Hill, who then took Chief Maquinna captive and demanded the release of Hewitt and his companion. Thus, our first view of the *Lydia* is in the guise of an angel of mercy. The ship traveled back to Boston by way of Canton. Although it may have made another western voyage in the intervening years, our next record of the ship was its departure from Boston in 1809 under the command of Thomas Brown. She sailed under a joint contract between her owner, George Lyman (son of Theodore Lyman) and the Perkins Brothers (James and Thomas Handasyd Perkins) with orders to engage in the northwest trade.

Based on these two sources, the *Lydia* was well on its way to the northwest coast in 1809 under the captainship of Thomas Brown, and probably in company with another of the Lymans' ships, the *Hamilton*. The brig *Lydia* is described as being a "foreign bottom," built in the East Indies of teak wood (Howay 1973: 85).

The *Lydia* sailed from Boston to the Pacific, where it touched in at Hawaii before coming across to the Pacific coast. It stopped in at the mouth of the Columbia River and then made its way up to the Puget Sound area, arriving at Kaigani on March 24, 1810. While on the northwest coast, the *Lydia* and Thomas Brown came to be involved with the Russian American Company in a dramatic fashion when they ransomed from local Indians the survivors of the ill-fated expedition of the *St. Nikolai*. One of these survivors, Timofei Tarakanov, stated in an account of his capture and ransom:

At long last, merciful God heard our prayers and delivered us. On the 6th [ed: 17th] of May [1810], early in the morning, a double-masted vessel came into view and soon approached the shore. My master, taking me with him, at once set out for the ship. This brig was a ship from the United States called the *Lydia,* under the command of Captain Brown. On this ship, to my great surprise, I found my comrade Bolgusov and learned that he had been resold to someone on the Columbia River, where he had been purchased by Captain Brown. The captain, having talked with me about our misfortunes, explained to my master as best he could that he should order all his countrymen to bring to the captain all captive Russians, whom the captain would buy back. My master departed and I remained on the brig. (Owens and Donnelly 1985: 64)

Tarakanov goes on to tell of how when the native chiefs asked for a much higher ransom for the last three captives they held, Captain Brown seized the brother of the chief and demanded that the others be turned over. When they eventually were returned, Brown paid the same ransom that he had for each of the other captives.

The *Lydia* then sailed up to Sitka/New Archangel, arriving in June 1810, and delivered the captives to Alexander Baranov. After a "near mutiny" in October 1810, the ship swapped masters with the *Derby,* and James Bennett took command of the *Lydia*. Bennett then sailed on to various Chinese ports (Howay 1973: 99), while Bennett returned to the northwest coast and continued to trade in 1812 and 1813. Sometime late in 1813 the *Lydia* was sold to the Russians, the price payable in sealskins. It appears that 20,000 sealskins each were given in exchange for her and the *Atahualpa*.[1] The Russians renamed the *Lydia* the *Il'mena,* and under that name she traded in 1814 along the California coast as far south as the Channel Islands.

Leaving Sitka/New Archangel in January 1814, the *Il'mena* was sent on a sea otter hunting expedition, traveling first to Bodega Bay and then on to the Farallon Islands, San Francisco, and the Santa Barbara Channel. The captain of the ship was William Wadsworth, and the supercargo was John Elliott d'Castro. On board was Antipatr Alexandrovich Baranov (son of Alexander Baranov), who left a journal of the trip.[2] A section of this journal relates the dramatic interactions of the *Il'mena* with Spanish authorities in the vicinity of Rancho Señora del Refugio, near Santa Barbara. After initially contacting the local rancher and Fr. Luis Gil y Taboada (then at Mission La Purísima) in order to trade goods, the *Il'mena* was warned by the rancher that it was in danger of being captured, but the Russians persisted. Finally, a group of Spanish soldiers appeared on the scene and arrested six people from the *Il'mena*. They were all taken to the port of Santa Barbara. Captain Wadsworth then sailed the *Il'mena* offshore to prevent the ship's capture but continued to send messages to Elliot d'Castro in captivity. Using Señor Ortega, owner of Rancho Refugio, as a go-between, Wadsworth was able to send some pantaloons, shirts, caftans, stockings, and shoes to Elliot d'Castro himself, as well as some small items of clothing to the crew, plus a roll of black silk, a half-dozen silk stockings, and a roll of canvas for the commandant of the Santa Barbara Presidio, per instructions from John Elliot d'Castro.

In addition, Elliot d'Castro passed on the news that the captured were being taken to Monterey. He also wrote that thirteen canoes, including that of [ed: Boris] Tarasov, were captured in San Pedro and were are being taken to Monterey to the new governor. Tarasov was the leader of a hunting party that had been dropped off by the *Il'mena* earlier to hunt in the southern Channel Islands. They were captured by the Spanish near San Pedro, where they had landed to make repairs to their kayaks.

Meanwhile, the *Il'mena* sailed to the island of San Miguel in the Santa Barbara Channel and then to Santa Rosa Island (called "Il'men Island" by the Russians), where they picked up a number of Kodiaks, including two women, who had been left there. From there the *Il'mena* sailed on to San Clemente Island and eventually left the California coast for Hawaii, on its journey back to Sitka. It was not until a year or so later that Russian captain Otto von Kotzebue aboard the *Rurik* came to California and was able to get the Spanish governor to release three of the *Il'mena* captives, including John Elliot d'Castro. Osip Volkov (a.k.a. José Bolcoff), another former prisoner, remained in Monterey and found employment working for Governor de Sola.

LETTER TO KUSKOV FROM KHLEBNIKOV
FROM THE SITE OF THE WRECK OF THE *IL'MENA* (1820)

The demise of the *Il'mena* came in June of 1820, while the ship was sailing from Sitka/New Archangel to Bodega Bay. From the site of the wreck, Khlebnikov (1990: 45) penned a letter to Ivan Kuskov briefly informing him of the circumstances and what was required to salvage the cargo. In his journal Khlebnikov (1990: 41–56) goes on at much greater length about the shipwreck and the subsequent efforts to salvage it. Of interest to those seeking the still undiscovered remains of this ship, Khlebnikov carefully noted the number of steps it took to walk from the site of the wreck to a bay adjacent to Point Arena, then the number of minutes of paddling to cross this bay, and finally the number of steps from the shore to a protected cove where *baidaras* from Fort Ross could come to collect the salvaged material. This sort of information is near and dear to the hearts of scholars, and many hope that one day Khlebnikov's calculations will prove the key to finding the remains of the *Il'mena*.

Dear Sir,

I have the honor of writing to you to inform you briefly of the shipwreck that we have suffered. Since my messengers met Aleuts on the way, the message I sent went no further, and so I am hastening to write you in greater detail.

We left Sitka on June 4 [ed: June 15, 1820] with goods to exchange in California for grain and with the material ordered by the Ross Office, along with ten men and their families bound for the Ross settlement. On June 17 [ed: 28], we sighted land and, at night, God knows why, we drifted into a bay at this cape. The night was overcast, and we tacked back and forth a long time trying to get out of the bay, but were unable to because of strong headwinds, and we ran aground. The *Il'men'* lost its masts, but did not take water, except in the cabin. Everyone was saved, and the cargo does not seem to be greatly damaged. Once on shore, I immediately sent you a message asking for help. Some Aleuts have arrived in the meantime and promised to help us unload. I am not sending you the papers from Chief Manager Semen Ivanovich Yanovskii, but I have the honor of reporting that he is well and presents his compliments. Awaiting you at the site of our shipwreck, I hope you will be able to send all possible assistance in the exceedingly difficult predicament we are in. I will then personally give you the details along with all the papers.

Please send instructions about transporting the men bound for Fort Ross with their families (21 persons in all).

Source: Khlebnikov 1990: 45. Reprinted by permission of the University of Alaska Press.

9

RUSSIAN ROUND-THE-WORLD ADVENTURERS
VISIT CALIFORNIA, 1822–1824

IN ADDITION TO SHIPS SAILING under the Russian American Company flag, other Russian vessels made their way to California, many of them navy ships part of round-the-world expeditions. Russia, under the Empress Catherine II (the Great), was very Western oriented and happily embraced the Enlightenment, which included an interest in scientific discovery. The Russian navy, like its British counterpart, was put into service to carry scientists to the far parts of the globe, with particular attention to the lands abutting the Pacific Ocean, especially the North Pacific, where Russia had a major colonial interest.[1] These expeditions were meant to parallel similar efforts by Great Britain (for example the voyages of Captains James Cook, George Vancouver, and William Beechey), France (Captains Jean François de Lapérouse and Cyrille Pierre-Théodore de Laplace), and Spain (Captain Alessandro Malaspina). Russia could not be left behind in this endeavor and enthusiastically entered into the enterprise. An additional practical matter for the Russian navy was the chance to provide their seamen and officers with additional training.

Ships that visited California under the Russian flag included the *Rurik* (1816), the *Kutusov* (1817), the *Kamchatka* (1818), the *Blagonamerenny* and the *Otkrytie* (1820–1821), the *Apollon* (1822–1823), the *Kreiser* (1823–1824), the *Ladoga* (1824), and the *Enterprise* (1824). Only some of these were intended as scientific expeditions; others were for military purposes alone (*Apollon, Kreiser,* and

Ladoga). Thanks to journals kept by ships' officers and supercargos, we have some valuable descriptions of California during this time. Skilled artists on board these vessels also left behind some of the most important images of California during the 1810s and 1820s.

In the late eighteenth and early nineteenth century, Russia had an established claim to the North Pacific, and through its Russian American Company it exploited the rich sea mammal resources of the area from the Kurile Islands, off the coast of Russia, all the way to southeastern Alaska. Increasingly, however, ships from other nations—particularly the United States—were encroaching on the region, and in 1821 Tsar Alexander I issued a *ukase* (royal decree) stating that the area was off limits to other countries. To enforce this rule, a sloop-of-war, the *Apollon*, was sent from Kronstadt (on the Baltic) to establish a naval presence. The voyage made stops in England, Rio de Janeiro, Port Jackson (Sydney, Australia), Kamchatka, Sitka/New Archangel, and California.

The arrival of the *Apollon* set the stage for visits by several other Russian warships, notably the *Kreiser* and the *Ladoga*, that were also on picket duty in the North Pacific the following winter of 1823–1824 (Ivashintsov 1980: 65–74). Despite Russia's protectiveness of its own areas, their ships were welcomed by Spanish authorities in California, a fact underscored by the latter's willingness to allow the Russians to construct bread ovens on the outer walls of the Presidio of San Francisco and to refurbish one of the rooms in the presidio for use by a visiting Russian officer. All in all, it seems clear that the relations between the Russian visitors and their hosts in California were quite amicable—and perhaps too amicable in some cases, when Russian sailors would jump ship to try to stay on land (a frequent occurrence on ships of all nations that stopped in California).

All of this was happening at a time when various areas of the Americas were gaining greater independence from their home countries (principally Spain). This was also the time the fledgling United States developed the Monroe Doctrine, which was directly stimulated by the aforementioned decree from the tsar of Russia. California itself was just then shifting from nominal Spanish rule to control by the new emperor of an independent Mexico, Agustín Iturbide.

The first document that follows is from the visit of the *Apollon* from November 25, 1822, to March 26, 1823, during which time the ship's interpreter, Achille Schabelski, visited many parts of the San Francisco Bay Area, and even went as far north as Fort Ross. Schabelski voices disgust at the treatment of the

Indians in the missions, an attitude that evidently reflected a developing sensibility concerning the rights of man, ideas that eventually came home to roost in the Decembrist Revolt against the Russian tsar in 1825.

Following that is an account by Lieutenant Dmitry Zavalishin, who came to California the following winter (1823–1824) and managed to find lodging in the presidio itself rather than remain on board the *Kreiser* for the length of his visit. He mentions that his room at the presidio, which had been nicely refurbished by the ship's carpenters, became a popular place to visit, and Zavalishin's account thus records more thoroughly the life of the Californios.

Finally, this chapter contains a brief section on visits to San Diego by some Russian ships. These visits occurred for the most part during the governorship of José María Echeandia, who chose San Diego as his seat of government. The Russians entered into commercial enterprises to hunt sea otters along the coast of southern Alta California and northern Baja California.

SCHABELSKI DESCRIBES A VISIT OF THE RUSSIAN WARSHIP
APOLLON TO CALIFORNIA (1822–1823)

The following account was published by the *Apollon's* interpreter, Achille Schabelski, in 1826. Schabelski sailed to California on this ship, although he did not return on it. Rather, after the ship's first visit to San Francisco in the winter of 1822–1823, Schabelski transferred to another vessel while the *Apollon* completed another summer's tour of duty and sailed back to San Francisco for the winter of 1823–1824. A well-educated Russian, Schabelski published his book in French in St. Petersburg.

The night of November 26² [1822] with a following wind, we entered the port of San Francisco.

The next day at daybreak after having hoisted our colors, we came to anchor in the middle of the Spanish settlement. [It was flying] a very new flag to us; Iturbide now reigned in Mexico, and California which in its political state is dependent on the Mexican government, had taken an oath of fidelity to this so-called emperor.³

During a stay of four months in this country, having occasion to travel over the land situated between San Francisco and Monterey, passing a month at the mission of Santa Clara and making an excursion from San Francisco to Port Bodega, I could learn through my own observations the state of things.⁴ The Spanish are careful what they will show to strangers, and it is in an abridged state that I will present my observations.

The changes which removed California from Spain, apparently did not alter the old order of things. As before, it is divided into presidios or military establishments, and missions. The former are inhabited only by soldiers commanded by military officers, and the missions are peopled by Indians under the direction of Franciscan friars.

A governor resident in Monterey has jurisdiction over New California.⁵ By the new rules, a governing body [junta] is established at Monterey. The deputies are chosen from among the inhabitants of California and recognize the Governor as their president.

When this land was part of the Spanish empire, the king sent it considerable sums.[6] The conversion of the Indians of California which he proposed as the object was laudable, but did the Spanish government know how this project was being executed?

The manner of converting the Indians being the same today as it was before [independence from Spain], and having had previous occasion of seeing it put into practice with my own eyes, you may judge from this description that it did not at all conform to the principles of Christianity.

The commander of the presidio sends a detachment of soldiers to the mission in order to augment the number of inhabitants. The missionaries give them the converted Indians who having embraced Christianity for a long time, speak Spanish well and serve as guides and interpreters for the soldiers.

Having left the mission, they travel over the country and as soon as they notice indications of some habitations, they stop to await the night, and send out the cleverest Indians to reconnoiter the area. Having assured themselves that it is a village, they swoop down on it during the night making loud cries. The natives, the most timid of indigenous Americans, who have only a bow as a weapon, rush out of their houses and are greeted with a fusillade of musket fire. This they hear for the first time and, seized by panic, they seek safety in flight. The Spaniards, profiting from the disorder, throw themselves on them and throw lassos [*lacets*] around their bodies. As soon as an Indian is caught, he is dragged to the ground and the soldier rides at a great gallop [dragging him] so that the Indian is weakened by the loss of blood from his wounds. He is then bound and turned over to the Indian allies.

If the soldiers, having trapped several dozen miserable Indians, perceive that their holy zeal will not produce any more captives, they return to the mission. The reverend Franciscan fathers receive their new infants and make them embrace Christianity. Such is the manner employed in California to make news proselytes for the Catholic religion.

The natives thus drawn into the Spanish establishment, by dint of punishment accustom themselves more and more to the new way of life and become trained in all kinds of labor.

The missions of California are built quite uniformly with the only difference that those found south of Monterey are richer. The church occupies the best place. Next to it is found the house of the priests, which always has nearby a barracks for the soldiers and a sort of convent in which, at nightfall, the fathers lock up the unmarried Indian women.

The village consists of several rectangular houses made of adobe, in which each room is occupied by a family. In the space which is found between these lodgings and the Indian village is always placed a huge cross.

Such a mission, containing sometimes more than 1000 Indians, is over-seen most often by two friars, which only have as guards a squad of soldiers consisting of three or four men. This number is more than enough to main-tain order among the timid Indians.

The type of life which the natives lead in the mission is very monoto-nous. When they get up they go to church. After having heard Mass, of which they understand not a single word, they assemble in a public place where they are given a light breakfast which is followed by hard labor until noon. At that hour the church bell beckons them and the Indians are obliged to quit work, throw themselves on their knees and enter into prayer. This, you understand, [occurs] when they are in the presence of priests. After this act of devotion, each one of them, a basket (*corbeille*) in hand, comes to the common kitchen where he receives his dinner consisting of cooked wheat grains which have been boiled in water [*atole*]. These baskets are made of tree roots with such craftsmanship that they hold water. [Mussel] shells (*coquille*) take the place of spoons. Having finished the noon meal, they work until sunset. Then they go to the church, from there to the kitchen to receive their supper and then they disperse to the houses.

The Indians, continuously subjected to wearisome work, do not have any possessions. Once in a while I found in the homes of a few of them a little salt and a few seeds. A shirt and a wool blanket, which they wrap around their bodies, are the only items which they receive from the fathers. Even these are made in the mission by the Indians themselves.

Some time ago, only the priests enjoyed the fruits of their [the Indians'] labor. But during the past 12 years the troubles in Spain no longer allowed the king to send money to support California.[7] The Governor and comman-dants of the Presidios were obliged to exact from the missions the supplies and equipment which were indispensable to the support of the soldiers. In vain the priests argued [that they should be exempted] by all divine and human laws. Their avarice was forced to give way to necessity and now the soldiers are outfitted and fed by the missions. The money which comes from the sale of commercial goods is divided between the priests and the officers.

Such an administration of California produced the most terrible results for the country. The Indian, deprived of all property and having no motive to encourage him to work harder, leads an extremely miserable life. The soldiers, inclined to indolence, see work as the worst evil. Only the priests and the officers possess things, so that the soldiers do not wish to do any work.

The Presidio is a large square structure of adobe bricks divided into several chambers and having more the appearance of a stable than of a European fort.

It's difficult to fully present the miserable state in which the Spaniards in California live. An observer among them believes himself transported into the 16th century. The construction of the dwellings, their dress and that of their wives, the weapons, the furniture, and their opinions and prejudices make them appear to be contemporaries of Cortez or Pizarro. Possessing a land which enjoys a delightful temperature and extreme fertility, they make not the least effort to profit by their wonderful situation.

The forts, built both at San Francisco and at Monterey, fallen into disrepair, are supplied with cannons on decrepit, old gun carriages which break at the first discharge of the cannon. I noticed in San Francisco such a one which dated from the year 1740. In visiting Monterey, I found only one soldier, asleep. Although it is true that to put this presidio (Monterey) in shape to defend itself would require a great deal of fortification, San Francisco, because of its position, presents a locale which one could very successfully defend against a superior enemy force because at the entrance of the port, which is extremely narrow, one could construct batteries on the two opposing sides.

One notices a similar lack of things which could better the condition of the inhabitants of this land. There does not exist any school, neither at Monterey nor at San Francisco, and a so-called doctor, a true student of Sangrado, comforts all the sick of California.[8]

Passing through the village, situated on the road from Santa Clara to San Juan [Bautista], I was surrounded by a large number of sick people who, with tears in their eyes, begged me to come visit them and to give them some remedies. These very people do not know that only six leagues from their village, near the mission of San José, are found hot sulfur springs which would be of great help to them. It was the Indians of this latter mission who showed them to me. Returning to San José, I did not fail to explain to the priests⁹ the necessity of building near these waters some house to obtain for the sick the means of curing them. But I strongly doubt that this counsel could produce any effect.

Vancouver was wrong in describing the Indians as savages, entirely deprived of intelligence and more resembling overgrown infants.¹⁰ This strong judgment was probably suggested to him by the priests, who hoped to hold them under an absolute guardianship as formerly the Jesuits had done in Paraguay. A more impartial observation showed us that these Indians are capable not only of all the aspects of agricultural work, but in time would even become artisans and it is to them that California is indebted for what little is produced.

It is agreeable and even consoling to find in the works of such as Châteaubriand sublime descriptions which paint the sacrifices made by the missionaries of the New World to propagate Christianity.¹¹ But in examining that which has actually occurred, one is forced to see them as brilliant illusions and to admit the opinion of La Rochefoucauld and of Pope that self-love rules also the actions of men.¹²

These verses of the English Poet [Pope]:

Two Principles in human nature reign;
Self-love, to urge, and Reason, to restrain;
Self-love, the spring of motion, acts the soul;
Reason's comparing balance, rules the whole,
Reason rules the whole, not self-love alone.

are only too applicable to the missionaries of California who, only speaking of eternity and of their contempt for passion, think only to satisfy their cupidity.

The [political] changes which have come over Mexico must influence California. The first act of power that one ought to exercise would be to abolish the military government which, in ruling this country, is completely contrary to its interests. Its commerce, far too limited by the existence of the missions, requires reforms needed to improve the state of the Indians and to provide them the means to acquire goods. They also ought to encourage agriculture among the inhabitants of California.

Wishing to see the Russian establishment near Port Bodega, I crossed the Bay of San Francisco and arrived at the mission of San Rafael. After having declared my intention to the missionary,[13] I received from him some horses and an Indian boy who, moreover knowing Spanish, could serve as an interpreter.

As I had to travel more than thirty-five leagues across a land entirely uninhabited by Europeans, prudence required me to take with me some weapons and it was with only two pistols and a saber, with no soldier for a guard, that I resolved to set out. The extreme timidity of the Indians assured me of my security.

The first day I traversed country which had a wonderful appearance, but the lack of trees rendered it not very appropriate for habitation. During this time I only saw several tents of unhappy fugitives from Mission San Rafael who, taking me for a Spaniard, fled to the mountains.

The next day, toward noon, I was stopped by a river which I was obliged to ford.[14] Resolved to await the ebb tide, I was happily surprised toward nightfall to see coming toward me about thirty Indians from the Mission San Rafael, having at their head a chief of their tribe who was sent out about a week earlier to capture fugitives. Immediately they cut down a large tree of which the trunk provided me with a launch and the branches for paddles. As they accompanied me to the establishment [Fort Ross], I had the occasion of seeing how they hunted the native peoples from whom they differ only by their cruelty and the knowledge of some superficial ceremonies of the Catholic religion.

The morning of the third day I perceived the Russian flag flying in the middle of the establishment of New Albion [Fort Ross]. The fort, which contained within it the house of the commandant and the storehouses, formed a square fortified with four bastions, provided with 24 cannon. All that I observed was in excellent order. Their forethought went so far that, despite there being a stream flowing very close to the enclosure, they had dug a well near the commandant's house so as not to lack water in case of a siege.

This establishment, lying nine leagues from Port Bodega, does not possess a bay adequate to receive ships and it had only been formed by the Russians with the sole intention of facilitating their relations with the Spaniards of California. These latter did not realize this plan, being previously very unhappy with their new neighbor, and not failing to claim their rights on all the [west] coast of America from Tierra del Fuego to the Bering Strait. But an uninterrupted possession of a number of years had legitimized the rights of the Russians to occupy Bodega and though still resenting all the implications of such an occupation, [the Spanish] had become faithful allies and good friends.

About a cannon shot from the fort, the natives of New Albion had built a village. They lived there peaceably. The smallest services which they rendered to the Russians were generously recompensed and the latter showed not the least inclination to dominate them. The huts of these natives, constructed of reeds, are set out in an orderly fashion and have a conical form. Having little passion and lacking courage, they wish only to be able to peacefully live their lives. The seeds which they grind into flour are the basis for their subsistence. Rarely do they occupy themselves with the hunt or catching fish. They wear almost no clothing and very few among them are tattooed.

With the intention of returning by water to San Francisco, I took from the establishment three baidarkas with seven Aleuts[15] and after six hours I entered the port of Bodega to allow the paddlers to rest. It is open to winds from the south quarter and is only appropriate for small ships. The Russians have built here a house and a bath. This latter is indispensable for a Russian establishment.[16] After having easily doubled the cape of Point Reyes, I visited the bay of Sir Francis Drake. It is not very good for an anchorage and it is only the name that it carries which makes it remarkable. The third day I arrived in San Francisco.

In taking the three baidarkas, I had hoped to use them to travel up the river of San Francisco [ed: the Sacramento River] which flows into the bay of the same name, and to investigate the cause for the light which we had noticed to the east northeast from our anchorage in the port. We could not attribute it to fire since the time had already passed in which the Indians burned the grasses to better the [growth of the] seeds. I assumed that this light came from the combustion of naphtha, or that it was due to some volcano of the Sierra Nevada in action. But my desire to satisfy my curiosity found great obstacles in the suspicions of the Spaniards who did everything they could to deter me from my project and I was forced to abandon it.

March 27 [ed: 26], 1823, aided by a strong current, in spite of contrary winds, we left the bay of San Francisco and directed our course toward the straits of the Northwest coasts of America to seek foreign ships but, required to spend some time at Sitka, we only visited Puerto Cordova of the Archipelago of the Prince de Galles,[17] named Caigane by the indigenous people. This port which holds the first rank among the places where United States citizens trade with the natives is vast and little peopled.

Source: Farris 1993a: 1–13. Reprinted by permission of Glenn J. Farris.

ZAVALISHIN'S ACCOUNT OF A VISIT TO CALIFORNIA
ABOARD THE *KREISER* (1823–1824)

Dmitry Irinarkhovich Zavalishin (1804–1892) was a young naval lieutenant aboard the *Kreiser,* a Russian frigate that had been sent to support the *Apollon* on picket duty in the North Pacific waters of Russian America. The *Kreiser* did not arrive on station until fall of 1823, which means she first visited California during the winter of 1823–1824, along with her sister ship, the *Ladoga,* and the *Apollon,* the three vessels and their crews taking advantage of the mild California climate during the cold season. This was an important time in the history of Russians in California because the new mission of San Francisco Solano de Sonoma had just been established (in 1823), in part to curb Russian movement

Lt. Dmitry Zavalishin visited California in 1823–1824.
Photo courtesy of *Southern California Quarterly.*

inland from Fort Ross, and yet the Spaniards nevertheless remained hospitable to their guests. Zavalishin includes in his account yet another story of Russians deserting their ships, and in writing of their capture, he emphasizes the assistance of the Spaniards to illustrate the amicable relationship of the two groups.

This period was also a time of increased Indian unrest, as evidenced by the insurrectionist activity of the Indian leader Pomponio, who happened to be incarcerated at the Presidio of San Francisco during the time these three Russian warships were visiting the area. Zavalishin's record of his encounter with Pomponio adds valuable insight to the activities of this audacious Indian revolutionary.

Zavalishin himself is an interesting character in that following his return to Russia he became involved in the famous Decembrist Revolt against the tsar in 1825. When this insurrection was put down, he was exiled to Siberia, and it was there during his copious free time that he wrote down his accounts of this visit to California. We are fortunate to have several portrait images of Dmitry Zavalishin that suggest why he was so charming to the señoritas of California when he was barely twenty years old.

❊ ❊

In early 1824 several sailors, mostly musicians, deserted the frigate *Cruiser* [ed: *Kreiser*] in San Francisco Bay in California. There were some grounds for suspecting that the desertions had not occurred without the connivance of the Franciscan monks who were in charge of the missions and who had long been in sore need of musicians. Capture of the deserters was very difficult because with the assistance of the Spaniards, especially the heads of the missions, the deserters were easily concealed somewhere nearby until an opportunity arose to send them farther away. Correspondence with the local authorities would evidently have resulted in a loss of time and only have made it still easier for the deserters to hide themselves. So the famous commander of the frigate, Michael [ed: Mikhail] Petrovich Lazarev (later an admiral and the commander of the Black Sea Fleet), decided to act on his own and to take forthwith decisive measures for quickly capturing the deserters. He entrusted me with this mission. For various reasons a plan that I had suggested was adopted; it involved the immediate dispatch at night of an armed party to Mission San Francisco, following such a route that nobody would meet us and warn the mission of our coming. Having taken the head of the mission unawares and shown him the basis of our suspicion of collusion by the missionaries in the desertion of the musicians, I hoped to persuade him to clear himself by giving me immediate and active assistance in the capture of the deserters, promising in that event to drop the matter completely if the deserters were to admit complicity on the part of any Spaniards. I wanted to add that in case the deserters were captured solely as a result of my orders and were to make the same admission, the head of the mission would be left to have only himself to blame for the unpleasant consequences of the affair. On the other hand, in appearing without delay at the nearest mission I hoped to intercept the deserters, who could not have gone far anyway, since their desertion had occurred only the previous evening. The route that I chose was very difficult; it mostly followed wet sand exposed along the beach by the outgoing tide. But our party spared no effort, not even stopping for a moment's rest, and before dawn, hardly able to distinguish nearby objects, we entered Mission San Francisco and approached the gates of the main building. However much we had tried to proceed quietly, there could not but have been some noise with the passage of an armed party. As a result of this noise—and perhaps quite accidentally—only when we passed the *casa* of the sergeant, who commanded a detachment of Spanish soldiers guarding the mission, were the windows opened and did this sergeant, who I knew well and liked, show himself. I had been coming to the mission almost daily, partly to study Spanish with the head of the mission, and as I passed his house the friendly sergeant had never failed to exchange greetings and a few words with me and sometimes he had persuaded me to drink some aromatic milk without dismounting. Having now seen me entering the mission with an armed party and myself armed from head to foot (there were no revolvers then, and I had perforce taken two pairs of pistols), he was dumbfounded with surprise, and the only words that he could utter were, "Aja! Don Demetrio!" Then the window slammed shut. Meanwhile, we approached the mission's main building. I ordered a gentle knock on the gates; commotion was heard inside, but there was no answer. We knocked again; a side window opened slightly, but then it slammed shut. Running was heard, but there was no reply to my request for admittance, and a dead silence ensued. Then we began to knock loudly at the gates with our gunstocks. This time the window was opened wide, and the head of the commandant of the mission, the fanatical Padre Tomás (Father Foma), appeared. His face, minus the usual sternness and seeming anger, expressed the greatest degree of amazement and indignation. *"¿Qué quieres hombre?"* (literally, "What do you want, mister?"—a familiar expression corresponding with our *"Chto ugodno?"* ["What can I do for you?"], he shouted in a voice expressing vexation but at the same time something like tender reproach, as it were, for he liked me very much. Not hearing my answer he gave vent to a whole stream of personal reproofs—that I had deceived him for so long, with him believing that the conjunction of such a number of Russian ships in San Francisco Bay [the sloops *Apollon* and *Ladoga* and two ships of the Russian-American Company, besides the frigate *Cruiser* {ed: *Kreiser*}] was accidental and that we did not have the slightest intention of taking California by force, whereas my present appearance with an armed party finally betrayed our long nourished design, etc., etc. It cost me much effort to stop his swift flow of words and to convince him that I had no intention whatever of making him a martyr or giving him an opportunity for heroic resistance (he spoke rashly to me of martyrdom and resistance in the matter of Saragossa [which heroically resisted the French sieges in 1808 and 1809], which was still well remembered then, and the like). I declared that it was only necessary to render me speedy assistance in the capture of the runaway musicians if he wanted to clear himself of suspicion of complicity in their desertion and even, perhaps, of inducement. I added that if the deserters, who were known to have taken firearms, were to offer armed resistance and it became necessary to use force, then I would shoulder everything myself so as not to expose the Spaniards to danger. I asked only that now I be given some chocolate to drink and that my men be fed and allotted a space where they could rest quietly (not the place that he had given us once in order to make us agree that there is a purgatory). I promised to pay all expenses. Although my words greatly annoyed him and evidently affected him because of the ready sureness I exhibited regarding the participation of the Spaniards in the desertion, he nevertheless reassured himself about the principal but imaginary danger and, although not much in favor of capturing the musicians, became very compliant about everything else, having rid himself of the fear of a forcible seizure of California by us. It was clear that he had tried to trick me and that he could easily catch the deserters, who he probably had somewhere nearby, certainly not far away. He now ordered the assembling of all available *vaqueros,* i.e., horsemen, and, having whispered something to them and his major-domo (*mayordomo*—properly speaking, a steward who supervises housekeeping at the mission), he issued a loud order in my presence to ride in different directions—in one direction to seek the deserters and in another direction to the neared *aldea* (village) to announce the desertion, informing all herdsmen encountered on the way. The deserters, of course, were soon found and delivered to us.

I relate this story at the beginning of my article on the condition of California in 1824 in order to indicate our relations then with the Spaniards. The following story will show how we were regarded by the Indians, who together with the Spaniards formed the two main groups of California's population at that time.

Once in the presidio (fortress) of San Francisco I and my late friend, Feopempt Lutkovsky, passed the prison, where the Indian Pomponio, who had terrorized all California before our arrival, was then held under close guard in dreadful irons; he was one of those people who are called marauders by conquerors but who in the eyes of the conquered people or tribe are important as national heroes in the manner of Robin Hood and the like. This sympathy on the part of the population explained Pomponio's successes and the difficulty of catching him, since he had connections everywhere and obtained news and warnings from every quarter. When he was finally confronted with the Indians who had lived with him in one of the missions and who therefore must have known him well, none of them indicated that he knew him; all of them stubbornly disavowed and denied that he was the real Pomponio. The fantastic notion that it was impossible to capture Pomponio could, of course, have contributed to this, but it is more likely that the main motive for disavowal was their unwillingness to betray him by revealing their relations with him. I should say that during my initial travels throughout California I was often threatened by the danger of falling into Pomponio's hands; indeed, there were occasions when not one Spaniard dared accompany me anywhere Pomponio might be hiding, and I had to travel those places alone, guided only by the general directions that were given me. There were even occasions when, because of a liking for me they simply obstructed me and hid the horses. It was impossible for me, however, to heed such danger, since on account of my duties and the continual missions that the head of the expedition gave me, I could not be absent long from the frigate, and I had received permission from Lazarev to travel always with the least delay. In order to save time I almost always had to lessen the distances by taking the shortest but most dangerous and uncomfortable routes; for example, on the direct road to Santa Cruz, which shortened the passage by a dozen miles, we had to crawl along a jagged mountain ridge, straddling it with a precipice on both sides, having let the horses go ahead on their own. But to return to the aforementioned event—when we passed the prison where Pomponio was held, as I said before, he was sitting by the door on the outside, where he was allowed to warm himself in the sun (the sole source of heat in the prison even in winter, which, of course, is generally not bad in California, although it is noticeable in a dwelling without a stove in San Francisco, where the thermometer approached the freezing point). Pomponio greeted us politely and affably, and a minute later one of the guarding soldiers overtook us and told me that Pomponio wanted to ask me something. Knowing that it was the custom among the prisoners to request rather than beg a cigarette or a cigar, I said that I did not smoke and therefore did not carry such things; but as Lutkovsky found a cigar, we were glad to have an opportunity to see Pomponio more closely and to talk to him, so we returned and approached him, and my companion gave him the cigar. He took it and thanked us in clear Spanish but said that he had not called us for that. "I wanted to talk to you, Don Demetrio!" he said to me. "I wanted to say to you: do you know me? Why, twice you were in my grasp. What a temptation it was! And what made me want to kill that Spaniard, José de la Cruz, who was your guide then? Ah! I would have destroyed all of them. But because of you I spared him!" Here he related in detail all the circumstances of one such occasion, namely, during my passage along a road which had been abandoned for a dozen years and which the family of this José de la Cruz, my guide, could barely recall having been passable. Pomponio added that when José and I descended to the bottom of a gully to drink from a stream flowing there and, alighting from the horses, sat under a huge sequoia and discussed the unusual size and straightness of the Californian pine, he was several steps from us behind some bushes, so that he heard our conversation. He said that at first he wanted to show himself and talk to me about what interested him most of all, but he was afraid that we would have misunderstood and fired and then his gang, having been aroused, would have come running and attacked us before the misunderstanding had been explained. "But why did you spare me, who simply fell into your hands, when, as is well known, you never spared anybody?" I asked him. "Because you alone have always been affectionate and kind to the poor Indians: why you are fairly well known everywhere, including the missions and rancherias. But, in addition, we know that you came to take this land from the accursed Spaniards and to free the poor Indians! Then the Indians will be all right!"

The above incidents typified our relations with the Spaniards and the Indians, however impossible it is to attest the relative situation of California and Russia's possessions in America at that time. On the one hand, the occupation of California by the Russians, which was proposed by the inhabitants of that land themselves, seemed very natural and very feasible to those most concerned. It only remained to find a form of agreement which would firmly link Russia's interests with the interests and wishes of the population and thereby form a strong force from the very beginning. I hoped to resolve this question very simply by explaining to both sides without misreading or exaggerating the reasonable desire for mutual benefit and fairness. I add that a good knowledge of Spanish, and some Latin, made me generally necessary as an intermediary in all relations with the inhabitants, and supervision of the expedition's stores—in accordance with my official duties and missions—put me in direct contact with all classes of California's population. I had access to a domestic circle of many families, and I was accepted as a kinsman in the home of the sister of the president of the province [ed: Luis Antonio Argüello]. On the other hand, because of my official missions and my own wishes I succeeded in travelling throughout much of California and becoming personally acquainted with the peculiarities of the country and the position of places, so that I could justifiably think that hardly anyone then could have known California's situation or foreseen its future better than I.

[In this later passage, Zavalishin describes the presidio of San Francisco where he took up lodging.]

In its original form a presidio comprised a large, quadrangular, one-story building of unfired brick whose exterior was blank and hence had to be replaced by a wall or rampart to form the main defense against the attacks of savages. Inside, around the entire building, ran a gallery or ledge which connected all the quarters. In front of the single gate on the inside stood two cannons; in San Francisco's presidio there was a special commander of this artillery. He also commanded the battery erected on a promontory at the entrance to the bay, and ships had to pass under its line of fire. In case of danger livestock and fowl were driven into the spacious interior courtyard, and all belongings were brought there, since in such cases the residents of all the surrounding settlements and missions withdrew to the presidio. But as the danger of attack from savages diminished or, at least, came to affect only the more remote missions, they began to permit outside buildings at the presidios, and as a result it became necessary to make passageways through the heretofore blank outer wall. Lately even Russian expeditions [ed: *Blago-namerenny,* for example] have had bakeries attached to the outer wall for the baking of both fresh bread and extra rusks for a cruise. This is how San Francisco's presidio became a rather formless pile of half-ruined dwellings, sheds, storehouses, and other structures. The floors, of course, were everywhere of stone or dirt, and not only stoves but also fireplaces were lacking in the living quarters. Whatever had to be boiled or fried was prepared in the open air, mostly on cast bricks; they warmed themselves against the cold air over hot coals in pots or braziers. There was no glass in the windows; some people had only grating in their windows. The entrance doors to some compartments (for example, to the president's room) were so large that one passed from the interior courtyard to the outside through the wall on horse-back. Since my duties required a permanent room ashore where all who had to do business with me could present themselves, one room in the president's quarters was remodelled for me by our frigate's craftsmen in the European style with a wooden floor, glass-paned windows, and European furniture. In it was put a spare copper hearth from the frigate. During my off-duty hours this room became a gathering place for female company, who came there with work. Generally the president's room was occupied after his move to Monterey (he was formerly commandant at San Francisco[18]) by his married sister, who lived here with her husband and daughter, and furthermore it served for the balls that the Russian officers gave for Californian society. I mention all this to show that then the local residents knew very well how to appreciate the comforts which were provided by another way of life but which they themselves had no chance or way of providing. This was not the only reason why they favored me with their plans for the disposition of California's future. In their fulfillment they saw the sole possibility of achieving much that was precious and desirable without, however, paying such a high price as they later had to pay the Americans, about whom I shall warn in due course.

Source: Zavalishin 1973. Reprinted by permission of James R. Gibson.

THE RUSSIAN-BUILT "KANAKA HOTEL,"
FROM *TWO YEARS BEFORE THE MAST,*
BY RICHARD HENRY DANA, JR. (1840)

Visits to San Diego were rare for Russian vessels, however, when California Governor José María Echeandia established his government there in order to oversee both Baja and Alta California, it made more sense for the Russians to visit the southern city.

From his travel journal, we learn that Russian American Company agent Kirill Khlebnikov had made his first trip to San Diego in November 1826, aboard the *Baikal*. He arrived on November 6/17 and left on November 22/December 3. He also went to San Diego aboard the *Okhotsk* on January 2/13, 1829. We know this because of his travel notes (Khlebnikov 1990: 30) and because Governor Echeandia addressed two letters to him, dated January 8 and January 16 of that year. It is very likely that one of these ships was responsible for building the bread oven on the beach of San Diego that was later described by Richard Henry Dana, Jr., in *Two Years before the Mast*, based on his visit in 1836. The oven was apparently so big it was later used as housing by a number of Kanakas who lived on the beach.

There was a large oven on the beach [ed: at San Diego], which, it seems, had been built by a Russian discovery-ship, that had been on the coast a few years ago, for baking her bread. This the Sandwich-Islanders took possession of, and had kept ever since undisturbed. It was big enough to hold eight or ten men, and had a door at the side, and a vent-hole at the top. They covered the floor with Oahu mats for a carpet, stopped up the vent-hole in bad weather, and made it their head-quarters. It was now inhabited by as many as a dozen or twenty men, crowded together, who lived there in complete idleness, drinking, playing cards, and carousing in every way.[…] [It] was called the "Kanaka Hotel," and the "Oahu Coffee-house."

Source: Dana 1965: 112.

℁ 10 ℁

RUSSIAN AND KODIAK DESERTERS, CAPTIVES, AND MARTYRS: BOLCOFF, EGOROV, AND ST. PETER THE ALEUT

THE FOLLOWING STORIES of a Creole, an Alaskan native, and a Russian help broaden our image of people from the Russian American Company who visited California in the early nineteenth century. In this section, we begin with Osip Volkov, whose name was Hispanicized to José Bolcoff. He became well known in the Monterey Bay area through his association with the last Spanish governor, Pablo Vicente de Solá, his marriage to Candida Castro, and his appointment as the first alcalde of Santa Cruz. The second individual was a Kodiak native named Chunagnak, who was reported to have been captured while hunting sea otters near San Pedro, California. According to Russian accounts, provided to them by another Kodiak native (Kegli), this man was brutally tortured and killed by Spanish ecclesiastical authorities because he refused to surrender his Russian Orthodox faith. Whether that story is real or not is yet to be determined, however, Chunagnak was accorded sainthood as "St. Peter the Aleut" by the Orthodox Church in America and so holds a special significance. The third person we will consider here was a Russian named Prokhor Egorov, who came first to Fort Ross, then deserted to live with the Spanish at Mission San José, and finally moved down to the Santa Barbara area, where he became involved in the abortive Chumash Revolt of 1824. Whether he was an idealist or an opportunist is hard to determine.

OSIP VOLKOV, AKA JOSÉ BOLCOFF

Osip Volkov was born sometime between 1794 and 1798 in Petropavlovsk, Kamchatka, to a Russian priest father, Yakov Volkov, and a Kamchadal mother, Ana Macorio. His mixed-race ethnicity classified him as a "Creole" in the parlance of the times in Russian America. Virtually nothing is known of his early life, however, he evidently became a seaman and arrived in California in 1815 aboard the *Il'mena*, as noted in the journal of Antipatr Baranov. Volkov was captured while on a shore expedition seeking water and food at Rancho Refugio, near Point Conception, on September 25/October 6, 1815, and from there he was taken to Santa Barbara.

Wind from NW and a nice weather with sunshine. I sent Mr. Elliot to Padre Mariano [ed: Payeras, the principal missionary at La Purísima] with a note. The note said that we're asking him to come and do some trading with us. At midnight, an Indian has come with an answer that he would like to trade; also the note said that he is afraid of the new governor who is in Monterey. In the morning, Olfama [ed: "Old Farmer," a nickname given to José Maria Ortega by the American sea captains] has come with his sons and brought some cattle for provisions. At 9 o'clock I went ashore to notify Olfama that we need no more than 6 bulls but as soon as I arrived, he asked me to go back to the ship since there are horseback soldiers. Also, Olfama instructed me to notify Mr. Elliot and Vozdvit not to come ashore but they did not listen, went both ashore and no more than in ½ hour they were surrounded by soldiers. Mr. Elliot was captured but Vozdvit and 3 more of his people escaped in a canoe. Along with Mr. Elliot were captured the following people: Fedor Sokolov, Dmitrii Shushkov, Petr Drushinin, American from Boston Liza [ed: Elijah?] Coal, Osip Volkov and Afanasii Klimovskij. All were taken to the port of Santa Barbara. In the afternoon I went ashore and met there Olfama's son with a soldier. He brought a note from Mr. Elliot who asked to send him some clothes. But we did not send it to him as we were going to go to Olfama and give the clothes to him (Baranov 1815, 239).

Volkov subsequently came to Monterey and into the household of the Span-ish governor of California, Pablo Vicente de Solá. The governor found Volkov (renamed José Antonio Bolcoff by the Spanish) to be useful in his dealings with the Russians, not only for his knowledge of Russian but also because he was literate. Although the Russians sought to have Volkov/Bolcoff returned to them, it never happened. (In 1820 the same ship on which he had arrived in California, the *Il'mena*, was on its way from Sitka/New Archangel to Monterey, expecting to pick up Bolcoff there, when it ran aground near Point Arena and was lost.)

Bolcoff stayed in the Californian community. It appears that the gover-nor sent him to Mexico soon after his arrival to learn about commerce, and although we know nothing of his time there on this occasion, there is a pos-sible clue in the 1860 U.S. Census, in which Bolcoff reported that the last place he had lived prior to settling in California was Vera Cruz, a major port on the east coast of Mexico. By about 1817 Bolcoff had returned to California and is said to have been rebaptized a Catholic, reportedly at Mission Soledad. For their part, the Spanish priests were uncertain as to whether Orthodox baptisms were valid, and in many cases they rebaptized people into the Roman church.

A few years later, Bolcoff met and married Candida Castro, daughter of José Joaquin Castro and Maria Antonia Amador, sometime between November 21, 1822, and January 1, 1823. This marriage caused a fair amount of concern among the Mission fathers; both Fr. Payeras and Fr. Sarría, the father-president of the mission, expressed their concern over the validity of Bolcoff's Ortho-dox baptism and whether he needed to be rebaptized yet again as a Roman Catholic.

Bolcoff then went to Mexico a second time, following the successful Mexi-can War of Independence of 1810–1821 against Spain. A new government had come to power under self-styled emperor Agustín Iturbide. In 1822 Iturbide sent a representative to California named Agustín Fernández de San Vicente. The Canonigo Fernández, as he was called, made a visit to Fort Ross, accompanied by Fr. Mariano Payeras, Comisario of the California Missions, in October 1822. At the end of the year the former Spanish governor of California, de Solá, returned to Mexico with the *canonigo* and took Bolcoff with him. (On January 7, 1823, while in San Diego, on the way to Mexico, Fernández wrote to the new gover-nor of California, José Argüello; he asked if, since Bolcoff's trip to the court of

Mexico was for the convenience of the empire of Mexico, the governor would request that Fr. Luis Gil y Taboada of Mission Santa Cruz would personally look after Bolcoff's wife, who was residing in the nearby Villa de Branciforte.)

Although we don't know exactly when Bolcoff returned to California, we know that he was not as well favored by Governor Argüello as he had been by the previous governor, de Solá. He therefore had to find other ways to make his living. In January 1824 Bolcoff, along with a Corporal Rodriguez, was accused of smuggling goods from the Russian ship *Buldakov* and was arrested briefly. There is a note in Khlebnikov's journals from July 1824 that Bolcoff was thought to have "escaped" aboard an English ship, but I believe he may have confused José Antonio Bolcoff with another man, Terencio Bolcoff, who was mentioned in a note written by Fr. Payeras in late 1822 as having passed by La Purísima in the company of two other Russian deserters, one of whom was Prokhor Egorov (see section on Egorov starting on page 132). At any rate, by September Bolcoff was in Monterey again helping Khlebnikov with some matters of translation. In 1825 Bolcoff set up a shop in Santa Cruz and in 1829 was noted as being a shoemaker there.

CHUNAGNAK, AKA ST. PETER THE ALEUT

Numerous Alaskan native peoples were brought to California by the Russians, and their interactions with the local California Indians and the mission system are described in a number of little-known but intriguing incidents. The story of Chunagnak—later St. Peter the Aleut—is an illuminating story.

In 1815 near the Alta California port of San Pedro, a party of Kodiak Islanders out hunting sea otter under the command of Russian Boris Tarasov was captured by the Spanish authorities. During their captivity at Santa Barbara, a zealous cleric is said to have insisted on their renouncing their Orthodox faith in favor of Catholicism. Two of the Aleuts refused. One of these, named Chunagnak, was subsequently tortured to death and the other, Kykhlai, was saved only by a last-minute reprieve from a higher authority. He eventually made it back to Sitka/New Archangel to tell his tale.

The earliest account of the capture and torture of Chunagnak comes in a Russian American Company official report from the governor at Sitka, Semyon I. Ianovskii, to the main office in St. Petersburg, dated February 15, 1820.

Icon of St. Peter the Aleut. From the Holy Configuration
Monastery, Boston. Photo by Glenn J. Farris.

Here is an example of the inhumanity and ignorance of the Spanish
clergy: In June 1815, on the coast of California near the Mission San
Pedro, they seized 15 baidarkas of Kadiak men under Tarasov, of
whom two Kadiaks fled to Il'men Island [possibly a Russian name
for San Nicolas Island[1]] where one of them died, and the other,
Keglii Ivan [ed: Kykhlai], lived with the natives of this island until
by chance the Russian-American Company brig *Il'men* came in
March, 1819, when he appeared before the commander of the vessel, Mr. Banzeman [ed: Benzeman], and was taken to Fort Ross. I
enclose the original testimony of this Aleut taken by Mr. Kuskov.
He has now been sent here on the brig *Il'men* and tells me the same
thing. He is not a type who could think up things. The Spanish tortured his unfortunate comrade, who until the very end replied to

his torturer that he was a Christian and wanted no other faith, and with these words he died. One must note that this victim though baptised like the others was not taught Christianity, probably did not even know the dogmas of the faith except God the Father, Son and the Holy Ghost. I suggest that the Government intervene so that the Spanish do not do the same with the rest. But we have to keep in mind that the colonies cannot get along without grain from California (Bearne 1978: 177).

This report was followed by a lengthier one from the main administration of the company to Tsar Alexander I, said to be dated "not later than December 20, 1820." The relevant portion is as follows:

A Company promyshlennik (hunter), a native of the island of Kodiak by the name of Kykhklai, who had been taken prisoner by the Spaniards in 1815 and returned to our settlement at Ross and then to the headquarters of the colony on Sitka Island in 1819, gave the following account of inhuman treatment by the Spaniards of one of the Company promyshlenniks.

In 1815 a Company servitor named [Boris] Tarasov was on Ilmen Island, which did not belong to any nation. He was the leader of a group of promyshlenniks who were there to hunt. Since they were unsuccessful there they decided to set out with fifteen dependent islanders from our Kodiak colony to go to other islands, Santa Rosa and Ekaterina [ed: possibly Catalina]. During the voyage his baidara began to leak, and he had to proceed to the coast of California. They stopped at the bay on Cabo San Pedro, where bad weather detained them until the next day. While they were there a Spanish soldier came to them from the mission of San Pedro [ed: probably San Gabriel] and informed Tarasov that in exchange for some gifts, he would bring to him two of our Kodiak men who had previously run off from another such hunting party and were presently in the mission.

When the soldier left, although the weather was calmer and they could proceed on their projected route, the desire to see and to free their fellow islanders persuaded them to remain there longer.

On the fourth day of their stay they were suddenly attacked by some 20 armed horsemen, who tied up all of our people and wounded many of them with their sabers. One of the Kodiak islanders named Chunagnak was wounded in the head. The attackers looted all their possessions and all the Company trade goods. The prisoners were then taken to the mission of San Pedro [ed: sic] where they actually did find the two Kodiak islanders who had fled from the island of Clement [ed: probably San Clemente] from another party of partisans. When they reached the mission, a missionary who was head of the mission wanted them to accept the Catholic faith. The prisoners replied that they had already accepted the Greek Christian religion [ed: Russian Orthodox] and did not wish to change. Some time later Tarasov and almost all the Kodiak people were taken to Santa Barbara. Only two of them, Kykhklai and the wounded Chunagnak, were thrown into prison with the Indians who were being held. They suffered for several days without food or drink.

One night the head of the mission sent the runaway Kodiak islanders with a second order for them to accept the Catholic faith, but again they remained steadfast in their own faith.

At dawn a cleric went to the prison, accompanied by Indians. When the prisoners were brought out, he ordered the Indians to encircle them. Then he ordered the Indians to cut off the fingers from both hands of the above mentioned Chunagnak, then to cut off both his hands; finally, not satisfied with this tyranny, he gave orders that Chunagnak be disemboweled.

Tortured in this manner, Chunagnak breathed his last after the final procedure. The same punishment would have awaited the other Kodiak, Kykhklai had it not been for the fact that the cleric received a timely piece of paper. When he read it, he ordered that the man who had been killed be buried, and that Kykhklai be returned to prison; several days later they sent him to Santa Barbara. There was not one of his comrades there who had been taken prisoner with him. All of them had been sent off to Monterey. Kykhklai was assigned to the same work as other Company promyshlenniks who had been taken prisoner by the Spanish.

Wanting to escape from a life of such torture, Kykhklai and another man conceived the idea of breaking away. They stole a baidarka and went in it to the bay on Cabo San Pedro, and from there to the island of Catalina, then to Barbara and finally to Ilmen, where one of them died and where Kykhklai was taken aboard the Company brig *Il'men,* which had come to the island and then went to the Ross settlement. The others who had been taken prisoner at the same time were freed on the insistence of our captains Hagemeister and Kotzebue.

This incident, just one of many, is a striking example of the inhuman way in which the Spanish treat Russian promyshlenniks. Many who had previously been in their captivity were so exhausted with labor and so abused from beatings that they will carry the results with them to the grave. The suffering inflicted on the poor Indians is impossible to conceive without shuddering. Not only do they not consider the Indians human beings, they consider them below animals. The Spanish take great pleasure in beating innocent Indians and then bragging about it to other Spaniards (Dmytryshyn et al. 1989: 332–334).

The story behind this strange happening involves the interplay of European political and economic interests as well as varying notions of dogmatic religious allegiance. When word of the death of Chunagnak reached the governor of Russian America, Semyon Ianovskii, he went to see a highly regarded hermit monk named Fr. Herman. Upon hearing the story, Fr. Herman is reported to have proclaimed Chunagnak a martyr to the faith, calling him St. Peter, thus expressing an antagonism between Roman Catholicism and the Orthodox Church, although this was little in evidence in most of the interaction between the Russians and mission fathers. More likely, the point was for the story of Chunagnak to act as a warning for the Alaskan native hunters, and even the ethnic Russians, not to desert or they might meet the same fate.

PROKHOR EGOROV

The year 1824 saw perhaps the most dramatic and concerted uprising of the California mission Indians against the civil and ecclesiastic authorities in

Detail of notes by Fr. Mariano Payeras mentioning
"Procoro LLegorof." Mission Santa Barbara Archive-Library.

Alta California. The incident occurred chiefly among the missions in Chumash territory: Santa Inés, La Purísima, and Santa Bárbara. The revolt began on February 21, 1824, with the razing of Mission Santa Inés, and from there it spread to La Purísima and Santa Bárbara. The Indian insurgents made a stand at Mission La Purísima for about a month, until they were attacked by soldiers sent from the Presidio of Monterey, who finally managed to rout them. They then fled to Rancho San Emigdio and from there on to an island in Buena Vista Lake, in the southern San Joaquin Valley, where they held out until persuaded by some missionaries to return to the missions. Various authors have written extensively about the revolt (Bancroft 1886; Beebe and Senkewicz 1996; Blackburn 1975; Geiger 1970; Sandos 1987; Stickel and Cooper 1969), but one facet that seems to have gone largely unnoticed by historians—despite its being mentioned prominently by several priests in their letters at the time of the revolt—was the participation of a Russian man on the side of the Indians.

Only one of the Spanish documents provides a name for this individual: José (Ord 1878: 8). He was generally referred to as *"el Ruso"* (Ordaz 1824) or, worse, *"ese indigno Ruso"* (this contemptible Russian) (Durán 1824). However, in the journal of Russian American Company official Kirill Khlebnikov (1990) are found two passages (July 2/13 and July 10/21, 1824) in which he specifies that the Russian involved was Prokhor Egorov, a Russian *promyshlennik* who had deserted from Fort Ross. Khlebnikov (1990: 153, 156) goes on to say that Egorov was killed by the Indians after he had fled with them into the southern San Joaquin Valley. Several Spanish accounts of the investigation that followed the uprising provide the testimony of various Indians that the Russian had indeed been killed on an island in Buena Vista Lake in the southern valley, although in one of these accounts his death is attributed to the Mexican military force that pursued them, not the Indians themselves (Cook 1962: 153).

It is important to consider the situation leading up to the revolt of February 1824. The success of the Mexican revolution against Spain in 1821 led to development of the "Plan of Iguala" that same year, a key provision of which was the call for equal rights among all the citizens of Mexico, including Indians. The fact that several years later there was little or no change in the status of the mission Indians may well have caused discontent, especially among the Indian leaders, who were likely deeply disappointed by the failure of the missionaries to implement these equal rights to the Indians in the missions of California (Farris and Johnson 1999: 17–18).

Another factor that affected the atmosphere at Mission La Purísima was the death, in April 1823, of the long-time padre of that mission, Fr. Mariano Payeras, who had for many years been a powerful and respected figure in the mission system. By contrast, the priest at Mission Santa Inés at this time, Fr. Blas Ordaz, was one of the most immoral priests in California, having fathered several children by Indian women, among other misdeeds. Add to this environment the presence of a Russian deserter from Fort Ross who would have had little love for his country's practice of serfdom, and here is the recipe for discontent and revolt.

Our first knowledge of Prokhor Egorov is his arrival at Fort Ross in December 1820. He was sent there from Russian American Company headquarters in Sitka/New Archangel and arrived on the brig *Golovnin* (Pierce 1990: 133). In the list of crew and passengers aboard the *Golovnin,* he is listed as a farmer, although he has also been called a *promyshlennik,* which, though often said to mean hunter, in company parlance tended to mean a "jack of all trades" employee who was ethnically a Russian. Perhaps the modern term "frontiersman" fits best.

We don't know when and how Egorov reached the Santa Barbara area, only that he was mentioned in a brief list of Russians that Fr. Mariano Payeras had noted for inclusion in his report of his trip to Fort Ross in October 1822. In

Fr. Mariano Payeras. Painting at La Purísima Mission
State Historical Park. Courtesy of California State Parks.

Payeras's note of 1823 (1995) he mentions, "three who came by La Purisima...
Terencio Bolcoff, Procoro Llegorof [Prokhor Egorov], and Rodivon Chavano" (see
image on p. 133). It appears that Egorov was one of three Russian deserters
who made their way to Mission La Purísima at the end of 1822. These same
three men are mentioned in a letter by Kirill Khlebnikov (1990: 156), dated
July 10/21, 1824, and addressed to the chief manager of the Russian American
Company in Sitka:

> In California, the uprising [the Chumash Revolt of 1824] that
> began in Santa Inés and Purísima missions, and, the day after, in
> Santa Bárbara has ended. Santa Inés was razed to the ground, and
> the other two missions were badly damaged. Our runaway, the pro-
> myshlennik Prokhor Egorov, led the uprising, ran off with the rebel-
> lious Indians, and eventually was killed by them.

This account was duly forwarded by Governor General Matvei Muravyov
to the Main Administration of the Russian American Company in St. Petersburg

(Russian American Company Correspondence 1818–1867 [1825]). This message adds some more details: "According to the Governor [Luis Argüello] 3500 *fanegas* of wheat, 1200 *fanegas* of corn, and 350 sacks of tallow and lard were lost in supplies, along with the destruction of these missions. The Indians fled to an island located in the center of a large lake near Santa Barbara and stayed there a long time. Along with them was our Russian, Prokhor Yegorov, who was killed here or elsewhere."

What were the details of Egorov's involvement in the uprising? Spanish sources provide some clues. It is clear that Egorov was known to priests at several of the missions. Fr. Narciso Durán of Mission San José wrote a strongly worded letter to the governor following the revolt in which he commented on Egorov (which makes me believe that the Russian had first gone to that mission after fleeing Fort Ross). Then we have the mention, quoted earlier, by Fr. Mariano Payeras of Mission La Purísima that cited Egorov as one of three Russians who passed by that mission in late 1822. We also have Fr. Blas Ordaz of Mission Santa Inés complaining of Egorov's participation in the revolt: Fr. Ordaz, a Franciscan missionary at La Purísima when the revolt began on February 21, 1824 (he transferred to Mission Santa Inés afterward), wrote a report of the uprising to the governor of California, Luis Antonio Argüello. The letter, dated March 21, 1824, and datelined Mission Santa Inés, states:

> The Indian Andres [ed: Andres Sagimomatsse (Johnson 1984: 10)] and his companion, Jaime, together with a Russian who had lived in Santa Bárbara, [ed: now] are at the Rancho San Emigdio with the armed Barbareño neophytes, all with plenty of force of arms [ed: i.e., weapons], led by the aforementioned Russian. He instructed them how to shoot at targets [ed: *a tirar al blanco*] and they have no lack of munitions with which to carry out his depraved intention. Moreover, it is known that the Russian has taken for his woman a married neophyte woman. Further, I have been advised that the above-mentioned Indians with their Director, the Russian, took all the treasures of the mission of Santa Bárbara, both in goods and in money, of which the latter alone amounted to 11,000 or 12,000 pesos. They took in their group all the people of the Tulares, saying that they would them give them anything, provided they joined in their undertaking (Ordaz 1824: 93–95).

Apparently Egorov's involvement was cause for special concern. The support of a European on the side of the Indians in an uprising was unusual, and the fact that he was skilled with firearms was likewise troubling. The Mexicans generally had no thought that the mission Indians could be dangerous, and a mission typically had a squad of only five soldiers and a corporal to keep its thousand or more Indians in check. Thus, a revolt like this was quite extraordinary, and it was easy for the Spanish to single out a European participant as being the source of its success. On March 31, 1824, Fr. Narciso Durán (1824), wrote from Mission San José to Governor Luis Argüello:

...but the latest news of the gathering of the Indians at San Emigdio worries me very much, especially with this contemptible Russian (*"ese indigno Ruso"*) at their head seems to me to bode serious results and [ed: word uncertain] which could result in another Pomponio.[2]

When the revolt collapsed, the leaders retreated first to the Rancho of San Emigdio (near today's Grapevine Pass on Interstate 5 in Kern County [Beck and Haase 1974: 22]). They took refuge there for at least a month before retreating farther inland to the marsh and lake country of the southern San Joaquin Valley. They were finally cornered on the island known as Mitochea (Cook 1962: 155) or Pelican Island.[3] There, by various accounts (Cook 1962: 153; Khlebnikov 1990: 153) the Russian was killed, although there is a discrepancy about whether he was killed by his former Indian friends (Khlebnikov 1990: 153) or by members of the punitive expedition (according to testimony by Senen, a Christian Indian[4]). Other details are also murky, such as the identity of Egorov's Indian neophyte mistress.

Whatever his reasoning for participating in the 1824 Chumash Revolt, Egorov's choice to side with the Indians against the missionaries was certainly unusual for a European at this time, despite the frequent comments of sympathy for the plight of the Indians found in various journals of Russian visitors. The idea that Egorov's decision might have been due to a love affair with one of the neophyte Indians has a romantic appeal.

By all accounts, Egorov was dead by the end of the revolt or shortly thereafter. And what of the Indians who participated? After Egorov's death, the missionary priests managed to convince many of the revolutionaries to give up their arms and return to the missions, although it appears that a certain number retreated farther into the San Joaquin Valley. An epilogue to the story of the revolt came ten years later, when mountain man Zenas Leonard, who was accompanying the Joseph Walker fur hunting expedition, reported finding a large (700 to 800 persons; this is a remarkably large number for an Indian village in that area and is probably inaccurate) Indian village near a river coming out of the Sierra (probably the Kern River). His description (Leonard 1978: 199–200) is worth quoting:

> We at length arrived at an Indian village, the inhabitants of which seemed to be greatly alarmed on seeing us, and they immediately commenced gathering up their food and gathering in their horses— but as soon as they discovered that we were white people, they became perfectly reconciled. After we halted here we found that these people could talk the Spanish language, which we thought might be of great advantage to the company, and on inquiry ascertained that they were a tribe called the *Concoas*, which tribe some eight or ten years since resided in the Spanish settlements at the missionary station near St. Bárbara, on the coast, where they rebelled against the authority of the country, robbed the church of all its golden images & candle-sticks, and one of the Priests of several thousand dollars in gold and silver, when they retreated to the spot where we found them—being at least five or six hundred miles distant [ed: there are several missions within one hundred fifty miles, so these numbers seem unlikely] from the nearest Spanish settlement.

Leonard's descriptions of the Indian people and their story appears consistent with the events of the uprising, despite the fact that John Johnson, a modern scholar of the mission records dealing with the Chumash, has told me that virtually all of the Indians involved in the revolt can be accounted for as either having returned to the missions or died (John Johnson, personal communication, 1993). On the other hand, it seems unlikely that Leonard would have conjured up the story of the village and its people without some basis in fact. At any rate, the Chumash Revolt, even if an ultimate failure, has gone down in history as one of the major attempts of the California Indians to throw off the burden of colonial control over their lives. Its connection to the story of Russians in early California is little known but nonetheless significant.

✷ 11 ✷

TRIPS UP THE RUSSIAN (SLAVIANKA) RIVER

(1820 AND 1833)

THE RUSSIAN RIVER remains, in addition to Fort Ross, one of the most recognizable geographic names recalling the Russian period of occupation in Northern California. The river itself flows some 110 miles from its origins in the interior to its mouth on the Pacific coast near Jenner; the lower section lies about midway between the Russian port at Bodega Bay and Fort Ross, and was therefore thoroughly explored by both the Russians at Fort Ross and visitors to Russian California. Although the river is virtually impossible to navigate by most vessels coming from the ocean due to the sandbars that fill the mouth during the summer months, it was possible for the Alaskan natives who worked for the Russians to travel up it in their light kayaks. In order to try to record a flavor of this beautiful river in the time prior to the heavy redwood logging that occurred in the early American period, what follows are several descriptions of travel up the river during the Russian era.

KHLEBNIKOV ON THE RUSSIAN RIVER
(JULY 20/31, 1820)

We had some free time, and so we took three baidarkas and set out for the Slavianka River. The mouth of the river had filled with sand, so we had to carry the boats across, and then we went up the river about 15 versts [ed: 9 miles]. It was a rather pleasant area, with woodless hills on both sides and then shrubs beginning farther up. Timber was found about 10 versts up the river on the right bank. In its straight stretches, the river is deep and about 50 to 100 sazhens [ed: 350 to 700 feet] wide. In the deep spots we saw larger numbers of sturgeon, and the Aleuts shot their arrows at them, but missed. The few birds sighted were too far off to be hit. On some of the sand bars near the mountains, we found several shiny pyrite pebbles and small talc-like stones. When the tide receded, a black, ferrous sand was observed on the bank. There were a number of indications that the rocks here contain copper ore. We returned safely.

Source: Khlebnikov 1990: 65. Reprinted by permission of the University of Alaska Press.

WRANGELL ON THE RUSSIAN RIVER (SEPTEMBER 1833)

Baron Ferdinand von Wrangell, in his capacity as the governor of Russian America, was interested in developing the various colonies within his realm, including the California establishment at Fort Ross. It had become abundantly clear that the agricultural endeavors of the colony would not succeed if they remained on the coast, the climate of which was not conducive to growing grain crops. He therefore sought to explore the interior of the Russian domain, and the most obvious area to examine was the lands lying along the Russian River, the dominant watercourse in the area. In his report to the directors of the Russian American Company following his visit to Fort Ross in 1833,[1] he made a point of describing the country flanking the river in consideration of potential development. His dream of taking over this land, however, was circumvented by the Mexican government's making land grants for property on the middle and upper portions, particularly the El Molino grant, located at the confluence of the Russian River and Mark West Creek,[2] which went to Captain John B. R. Cooper. Ultimately, the only Russian farm established on the Russian River was the Kostromitinov Ranch, which was close to the mouth of the river.

The necessity of occupying the valley of the Slavyanka [Russian] River. Between Ross Settlement and Little Bodega Bay there flows into the sea a river whose mouth is dry in summer, but above the mouth there is abundant water. In its course this river crosses extensive plains alternately forested and unforested and covered with succulent grasses, having its beginning about 80 verstas [53⅓ miles] upstream from its mouth and separated from Ross by a ridge of hard-to-cross hills and from the plain of the nearest Californian mission by two rows of hills not as steep as the former. On these plains roam Indians that war among themselves, of which one settlement, being a collection of runaways from the mission, is hostilely disposed toward all Christians, and others to the contrary. The Californian Spaniards pursuing Indians that had fled the missions became acquainted with these places and could not hide their desire to settle on them. Private persons are not strong enough to do this; and if the Californian government recognizes the necessity to build a mission here, then of course it will seize Little Bodega Bay, whither a vehicular road can be conveniently built and the output of the mission can be taken for sale to foreigners. In such a way can we be driven from here and we would be deprived of much, i.e., a fairly safe (in summertime) port and extensive fields suitable for the establishment of grain cultivation and stock raising on so vast a scale that not only all parts of the colony but Okhotsk or Kamchatka itself could be supplied with grain, salted beef, and butter by the Company. The occupation of these places having secured the colony with the most necessary requirements of provisions, the Company could derive many other advantages. For example, the continuously increasing number of old promyshlenniks, with families on their hands, remaining a burden to the Company and to all inhabitants of the colony, would be better settled on the Slavyanka River, where their children would grow healthfully and hence the latter could enter the temporary service of the Company. Here, then, it would be possible to establish the main school, and the modernization together with the perfection of agriculture under experienced and sensible management would revive several useful manufactures (namely, thick broadcloth and blankets, rope, and a soap plant) and would derive an abundance of productions useful for the colony and profitable in trade turnover with our neighbors.

Thus, on the one hand the fear of losing that which we own, and on the other [hand] the hope of substantially useful acquisitions, especially arouse the desire to occupy the plains of the Slavyanka River for the Company.

There are very sufficient means for this in the colonies, but the proposal for the occupation of the plains will destroy Ross Settlement. The sole difficulty in the fulfillment of this plan stems from the fear of the Colonial Administration that such an undertaking will arouse the envy of foreigners living in California and through their intrigue will set the Government of Mexico itself against us, or will even be subject to the displeasure of our Government for the spontaneous occupation of a place so remote from the established borders of Russian possessions in America.

On the other hand, in my opinion all these difficulties could be removed if our Government entered into direct relations and negotiations with the Government of Mexico on this subject. There they will understand well that the proximity of a handful of Russian muzhiks [peasants] isolated, so to speak, from their homeland can never be dangerous to the safety of the possessions of Mexico, but on the contrary a Russian settlement on this site can stop or at least hamper a much more dangerous encroachment for Mexico by the English and the Northern United States. Besides, the supposed goal of the Russian-American Company would be attained if it were allowed to freely use for 50 years or less Bodega Bay and the plains adjoining the Slavyanka River and protected on both sides by mountains like a natural boundary; and after the expiration of the agreed term these places can be taken by the former owner. In such an agreement it seems that it would be possible to succeed under the pretense of purchase or other means of policy, keeping in mind not to give foreigners cause to bar Russia from actual possession of the aforementioned country.

Such are my opinions; submitting them for the consideration of the Main Administration, I should still mention that it is necessary to hasten the start of negotiations with the Government of Mexico about the aforementioned subject; slowness may damage success, permit the English or citizens of the United State not only to impede us but also to occupy the places themselves and deprive the Russian-American Company of one of the best acquisitions in this territory.

Praising the plains of the Slavyanka River, I am based on a personal inspection of them,—for which, accompanied by the Manager of the Factory [ed: Peter Kostromitinov] and 20 Russians, Aleuts, and Indians, I undertook a trip there lasting from the 11th/22nd to the 14th/25th of September. On the 2nd day of the ride we reached the beginning of the plains, which we inspected for a distance of 40 verstas [26½ miles] and found places very suitable for settlement; in the Slavyanka and other rivers flowing into it the Indians procure fish; superb groves of oak are inhabited by numerous wild goats [ed: sic, mule deer]; the grass is succulent; the land is excellent and capable of growing all kinds of grain, the vine, and the fruits of southern Europe, and I see so much that it is possible to build an entire town and to reap up to 50 thous. puds [30,094⅙ bushels] of wheat and keep up to 40 thous. horned cattle.

If it is resolved to occupy these places, then in my opinion it would be necessary to send a detachment (15 Russians) there in May in order to clear an enclosure with guardhouses, magazines, and barracks on the sheltered slope of the Slavyanka River near a plain between this river and another river, while others will try to go there, too, on wheels from the Bodega side and take an entire year's necessary supplies for the detachment, which, conveniently for planting time, will at the first opportunity sow no more wheat than is necessary for the maintenance of the whole settlement for one year. Then the following May it will be possible to move all property from Ross on a special ship to Bodega and to drive all cattle overland to the plains: so that the occupation of the plains and the transfer of Ross will be brought to a finish in the 2nd year. For initial acquisition and organization it will be necessary to act under the leadership of an experienced, enterprising, well-behaved, and good manager versed in rural practices.

Source: Gibson 1969: 212–213. Reprinted by permission of James R. Gibson.

12

BOTANISTS ON RUSSIAN EXPEDITIONS
TO CALIFORNIA (1816 AND 1824)

RUSSIAN EXPEDITIONS under the command of Lieutenant (and later Captain) Otto von Kotzebue aboard the ships *Rurik* (1816) and *Predpriatie* (*Enterprise*) (1824) carried with them botanists who made collections in the vicinity of the Presidio of San Francisco and surrounding lands. A total of eighty-two species of California plants was collected by Adelbert von Chamisso and Johann Friedrich Eschscholtz, and many of the names given to the specimens have been associated with members of the crews of these ships. Perhaps the best known is the California state flower, the California poppy, which was named by Chamisso after his colleague: *Eschscholtzia californica.* Another plant, the skunk weed— *Polemonium captitatum* (*Gilia Chamissonis Greene*)—was obviously named for Adelbert von Chamisso himself.

It is important to appreciate that the Russian expeditions were interested in more than simply sea mammal skins and foodstuffs. The natural and cultural history collections compiled by people like Chamisso, Eschscholtz, Emile Botta, and Il'ya Voznesenskii were significant additions to the world's knowledge of California and provided important baseline information on species of continuing interest to naturalists even today. (The naturalists also collected animal specimens, and several of these still bear names honoring Russians Il'ya Voznesenskii[1] and Egor Chernykh.) As noted by scholar Alice Eastwood more than half a century ago (1944: 17), their contributions are even more valuable now that so many of the species they studied in their time are extinct.

ALICE EASTWOOD ON THE BOTANICAL COLLECTIONS
OF CHAMISSO AND ESCHSCHOLTZ IN CALIFORNIA (1944)

The following article, published in 1944 by the renowned California native plant botanist and historian Alice Eastwood, lists the author's commentary alongside the collections made by Adelbert von Chamisso and Friedrich von Eschscholtz during their visits to California in 1816 and 1824.

Otto von Kotzebue, commander of two
expeditions to California (1816 and 1822).
Courtesy of the Fort Ross Interpretive Association.

Otto von Kotzebue of the Royal Imperial Navy of Russia made two trips around the world and visited California on both. The first was in the ship *Rurik*, the main object being the discovery of the Northwest Passage. With him as naturalists were Adelbert von Chamisso, a noted poet and author, and Johann Friederich Eschscholtz, entomologist, zoologist, and ship's doctor. The *Rurik* arrived in San Francisco October 1, 1816 [Chamisso says it was October 2], and remained one month. This was an unfavorable time of the year for collecting plants or insects, but judging by the number of distinct species of plants collected, it must have been a year of early rains. I have collected in San Francisco on Thanksgiving Day nearly a hundred species of plants in bloom on such a year, when

"…smiling spring its earliest visit paid,
And parting summer's lingering blooms delayed."

The account of the plants and descriptions of the new species were published in Linnaea, a botanical journal published by D. F. L. von Schlechtendal and founded in 1826. Chamisso and Schlechtendal were joint authors of most of the new species, but some were described by Chamisso alone. The locality cited was "ad portum San Francisco" and all were collected, according to Chamisso, in the hills and downs about the Presidio. Very few, if any, are to be found there today.

Source: Eastwood 1944: 17–32.

THE COLLECTIONS OF ESCHSCHOLTZ (1826)

In 1824, Kotzebue made a second voyage in the ship *Predpriatie (i.e., Enterprise)* and Eschscholtz came as naturalist. They landed in San Francisco September 27 and departed November 23, a stay of nearly two months. During this time Eschscholtz visited Mission Santa Clara and Mission San Rafael and from there rode across valleys and hills to Sonoma and Bodega Bay [ed: and on to Fort Ross]. He remained at the Russian settlement a week and returned by sea to San Francisco. Off Point Reyes they were driven ashore by a violent storm and finally entered the Golden Gate on October 12. In November another trip was taken on which they ascended the Sacramento River in small boats as far, supposedly, as Rio Vista. Eschscholtz does not give the exact place where his collections were made, but from the plants collected all but one could have come from San Francisco. The new species were published in "Mémoires de l'Academie Impériale des Sciences de St. Petersbourg," vol. 10, 1826. An abstract of this publication was given in Litteratur-Bericht in *Linnaea*, vol. 3, pp. 147–153. In these abstracts the

Portrait of Johann Friedrich Eschscholtz.
Courtesy of the Rasmuson Library, University of Alaska, Fairbanks.

description of the new species by Eschscholtz were republished and have been considered authentic:

Abronia latifolia, "in arenos [ed: arenas] marit." Yellow sand-verbena. *Hoitzia squarrosa (Navarretia squarrosa* H. & A.), "in arenos [ed: sic]," skunk weed. *Polemonium captitatum (Gilia Chamissonis Greene),* "in arenos [ed: sic]." *Solanum umbelliferum,* "fruticetis," nightshade. *Ribes tubulosum "fructicetis."* This must have been *Ribes malvaceum* and not *R. glutinosum* Benth., the common wild currant of San Francisco, as the leaves are described as white-tomentose on lower surface. *Ribes malvaceum* has not been found in San Francisco. *Velezia latifolia (Frankenia grandifolia* C. & S.). *Eriogonum arachnoideum (E. latifolium* Sm.). *Lonicera Ledebourii,* "fruticetis," twinberry. *Ceanothus thyrsiflorus,* "fruticetis," California lilac. This was described as twice the height of a man. *Rhamnus californica,* "fruticetis," coffee-berry. Hendecandra procumbens (*Croton californicus* Muell. Arg.), "in arenos [ed: sic]." *Lupinus Chamissonis,* "in arenos [ed: sic]," blue sand lupine. *Lupinus sericeus* Pursh (*L. arboreus* Sims), flowers described as yellow.

On the first expedition, during the month of October, sixty-nine specimens were collected. Among them were two new genera and thirty-three new species. Three were synonyms having been previously described by other authors. On the second expedition, Eschscholtz named and described thirteen species, three among them previously described.

Source: Eastwood 1944, 19–20. From "Litteratur-Bericht," in *Linnaea,* vol. 3 (1829), pp. 147–153.

EXCERPTS FROM CHAMISSO'S JOURNAL (1816)

It is interesting that in his journal account of the visit to San Francisco in 1816 Chamisso only briefly alludes to botanizing, instead focusing on his experiences in California as a whole. This was probably because his natural history collections were more specialized and due to be published later in professional journals.

California poppy (*Eschscholtzia californica*). Original in the New York Botanical Garden. Courtesy of the Fort Ross Interpretive Association.

Adelbert von Chamisso, naturalist aboard the *Rurik* in 1816. Courtesy of the Fort Ross Interpretive Association.

The year was already old, and in the area, which in the spring months, the way Langsdorf saw it, should resemble a flower garden, now offered the botanist nothing but a dry, dead field. In a swamp in the vicinity of our tents a water plant is said to have been green, and Eschscholtz asked me about its pedigree. I hadn't noticed it, but he had calculated that a water plant, my special fancy, would not have escaped me and so had not wanted to get his feet wet. That's the kind of thing you can expect from your closest friend.

[...]

Don Pablo Vicente [ed: de Solá], when he descended the hill to our tents, once brought a present *a su amigo don Adelberto,* a flower, which he had plucked by the wayside and which he solemnly handed to me, the botanist. By chance it was our cinquefoil or five-finger (*Pontentilla anserina*), as beautiful as it could grow near Berlin.

Source: Chamisso 1986: 104, 106.

FAUNA NAMED BY OR FOR RUSSIANS (1984)

Aside from their botanical finds, Chamisso and Eschscholtz identified and named numerous animal species during their visit to California. Frederic Kaye Tomlin, a grandson of the Call family that bought Fort Ross in 1873 and continued to live there until the 1960s, put together in 1984 a list of fauna that were named by or for various Russians; an excerpt appears below.

The last item on the list is especially interesting because it appears to have been named for Egor Chernykh, the agronomist sent to Fort Ross in 1836.[2] The species is officially called *Brachinus tschernikhi Mannerheim*; it was collected by Chernykh in California and sent to Carl Gustaf von Mannerheim (a Finn), who provided it with its scientific name.[3]

Tiger beetle (*Omus californicus eschscholtzii*)
Monterey salamander (*Ensatina eschscholzii eschscholzii*)
Steller sea cow (*Hydrodamalis gigas*)
Steller sea lion (*Eumetopias stelleri*)
Steller jay (*Cyanocitta stelleri*)
Gumboot chiton (*Cryptochiton stelleri*)
Yellow-faced bumble bee (*Bombus vosnesenskii*)
Isopod (*Idotea wosnesenski*)
Live oak cluster beetle (*Cibdelis blaschkei*)
Bombardier beetle (*Brachinus tschernikhi*)

Source: From Frederic Kaye Tomlin, "Flora and Fauna Named after Russians or Their Employees as a Result of Activities in Russian America." Unpublished; handwritten copy dated August 1984 in the personal files of Glenn J. Farris.

13

THE TRANSFORMATION OF FORT ROSS'S PRIMARY FUNCTION FROM FUR HUNTING TO AGRICULTURE AND LIGHT INDUSTRY

ALTHOUGH FORT ROSS was initially established as a base for fur hunting operations, by the early 1820s the Russians were reporting a steep decline in the number of sea otter furs taken each year, a situation that in turn led to a shift in priorities to the community's alternate purpose: provisioning the Alaskan colonies with grain and products of light industry. In addition to various farming ventures, the colony was active in building ships and launches suitable for sailing along the coast and within San Francisco Bay. Other projects included brick-making, tanning hides, milling grains, and even building prefabricated wooden structures. When Karl Schmidt took over as the second commandant of Fort Ross, he made greater efforts toward the development of gardening, cattle husbandry, and the growing of crops, and also continued the colony's shipbuilding industry.

Schmidt was a very young man, only twenty-two at the time he assumed command of Fort Ross, and it seemed that some of the other Russian American Company officials took a dislike to him. RAC chief agent Kirill Khlebnikov, especially, is condemning in his comments about Schmidt; Otto von Kotzebue, meanwhile, was complimentary, saying of his visit to Fort Ross in 1824:

The Spaniards should study farming at the settlement of Ross under Schmidt. He manages the economy here with astonishing and praiseworthy perfection. All of the agricultural implements are made here under his direction and are not inferior to the best European models. Our Spanish companions were likewise staggered by all of this. But what amazed them most of all was the windmill; they had never seen such a perfect and useful machine.

Kotzebue went so far as to say that "the settlement of Ross brought much benefit to the Spaniards. Neither a single locksmith nor a single blacksmith is found in all of California. So all of the iron implements of the Spaniards are manufactured or repaired in the Russian colony for good payment. The [ed: Mexican] dragoons accompanying us brought many broken rifle bolts with them to be repaired" (Kalani 2011: 222).

Schmidt was a smart and enterprising man, even able to write in Spanish (surprisingly, not all the commandants were), but eventually the governor of Alaska, Matvei Ivanovich Muraviev, heeded the complaints against Schmidt and replaced him with a clerk from his own office, Paul Shelekhov.

Paul (Pavel Ivanovich) Shelekhov, the third commandant of Fort Ross (1825–1829), also promoted light industry and, according to French visitor Auguste Bernard Duhaut-Cilly in 1828, oversaw construction of "prefab" wooden houses to sell in California and Hawaii. As far as I know, none of these structures has survived, and corroboration of their being received in either Hawaii or California has not been found, so this may have been a short-lived enterprise. Overall, remarkably little is known about life at Fort Ross during Shelekhov's tenure. It is probable that the Fort Ross chapel was constructed sometime during his command, but even that is unconfirmed.

Following Shelekhov was Peter Kostromitinov, the commandant who perhaps held the longest tenure at Fort Ross. (Kuskov may hold that title.) We are much more familiar with life at the fort while Kostromitinov was in charge, since there were a number of visitors who left accounts of their time there. Perhaps the best description is found in the report submitted by the Governor General of Russian America during the first half of Kostromitinov's command at Fort Ross, Baron Ferdinand von Wrangell, whose report from 1833 follows. The year 1833 was a very busy one for visitors, among them John Work and his Hudson's Bay Company Brigade, American fur trapper Ewing Young, Commander of the Presidio of San Francisco Mariano Vallejo, merchant William Hartnell, and even a trio of Hawaiian sailors in a commandeered Pacific Northwest canoe; accounts from some of these people are also found in this volume. The amount of documented activity around Fort Ross during 1833 makes it one of the most notable for purposes of interpretation of life in the colony. (The other two important years are 1822 [the visit of Canonigo Agustín Fernández de San Vicente and entourage] and 1836 [Fr. Veniaminov's visit.])

Mariano Vallejo's trip to Fort Ross in 1833 was part of an unusual overture on the part the new governor of California, José Figueroa, who sought more friendly official relations between the Russians and Californians. In fact, Figueroa's own trip to Fort Ross the following year (August 23–25, 1834) was the only instance of a California governor actually visiting the Russian settlement. Unfortunately, Figueroa's notes of the trip (Mathes 2008: 218–221) are very brief and not worth including here. Nonetheless, the visit itself is noteworthy. Figueroa's untimely death in September 1835 marked the end of the cordial official relationship between the California government and the Russians at Fort Ross.

GOVERNOR WRANGELL'S REPORT
CONCERNING A VISIT TO FORT ROSS (1833)

Baron von Wrangell's account of his 1833 visit to the Russian American Company's settlement in California provides some wonderful detail of how the community appeared in the physical sense, and it also showed his interest in the welfare of the people. He tells us what life was like for one representative family (a husband, a wife, and five children) at Fort Ross, providing a list of material goods given them by the officials and an account of their costs, and he included his own personal commentary that the value of these items far exceeds the salary earned by the man. Since the Russian American Company operated a closed economy for its employees, in which RAC scrip was used instead of cash and could only be spent in the company store, we see how easily an employee could grow deeper in debt over the years. Wrangell also

Baron Ferdinand Petrovich von Wrangell. From the Central Naval Museum,
St. Petersburg. Courtesy of the Fort Ross Interpretive Association.

showed compassion for the local Indians, who were brought in to work the fields at harvest time, sometimes under duress; he observed that such actions would result in creating enmity among the local people that was not to the advantage of the Company.

Wrangell had tallied up the production of the colony as of the last full year (1832) before his visit, and he points out how agriculture confined to a coastal environment does not provide adequate yields. He then suggests the need for expanding the colony into areas inland from the coast and includes an exploratory trip up the Russian River to investigate its valley. He also notes the somewhat decrepit condition of the buildings in the fort. Overall, Wrangell seemed to feel that it was worthwhile to put more resources into Fort Ross to make it more successful. His report stimulated efforts to improve the situation, and within a couple of years a trained agronomist (Egor Chernykh) had been sent, and, judging from comments in the final inventory, apparently a number of buildings were repaired or built anew, including a kitchen and a warehouse.

Report to the Main Administration [of the Russian American Company, submitted on April 10/21, 1834, as Dispatch 61]

With the departure of the ships from Novo-Arkhangelsk, and having entrusted command of the port and affairs to my assistant, Mr. Captain Lieutenant Etolin, on June 13/24 of last year [ed: 1833], I left Sitka Bay on the sloop *Baikal* under the command of Lieutenant Illyashevich,[1] bound for Ross Settlement, where I left the sloop on the evening of July 1/12. According to the report of Mr. Kostromitinov, Manager of the Factory [ed: of Ross], everything is fine; in spring an infection raged here, from which almost the entire command was sick, but none died and now, thank God, they are well again; many of the Indians living nearby perished.

I inspected the buildings, magazines [ed: warehouses], and economic establishments and became acquainted more closely with all circumstances, conducements, and impediments concerning the agricultural and manufactural production of Ross Settlement, and I do not think it superfluous to state to the Main Administration a general summary of the observations made by me on these subjects.

Buildings. On flat, clayey ground atop a hill sloping steeply to the sea has been erected a wooden palisade along the edges of a fairly extensive area forming a regular square; at two diagonally opposite corners in connection with the palisade have been erected two watchtowers with cannons defending all sides of this so-called fortress, which in the eyes of the Indians and local Spaniards, however, seems very strong, and perhaps unconquerable. Within this enclosure by the palisade itself stand the Company buildings: the house of the Manager of the Factory, barracks, magazines, a storehouse, and a chapel, all kept in cleanliness and order, conveniently and even prettily situated. However, almost all the buildings and the palisade itself with the watchtowers are so old and dilapidated that they need repairs, or they will have to be replaced by new structures. On this hill, outside the fortress, facing and paralleling its sides, are located two Company cattle barns with pens, spacious and kept in excellent cleanliness, a small building for storing milk and making butter, a shed for Indians, a threshing floor, and two rows of small Company and private houses with gardens and orchards, occupied by employees of the Company. On a cleared spot beyond this outskirt stands a windmill. Below the hill by a landing for baidarkas [kayaks] have been built a spacious shed and a cooperage, a blacksmithy, a tannery, and a bathhouse. Everything is situated conveniently and in accordance with the purposes of the settlement and its local circumstances; but as stated above, most buildings have deteriorated. The brickworks was moved last year to Bodega Bay, where a spacious shed was built for storing bricks and other necessary supplies that are cargo on ships arriving here annually from Sitka with the sub-division's supplies.

Cultivation. In the vicinity of the settlement the land is hilly, dissected, cut by deep ravines, and covered with trees; the soil is mostly loam, but there is also chernozem[2]; it produces high and pleasant-smelling grass nutritious for cattle, and in some places protected from sea winds and fogs the farmer's labor is rewarded with a wheat harvest of 10-fold to 27-fold the seed. Unfortunately, however, such places found here that are not subject to the baneful influence of sea fogs are very few and are small patches on the slopes of high, steep hills accessible only on foot or on horseback, so that, having overcome cultivation of this steeply mountainous plowland with no little labor, after harvesting there remains the extremely difficult and slow work of hauling the sheaves on shoulders to the threshing floor or to such places whence they can be conveyed by horses. To this inconvenience are added others by the necessity of sowing all places suitable for plowland every year without interruption, from which much plowland has now already lost its strength, does not return the seed, and should be abandoned, while they cannot be replaced by other places; on other plowland wild oats grow in such abundance that they smother wheat, and the sole method used to eradicate them is leaving them for trampling by cattle for two or three years—meaning that again part of the cultivated land is lost; to crown everything ground mice and hamsters [gophers?] make real raids and eat standing grain.

After this nobody will expect good successes from grain cultivation at Ross and will not be surprised that from 1826 to 1833 (inclusive), i.e., in the course of 8 years, about 6,000 puds [about 4,000 bushels] of wheat and barley were sent to Sitka, comprising around 750 puds [about 500 bushels] per year, a very insignificant amount! The year 1832 was one of the best harvests: then on Company and private plowland altogether 542 puds, 11 funts [304½ bushels] of wheat and 191 puds, 26 funts [144⅕ bushels] of barley were planted and 6,104 puds, 32 funts [3,674⅜ bushels] of wheat and 942 puds, 30 funts [709¼ bushels] of barley in 30,000 sheaves were harvested. In that year from the stated harvest of grain were derived 37,328 rubles in favor of the Company and 5,748 rubles in favor of private individuals, figuring a pud [36 pounds or ⅗ of a bushel] of wheat at 5 rubles. After local expenses and retentions for planting there remained in surplus about 1½ thousand puds [902⅚ bushels] of wheat, which was sent to Sitka: this is beyond any gain that could be expected from grain cultivation at Ross under its present condition.

Last year, 1833, were planted 377 puds, 32 funts [227⅖ bushels] of wheat and 204 puds, 18 funts [153⅘ bushels] of barley, and 3,759 puds, 26 funts [2,262⅞ bushels] of wheat and 1,084 puds [815⅗ bushels] of barley were harvested. For experimentation 6½ funts [5⅚ pounds] of hemp were planted, and 2 puds, 35 funts [103¾ pounds] of seed were harvested, which this year should be used for planting. In the future a useful experiment will be made in the planting of millet, buckwheat, flax, oats, and rye, and hence for this purpose I most humbly ask the Main Administration to order at the first opportunity the dispatch to the colony of a certain amount of the above seeds.

The local farmers scarcely have an understanding of the cultivation of fields; generally like promyshlenniks [frontiersmen] arriving in America, they consist of all kinds of riffraff; the Manager of the Factory himself, who supervises agriculture here, has never had any experience whatsoever in these matters: consequently, in all fairness should it be surprising that with great local difficulties and without the benefit of practical experience agriculture has been reduced to that mediocre condition in which it is now found [?]

Perhaps with the introduction of intercropping and other auxiliary means the fields would not have depleted so quickly, and with the improvement of threshing and winnowing they would not have lost so much as now. Here only wheat and barley are sown; the fields cannot be fertilized with manure, and they are not left in fallow on account of the impossibility of replacing them with others; the grain is threshed by horses, 30 or more of which are mobilized in an enclosure covered with sheaves, from which the kernels are dislodged by the running hoofs. By this method they thresh 900 sheaves per day with 50 horses under 8 drivers. On account of the shortage of men, it is not possible to use flails. If they had a simple, mobile threshing machine, then the sending of such a machine by the Main Administration would afford very considerable benefit; and I think it most properly concerns the Imperial Moscow Agricultural Society in order not to err in selection in buying a threshing machine. Somewhere in a periodical they extol the Chaplygin and Makhov machines, especially for their cheapness; however, it is best to ask the Moscow Society for sensible advice in order not to incur expenses in vain and uselessly lose time besides.

I do not mention gardening and orcharding at Ross because neither one nor the other brings the Company profits and should remain pursuits of private persons only.

Stockbreeding constitutes another agricultural subject at Ross. The mountainous site and the forest pose an insurmountable obstacle to the considerable propagation of cattle in the vicinity of the settlement. From July to

November or December the cattle are scattered 20 verstas [13¼ miles] on all sides, seeking grass that in summer fades from the sun and is plucked by the cattle in the vicinity of the settlement, so that it is impossible to carefully tend the cattle, and, being driven twice a day from distant places to the barn for milking, the cows tire and give so little milk that in 1832 with every care only 116 puds [4,189 pounds] of churned butter were obtained from 147 milk cows. After local outlays about 85 puds [3,069⅗ pounds] from this amount were sent to Novo-Arkhangelsk. Besides butter they get from the cattle: salted beef for Sitka and a small proportion of tallow and hide made at the factory here for local use and for sending to Sitka. On September 1/12, 1833, there were reckoned on hand at the settlement:

horned cattle . . . . .719 head
horses . . . . 415 head
goats and sheep . . . . 605 head
pigs . . . . .34 head

Total   1,773 head.

From this stock breeding there were derived in the course of the year for the benefit of the Company butter, tallow, hide, and sheep's wool at

3,300 rubles

salted beef . . . . 2,472 rubles
fresh meat sold to employees . . . . 1,205 rubles
and used as food for the command at. . . . . . 1,005 rubles

Total   7,982 rubles.

From year to year all breeds of cattle multiply considerably by breeding, but because of the smallness of the place up to 2,000 head altogether should not be allowed, although for sufficient feeding of the people (for want of fish) and for the preparation of salted beef for Novo-Arkhangelsk no less than 1,500 head of horned cattle alone would be required; then depletion of the herd would not be hazarded, and it would be possible to feed the inhabitants and to send to Sitka one-half of its annual needs of salted beef, i.e., 400 puds [14,445⅕ pounds] per year.

Various items of industry that bring benefit to the Company, apart from grain cultivation and stock raising, include:

1. the hunting of animals, which at the beginning of the settlement were considerable but are now limited to two hundred fur seals and occasional, fairly rare ventures for sea otters by local Aleuts along the Californian coast. This hunting is strictly forbidden by the Californian government and that is why it is seldom managed to obtain temporary permission, and according to many assurances this animal [sea otter] will soon utterly disappear from this coast, being continually driven by skippers of the United States with the help of Kolosh [Tlingits; ed: possibly all of the tribes in the northwest coast area], despite the prohibition of the Spaniards. In the last 7 years the Aleuts of Ross Settlement bagged the following:

	in 1826	1827	1828	1829	1830	1831	1832
sea otters [adults]	287	9	I	18	12	112	I
young sea otters	13	3	0	5	4	0	0
fur seals	455	290	0	210	287	205	118

2. various wares ordered by the Californian Spaniards, like cooking utensils, wheels, long-boats, etc., and for such articles they formerly paid fairly profitably and Ross Factory sometimes derived profit for the Company of up to 6 thousand rubles per year. Now such transactions are rare and negligible because the foreigners controlling trade in California have brought all the possible needs of the inhabitants and supply them at such low prices that it is not possible for us to compete with them.

3. the supply of Novo-Arkhangelsk Port with a small amount of tar, good quality bricks, and sturdy timber (laurel) necessary for various articles on ships. It is impossible to get more of these items from anywhere but Ross, and they are of course important to us on account of the vital need for them. The procurement of laurel, however, is becoming extremely difficult now because suitable trees near the settlement have been felled and it is necessary to seek them in deep ravines.

Population and Condition of the Inhabitants. On July 1/12, 1833, there were reckoned in the settlement

	adults		children younger than 16 years	
	males	females	males	females
Russians	41	4	3	2
Creoles[3]	10	15	30	33
Aleuts	42	15	21	5
Indians	35	37	uncounted	uncounted
Total	128	71	54	40
	199		94	

Grand total   293 souls of both sexes.

At the time when they reap grain Indians from the nearby tundra gather in the settlement for commensurate pay, or by necessity, when there are few hunters, then they forcibly collect as many Indians as possible, sometimes up to 150 persons, who for 1½ months are occupied without rest in Company field work, and without their assistance it would not be at all possible to reap and to haul the wheat from the plowland to the threshing floors. As an example, I noticed during my stay at Ross that they put to work:

Russians and Creoles (the Aleuts were hunting sea
    otters). Sentries, artisans, carpenters, cooks etc. . 49 pers[ed: persons]
Indians (for reaping and hauling sheaves to the
    threshing floors, hauling clay for bricks, etc.). . . 161 pers
                                        at work 210 pers

From this the necessity of the assistance of the Indians is strikingly obvious.

Russians, Creoles and Aleuts are on salary or on daily pay while working, and Indians receive food and sometimes pay from the Company. Those receiving salary are given 1 pud [36.113 pounds] of flour per month and 1 funt [.90282 pounds] of meat (including bones) per day, and others are allotted only flour for gruel as food: from this meager food and with the strenuous work the Indians toward the end are in extreme exhaustion! However, complaints and requests were received by me not from these people but from promyshlenniks on salary.

All assert that there is no way whatever for them to live and to feed a family with one salary and one ration of flour and 1 funt of meat (with bones) per day: as a result of which the Factory can in fact by no means lessen duties, but on the contrary they are increasing from year to year. In order to give an idea of the expenses of a Russian promyshlennik at Ross, I add here the debts of one of them, Vasily Permitin,[4] who has a wife and five children. For 1832 he received on his salary's account:

Wheat	3½ puds		[126⅖ lbs.]
Wheat flour	42 puds	10 funts	[1,525¾ lbs.]
Barley do.	2 puds		[71¼ lbs.]
Dried Meat	1 pud		[36⅒ lbs.]
Fresh Beef	1 pud	35 funts	[67⅗ lbs.]
Lard		24 funts	[21⅗ lbs.]
Cow's Butter		11 funts	[9⁹⁄₁₀ lbs.]
Tallow Candles		14 funts	[12⅗ lbs.]
Salt		14 funts	[12⅗ lbs.]
Beef Fat		2 funts	[1⅘ lbs.]
Copper Utensils	4½		[4 lbs.]
Millet		10 funts	[9 lbs.]
Circassian Tobacco		22 funts	[19⅘ lbs.]
Soap		27 funts	[24⅓ lbs.]
Tea		10¾ funts	[9⅔ lbs.]
Sugar	1 pud	7½ funts	[42⅞ lbs.]
Treacle		10½ funts	[9½ lbs.]
Wool felt	2 bundles		
Cotton stockings	1 pair		
Flannel blankets	2 bundles		
Cotton dress	1		
Soles	21 pair		
Uppers	10 pair		
Cotton ends	5 pieces		
Medium sheepskins	2 pieces		
Flemish linen	21 arshins		[49 feet]
Calico	32 arshins		[74⅔ feet]
Ticking	17 arshins		[39⅔ feet]

Trouser burlap	15 arshins	[35 feet]
Gingham	7 arshins	[16⅓ feet]
Soldier's broadcloth	2 arshins	[4⅔ feet]

All these total 728 rubles, 17 kopeks at existing prices, while Permitin's annual salary is 350 rubles. Added as an example, the order of things and supplies bought by Permitin shows that nothing unnecessary was taken; consequently it is impossible not to recognize the impossibility of these men maintaining themselves with one salary of 350 rubles per year. Having received this circumstance with respect, I found it necessary to make certain privileges for the local promyshlenniks that are stated in proposal No. 260 for the Factory, which I submit to the Main Administration in a supplemental report for examination and approval. In due course, it will be necessary to build a school in the local division for the care of the children who abound here: however, assuming a transfer of the settlement to another site I did not proceed to establish either a school or a hospital. In the aforementioned proposal I have authorized providing the Indians and the Aleuts the best food, as against formerly, and especially paying the Indians somewhat more generously for work. Not only humanity but also wisdom demand that the Indians be encouraged more: from the bad food and the negligible pay the Indians have stopped coming to the settlement for work, from which the Factory found itself forced to seek them in the tundras, attack by surprise, tie their hands, and drive them to the settlement like cattle to work: such a party of 75 men, wives, and children was brought to the settlement during my presence from the distance of about 65 verstas [43 miles] from here, where they had to leave their belongings without any attention for two months. It goes without saying what consequences there must be in due course from such actions with the Indians, and will we make them our friends? I hope that the Factory, having received permission from me to provide the Indians decent food and satisfactory pay, will soon see a change in their disposition toward us, and the Main Administration will of course recognize these increased expenses, justifiable and useful, as against the former expenses. I also recognized the necessity to increase the daily pay of the Aleuts for working days, as stated in proposal No. 275 to the Factory (see the report), and in which I ask the approval of the Main Administration.

Capital and Upkeep of the Division. According to the reckoning of the Factory, by January 1/12 of 1833 the capital included the following items:

Cash	4,398 rub. 22 kop.
Supply magazine	41,465 rub. 87 kop.
Public magazine	64,445 rub. 49 kop.
Trading store	5,133 rub.
Pharmacy	132 rub. 24 kop.
Chapel	2,474 rub. 86 kop.
Tannery	466 rub. 50 kop.
Household property	42,645 rub. 43 kop.
Company plowland	18,009 rub. 72 kop.
Debts of employees	44,797 rub. 63 kop.
Do. of Aleuts	3,397 rub. 11 kop.
Do. of Californians	3,096 rub. 26 kop.
Company stockbreeding	40,230 rub. 10 kop.
Total	270,693 rub. 33 kop.

From this capital should be excluded 14,484 r., 49 k. of devaluation made by me on unfit materials and things that have arrived, as in report No. 266 to the Main Administration, if it pleases to see it.

For 1832 there were spent on upkeep of the division:

on salary . . . . 25,227 rubles
on other items . . . . .30,151 rubles

Total   55,378 r. expenses

For this same period by reckoning 45,119 rubles in profits and invoices were due in favor of the Company, to which I add probable profits from the hunting of fur seals

2,660 rubles

Total   47,779 profits

Consequently, in the course of 1832 the Company compiled a net loss from the production of Ross Factory of 7,599 rubles. It was remarked above that on account of the harvest of grain the aforementioned year was one of the best; except for 1¼ hundred fur seals, there was no fur trade. Concerning the fur trade throughout the Ross Division, at the present time it cannot be taken into discussion with the compilation of the expenses and receipts of this Factory,—it has been stated above and explained by the extract placed there of output for 7 years. Consequently, it is possible to say affirmatively that from the maintenance of the Ross Division in the best harvest years the company will always suffer losses if the settlement remains on the sites now occupied, which do not permit substantial improvement on the part of agriculture,—which in my opinion should be the only sensible aim of the establishment.

[Paragraphs on the Slavianka River were moved to pages 141–144, in the Russian River section of this collection.]

In caution I still should mention that the plains along the Avacha River [Estero Americano] flowing into Bodega have been found to be quite unsuitable for grain cultivation: a dense fog from the sea almost always stands on them, the land is clayey and there are no trees, so that it is impossible to expect good harvests.

Finishing this report about Ross Settlement, I add with pleasure that the Manager of the Factory, Mr. Kostromitinov, observed by me in the administration of the division entrusted to him, is a diligent, energetic, and observant credit to the Company, and that is why I have beseeched that he remain for two more years, although he asked to leave. On these grounds I ask the Main Administration to try to find and to send here next year a man capable of occupying this post: here I do not have in view suitable men for such duty.

Source: Gibson 1969: 205–215. Reprinted by permission of James R. Gibson.

KOSTROMITINOV'S REPORT TO THE

HEADQUARTERS OF THE RUSSIAN AMERICAN COMPANY

(JULY 31/AUGUST 10, 1833)

This report prepared by Peter Kostromitinov and dated July 31/August 10, 1833, is interesting as it relates to the inspection report prepared by Governor von Wrangell (see previous selection) and to the various incidents that happened during 1833 and the visitors who came by Fort Ross that year. As noted in Wrangell's report, Kostromitinov had requested several times to be relieved of his position as commandant at least as early as 1833, a detail that suggests he was not happy at Fort Ross, and yet he was not finally replaced as manager of the fort until November 1838, when Alexander Rotchev took command. For some reason, when the agronomist Egor Chernykh came to Fort Ross at the beginning of 1836 as a possible replacement for Kostromitinov, the latter evidently changed his mind about leaving and stayed on in the position for several more years. After the sale of the fort in 1841, he moved back to Russia and then to Sitka/New Archangel, only to return to San Francisco in the early 1850s, after which he ran the RAC emporium and was given the title of Vice Consul. The following report by Kostromitinov was relayed by Governor Wrangell to RAC headquarters, probably along with his own report of his visit.

※ ※

The Office of the Settlement Ross on July 31 [ed: August 10] of the previous year [ed: 1833], reports to me the following:

On the 11th [ed: 22nd] day of March of the previous year [ed: 1833], four trappers from the river Columbia arrived to the outer settlement [ed: Bodega Bay?] and to the questions from the Office Manager, replied that their party is staying at the Mission of San Francisco Solano to purchase provisions and powder, but since the Mission had no powder, their Chief [ed: John Work] sent them here for this purchase. When they departed from the fort of Vancouver, they had enough powder but during the crossing of a large river they have lost it together with some other things.

The Ross Office had decided to provide them with 5 pounds of powder and 10 pounds of lead [for] which they paid three river otter pelts[5] and have left the next day.

The Office Manager learned from them also that they started hunting for the river otters [ed: beaver?] in December of 1832 and until March of 1833 trapped no more than 800 pelts. During all this time they had continuous rains and encountered deep snows while crossing the mountains.

In January of the last year, when the Office Manager of the Ross settlement was visiting the port of San Francisco on the sloop *Urup,* Messrs [ed: William E. P.] Hartnell and [ed: John Rogers] Cooper asked that assistance be given to an American, Mr. [ed: Ewing] Young, who was trapping the river otters and in case he delivers them to the Settlement Ross, to store them in our warehouse for safekeeping which was promised to them with the permission from Mr. Etolin. Mr. Young arrived at the settlement on March 13 [ed: 24] in company with seven people and brought with him 199 pelts of river otters which were later removed to California by Mr. Cooper. His party consisted of 25 trappers and after circling the Bay of San Francisco, he arrived at our Settlement from the North: he talked about the lack of success in trapping and blamed it on the bad weather and the above mentioned Columbians[6] whom he met twice.

In order to assist him, various materials and craft pieces worth 160 piasters were given to him with charges transferred to Mr. Cooper.

On April 7th [ed: 18th] the Office Manager, while travelling from the Settlement to the river Slavianka in order to collect plants, has noticed on the other side many people and horses. He sent to find out about these people and the man who arrived from there declared to him that he is the Chief of a party of trappers from the river Columbia and asked for permission to pass through our Settlement because, planning to return from the Mission San Francisco–Solano by the old road, he encountered snows in the mountains and extensive muds in the Valley and so decided that the voyage along the sea coast will be better.

After receiving this permission he ordered his people to stay overnight near Slavianka and proceeded with the Office Manager to the Settlement Ross.

Next day, his party consisting of 163 persons, including women and children with 450 horses, passed through the Settlement continuing in a Northern direction along the sea shore. On the request of their Chief, Mr. John Hork [ed: Work?], some materials and provisions were given to them for which we received in exchange 19 river otters large, 2 small otters and one pelt of otter.

On June 7th [ed: 18th] a Kolosh [ed: usually meaning Tlingit, but could be any northwest coast Indian] boat had landed at the Settlement and three Sandwich [ed: Sandwich Island natives] declared that they are from the American vessel that perished on the other side of Trinidad [ed: Trinidad Bay] and are on the way to Monterey in order to return to their homeland[ed: ;] they travelled by boat for about 45 days. Captain of the wrecked ship had departed by another ship with some sailors and these 11 men were left because of the lack of space. They were promised another ship but were not sure about this and so these three decided to reach Monterey, while the remaining 8 decided to wait for the ship.

It was impossible to get more from them because except of their own tongue, they did not speak any other. Two days later they departed and whether they have reached the port of San Francisco or Monterey, is unknown.

The Office Manager bought from them 3 sea otters. These people told us that the Indians at 15 days travel from the Settlement have many sea and river otters and would trade them readily for iron knives and other things. I consider it my duty to report this to the Company Headquarters.

Source: Peter Kostromitinov report, forwarded by Governor Wrangell to Head Office, No. 197, report dated April 28/May 9, 1834. Russian American Company Correspondance 1818–1867. Records of the Russian American Company, microfilm roll 36, National Archives, Washington, D.C. Typescript translation dated 1990 by Oleg Terichow.

CHERNYKH AND THE SCOTTISH THRESHER
AT FORT ROSS (1836–1841)

The procurement and ultimately production of grain to feed the Russian colonies in Alaska was of major importance to the Russian American Company. In
the early years of the Fort Ross settlement, the grain was mostly grown in fields
adjacent to the fort, and a windmill had been constructed to grind the grain
(Farris 2001). In the 1830s, attempts were made to expand the areas of production, and as many as five ranchos may have been founded by the Russians, of
which three became firmly established and were fairly successful.

In 1836 a Russian-trained agronomist arrived at Fort Ross. Egor (Georgii)
Leontievich Chernykh was born around 1813 in northern Kamchatka, the son
of a Russian priest and a Kamchadal (or Itelman) native (Pierce 1990: 86).
Chernykh was sent to the Moscow Agricultural School in 1823, and after graduation he first returned to Kamchatka, where he entered into various enterprises
to improve agriculture in the area. A series of crop failures eventually ruined the
company he had joined there, and Chernykh thereafter took up employment
with the Russian American Company as an agronomist. In an effort to improve
their agricultural enterprise in California, the RAC sent Chernykh to Fort Ross,
where he arrived on January 14/25, 1836.

Following his arrival Chernykh wrote several letters that described the state
of agriculture in California at the time. He described at length the "wretched
fashion" of threshing using horses to trample out the grain, a technique common in California at the time. Observing this inefficient method prompted him
to build a threshing machine, which he discusses in the document that follows.

The thresher was mentioned in an account of a visit to Fort Ross in late
September 1839 by Captain Edward Belcher of the H.M.S. *Sulphur*. Belcher's
report (1843: vol. I, 315) states: "...on the N.W. from the stockade are situated
the stables for the cattle, a large granary, with a threshing machine capable of
cleaning one hundred bushels of corn per day; a windmill..."

In a curious footnote to this story, the thresher shows up once again in
the inventory of goods sold in 1841 by the Russians to Captain John Sutter of
New Helvetia. The original French inventory reads as follows: "Une machine
écossaise pour battre le blé (en fer de fonte)." This translates to "A Scottish

machine for threshing wheat (using 'slit iron')." Whether or not Captain Sutter (of gold rush fame) ever did bring the Scottish thresher up to Sutter's Fort to use on his extensive wheat fields has been lost to history, but it is intriguing to think that the machine may have made its way to California's Central Valley.

Throughout California reaping is done with sickles and threshing with horses in the most wretched fashion. They construct a round threshing floor, from 5 to 8 sazhens [35 to 56 feet] in diameter, and enclose it with a wooden or stone wall. They spread sheaves of wheat throughout this contrived thresher to a depth of 1 to 2 arshins [28 to 56 inches]; then they drive from 70 to 150 horses inside, and they spur them with whips, so that the kernels are dislodged by the hoofs in constant motion. At first the poor animals sink into the straw, until they trample it. This activity continues for an hour or an hour and a half; then they drive out the horses, take off the top layer of trampled straw, and throw it out of the thresher; then they again drive in the horses, continuing this operation until the loose sheaves spread in the thresher are turned into chaff. They winnow this chaff and get pure wheat. The unfortunate animals injure themselves while jumping inside the enclosure; mare in foal frequently miscarry and often die.

However, it should be mentioned that the local wheat is very firmly attached to the ear, so that it is hardly possible to thresh it cleanly with flails; with horses threshing grain is left in few ears; nevertheless, in throwing straw out of the thresher much grain is discarded with it.

Having found what difficulty and losses grain threshing entails at Ross, I decided to build a wooden Scottish [threshing] machine, and, to my greatest pleasure, I finished it fairly successfully. I built it according to the drawing and description of Mr. Flat [ed: Mr. Flota or possibly Fleet] in the *Agricultural Journal,* with an insignificant change.

The machine built by me is entirely wooden, except the coaks and the bearings, which are made from iron; the cams on all wheels, as well as the teats on the gears, are of hard laurel; the conveying cylinders are also laurel. It is set in motion by two horses; the drum with six beaters makes 180 revolutions per minute, which are insufficient, as I noted from experience; it can thresh up to 700 large sheaves in 10 hours; but with the help of 4-5

"La Trilla," threshing the grain in old California.
From Owen C. Coy's *Pictorial History of California* (1925), No. 93.

men and 4 horses (which are replaced every 2½ hours) it threshes from 350 to 550 sheaves per day, owing to the stubbornness of the workers in the face of this innovation and the unfamiliarity of the horses with circling. It should be mentioned that here and throughout California there are no barns, and that is why wet threshing always prevails; why does the machine not thresh wheat as cleanly as the threshing machines I saw in Moscow [?]. Concerning this it is necessary to consider the slowness of the turning of the drum and the small number of beaters.

Although the aforementioned number of sheaves threshed by the machine that I made is negligible, at Ross it is advantageous: because here 120 horses and 25 Indians are needed to thresh 1,000 sheaves of wheat per day. I cannot understand why almost half of the ears are removed and deposited together with the grain and straw by my machine. It was impossible, of course, to avoid defects with the first construction of this important and rather complex machine. Next summer (1837) I intend to correct the mistakes noted in my machine, and I shall try to build another wooden [one]. It is even more possible now that on the sloop *Elena*, just arrived from Kronshtat [sic], we have received iron parts of a Scottish thresher, purchased in Moscow from the Gutenop brothers. The wooden machine has been known to thresh up to 10,000 sheaves of wet wheat and not suffer any damage; the teats and the cams are quite intact, and even the iron coaks and bearings are very little worn; the coaks were made like balls. More rubbing is noticeable in the gear teats on the drum axle; but in case of need one has only to insert new ones in place of the worn ones, and if the cams on any wheel are damaged, then it is also possible to instantly install new ones, which are in stock. What a difference in repairing an iron machine in case of damage!

Source: Gibson 1968: 48–56. Reprinted by permission of James R. Gibson.

CHERNYKH'S REPORT ON
AGRICULTURE IN CALIFORNIA (1841)

Russian agronomist Egor Chernykh prepared a report—"Agriculture in Upper California"—that he sent to a journal in Russia, which published it in 1841. It begins with a lengthy background description of the climate and crops planted in Mexican California. Chernykh then discusses certain ways of threshing grain, his descriptions being of particular interest both in terms of his account of the threshing methods as well as his views toward developing good threshing techniques for Fort Ross and the ranchos. As an agronomist trained in Russia and sent specifically to California to attempt to improve crop production, much of Chernykh's report deals with crop yields. He arrived in California a few years after the secularization of the missions (1833–1834), which had resulted in dramatic declines in crop production that were not fully made up for by the growth of the ranchos, which were more apt to concentrate on cattle raising. One nearby land grant that did continue to grow and supply grain to the Russians was Rancho Olompali, which was then owned by a former mission Indian named Camilo Ynitia (Davis 1967: 103). The Russians were able to obtain the labor of a number of mission Indians, who brought with them knowledge of techniques for planting, harvesting, and threshing that had been common in the missions. Thus, the observations made by Chernykh on the grain production methods used in Mexican California were especially relevant to the future of the Russian farms. Despite the often crude methods used by the Californios, the Russian agronomist was impressed by their crop yields.

On the northwestern coast of America, between the Cape of St. Luke [ed: Cabo San Lucas] and the port of San Francisco, lies the blessed land, called California. It is divided into the Upper or New and the Lower or Old. The Upper California is the area between the ports of San Diego and San Francisco, and the Lower California the area between the port of San Diego and the Cape of St. Luke.

Having the honor of serving in the colonies of the Russo-American Company, namely in settlement [Fort] Ross, I had become acquainted with the climate of the Upper California and with the economy of its inhabitants.

[A lengthy description of planting various vegetable crops in Mexican California has been omitted here.]

Reaping is done with sickles; for easier threshing only the ears are usually cut off the bread plants. The straw remains in the field and is burned or used by cattle. The harvested ears are carted to the threshing ground in large clumsy wagons; these wagons are called here "carrets" [ed: *carretas*], the wheels being nothing but crosscuts of large whole logs.

Threshing is [ed: d]one with horses. For this purpose, threshing grounds are made of two kinds: earth and stone. [Original editor's note states: Wooden threshing grounds seem to be in use only in Ross.]

For earthen ground a smooth level place is selected on clay soil; it is surrounded by fence, and during the winter cattle [ed: sic, horses] are herded there so that the surface is tramped down and leveled. When rains end and weather becomes hot, such a place on clay soil gets as hard as rock. For a stone threshing ground, a level place, is likewise selected; the floor and the walls are made of brick or flat stones. The diameter of threshing grounds depends on the amount of bread plants and the number of horses, varying from 56 to 84 feet. A tall pole is sometimes placed in the center of the ground. Into the ground, so constructed, the harvested plants are brought, and either are scattered over the entire ground some 4 to 5 feet high, or are put up in the shape of a haystack in the center, around the pole, leaving between the sides of the stack and the walls of the ground a small space perhaps 10 feet for the horses to run in. Having laid down the bread plants in such manner, the farmers drive into the enclosure from 50 to 180 horses, depending upon the size of the area.

If the harvest is scattered over the whole ground, the horses sink into the plants until the plants are tramped down; for an hour or hour and a half [ed: the horses] are driven with long whips in order to keep them in constant motion, knocking the grain out of the plant heads. Then the horses are herded out while the plants are turned over and the horses again driven in, and so on. When it is observed that the grain is separated from the straw, the top layer is carefully removed and thrown away. The entire lot of the harvested plants is thus turned over several times and the horses driven in and out until all the plants on the ground are pretty well shredded. By sifting the shreds, the clean grain is obtained. The poor animals, jumping around in the crowded enclosure get injured, [ed: and] pregnant mares often abort and sometimes die.

Under this method of threshing, in order to finish 1,000 sheaves per day, it is necessary to use 100 to 200 horses and 20 to 25 Indians who take turns to drive the horses. The Indians hop around in the area with the horses and keep repeating in a plaintive refrain two words: *Evva, camya; evva, camya!* [Ed: Possibly he was hearing "Yegua, cambia!" or "Mares, change [direction]!"]

The second method of threshing is preferable to the first. The stack around the pole of bread plants is gradually lowered to the ground by a man who is seated on top of it; it is thus easier for the horses to thresh out the thinner layers. It is claimed that by this method 8 to 10 men and 150 horses can produce over 1,000 pud [ed: about 36,110 pounds] of wheat grain per day. In this case it is unnecessary to keep turning the plants over as in the former method, and thus it is not needed to have so many men.

Despite the inadequacy of threshing grain with horses, the method deserves attention because of its speed, particularly for threshing hard wheat.

The above described threshing grounds are to be found only at Mission[s?] and in well-to-do households handling large harvests. The poorer farmers have small threshing grounds in which they work the grain using domesticated saddle horses. For threshing the farmers always use droves of mares which are kept grazing separately and are practically never used for saddle; their entire use is restricted to threshing. Grain, threshed by horses, contains many impurities and many grains are damaged.

The volume of planting bread plants is generally insignificant. Each rancher plants mostly for his own consumption unless he has in mind a profitable sale.

It is also difficult to determine accurately the volume of harvest. No Californian will declare his true harvest: if he is selling bread [grain], he complains of poor harvest, and if he is not selling, then he exaggerates the harvest out of vanity. In spite of my earnest desire, I have been unable up to now to obtain any information regarding planting and harvesting of various grains in Upper California during the last recent years.

[Chernykh then draws on information published by Vasilii Golovnin from his visit in 1818 regarding the fertility of the soil.]

Such was the harvest twenty-two years ago when the Indians worked so to speak, under the club for the Missionaries. Now, however, after the downfall of the Missions' power, each Californian owns the land assigned to him, and works it for himself; and therefore harvests could be more plentiful than before. (The Spanish Californians call themselves *Rasones,* or *Hombres de rason* [ed: *razón*], i.e. reasonable men, while the wild Indians are called gentiles.)

In fact, now one frequently hears of a wheat harvest 60 to 100 fold, and maize harvest of 100 to 500 fold. It is understood of course that such harvest happens in a good year and for good farmers. The usual wheat harvest can be safely estimated between 10 fold and 70 fold. The good farmers here are the old settlers, Spaniards who immigrated from Europe and from Mexico. The latest generation pays little attention to agriculture.

The primary cause of low harvests in Upper California is rot which annually damages wheat, and grasshoppers which devour from time to time wheat, frijoles, and other grains still standing in the field. In July and August, Indians burning straw in the field occasionally set fire destroying not only the planted wheat but also all wild plants so the animals find no feed for themselves. Such accidental fires occur every year. It also happens that on rich soil wheat overgrows, falls over and begins to rot; however, this occurs seldom because there is no rain during and after the ripening of the grain.

How many grains are planted to a given area of land? This question cannot be answered satisfactorily by any local farmer. It should be noted that grains here are planted far apart from each other so that when the ground is covered with growing wheat, one can walk through the field without stepping on the plants. It is estimated that one desiatina [2.7 acres] takes not more than 4 to 6 pud of seed wheat. Some farmers plant wheat by hand in furrows made by plow, and produce the best harvest. One is naturally curious to know by what system California farmers produce plentiful harvests. Should you ask a Californian about it, he will fail to understand the question: these fortunate people have not yet come to the proper time to discuss the systems of agriculture. Maybe their distant descendants will be able to answer the posed question.

In California the very same land is planted until the weeds take over, and still the harvest is always excellent. When the weeds become too strong, the land is used for grazing if another piece of land is available for planting. If not, the weed infested field is used for crops requiring frequent plowing between the rows: maize, frijoles, peas, garbanzo beans, etc. Weeds among these plants are destroyed: during the summer the soil is plowed several times and heaped up against the plants. This is somewhat like crop rotation.

It is said that in California the very same piece of land is planted several years in a row: not two or three years and then fallow. No, the same land is planted 5 to 10 years and longer, the very same wheat, and yet they always get excellent harvest unless something unusual happens harmful for vegetation. Furthermore, the field is never fertilized.

One would think that there was hardly enough time (between harvests) for humus to develop in the blacksoil to yield so many harvests.

But this can be easily explained: one should only recall that, at the local annual temperature, humus forms in the blacksoil without interruption through the year. Therefore, the local blacksoil serves as an inexhaustible store of food for plants. This is what happens in fact.

The main sales of wheat from California up to now went to our American colonies [Alaska] which bought annually 3 to 4 thousand *fanegas* of wheat; the remaining wheat the local farmers convert into flour and sell it to the American merchants who ship it to Lower California where the shortage of water, heat, and frequent droughts are unfavorable for agriculture.

Mexico, having become independent, has permitted anybody and everybody to settle in California on granted land; it was required only to accept [ed: become] a subject of the Mexican Republic and to become a Catholic. The latter requirement, however, now receives less attention. This freedom of settlement attracted here many Americans, Irish, some Germans and Frenchmen. Each settler is given some land, two leagues long and one league wide. (One league equals 1,986¾ Russian sajen. One sajen is seven feet.) He who has money can obtain more land. This land is called a rancho. Each rancho owner, ranchero, has the right to use the land for any profitable purpose: bread grains and other plants, fruit trees, various farm animals.

As the number of ranchos increased, it became possible to obtain bread otherwise than from the missionaries, which has led to declining prices on bread. It is unlikely that the volume of planting increased with the number of ranchos; on the contrary, the total volume must have declined. The missions which used to plant 100 to 300 fanegas, now sow next to nothing because all Indians, who were proclaimed free men, left the missions and are now engaged in horse thieving: they drive droves of horses away from the "reasonable men" and plunder.

The increasing number of ranchos destroyed only the monopoly of the missionaries, reviving trade in bread and bringing benefits to all inhabitants of the country. Formerly, when bread was sown and sold almost entirely by the missionaries alone, wheat sold for 3 to 4 Spanish piasters per fanega, later on for 2 piasters, and during the recent years, namely since 1838, the price constantly changed and finally stood at 1½ piasters per fanega.

At this price, many ranchos, especially those better off, refused to sow bread for sale. To be sure, 1½ piasters per fanega of wheat, i.e. 2 rubles per pud, is a pretty high price, judging by plentiful harvests, but the handling of bread, that is reaping and threshing, costs very much because of the shortage of men. Indians can be induced voluntarily to work for high pay, one piaster per day (5 rubles), and despite all that, the Indians will run away on account of the least displeasure or urging.

It happens often that the owner, having lost hope to find workers for harvest, would take off whatever bread he needs for himself and leave the rest in the field. Often the ranchero would offer you a field full of excellent wheat to harvest if you would give one half to him.

Orchard keeping in California is used on a small scale. Small orchards of fruit-bearing trees and vineyards are found only in the Missions. When the orchards were owned by the missionaries, they were kept in good order; but now, under administrators (managers), everything is gone wild and, in places, destroyed. When private persons have orchards and vineyards, they are so insignificant as to deserve no attention.

The fruits which grow to considerable size are: apples, pears, peaches, apricots, quince, plums, etc. In general, fruits are coarse. Blue grapes are cultivated and yield good harvest and good taste. Vine slips are stuck into the ground, and some of them bear fruit in 3 to 4 years. Local grapes make good wine, but in small quantities and does not keep well.

Wild grapes are found in large volume along the banks of rivers and streams; the vines climb up the trees to considerable height.

In this year, 1841,[7] the local produce prices were, as follows:

		Piastre	*Real*
1 fanega of wheat		1	4
1 " barley	[ed: no value given]		
1 " frijoles		2	4
1 " maize		2	
1 " peas		2	
1 " garbanzo		2	4
1 aroba wheat flour (28 Russian pounds)		1½–2	4
1 " butter (from cow milk)		12	4
1 " dried meat		—	4
1 " lard, pork		1	4
1 " Monteka [ed: manteca] (beef suet)		2	
1 " soap, California-made		12–14	
1 " onions		2	
1 " apples		2	
1 steer, large (12–20 pud)		5–8	
1 hide, cattle, raw		2	
1 " " , tanned		6–8	
1 " , roebuck, raw		1	
1 " , goat, raw			4
1 horse, common		8–10	
1 " ", hire per day		1	
1 hog, large		6–8	
1 hen			4
1 ram		2	
12 eggs			2
1 gallon Calif. grape wine		3	

Prices on local products change very seldom because of little change in quality and variety, as well as of demand. If one should buy the above mentioned things through barter, then the prices are considerably cheaper, especially if bought on the ranchos.

Because of population scarcity, there are up to now no ranchos inland. Fear of Indian attacks forces the Californians to settle close to each other. In 1839, the first attempt was made to establish settlement on the Sacramento River which falls into San Francisco Bay. Sutter, a Swiss retired captain of the French service, together with several hired Hawaiians and Americans, settled on the above named river, the location being known as New Helvetia. It seems that the settlement has been established according to the wishes of Hudson's Bay Company whose active exploring parties constantly move around in all directions to the south of the Columbia River, and now they have frequent contacts with Sutter.

It is regrettable that this blessed country, California, raising happy-go-lucky people, is so sparsely populated. Lack of authority existing here under the guise of republic, and unreasonably high prices on all goods, due to high tariffs, frightens any prudent man away from deciding to settle here. Yet, in spite of everything, many poor Irish, English, and Americans have found their fortune in California, and many, many more unfortunates will find their happiness here also.

Member of the Society, E. Chernykh

1841, 12 January
Rancho Chernykh
Russian American Company
in Upper California

Source: Chernykh 1967: 10–28. Reprinted by permission of James R. Gibson.

14

RUSSIAN INTERACTION
WITH THE NEIGHBORING INDIANS

THE RUSSIAN SETTLEMENT at Fort Ross was made up of a small number of ethnic Russians, Finns, and Siberians, as well as a sizable contingent of "Aleuts" (actually a mixture of Aleuts, Kodiak Islanders, Tana'ina from the Kenai Peninsula, and other Alaskan natives) and an ever-growing number of "Creoles" (as people of mixed of Russian and Indian heritage were called). Since they brought few women with them, a number of the men who came to Fort Ross took local Kashaya, Bodega Miwok, and other Pomo women as wives. In the 1820 and 1821 censuses of Fort Ross by Ivan Kuskov, at least forty-five California women were counted as living with the settlers (Fedorova 1975; Istomin 1992); the distribution mentions four Indian women "from the region of Ross," one "Bodegin" Indian woman [married to a Russian], one Indian woman "from the region of Ross" [married to a Creole], and seventeen "common law wives from the region of Ross," ten "from the river Slavianka," and nine "Bodegin" [married to Alaskan native men] (Fedorova 1975: 12).

By 1833, Creoles, their numbers augmented by the children of the mixed marriages in the settlement, had become the largest part of the population. In that year there were sixty-three Creole children under the age of sixteen living at Fort Ross (Gibson 1969: 210).

The most lengthy description of the Indians in the vicinity of Fort Ross was prepared by Fort Ross manager Peter Kostromitinov, who took a serious interest in the neighboring native peoples. He had to deal with them both as laborers for the colony as well as possible enemies, as he mentioned to Mariano Vallejo during the latter's visit to Fort Ross in 1833 (Kostromitinov 1980: 14–15). Because of the perennially small number of ethnic Russians at Fort Ross (and indeed throughout Russian America), the settlement's success relied on the native populations for assistance, and so it was reasonable that Kostromitinov took note of the customs of the native peoples and reported on them to his superiors. It was during Kostromitinov's tenure as manager of Fort Ross that attempts were made to expand beyond Fort Ross and Bodega Bay to develop additional farms farther inland. For these, in particular, native workers were needed, and Kostromitinov made use of Indians who had been in the missions and learned skills as vaqueros. Of course, everything was not rosy in the relationship between the Indians and the people of Fort Ross, as was noted in Wrangell's report on his 1833 visit, in which the governor took Kostromitinov to task for having brought Indians in by force to help with the harvest (see Wrangell report on page 156).

Although Europeans recorded numerous observations of life at Fort Ross—among them Russian, Spanish, German, English, and French (see Lütke 1989, Kostromitinov 1980 [1839], Payeras 1995 [1822], Wrangell 1839, and Laplace 2006)—these, quite naturally, give us only the European perspective on life in the settlement. Accounts from the viewpoint of native peoples are far rarer. A few examples show up in the recollections of Peter Kalifornsky (Kalifornsky 1991; Kari 1983), whose Tana'ina great-grandfather, Nikolai Kalifornsky, lived at Fort Ross from approximately 1812 to 1820.

The richest trove, however, comes from the "Kashaya Texts," transcribed and translated by linguist Robert Oswalt in 1964. The Kashaya Pomo people lived in the immediate vicinity of Fort Ross; their tribal area is usually considered to extend from a little north of Stewart's Point down to Duncan's Point. This tribe managed to avoid Spanish missionization, in part due to the presence of the Russians, and so their experience was quite different from that of many coastal peoples. Even their neighbors who lived near Bodega Bay, the Bodega Miwok, were more often taken into the missions.[1] Since the Russians at Fort Ross were more interested in labor and commercial endeavors than in proselytizing, the relationship between the Kashaya and the people of Fort Ross was, for the most part, quite amicable, and this included the many relationships that developed between Kashaya women and Alaskan native men.

The following Kashaya stories touch on various aspects of life at Fort Ross during the Russian occupation. The overwhelming majority of the narratives derive from a woman named Lukaria; it makes sense that a woman made these observations considering Kashaya women were more likely to become deeply involved in the life of the people living at Fort Ross, as opposed to native men, who were mostly brought in for temporary labor. Round-the-world traveler Fedor Lütke (1989: 278), described in 1818 unions between Russians and Aleuts and Californian women in a way that illustrates the adaptability of the Kashaya women:

Some of the Promyshlenniks and Aleuts have married these Indian women. Our interpreter, whose wife is one of these people, told us that she had learned his language very quickly and well, and that she had also learned Aleut handicrafts, such as sewing the whale gut *kamleika* [waterproof outer garment] and other things. In one hut I saw a rather comely young woman preparing food, and when I approached her I was surprised that she spoke easily and in clear Russian. She invited me to eat her acorn porridge, and then complained about the rain. When I inquired I found that she had lived for some time in the Ross settlement with a promyshlennik, and then had returned to her people.

In articles on Russian and Aleut words that have been absorbed into the Kashaya language, Robert Oswalt (1958; 1971; 1988: 20–22) gives examples of not only Russian words that apparently came directly from the ethnic Russians but also numerous Russian words that the Kashaya learned from the Aleuts. These are distinguished by certain pronunciation peculiarities of the Aleuts that were taken up by the Kashaya even though the latter were perfectly able to render the correct Russian form. (For instance, the Aleuts replace the Russian "b" with a "p," whereas the Kashaya have no trouble with the "b" sound.)

KOSTROMITINOV'S OBSERVATIONS
ON THE INDIANS OF UPPER CALIFORNIA (1839)

Peter Kostromitinov, the longest serving manager of Fort Ross (1829–1838), wrote his "Observations on the Indians of Upper California" in 1839, the same year it was published alongside various reports on Fort Ross by Ferdinand von Wrangell.

The Indians living in the vicinity of Ross are divided into several tribes, distinguished by the following names: the Bodega (*Olamentke*), the Steppe (*Tundrenskie, Kainama*), the Northern (*Severnovskie, Chwachamaju*) and the Distant (*dal'novksie*) Indians. The latter are divided into many tribes, but their number and economic position are not known in Ross Colony.

The Bodega Indians [Coast Miwok] do not understand the Northerners, since both their language and manner of pronunciation are different. The Distant and Steppe Indians speak many dialects or languages, but their characteristics and relationships are not yet known.

It is difficult to determine the number of these nomadic tribes. Large villages used to exist on both Bodega Bays, large and small, but since two missions were founded on this side of the Bay of San Francisco, these settlements have disappeared. Many Indians were settled in these missions, the rest either emigrated to Ross or perished in the epidemics of 1815 to 1822. There are large settlements on the Slavianka plain and north of Ross, known as Kajatschim, Makoma and Japiam. About 2,000 souls are known to belong to the latter; however, it appears that these appellations refer to areas rather than to settlements, since the Indians live more dispersed than gathered together. Across the mountains which divide the Slavianka plain there is a large lake [Clear Lake] where there are many Indian settlements. When this lake was investigated, it was discovered that although these Indians differ little from the coastal Indians in outward appearance and customs, their language is quite different.

The Indians are of medium height, although some are tall; they are rather well proportioned, their skin being brownish, but the color seems more attributable to the sun than hereditary; eyes and hair are black, the latter being straight. The Bodega Indians do not decorate their bodies; the Northerners, on the other hand, tattoo their faces, chests, and hands with various designs and paint themselves with plant juice, from which the skin receives a dark blue color which remains permanently. Both sexes are strongly built and cripples are seldom seen; but as a result of the climate and their way of life they do not live to a great age. The women age very quickly and one therefore sees more old women than young ones. The physiognomy of the Indians in general bears the impression of good nature rather than savagery, and one often sees charming faces, among males as well as females. They are placid, peaceful and very capable, especially in the comprehension of material objects. They give the impression of great stupidity only because of their excessive inertia and lack of concern; yet they need only to see some not-too-difficult or finished piece of work and they attempt to copy it at once.

These true children of nature have no concept of clothing. The men go completely naked; the women cover the middle part of the body, both before and behind, with the skins of wild goats [ed: sic, mule deer]; the men tie their hair in a tuft on the top of their heads, while the women bunch theirs at the neck, sometimes letting it hang free; the men fasten the bunches of hair with tastefully carved little pieces of wood carved from the red palm. Both sexes adorn themselves with pearls from mussels; in their ears they wear small bones from eagles' feet and they always go barefoot. This is the entire dress of those yet unacquainted with our customs. The Indians who live closer to Ross and often work there have jackets, trousers, blankets and other things, which however they regard with complete unconcern. If they obtain something of this sort, they gamble it away or exchange it for some trifle. The differences between our articles of clothing are unknown to them and it is sometimes comical to see a savage dressed in a woman's gown with a chemise over it, or another wearing all the shirts he owns, so that he can hardly move. Without attachment to any material thing and ignorant of the worth of anything, they sometimes demand a great deal for the work they do, sometimes only a trifle. Their only purpose is to acquire something so that they can gamble it away again. [Ed: Cyrille Laplace makes similar comments on the tendency of the Indians around Ross to readily gamble away the articles of clothing they had obtained from the Russians (see "Cyrille Theodore Laplace's visit to Bodega Bay and Fort Ross," page 235).]

The men live in perfect indolence; their greatest pleasure is to eat until satiated and to have nothing to do. The preparation of meals and other domestic chores are the duty of the women; constantly nomadic, the women carry the children as well as all the other baggage while the men precede them, carrying bows and arrows and only seldom any burden. They have summer and winter dwellings. In summer, they find shelter in bushes, which are thinned at the bottom and tied together at the top. For the winter they build barabaras [ed: semi-subterranean dwellings]. Some upright posts are driven into the ground point first and covered with bark, branches and grass; one opening is left at the top, another at the side—the former to allow smoke to escape, the latter as an entrance to the barabara. A bow, arrows, a large pot and, sometimes, fishing nets are their few household utensils. The bathhouses are built in the same way as the barabaras. They dig a hole, stick posts around it and cover it, first with bark, then with earth; a small hole at the side allows smoke to escape and a hole at the bottom is made to allow entrance, but so small that it can be entered only by crawling.

The season determines the place they must visit to find sustenance. In spring, they live near rivers and other places where water is abundant in order to catch fish and gather roots and herbs; the summer brings them to the forests and steppes, where they collect berries and the seeds of wild plants; in autumn they lay in stores of acorns, wild chestnuts, and other nuts, and kill bison [!] and wild goats [ed: mule deer] with their arrows. The Indian's diet includes anything they can procure, large and small animals from land and sea, fish, crabs, roots, plants, berries and other things produced by the earth, and even insects and worms. Meat and fish are eaten slightly roasted over coals; everything else is usually eaten raw. Acorns, collected in great quantities, are their staple food. They prepare them as follows: after the acorns have been picked from the tree, they are dried in the sun and then cleansed and crushed in baskets [ed: probably using basket mortars], using special stones; a hole is then dug in sand or dry earth, the acorns are emptied into it and completely covered with water, which soaks into the earth. This rinsing is repeated until the acorns have lost their characteristic bitter taste;

they are then removed and cooked in a cauldron, into which red-hot stones are thrown. If the Indians wish to make pancakes or a kind of bread, the acorns will be ground somewhat coarser and, after their bitterness has been removed, they are left a little longer in the hole. In this way, the Indians made a kind of dough, which can be cut in flat cakes or pieces, wrapped in broad leaves and baked on coals. This bread always looks black. Wild chestnuts are prepared in the same way, but the Indians make no bread from them but eat them as a mash. At the beginning of July the Indians begin the leisurely gathering of acorns and seeds of wild plants.

When this is finished, they go on without loss of time to collect the seeds of a plant which grows abundantly on the plain. Its appearance is as follows: it grows 1½ to 2 feet tall, several sprouts start from the roots, the leaves are very small, narrow and covered with a soft fluff, they have a peculiar odor and stick to the fingers, the flowers are yellow and stand out in pointed clusters and the small black seeds resemble *Latuk*.[2] The seeds are shaken from the plant with a spade specially made for the purpose, ground into meal and eaten dry. The taste is similar to that of toasted dried oatmeal. They also collect wild rye and wild oats, and other grains, which after suitable preparation, are eaten either dry or as a sourish paste.

The Indians drink water only. They have no knowledge of strong drink. Sometimes, when they see the distribution of rum to the garrison at Ross, they ask for some. Some enjoy it very much, others like it not at all, but even the former do not become drunkards. They call rum and other strong drink *omy-liva*, i.e. bad water. Like all savages, however, they enjoy tobacco very much; they smoke it through a specially carved wooden tube, the pipe bowl being carved out of the same piece of wood. They hollow out an opening at the thick end, or pipe bowl, in which they stuff the tobacco, but since the pipe bowl and stem are straight, they smoke with their heads tilted back in order not to spill the tobacco.[3] They also have a special herb resembling tobacco, which chiefly grows near rivers in sandy soil, but the smoke of this herb has a most offensive smell. The Indians living near the settlement are beginning to abandon use of this herb since they do not lack the opportunity to obtain tobacco by working; those living farther away, however, remain faithful to their own tobacco.

It is not to be supposed that people living in such primitive conditions should have any concept of social life or culture. Occasionally, they do live together in large numbers, but for the most part they live in small dwellings and are not acquainted with subservience. He who has the most kinsmen will be recognized as a chieftain or toion; in the larger settlements, there are several such toions, but their authority is negligible. They have neither the right to command nor the right to punish disobedience. Therefore, the respect due to the oldest member of the family is without significance; sometimes, the elder's experience will be of service in advising on some undertaking and that is all. In their view, most of the work has to be done by the older men and women; the young people are reserved until needed. In other words, the tribal elders do not enjoy the respect given them by other tribes, for example, the Kolosh, Aleuts and similar peoples.

Their religious views and practices are as simple as their habits. No outside assistance is given to women during their confinements; they have recourse to an old woman only during difficult births, which by the way are very rare. The newborn child is washed, wrapped in a goatskin and placed in a basket; the babies are nursed as long as the mother has milk. In accordance with a curious superstition, the father of the child may not leave the hut for four days and must remain completely inactive. The child is named after some plant or tree or other visible object, but when he is grown the earlier name is changed into something similar but more descriptive of his character. Their affection for their children is very great, but when the latter are scarcely grown and can manage without their parents, they are no longer obedient, so that the fathers become indifferent to them.

Marriage is entered into without any kind of ceremony. When two young people like one another, the young man enters the barabara of the girl, often without even asking the parents' consent, and begins to live with her. If a quarrel develops between married people, they immediately separate; if the quarrel was merely verbal, there is sometimes a reconciliation, but if they came to blows, then settlement is rarely achieved. The children of the marriage remain with the mother, although the father does not lose his affection for them. Since the men do not love their wives wholeheartedly, jealousy is foreign to them. Even if the woman develops affection for another and the husband learns of it, he will not try to prevent it, even though he knows, but the other must live in the village or be a member of the same tribe; he never could permit the woman to go with an outsider—this could lead to quarrels and wars. Their desires also degenerate into bestial lust and one encounters men who offer themselves instead of women. The possession of more than one wife is not permitted, although the toions were accustomed to possess two in earlier times; but even then they were always the object of derision, and now the custom has disappeared entirely. Blood relationship is strictly observed and marriages within the first and second degrees of kinship are not permitted; even in the event of separation, the nearest relative may not marry the woman, although there are exceptions.

The dead are cremated; all the relations gather round the funeral pyre and display their grief by yelling and howling. The closest kinsmen cut off their hair and throw it into the fire, strike their breasts with stones and hurl themselves to the ground. Sometimes, out of a particular affection for the dead man, they beat themselves until the blood runs, or have even killed themselves, but such cases are rare. The dead man's most valuable possessions are cremated with the corpse.

There are annual commemorative rites, and it has been noted that they almost always occur during the month of February. These rituals are as follows: ten or more men are selected for presentation, according to the size of the settlement; they must first purify themselves by fasting, and for several days they eat very little; above all, no meat. After preparing themselves in this way, those taking part go, on the eve of the appointed day, to a barabara specially chosen. There they dress up, smearing themselves with soot and with various colors, decorating themselves with grass and feathers, and then sing and dance until darkness falls. They then go into the woods and run around singing, torches in their hands. They return to the hut and spend the night there, in song, dance and contortions. The next day, until morning, is also spent similarly, but on the third day they go to the kinsmen of the dead, who are waiting in their huts, and after a suitable welcome, commence lamentations all together; the old women scratch their faces and beat their breast with stones. The relatives of the deceased positively believe they are seeing their dead kin in this spectacle. During this presentation, the whole settlement practices strict abstinence from food and sometimes they do not eat meat for a long period.

They were very reluctant to answer questions about these rites, so that it was impossible to learn more details.

Their weapons consist of a bow and arrow and a spear, usually made from young fir. The points of their arrows and spears are sharp trimmed stones, and their bowstrings are made from the sinews of the wild goat [ed: mule deer]. They also make a kind of catapult [ed: sling-shot], by means of which they hurl stones for long distances, for use in times of war. Peaceable by nature, the Indians seldom make war on one another; and especially now no great attacks have been reported in the neighborhood of Ross. On the plains of the river Slavianka some years ago, the Makamov and Kajatschin Indians of the Slavianka plain quarreled. The cause of it was that the Makamov Indians had invited a toion to visit them, and strangled him in the bath house. The conflict lasted for almost a year, and about 200 men were killed on both sides at different times until finally, tired of war, they settled the quarrel amicably and presented one another with various gifts.

They kill a captured enemy on the spot and hang him from a tree, but they rarely take more than one or two men prisoner, for they always move about in large numbers, and although a few bold men will be able to approach a hostile settlement at night time, they will usually be satisfied if they let fly a few arrows before making themselves scarce. Both sides usually place lookouts on nearby hills or mountains who will shout when they become aware of someone not belonging to the settlement. During a war, the women, children and old people will be taken to a safe place. He who surpasses all others in bravery will be held in the same esteem as a toion.

I include here a war song of the Bodega Indians, with the translation:

When beginning or preparing for war, they sing

Temoi hoibu	Let us, O leader
Onigi tschinami	go to war!
Temai ilawak	Let us go and capture
Temai o tomai	a pretty girl!

On approaching the enemy settlement:

Indi mi schujugu	When do we cross the mountains?
Pari o londo	Who do we see first?

Upon beginning to shoot:

Buteki landa	Accurate are our shots
Junawschi landa	Keep putting forth yours!

Then the toion sings to inspire his warriors with courage:

Otilek—otilek lilem	Bestir yourselves, bestir yourselves,
Lile oje lippe	Into battle now,
Lile oje ile lippi	Stouthearted, follow me!
Nawu elendu	Fear nothing, enemy arrows
Indi koscht ma iwid elendu.	Will do you no harm.

Each of these couplets is repeated several times, as appropriate.

A celebration is usually held when a sick person reaches convalescence. The recovered person invites all those living in the neighborhood to be his guests, but the rich and the toions even send for Indians living farther away, if they are on good terms with them. When the guests arrive, the host sets all that he has before them. In a single hour they consume stores which have been difficult to gather and which would feed the host's family for several months. When all are satisfied, they begin speeches of goodwill, undertaking to live in peace and harmony and not quarrel. Singing and dancing follow—some sing, others dance and play all kinds of tricks; sometimes a young woman comes into the middle and sings, but the men join hands and turn and jump around her. Some of the men have eagle's bones in their mouths and whistle a merry tune. At the end of one song, all cry *hoi,* and continue with their singing. The song usually consists of a few short words, for example, "You love me and so I love you too." This is repeated again and again during the dance. The tune is pleasant but almost always melancholy.

Both sexes are exceptionally fond of gambling, which may explain why their dances are not particularly varied, or much practiced. Their hunger satisfied, they will devote the rest of their time to gambling. Their first and favorite game is the guessing of a riddle. Those who wish to play divide into two sides, sitting opposite one another. A goatskin [ed: mule-deer skin] is laid between them, on which each side places small sticks. One man takes a little grass or something similar in his hand. Holding both hands behind his back, he makes all kinds of gesticulations, moving the object from one hand to the other. His opponent must now note which hand holds the grass. If he thinks he has guessed correctly, he strikes the hand which he believes holds it. If he is right, he receives more sticks; if not, he must forfeit some of his own. Then the next pair continues the game in the same way. The side which gains all the rods wins the game and divides the articles won. The spectators, usually numerous, sing during the game and spur the players on with all kinds of jests and jokes. It is an indication of their sweet temper that the players never quarrel. The Indians' love of gambling is such that those who work in Ross, disregarding fatigue after a full day's work, sometimes enjoy playing until four in the morning, and they return to work without having had a full night's rest.

The Indians trace their origin back to the wolf [ed: sic, Coyote]. According to an old tradition, a wolf whose family has now died out stuck two sticks in the earth and decided that one should become a man, the other a woman. He then made a bow, shot a blunt arrow into the middle of one rod and so made a man. The latter shot at the other rod and brought forth a woman. Such absurd notions about the origin of mankind are general among them.

Of the Supreme Being, the Indians entertain a hazy conception. They believe that after making heaven and earth and all things visible, he is no longer involved in anything and, having yielded up his powers to other spirits, he is incapable of doing either good or evil. They have probably derived these ideas, with some distortions, from the celebrations of the baptized Indians of California. They distinguish the good from the evil spirit merely by the fact that the one does good, the other does evil, he is more to be feared, and should be held in greater honor. There are no religious customs at all.

Their magicians, or shamans, do not exhibit the same dexterity and agility as do those of other savages. When they are about to practice their magic, they go deep into the forest, and after their return they will prophesy for those who wish it. The shaman takes glass beads or something similar with him into the woods, in order to appease the evil spirit and avoid misfortune, thus ensuring that he has something to sacrifice to the fiend. He brings the things back after a while, passes them off as his own, and gambles them away. The chief art of the shaman is the cure of diseases.

One would suppose, because of their way of life, that these natives would be less subject to sickness than others, but various illnesses do prevail among them, principally high fever, colic and those associated with syphilis. Frequent and sudden changes of temperature of the air, from hot to cold and vice versa, are the cause of the first two; the last has the same cause as everywhere else. The shamans use herbs and roots as cures, but generally suck blood from the affected spot and put small stones or snakes into their mouths, averring that they removed them from the wound. Frequent hot baths are also used to cure venereal disease.

Simplicity and good nature are the principal traits in their character. Theft and homicide are almost unknown among them, and if one does not irritate or insult them, one is completely secure. But this stems more from their great timidity. For example, the sound of a cannon shot puts them in terror, and some tremble visibly. Suicide is completely unknown, and if one asks them about it, they cannot even understand how such a thing could occur.

Much more could be told about these savages, but because of their strange delusion that they will die if they tell a stranger about their customs, they answer every question with "I don't know." I once asked them if the year was divided into twelve months. The answer was, "I don't know."

"Then who does know?"

"Oh, there are learned people who know everything."

"Where do they live?"

"Deep in the plains."

Such evasive answers were customary.

Their inattention and indifference go further. They were not interested in our watches, burning glasses and mirrors, our music and the like, and do not ask how and why all this is produced. Only those things which frighten them made some impression, and that was probably the influence of fear rather than thirst for knowledge.

The Indians of the California missions are equally simple in their habits and customs. They are indeed still primitive in arts and crafts, but have learned all the vices of their teachers. Theft, drunkenness and murder are now quite common among them. They observe the usages of the Roman Catholic Church more from fear of punishment than out of adherence to its beliefs.

The change from the most abject subservience under the former [ed: mission] regime to complete freedom under the present one [ed: this was written at about the time of secularization of the missions] will corrupt their morals still further.

―――――――――

Source: Kostromitinov 1980 [1839]: 34–49.

KASHAYA ACCOUNTS OF LIFE AT FORT ROSS (1964)

Among the many stories in the "Kashaya Texts," nine of them touch on the lives of the Kashaya near Fort Ross, in a settlement the natives called Métini. The majority of the accounts were passed on by Herman James in 1958, who learned them from his grandmother, Lukaria Yorgen Myers. She was said to have been born eight years before the Russians came, which would have been about 1804. (See her photo on page 229.) Also included here is one story about the Russian period by Essie Parrish, who learned it from her father. Following are seven stories from the Kashaya people; two more are related in a later section, about a Hudson's Bay Company Brigade that visited Fort Ross in 1833 (see pages 226–234).

THE FIRST WHITE FOOD

[Essie Parrish] (Oswalt 1964: 251)

It was also there at Métini that the white people first discovered the Indians—having come up, they found them. After they discovered the Indians, they wanted to domesticate them. In order to feed them food, in order to let them know about the white man's food, [the white men] served them some of their own white food.

Never having seen white men's food before, they thought that they were being given poison. Having given [the Indians] their food, they left and returned home but [the Indians] threw it in a ditch. Some they buried when they poured it out. They were afraid to eat that, not knowing anything about it—all they knew was their own food, wild food. They had never seen white people's food before then.

That is what our old people told us. This is the end.

Over time, the Indians became used to many of the introduced foods, especially as many of their own native foods were becoming harder to obtain.

THE LAST VENDETTA

[Herman James] (Oswalt 1964: 255–259)

Now I am going to tell another story about enemies. They couldn't just let it be [unavenged] when a relative of theirs was killed by an enemy. Now one family lived at Métini and another at Forest Depths.[4] It turned out that [those from Forest Depths] had killed one man from Métini while he was wandering around in the woods; they had shot him. That's the way they acted to stir up a kin group when they wanted opponents, when they wanted to kill people.

When [the dead man] did not show up for a while, [his relatives] went looking around in the woods where he had gone hunting deer. They didn't find him anywhere. After a while, when the body was decaying with vultures sitting on it, they found that person— their [kins]man who had been killed.

Although he was decayed, they picked him up in a litter, carried him off, and set him down at home. Notwithstanding [his condition], they prepared him, strung beads around his neck, and packed everything of his—all of his personal possessions—off to the woods on the following day in order to burn them up together. Having carried him to where they had piled up wood, they cast him up on it and threw all his things up there too: bow, quiver, and beads. Then they lit the fire. It burned him up.

The situation remained thus for a little while—at first they said nothing. Then one said, "Although we were enemies of that place, now we have become [greater] enemies." "Let us quit being enemies now," said the relatives. "Tomorrow let us go there where they live," they said. "You others [nonrelatives] come along with us." Accompanied by about four [nonrelatives] they set out for that place to battle the enemy.

One man [at the place they were going to] was an expert shot. The arrow he shot never missed: it always hit the mark. Those approaching that place were a little afraid of him, as they prepared to attack. While still walking some distance off, they asked that man if he was going to help the people they were going after. "No," he said, "I'm not in it. I'm not going to participate." When he had answered so, they said, "OK" and approached that place.

[The one they were after] turned out to be hidden in the house; he wasn't walking around outside. "Where is he?" they asked while standing off in the distance. Having aimed their bows and arrows, they stood ready. "He's not here," said a woman at first. "He hasn't come here," they said. "We know he's there anyway," said the attackers.

After a while the enemy man said, "I'll just let them kill me," and was about to go out, but the woman blocked the door with her body. For a long time [the attackers] didn't shoot, they just stood holding [their weapons], watching ready to aim. The woman stood protecting him. Fearing to shoot the woman, they didn't shoot at first but waited alert.

After a while, when the woman got a little tired, when she left a small gap, [an attacker] shot with one arrow. [The man] fell back into the house. He lay there like that. "Don't shoot any more. You have bloodied up my whole house. Don't come here nor shoot anymore," said the woman still standing there at the door. The leader still wanted to drag him out. "No, go back home," the woman still said—the men [inside], seeing the many weapons, were too afraid to say [what she said].

Then the youngest brother said, "Let's go home. He will still die even though he was shot with only one arrow." Saying, "All right," they went off a ways. When they finished killing a man like that, they stood in a group and gave a victory cheer. That was their way when fighting an enemy. They did that when completing the mission.

At that time an undersea boy [a member of the Fort Ross colony] with a gun had been riding around on a horse. From where he was sitting on his mount he saw them cheering, standing huddled together. The undersea boy said that he wanted to shoot one—he had said that he wanted to shoot several. But he just let it be.

Then the Indians, having slung their bows and put their arrows in their quivers, returned home. They set off to go back to Métini.

They lived there. "Let this now be the end," said the old people in council. "We aren't going to kill any more; we aren't going to be enemies with Indians any more. Now we'll just live peacefully. Battling enemies comes out to be a bad deal—people keep dying."

Into what we call a "cross house" [church] some people drifted in. Some people drifted into the church belonging to the undersea people [the chapel at Fort Ross]. Thereafter there was no more killing of people—what was called enemy-killing.

My grandmother [Lukaria] told this, saying that she herself saw and heard it. From where they were living, men set out and killed a man. Then my grandmother said, "Thereafter the Indians didn't kill each other. They lived peacefully." This is true. This, too, really happened. They really did it. They really killed people at first. They battled the ones they called enemies. When one of their own relatives was killed they remembered it for a long time; they couldn't forget it until they had killed back. Only when killing that man could they quit satisfied. But after that time they all stopped doing that, said my grandmother. She told me that this is also a true event that she saw herself. This is the end.

This is a tribute to the Russian attempt to keep peace among the peoples with whom they associated by suppressing an age-old form of vengeance feuding which was not infrequently found among the California Indians. It also suggests that some of the Indians became interested in the Orthodox religion. The Indians referred to the inhabitants of Fort Ross as "undersea people" because they first arrived in *baidarkas* that were so low to the water their passengers seemed to be emerging up from the ocean.

GRAIN FOODS

[Herman James] (Oswalt 1964: 267–269)

My grandmother told me this too about what the undersea [Fort Ross] people did. What I am going to tell about now is how they ground their flour when they raised and gathered wheat.

Where the land lies stretched out, where all the land is at Métini, they raised wheat which blanketed the land. When it was ripe everywhere, then the people, by hand, cut it down, tied it up, and laid it there. Then, in a sea lion skin, they dragged it to their houses.

They had made a big place there, with the earth packed down hard by wetting—there they threw down what they had tied up. Next they drove horses down there. The person who drove the horses around there in a circle was one man who took turns with various others. When it was that way [threshed], when it had become food alone, they put it in sacks. While loading it in sacks, they hauled it off in stages to where their storehouse was. They filled that place up with flour [ed: sic, probably unmilled grain], and hauling it away as before, they piled it up in a building. There was a lot for them to eat in winter.

Once, while a woman was walking around there, she happened to get too close while the wind was turning [the grindstone]. At that time, women's hair was long. [The woman's hair] got caught and turned with it. The woman, too, was spun around, all of her hair was chewed off, and she was thrown off dead.

They picked her up, carried her home, and cremated her—at that time they still cremated. That is the way it happened; the flour grinder snared the woman and she died.

They also used to tell that the Indians in their different fashion also gathered grain when it was ripe by taking a tightly woven packing basket and knocking [the grain] so that it would fall into that. When they filled [the baskets] they too would store that at their houses. They too [had] a lot, a lot like that for winter, and pinole too.

Then they found out; they saw how they, the undersea people, stored their own kind of food. At that time, the Indians didn't yet know much about flour. Later on, when [the Russians] had lived there a while, [the Indians] ate flour too. And they also still ate pinole in their own way.

This has been a true story that our grandmother used to tell me, one that she saw herself—at that time when she saw those things, she was still a young woman. When she had grown old, she told me that true story. That is what I have told, the true story that our grandmother told. This is all.

Having their own tradition of harvesting grass seeds, the Kashaya clearly took an interest in the agricultural methods of the Russians. Their description of the threshing floor being of beaten earth differs from European accounts of tightly laid plank floors, although the latter were indeed used by the Mexicans, according to agronomist Egor Chernykh (see section on the Scottish thresher, page 171). The description of the use of stampeding horses to thresh the grain is substantiated by numerous other accounts of observers both at Fort Ross and in Spanish California. The story of the woman who got her hair caught and was killed brings up an intriguing comparison with a story of a similar tragic death retold by the late-nineteenth-century romantic author Gertrude Atherton (see page 311). The year before Atherton published this story, she wrote an article about a visit to Fort Ross in which she describes meeting with an old woman who was "half Indian, half Russian" (Atherton 1893). This woman told Atherton many stories of Fort Ross at the time of the Russians. Atherton did not give the woman's name, but it was almost certainly Lukaria. Although Atherton's story of a Russian heroine decapitated by a windmill is clearly fiction, finding this antecedent in Kashaya folk history suggests that some such event actually occurred.

The sense of cultural continuity implied by the Kashaya persistence in storing and eating foods in their own way is echoed in the observations of Cyrille Laplace (Farris 2006), who visited in August 1839, toward the end of the Russian period (see page 235). Laplace even remonstrated to his host, Alexander Rotchev, that the Russians were having very little obvious effect on the customs of the local Indians. Rotchev's reply was that they actually were, although perhaps in more subtle ways, as evidenced by the Indians' becoming increasingly settled and attached to the fort.

THE WIFE-BEATER

[Herman James] (Oswalt 1964: 269)

This that I am about to tell about was also at Métini. This my grandmother also told me—it, too, is true. People lived there, in the manner I have described.

One time there was a man and an Indian woman living there together. Once, early in the morning, he arose cranky. He growled at his wife. He got meaner and meaner, and suddenly grabbing an axe, he cut her head with it.

At that time, the undersea [Fort Ross] people already lived there. They already had a sheriff then, and when they told him, he led him [the husband] away. He was shut up at a place where a little house was standing. They locked him up for about one week.

Then, in the woods, they cut off small hazel switches to whip him with. They brought them to the settlement. They laid them there.

Then, leading the man out, they made him stand at a certain place. So that he couldn't run away, they had tied his hands, tied his feet, and stood him up. Next they started in to whip him. When one [switch] wore out, they took another, and thus whipped him for half a day. He fell down unconscious. Then they carried him home.

Unexpectedly, he became conscious. After a while he recovered. When he had recovered, he told what had happened to him. He said that that was the only thing that could tame him. After they whipped him, he said that he started to think of good, righteous things. Intending to tell about that, he caused the people to assemble and spoke. "Don't ever want to try that," he said. "I am telling you that I could only stand going through that because I am strong," he said.

That woman left the man. They separated. Then they lived there like that. For a long time the man was alone. The woman, too, was alone. She didn't want to stay with him any more.

This is what was told to me. It, too, is true. This is all.

Ill treatment of Kashaya wives was apparently not condoned, and wife beating was severely dealt with. The brutality of the whippings obviously made a deep impression on the Kashaya (see also the next story), and they were undoubtedly impressed with the sense of justice of the Russians to punish one of their own in such a fashion. (The story does not specify whether the man was a Russian, Creole, or Aleut, but it seems to imply that he was not a native Indian.)

The description of the jail as a little house standing by itself is notable as well. Although the current interpretation at Fort Ross has a cell within the Officials Quarters inside the stockade, I believe this grew out of a misreading of some documents describing the buildings at Fort Ross. A closer look at the historical texts reveals that the jail actually adjoined one of the warehouses inside the stockade.

THE SUICIDE OF A WIFE

[Herman James] (Oswalt 1964: 271)

This, too, my grandmother told me of what she saw herself. That was at a time when the undersea [Fort Ross] people had come up [from the ocean].

One time, a woman arose early in the morning. That Indian woman was married to an undersea man. They had been quarreling with each other. The man walked out saying, "If I find you here at home, I will kill you." Then he left to go to work.

When she had finished eating, she gave food to her children, went into the bedroom, and put on her good, new clothes.

"Where are you going, Mother?" said her oldest girl. She replied, "I am going to walk over to coastal cliff for a little while." "Let me go along, Mother," said [the girl]. "No," she said at first. But still, when she left, when she had gone some distance, [the child] followed. When [the mother] reached her destination, [the child] came closer to her mother. She stopped at the top of the coastal cliff.

"What are you going to do?" she asked her mother. "I am going to die today," she replied to her daughter. "No," said the daughter. "Who would take care of us?" "Your father growled at me so much that I can't go home any more," [the mother] said.

Then the child grabbed her dress. When she did so, [the mother] didn't listen. After a while, she suddenly threw herself way down onto the gravel beach. When that happened, when she threw herself down, the child let go.

Then she ran home and told. The others came, carried her up, and laid her down over at her house. The next day they buried her—at that time they already buried people [no longer cremated them].

Then her husband arrived home and she wasn't there. Subsequently they locked him up as a prisoner—the undersea [Fort Ross] people did. One week later, they took him out, led him off a little way from the house, and arrived at a place where they used to whip people. Then they whipped him; they whipped him for almost a whole day. When they did so, he fainted and fell to the ground. He didn't regain consciousness; he died. Then they buried him.

This is also a true event that was told to me. [My grandmother] really saw it herself. This is all.

This story provides ample evidence that this Kashaya woman was well on her way to being acculturated to the Fort Ross lifestyle. She was apparently living in one of the Russian-style houses adjacent to the stockade, and it is noteworthy that before committing suicide she went into her bedroom to put on "good, new clothes," evidently a dress. It is also significant that the woman was buried rather than cremated. It is not clear where she would have been buried, although one might conjecture it was in the Christian cemetery across the gulch from the stockade. If so, she had clearly separated from her native peoples' ways.

TWO UNDERSEA YOUTHS FREEZE TO DEATH

[Herman James] (Oswalt 1964: 273–275)

This, too, is a true story that I am about to tell. My grandmother told this. Undersea [Fort Ross] youths were living there growing up. The Russians had landed a little earlier, and having lived there for ten years, the children had become big.

One time, when the winter rains were falling, [two youths] said that they would go hunting birds—what are named "black birds" [coot]. It was at Shohka.[5] Among the piled up driftwood, they had been accustomed to gathering coots [killed in the storms]. They set out for that place, having heard that many were there. They traveled along towards there for a long time. Having done so, they camped.

The next day they went towards the place where they customarily gathered the birds. High water was flowing at Shohka. They found many birds and gathered them—all day they gathered them. Their clothes got soaked all the way through. At first they didn't realize it, while they were wandering around in the wet. Suddenly, when dusk arrived, rain fell again—it rained heavily so that even their bodies were soaked.

"Let's climb up out," said one. "All right," said [the other]. When they had got themselves a little way up out from there, unexpectedly their bodies felt numb, they said. When they had gone on a little further, they sat down leaning against a rock. There they sat. After a while it got so that they couldn't get up—their legs felt rather heavy. When it had become evening, the rains fell harder and harder.

They sat there like that at first. Many coots were lying there in the sacks they had been packing around. Then one said, "I wonder how it would be if we stuffed the feathers against our bodies." "Perhaps if we did that, it would warm us up," said the older one. "Let's try it," he said. Taking the coots up out of the sack, they plucked them and stuffed them inside their clothes. They stuffed that way.

The rain pelted down steadily. There wasn't a dry spot on their bodies—they were all soaking wet. They sat there like that. They stuffed like that. The feathers having got wet, they never warmed up. They really began to freeze stiff when the middle of the night came. At the stroke of twelve it got so that they couldn't talk. Then, probably at one o'clock, one suddenly just died, fell over and lay there, having frozen stiff from the great cold. The other one must have died soon afterwards.

When they didn't show up for a long time, the undersea people said, "I wonder why the boys haven't come back." They looked everywhere; even over where the Indians were living [apart from the Russian settlement]. There was nothing. They didn't find anything. "They must still be way off to the south," they said. "Let's go search."

At that time the undersea people rode around on horses. In the evening they rode off toward Shohka with four horses. It was far from there. They rode along. They found where [the youths] had been first—where they had collected coots. Saying, "Where could they have gone?" they looked around there for a long time. They didn't find them.

Then, suddenly, one person, on seeing them leaning against a rock said, "There they are." He must have thought they were alive, seeing them at a distance at first. When they rode up towards there, suddenly they were lying there dead, frozen stiff from the bitter cold. They had become rigid like a stick.

Having put both of them up on horses, they led them off home-wards. Then they set them down at home. Unexpectedly [to their mothers] they set down those dead youths. Their mothers looked pitiful—they felt sad. Subsequently, they stayed there for a while.

Because of that, the Indians said that cold was a terrible thing. Even if he wore a lot of clothes, a person would die if he got drenched in the rain. "When the body's blood grows cold, one becomes numb," said the Indians. They [Indians] wore a bear skin underneath so that the cold could not get in. Even the rain couldn't penetrate that bear skin or panther skin—or the buckskin that they wore in summer time. That's why the Indians never sickened from the great cold, even when the rain beat against them. [The Russians] asked why it didn't happen to them [the Indians]. Then they told the undersea people.

This that my grandmother told me is also true; she saw it her-self. She also saw when they buried them in the ground. Before they buried them, they had borne them into the church. Having prepared them, they set the two youths down into the ground. This is what she told me she herself saw—saw with her own eyes—this is also true. That's the way she told me the story. I know a lot of the true stories that she told me. This is the end.

The Kashaya were said to have worn very little clothing, but what they did wear was apparently better suited to the environment than what the Russians had. A modern-day Kashaya, Otis Parrish, son of Essie Parrish, explains that his peoples' view of cold was that one learned to mostly ignore it, that it affected only the outer layer of one's body but did not penetrate. In harsh conditions, the natives would wear natural coverings, like bear or rabbit skins, which better retained heat and repelled water than the processed cloth (e.g., cotton and wool) of the Russians.

The story, said to have occurred about ten years after the Russian arrival (circa 1822[6]), is intriguing in that it is one of the very few descriptions of activities of young people living at Fort Ross. It is also interesting to note that even though they were of mixed parentage, the boys had adopted their fathers' attitudes about clothing and not learned from the native side of their heritage.

TALES OF FORT ROSS

[Herman James] (Oswalt 1964: 277)

This, too, my grandmother told me. She also really saw this herself. I am going to tell about the land at Métini. They lived there. Where they originated, where our ancestors originated, at Métini, is the place where they first lived. They lived there for a long time.

Then, unexpectedly, they detected something white sailing on the water. It later proved to be a boat, but they didn't know what it was—the Indians hadn't seen anything like that before. Then it came closer and closer, and unexpectedly it landed, and it proved to be a boat. They turned out to be the undersea people—we Indians named those people that.

Having landed, they built their houses close to where the Indians were. After staying for a while, they got acquainted with them. They stayed with them. The Indians started to work for them. They lived there quite a while; having lived there for thirty years, they returned home.

Then the white people [literally, "miracles"] arrived. They, the white people, took over the land where all the Indians had been living. But the Indians still stayed.

[The passage continues with comments about life with the Benitz family, who took over Fort Ross when the Russians left.]

Since the Russians would have initially arrived at the beach at Fort Ross in *baidarkas* or perhaps longboats, both of which sat low enough to the water that it made the passengers appear to be floating on the surface, the image of people appearing to come out of the sea would certainly have inspired the Kashaya to call them the "undersea people."

This story continues the history of Indians in the area through the period of the next occupants, a German immigrant named Benitz and his family (at Fort Ross from1843 to 1867), and the eventual forced departure of the Indians from the settlement under a subsequent owner. It paints a broad, although sketchy, picture of Kashaya history from just before the arrival of the Russians and Aleuts and carries it beyond, as if to demonstrate the enduring nature of the Kashaya people in their homeland. Despite many comings and goings of other people, the Kashaya remain.

The series of seven stories reprinted here offers a rare vision of life in a Russian settlement as observed by the native peoples who became part of that life. In an earlier paper (Farris 1989) I was able to demonstrate the validity and accuracy of at least two stories told by natives about Fort Ross, even pinning down some details to a specific historical event (the passing of a Hudson's Bay expedition). These verifications lend an amount of credibility to other parts of the Kashaya oral history, and as we delve more deeply into the archival material related to Fort Ross, we may find additional corroboration of some of the events portrayed in Kashaya oral histories, particularly the deaths and perhaps the whippings. It may even be possible to ferret out the names of the individuals featured in these stories. The point of retelling the stories here, however, is to deepen our knowledge of the everyday lives of the people living in this settlement.

Source: Farris 1992b.

❧ **15** ❧

FOREIGN VISITORS TO
BODEGA BAY AND FORT ROSS

THE RUSSIANS WHO LIVED AT FORT ROSS left few accounts of daily life at the settlement, most likely because it was familiar to them and thus hardly worth mentioning. It is a pity that no journals or diaries kept by any of the inhabitants of Fort Ross have turned up so far. It seems particularly surprising that some of the educated residents, like manager Alexander Rotchev and his wife Elena, did not keep diaries, given the popularity of writing personal journals at the time. If such a diary were ever to appear, it would be a real treasure.

Russian visitors who did record some of their recollections of Fort Ross (Vasilii Golovnin, Achille Schabelski, Otto von Kotzebue, and Fr. Ivan Veniaminov, among others) were notably vague in their comments compared to visitors from other countries, and even Ferdinand von Wrangell, despite providing an exhaustive report on activities at the colony, provides more statistical data rather than a sense of the flavor of life at Fort Ross.

Thus it is that we look to journals of foreign visitors who found things at the settlement strange and interesting and thus more worthy of comment. Starting with soldiers sent to reconnoiter the new settlement (see accounts by Gabriel Moraga and Gervasio Argüello, page 80), and then following up with sea captains (Auguste Bernard Duhaut-Cilly, page 218, and Cyrille Laplace, page 235), we have a variety of observations that help us better view the scene of

Fort Ross. Mariano Vallejo's visit in 1833 is fairly informative, although it focused on military intelligence above all else. Probably the accounts that provide the most details about life in the colony were penned by Fr. Mariano Payeras in 1822 and French naval captain Cyrille Pierre-Théodore Laplace in 1839.

CANONIGO FERNÁNDEZ DE SAN VICENTE,
ACCOMPANIED BY FR. PAYERAS (1822)

The Canonigo Agustín Fernández de San Vicente was sent to California in 1822 by the short-lived imperial government of Agustín Iturbide, the self-styled emperor of Mexico. His job was to inform the Californians of their status as citizens of the newly independent Mexican state, as opposed to being subjects of the Spanish king. While in California Fernández de San Vicente took it upon himself to travel up to Fort Ross in the company of officers from the Presidio of San Francisco, as well as the *comisario* of the Franciscan missions in California, Fr. Mariano Payeras. The deputation was graciously welcomed by Russian commandant Karl Schmidt, but the *canonigo* duly registered the official objection to the Russian American Company occupying land in what the Mexican government considered to be a part of its province of California. Kirill Khlebnikov, though not present at the meeting at Fort Ross, had met the *canonigo* while in Monterey; this is his description: "He was born in Guadalajara, Mexico, and is a Creole. Educated in Europe, he is a canon by rank. He wears a small calotte,[1] a blue frock coat and a three-cornered hat, and he is addressed by the title 'Your Honor.' He is polite, but grimaces with each word, as if to indicate that he finds being polite repulsive. As he has taken up a political career, he probably has read Machiavelli and regards the Creator's work with disdain" (Khlebnikov 1990: 108).

The meeting resulted in a written protocol that read as follows (Khlebnikov 1990: 110):

No. 8, October 13, 1822   Protocol

On 12/23 October, 1822, the envoy of the Mexican Court, Don Agustín Fernández de San Vicente, visiting the manager of the Ross settlement in the so-called "Kuskov House" together with the head of all the missions of New California, Mariano Payeras, the Commandant of the San Francisco fort [ed: presidio], Don Luis Argüello, and the Lieutenant of the San Blas infantry regiment, Don Antonio del Valle, urgently requested documents concerning the right of the Russians to settle at Ross. In reply,

Mr. Schmidt, in the presence of Mr. Vasilii Starkovskii, Iakov Dorofeev, Fedor Svin'in and Vasilii Grudinin, showed him the documents he had concerning the settlement and pointed out that all
the documents received from the Spanish Court were with the Chief
Manager in Sitkha. He also showed him an agreement that had
been signed by the Spanish and Russian courts on October 17, 1812,
and the letter signed by the RAK [ed: RAC] directors on June 30,
1812, and addressed to the Spaniards living in California. The envoy
pointed out that the Mexican Government would insist upon the
return of this territory and asked Mr. Schmidt to inform the Chief
Manager of that fact without delay. Mr. Schmidt suggested referring
the matter for a decision to the Chief Manager's representative, Mr.
Khlebnikov, who is now at the port of Monterey on board the brig
Buldakov under the command of Mr. Etholen.

Signed by:

Karl Schmidt
Agustín Fernández de San Vicente
Vasilii Starkovskii
The hieromonk Mariano Payeras
Iakov Dorofeev
Luis Antonio Argüello
Fedor Svin'in
Antonio del Valle
Vasilii Grudinin
José Joaquin Estudillo, Secretary
Vasilii Starkovskii, Secretary

The document that follows explains the *canonigo*'s own version of the meeting
with the Russians. It appears to have been an introductory or cover letter for a
package of documents that he brought back to Mexico, which has since gone
missing. I have made numerous queries to people who have worked extensively with the Mexican archives in hopes of finding some of the items listed by
Fernández de San Vicente, but with no luck; maybe one day they will resurface.
It would be fascinating to find, for instance, the "legal deposition from one of

the three Russians whom I have brought with me." Although he may have been referring to José Bolcoff (Osip Volkov), that person may also have been one of the other two Russians who accompanied him back; in any case, the document might shed more detail on their own experiences in the missions after deserting from either Fort Ross or a Russian ship. Likewise, the declaration of "one of the Russians living at Mission San José" would be intriguing, as conceivably it might have been from Prokhor Egorov, who was later involved in the Chumash Revolt.

Most Excellent Sir: In your order of the 9th of the current month, Your Excellency informs me that my statement to the national government dated March 3, regarding the plans of the Russians to engage in hostile acts against Upper California,[2] has commanded the complete attention of His Majesty,[3] and that having offered to provide a detailed, documented report, I do so as quickly as possible: in due compliance of said superior order, I annex to Your Excellency the original letters, numbered from one to five, written by the most prudent missionary of that Province,[4] as well as the declaration of one of the Russians living at Mission San José.[5] Although it is in the Russian language, the interpreter[6] who has brought the letters can inform Your Excellency of the content of the declaration: also attached and marked with the number two is the legal deposition from one of the three Russians whom I have brought with me; on different occasions, I have questioned the other two[7] about the intentions of their countrymen and they have confirmed what the said Estevan[8] has said, with some other information which leaves no room for doubt, from which the government can be informed, since this is the sole purpose for my bringing them to this court.

I must [not] omit stating to Your Excellency what I myself observed in Monterey upon the arrival of the Russian brigantine called *Buldakov* under the command of Captain Adolf Etholén. As soon as he arrived he published the manifest of the goods he was carrying and on seeing it the new Californians boarded the said ship to purchase and were well received; but with the Provincial Deputation established, the commandant of Ross, don Kiril Khlebnikov[9] who came aboard said ship (and who I understand is the principal agent of their plans) requested that the said Deputation provide him with exclusive privileges to hunt sea otters pelts as Your Excellency will see in document number three in which that Deputation consulted if it would be convenient or not to accede to his request, and having made them understand by written order and verbally the harm that could result from this concession, he was answered in the negative; from that day they varied even their friendly dealings, looking at us with frowns and not wishing to sell anything to those inhabitants.

To simplify my report even more and save Your Excellency the trouble of searching in the Secretariat of State for the treaty of friendship, settlement of differences and boundaries between His Catholic Majesty and the United States of America, I include for Your Excellency three copies with a copy of the principal part of my instructions and they are marked with the number four: In that in them I am warned that I inform myself of what might be feared with respect to the Russian and American establishments in those parts; if the latter have traveled down the Columbia River[10] and situated themselves on the shores of San Francisco: if the force is respectable that the former have in the Port of Bodega are considerable, and if through the proper number of copies of the treaty of limits that should be given to me by the Secretariat of State so that those colonists may be instructed that the dividing line should not go beyond 42 degrees: in compliance with such sacred precepts and attempting to inform myself in Monterey relative to the Russian and Anglo-American establishments, there were so many reports that I thought it well to travel by land from Monterey to Ross, alias Coscow [Kuskov],[11] about 30 leagues to the north of Bodega: there I dealt with the greatest of harmony with the commandant don Carlos Schmidt, and having presented him with a copy of the treaty of limits, he responded to me what Your Excellency will see in document number five.

Upon my arrival at Bodega, I found only two Kodiak Indians with their wives. The force at Ross consists of 30 soldiers, 50 Kodiak Indians, [blank] cannons of all calibers, and some wild Indians who help in the construction of ships. If the government takes appropriate measures, I have no doubt that we will be able to retain our boundary line: but if this is ignored and not attended to quickly, my opinion is that we will lose this precious and fertile province of the Californias, the western key to our continent.

I conclude then, stating to Your Excellency that as much through the reports that have been given to me privately at Bodega and in the same Ross as well as from what is well known in that province after General Resanoff [Rezanov] having been there in 1806, fixing as a principle that the Russian establishments of the northwest cannot be sustained without California, that is without the seeds and meats that are so abundant, since they are totally lacking of these items, being almost reduced to eating pure sea lion meat, and even this is scarce, this being the motive for those of Ross frequently fleeing, and the same and even more so with those of Sitka if they were not so far away, after seeing uncovered and null the desirable hopes for which they had been recruited from Europe, crossing half of the world, whose recruitment would be more simple and numerous according to the three Russians who are with me, always with the likelihood California would succumb to Russia, because then the piastres and rubles would not become scarce with the hope of reintegrating themselves later with the possession of the province.

Finally, Sir, I repeat what I have said in my report of March 3, and as much through the former as in this Your Excellency will appreciate that my fears are not limited to the forces they have in their establishments that are in contact with ours in respect to the preparations for example the canton of the Island of Sitka, alias New Archangel. This is the extent to which I may inform Your Excellency limiting myself to the matter of the Russians.

God guard Your Excellency many years.
México, April 12, 1823.
Most Excellent Sir
Agustín Fernández de San Vicente
Most Excellent Sir don José Ignacio García Illueca,[12]
Secretary of State and chargé of three ministries.

Source: Glenn J. Farris, trans. and annot. Document 70 in Mathes 2008: 175–179. [Note: The original version of this document is located in the Beinecke Library at Yale University.] Reprinted by permission of the Fort Ross Interpretive Association.

AUGUSTE BERNARD DUHAUT-CILLY (1828)

Born in St. Malo in March 1790, Auguste Bernard Duhaut-Cilly was the son of Bernard du Haut-Cilly, a French nobleman. Auguste went to sea at age seventeen during the Napoleonic Wars and saw action against British naval vessels, especially in the Indian Ocean. He was aboard the frigate *Aréthuse* in 1813 when it won battles against a number of British ships off the West African coast, and for his part he was knighted in the Legion of Honor. With the peace that came upon the defeat of Napoleon in 1814, Duhaut-Cilly shifted over to the merchant marine and commanded a number of voyages to the Indian Ocean, South America, and the West Indies. In the mid-1820s he commanded a merchant ship, the *Héros,* to the Pacific coast. It was meant to be a trading expedition but was largely unsuccessful, in part because of the large number of

Captain Auguste Bernard Duhaut-Cilly. From Duhaut-Cilly 1997.

View of Fort Ross drawn by Auguste Bernard Duhaut-Cilly, June 1828.
From Duhaut-Cilly 1997: 188. Image courtesy of the Fort Ross Interpretive Association.

other vessels, especially American ones, that always seemed to sell their goods just before his arrival in a given port.

Duhaut-Cilly spent the better part of 1827 and 1828 travelling up and down the California coast and visited Fort Ross in June of 1828. The following portion of his travel journal relates his time at the Russian establishments. Duhaut-Cilly was something of an artist and we are fortunate to have a drawing he made of Fort Ross during the visit. He was impressed with the Russian colony and apparently developed a good rapport with the manager of Fort Ross at the time, Paul Shelekhov, although as Duhaut-Cilly points out, he and his companion, scientist Paul-Emile Botta, did not speak Russian and Shelekhov was unable to converse in French, English, or Spanish; somehow, however, they did manage to use Spanish as a medium, probably with the help of other members of Fort Ross who had learned some of the language. Duhaut-Cilly's comments on the lack of Russian women at the settlement make the point that life at Fort Ross was not merely a transplant to the New World of an otherwise typical Russian community.

Duhaut-Cilly's observations about Fort Ross are important in several regards. First, this is the only extensive account of life there during the second half of the 1820s, when Paul Shelekhov was commandant. The drawing made of the fort (above) is also the first one since the construction of the chapel, believed to have occurred in about 1825. The Frenchman's comment on Shelekhov's commercial enterprise of making "prefab" wooden buildings meant to be sold in California and Hawaii is the only mention we have of this enterprise.

On 2 June [1828] toward evening we found ourselves a few leagues from land on that part of the coast where I supposed the Russian colony to be and in fact we discerned with the telescope something that resembled a group of houses. At sunset we lay closer. Convinced now that we were not mistaken, I ran up the flag and shot off a cannon. Almost at once a puff of white smoke told us that they were responding in the same way, and we could make out a Russian flag. But since it was too late for a landing before nightfall, we shortened sail and maintained our position until the following day.

On the morning of the 3rd, as we were lying to at a distance of several miles, examining the coast without discerning any opening or recess that might indicate a harbor, we suddenly noticed three baidarkas coming toward us, each carrying three persons. Several minutes later these boats arrived alongside, and we were paid a visit by the Russian commandant himself, Paul Shelekhov, to whom I communicated my reasons for going there. At the same time I requested permission to anchor in his harbor in order to display those things in the cargo that might suit him. Although he was not in need of much and was rather short of trading goods, he welcomed my proposal and, ordering one of his men to serve us as pilot, he said he would accompany me to the port of Bodega, the only anchorage in use by the colony. He sent two of the boats back to shore and asked me to have the other hoisted on board, after which we took our way parallel to the coast.

From where we had been lying to the settlement had quite a different look from that of the presidios of California, models of rude design and indifferent execution. Houses of elegant shape with roofs well constructed, fields well planted and surrounded by palisades gave this place an appearance that was quite European.

After fifteen miles we reached a small peninsula that sheltered the roadstead of Bodega. Three hundred cables to the east of this point there is a small, flat island where we could see some greenery. The sea was breaking violently on the rocky peninsula [Bodega Head] and against a cliff on its east-southeast side. Our Russian pilot had us pass in mid-channel between the island and the peninsula with a depth of four to five fathoms, and we soon anchored inside in the middle of a sort of bay surrounded by land from south to east-by-north, that is to say on three-quarters of the horizon.

Toward evening Commandant Shelekhov returned to shore where horses had been brought for him, having made me promise to visit him the next day.

On the morning of the 4th, remarking the horses he had sent for us, I went on shore with Dr. Botta and our pilot. The landing place is in a small harbor at the mouth of a saltwater lagoon, sheltered from all winds. Ships drawing little water could find haven there. There they have built some fine wooden storehouses for use by the Russian ships.

Mounting our horses we began the journey, accompanied by several Russians and by our pilot; after having performed skillfully his nautical functions on the previous day, he steered us equally well over a different element, bearing now the modest title of guide. Having crossed the isthmus of the peninsula, we rode for a league along a fine sandy beach and then ascended a cliff of moderate height. After that we took our way over an esplanade carpeted with grass mixed with strawberry plants bearing fruit and ensplendored with a multitude of flowers of every color. The sea was breaking at the base of the cliff, its snow-white foam contrasting with the dark color of the rocks and the rich green of the fields, which our horses trod with no more sound than if they had been stepping on eiderdown. Two leagues along this plain brought us to the bank of a considerable river, called Sacabaya[13] by the Indians and Slavianka by the Russians. It was too deep even in the summertime to be forded, and in winter it becomes fearsome, swiftly carrying off immense tree trunks uprooted by storms. The retreating water had left some huge ones on both banks.

The crossing has been disastrous for many travelers; two years before this an American captain was drowned here. As for us, we passed over safely enough in a baidarka that Mr. Shelekhov had sent for the purpose. Since this boat, made of sealskin, held only two persons, it was necessary to make a trip for each one of us. Conducted skillfully by a Kodiak Islander, it had more than one point of resemblance to the bark of old Charon. Its lightness and instability could make one think that it was meant only for the transporting of shades, and the guttural grunting of the Kodiak when he pointed out the person who was to enter the baidarka with him must have sounded like the hoarse voice of the pitiless boatman of Hades, scolding souls on the banks of the Styx.

One had to exercise great care in sliding oneself into a round hole up to the middle of the body, when the slightest movement to right or left was enough to make the light craft tip in a disquieting way. Nevertheless, I had no wish to sit idly while we crossed, and in my capacity of seaman I seized a paddle and wielded it in a way to satisfy the old pilot of the Slavianka. It is in these cockle boats of skin that the natives of the Aleutian Islands, braving the high seas, hunt the Saricovian otter [sea otter] and do battle with the most monstrous whales, whose flesh and oil are their favorite food and drink.

[Duhaut-Cilly then digresses to comment on hunting methods used by the Alaskans.]

Our horses were accustomed to the passage of the river and they swam across by themselves as soon as they were relieved of their saddles. Starting out once more we ascended by so steep a road that we found it hard to believe that the horses could avoid falling back on their riders.

The mountain whose summit we reached, not without difficulty and even some danger, was covered with enormous conifers, mixed with sycamore, bay trees, and several species of oaks. At a height of two thousand feet we looked out over the sea, which was beating against the land below; the waves, silent at this distance, looked like small whitish patches scattered over a cloth of azure.

We descended the far side by a slope as steep as the first one, and at every opening we could see through the trees or over their tops and more and more distinctly the Russian establishment, lying below us and on the northwest side of the mountain. Fearing that our horses after a journey of four leagues, would not be able to carry us over both dangerous slopes, Mr. Shelekhov had had the foresight to post fresh ones at the high point.

At eleven in the morning we arrived at the colony called Ross by the Russians. It is a large square enclosure surrounded by a thick wooden palisade twenty feet high, strongly constructed and topped with iron spikes of proportionate size and weight. At the northeast and southwest angles are two hexagonal towers pierced with ports and loopholes. On the four sides, which correspond to the cardinal points, are four gates, each defended by a carronade of fixed breeching set in a port as on a ship. Within there were also two bronze field pieces with caissons. A handsome house for the commandant or governor, pleasant lodgings for the subalterns, large storehouses, and workshops occupy the square. A newly constructed chapel serves as a bastion in the southeast corner. This citadel is built near the edge of the cliff on an esplanade about two hundred feet above the sea. On the left and right are ravines that protect it from attacks by the Indians from the north and south while the cliff itself and the sea shield it from the west. The ravines open onto two small coves which serve as shelter and landing place for the small boats of the colony.

All the buildings at Ross are of wood but well built and well maintained. In the apartment of the governor are found all the conveniences valued by Europeans but still unknown in California. Outside the compound are lined up or scattered the pretty little houses of sixty Russian colonists, the flat huts of eighty Kodiaks, and the conical huts of as many native Indians.

East of the settlement the land rises gradually to great heights covered with thick forests that block the wind from the north to the southeast. All these slopes are partitioned into fields of wheat, beans, oats, potatoes, and the like, fenced off to protect the crops not from thieves but from farm animals and wild beasts.

In spite of its military appearance the colony is a commercial establishment owned, along with those of Sitka and Kodiak Island, by a company of merchants. It appears, however, that the emperor has granted it great privileges, and that many in the Russian court own an interest, large or small. The governors have military rank, and the ships of the company fly the national flag and are commanded by officers of the imperial navy.

There appears to be great order and discipline at Ross, and although the governor is the only officer, one notes everywhere the signs of close supervision. After being busy all day in their various occupations, the colonists, who are both workers and soldiers, mount guard during the night. On holidays they pass in review and drill with canon and musket.

Although this colony, in existence for fifteen years, appears to lack nothing, it cannot be of great account to the company that founded it. As the principal source of revenue they counted on the hunt for sea otters and seals.

The first of these is nearly exhausted and no longer provides anything; as for the second, the governor keeps about a hundred Kodiaks on the Farallons throughout the year, as I have said elsewhere, but that hunt, once quite productive, declines with every passing day and in a few more years will amount to nothing. Looking on these products as now secondary, the governor has for several years concerned himself primarily with husbandry. Not only does he grow the wheat and vegetables that were once obtained from California, but he also provisions the larger colony of Sitka. With only six hundred cows he was producing more butter and cheese than all of Alta California with its countless herds.

In spite of all these advantages the colony of Ross inspires in the traveler's mind only somber and melancholy thoughts. The reason, I believe, is that this society is incomplete. The governor is a bachelor and has no woman in his house; all the Russian colonists live in the same state. In this establishment there are only the women of the Kodiaks and those of the Indians. No matter what relations may exist between them and the Russians, the visitor, to whom these women are objects of disgust, cannot help regarding this little community as deprived of that sex whose sole presence makes life bearable. The tasks that usually fall to women are here the portion of men, and this difference shocks the eye, weighs on the heart, and causes a pain that one feels in spite of oneself and before discovering the true reason for it.

We went with Mr. Shelekhov to view his timber production. In addition to the needs of his own settlement he cuts a great quantity of planks, beams, timbers, and the like, which he sells in California, in the Sandwich Islands, and elsewhere; he even builds entire houses and ships them disassembled. The trees felled are almost all conifers of several kinds and especially the one called *palo colorado* (redwood). The only virtues of this tree are that it is quite straight and splits easily; for the rest, it has little resin and is very brittle. It is the largest tree that I have ever seen. Mr. Shelekhov showed me the trunk of one that had been felled recently; it was twenty feet in diameter measured two feet from the ground and from one burl or buttress to the other; the main trunk was more than thirteen feet in width. I measured two hundred and thirty feet from the stump to the crown, lying where it had been parted from the bole. Imagine what a huge quantity of boards can be obtained from a tree of this size. The stacks of them from one such covered a considerable stretch of ground. Not all the palos colorados are this prodigious, but one can see many that three men would have difficulty stretching their arms around and that would make, as a single piece, the lower masts of our largest ships of war.

Mr. Shelekhov treated us with the most refined hospitality, and we passed a comfortable night with him. Unfortunately neither Dr. Botta nor I understood Russian, and the governor spoke neither French nor English nor Spanish. This inconvenience caused us to miss much of the charm that his company should have provided. It was in Spanish that we made ourselves understood best. I did only a little business with him; an American ship had preceded me here and had taken nearly all the pelts possessed by the establishment. I sold him only the value of a few hundred sealskins. Arising early the next day I positioned myself on a hillside to the east and sketched the citadel, as shown in the plate that accompanies this volume. After breakfast we mounted our horses to return to the port, from where we set sail the next morning.

During the three days that we remained in the bay at Bodega the wind blew fresh from the northwest, and although the ship was sheltered and the waters there were calm we broke our best bower cable. This was the second such accident to it; on our return from Peru to Monterey it had broken in a strong northwest breeze. At that place we found a smith who was skillful enough to repair it and who also changed seven links that were unsafe. This iron cable had been in excellent condition on our departure from Le Hâvre, and during two years of use we had on numerous occasions remarked its strength. But after having held in big winds and heavy seas it now failed us under quite ordinary circumstances. We must not believe, then, that chains are everlasting; they wear out like everything else.

Source: Duhaut-Cilly 1997. Reprinted by permission of the University of California Press.

JOHN WORK, MICHEL LAFRAMBOISE,
AND THE HUDSON'S BAY COMPANY BRIGADE (1833)

The year 1833 had already been a peculiar one for the inhabitants of Colony Ross. One month before the arrival of the Hudson's Bay Company Brigade, led by John Work, seven American fur trappers, headed by Ewing Young, had come to the fort from the north to leave 199 river otter skins for his agent. The Russians advanced Young 160 piasters worth of supplies for his main party of twenty-five, waiting for him up the coast. Young's visit was anticipated, having been arranged by merchants William E. P. Hartnell and John B. Rogers Cooper of Monterey the previous January, when Peter Kostromitinov, manager of Fort Ross, was visiting San Francisco aboard the Russian sloop *Urup*. In contrast, the surprise visit by the Hudson's Bay Company Brigade—made up of a party led by John Work and supplemented by a second group headed by Michel Laframboise, for a total of 163 men, women, and children, as well as 450 horses and mules—was quite a different story.

The Hudson's Bay Company, based at Fort Vancouver on the Columbia River, dominated the beaver trade on the West Coast. Periodically American mountain men (Ewing Young, Joseph Walker, and Jedediah Smith among them) would enter the Central Valley of California in search of these valuable furs, and fearing these outsiders' eventual encroachment on territories hunted by

John Work, leader of the Hudson's Bay Party, 1832–1833.
Courtesy of the Provincial Archives, Victoria, British Columbia.

the HBC, the "Honorable Company" sent a number of expeditions south into California in the late 1820s and 1830s not only to hunt beaver but to attempt to exterminate them in a sort of scorched-earth policy that would dissuade the Americans from hunting farther north into the Oregon country. For the most part the HBC kept to the Central Valley, usually setting up their main camps a little south of today's Stockton, at a place even today called French Camp.[14] In the expedition of 1832–1833 the main brigade was led by John Work, an Englishman, however, he was joined by a second brigade that had been sent out along the Oregon coast under the command of French Canadian Michel Laframboise. The combination of the two parties made this a much larger group of hunters than usual. The ethnic makeup of HBC brigades was generally in large part mixed-blood French Canadian men and their native wives from tribes in the Pacific Northwest.

John Work had been ordered by the Chief Factor of Fort Vancouver to take some time to explore the California coast north of San Francisco to determine whether there were beaver there. This order was how the large hunting party found itself travelling up past Sonoma and Fort Ross in the spring of 1833. The Russians were, understandably, nervous about such a large and very well-armed group entering their territory, but in the course of a meeting between Peter Kostromitinov and John Work, it was decided that the hunters would be permitted to pass through even though the former told the HBC chief that he had personally traveled a long way to the north of Fort Ross and had seen no beaver.

Presented here are the terse journal notes of John Work, leader of the Hudson's Bay Company Brigade of 1832–1833.

THURSDAY 18 [April 1833]. Stormy cold weather. Raised camp and proceeded over a succession of hills 15 miles Westerly to the sea shore and along the shore to the Russian river, which we crossed immediately, and encamped. Here we met the governor of the Russian establishment [Peter Kostromitinov; he] objected to our passing his establishment and said there was no road except right past the fort. We told him that we meant to pass but that we meant to pass it at a distance[;] he was told that our two nations were at peace and that we did not see any reasons for his objections and that we must pass. [H]e then said that as there was no other way he would allow us to pass [words obliterated] to accompany him [words obliterated] it was after dark when we arrived. I took two men with me and left Michelle [Michel Laframboise] to come on with the camp in the morning. The governor speaks but a few words of French, so that we had not much conversation[;] he treated me very politely.

FRIDAY 19. Raw cold weather. The camp passed the fort past noon & proceeded 5 miles farther on[. W]here we encamped, the governor and a number of his people accompanied us to the encampment[. H]e invited me to dinner with him at the fort in the evening[. H]e had been along the 100 miles on discovering the road we are going[. H]e represents the road as passable but intrenched by a great number of deep gullies which are difficult to pass. There are also some point of woods.

Source: Maloney 1944: 19–40.

KASHAYA VERSIONS OF THE HUDSON'S BAY
COMPANY BRIGADE AT FORT ROSS (1833)

Thanks to linguist Robert Oswalt, we have English translations of two fascinating Kashaya accounts of the mysterious strangers' passage by Fort Ross. The first story, "The Ayash Expedition," was told to Oswalt in September 1958 by Kashaya leader Essie Parrish. The second story, "The Big Expedition," was told in the same month by Herman James, who had learned his stories from his maternal grandmother, Lukaria. (See page 197 for more on these Kashaya narrators.) A wonderful detail about these two writings is their dual-language presentation, with Kashaya and English texts side by side, which helps preserve the rhythm and flavor of the originals instead of losing them to the spruced-up "as told by" feel found in many native stories available only in English.

Lukaria Yorgen Myers, Kashaya matriarch and oral historian.
Courtesy of the Fort Ross Interpretive Association.

In his introduction to the stories (properly included under the heading "Folk History") Oswalt suggests some ambiguity about the timing of the event both stories address. Essie Parrish stated that it occurred "long, long ago before the white men arrived," whereas Herman James said it occurred at a time when "the undersea people had landed there." It is important to understand the terms "undersea people" and "white people" as used here and in another work recorded by Oswalt, "Tales of Fort Ross." In this narrative, "white people" refers to post–Russian period American settlers, such as William Benitz, who took over Fort Ross when the Russians left. Thus, when Essie Parrish says, "before the white men came," she actually means before the *Americans* came, i.e., prior to 1843. The term "undersea people" refers to inhabitants of Fort Ross, who arived on low *baidarkas*, making them appear to have emerged from the ocean.

On the morning of April 19, 1833, the Hudson's Bay Company Brigade climbed the steep coastal hills leading up from the Russian River and followed the ridgetops along the road established by the Russians, until they saw Fort Ross below. Descending the ridge over a series of benches, the contingent stretched out in single file and thus became a long, sinuous body of humans and animals coming down slowly past the Kashaya village of Métini, and then that of the Kodiak hunters, built outside the walls of the fort.

The Kashaya people in their small village were surprised and clearly alarmed to see the strange apparition of a seemingly endless line of unknown people crossing territory occupied by the Russians. As Herman James, grandson of one of the witnesses, told Oswalt, "They went on and on—they are said to have been coming down for about half a day, as if the column would never cease." It's easy to imagine the HBC brigade strung out for perhaps a mile, coming down the hill above Fort Ross and passing silently upcoast to the north, where, as agreed, they would encamp some five miles farther on, probably somewhere in the area between today's Stillwater Cove and Ocean Cove.

The party the Kashaya saw included tall men and women, with their babies on cradle boards and fastened to mules. They were all mounted and wore long robes, many with cloths wrapped around their heads like turbans. Both the Kashaya and the Kodiaks were confused by the appearance of these strangers and the latter offered them some wheat flour, the new staple the Russians had taught them to use. Although the Hudson's Bay people did not converse with either the Kashaya or the Kodiaks, they took the flour and moved silently ahead toward their next campsite. This strange behavior made a deep impression on the Kashaya. Not knowing what to call these people, they fixed on a word that they heard repeated many times by the strangers: "Ayash."[15] When they asked the Russians who these people were, they were told that the strangers were Indians like themselves. In fact, many of them were French Canadian metis and their often Indian wives from tribes in the Northwest.

Perhaps because the Hudson's Bay people were of such an outlandish appearance in the eyes of the local people, the Kashaya oral tradition that grew up around their passage included many graphic details of their appearance. Apart from the notable height and clothing of the strangers, such details as the long tepee poles pulled along in travois fashion made an indelible impression. One peculiarity passed down was that the strangers did not seem to cook their food but rather ate it raw; one of the Kashaya who was a captive of the Hudson's Bay people for a while attested to this odd behavior. Generations later, the story of this passing was still being told over and over, but yet no one really understood who the people had been.

As I read over these stories and envisioned the horses pulling a travois-like structure, I remembered the John Work party and put the two together. The result was an article first published in the *American Indian Quarterly* in 1989 titled "Recognizing Indian Folk History as Real History: A Fort Ross Example." I had long felt that too often Indian tales were rejected as having any historical merit, often because of modern scholars' inability to tie them down to known historical events. Connecting these two Kashaya stories to the historical event of the passing of an HBC brigade by Fort Ross seemed a good example of how, seen in the right light, such a story could be recognized as a record of a real historical event.

꿿 鸞

THE AYÁSH EXPEDITION

[Essie Parrish] (Oswalt 1964: 246–249)

I am going to tell about something that happened in the old days—something my father used to tell. It was over at Métini, long, long ago before the white men arrived.

The Indians didn't know what could be coming over. They were suddenly coming over where the ridge slopes down at Métini. It was at daybreak, when the sun was just rising, that they started to come over.

Some were riding on mules. Their possessions had been tied on. [Some] were packing their babies in baby baskets; others had tied [their babies] on the animals. Both the men and women all wore long clothes. And on their heads something like cloth was wrapped around and around. They were tall men, tall women. They came down the mountain endlessly.

Then they turned north. The Indians watched them going. Even when they turned it was as if they were coming down in an endless series—like the waves of the ocean. They turned, they went away off to the north, after a long time they were past. After they had finished passing by, there was a cloud of dust kicked up along the trail they had come down—because there were so many of them, I suppose.

There was one Indian who had gone off casting for fish at a gravel beach just at the time when those people were coming down. And it turned out that they caught that man. Having caught him, they took him along. After they had turned north that man didn't return—he was [discovered] to be lost. [The Indians] searched far and wide for him at the beach where he had said he was going. He wasn't anywhere; they thought he had been carried off by the ocean. Unexpectedly, on the next day toward evening, he returned.

Then he told about how some people had captured him—those who had turned to go along the ocean. He said that after having caught him, they led him away. They stopped to take a rest—probably at some place far to the north. Having stopped, some of them detached their baby baskets from the animals. Having detached them, they drilled a fire on the babies' [cradleboards]—on them they drilled. They then let the fire blaze up. I don't quite remember if they did it to warm themselves or to cook—but [the captured man] said that they ate their food raw.

I also don't remember how he happened to escape from them. Having run off he crawled into his home—somehow they didn't chase after him. When he arrived home, he collapsed sick. From some cause, perhaps from being so scared, that happened. That man kept on getting sicker and sicker. No one being able to cure him, he died in his home.

That is the end of what I heard of the story.

I forgot to say this. When they came over there, they were talking, talking a lot. But they [the Indians] couldn't understand them, they were speaking another language. The only word they detected was /☐ayá•š/. While saying other things, they were saying /☐ayá•š/. Consequently, they were named Ayásh, but I don't know what kind of people they were.

THE BIG EXPEDITION

[Herman James] (Oswalt 1964: 252–253)

In the old days people lived at Métini. They say that at that time the undersea people had landed there. They lived there together close by, having become acquainted with each other.

Then one day they looked across [a canyon] there was something like a cloud of dust flowing along. Unexpectedly there were people coming— many. They had horses and everything—even their children were suspended on the horses, and food too. They were dragging along long poles fastened to the horses. Then in places such as where creeks flowed down, they made what are called "bridges" and went across them.

At first [the natives] thought they were few. Then when they came down the near face of the mountain [they saw that] there were many people with horses, dragging the poles along. They kept coming and coming. Now they approached where [the natives] lived. "They are apparently people of some kind," [the natives] were saying. Having become frightened, they went into the houses. With no one in plain sight, they watched [the expedition] while thinking that [the strangers] would kill them. Even the undersea people did the same—they had never seen anything like that before; nor had the Indians.

They came down like that—all in a row they came down—many— many hundreds—thousands. They were going along as if they would never come to an end. When they came close to where the undersea people were living, a few people straggled out and gave them some of what they [Indians and Russians] had to eat. They gave flour, being afraid. [The strangers] took it willingly—at that time. They gave it to a lot of them.

They went on and on—they are said to have been coming down for about half a day, as if the column would never cease. [The Indians] watched while they were coming down with everything, quivers and bows strapped across their chests. They kept going like that, like I described. Those things that they were dragging along they laid across the gulches and went across. They went on and on like that. Finally, after a long time, the column came to an end.

In two places guards were standing; one boss was at the head and another at the rear, wearing different clothes. The one in front was the leader. The rear one was a guard. For a long time they didn't finish filing by. For nearly a day they went by.

After that, after three or four days had passed, [some Indians] having gone northwards saw what they had given all poured out on the ground—it looked terrible. They hadn't known what it was for. Everything they had received from the undersea people, all of the food, had been dumped out. They had apparently just left it on the trail, as [the Indians] found it. When those people who had gone there returned, they told that the food they had given was all dumped. "Apparently they didn't eat that kind of food," they said. "They probably didn't know it was something to eat."

After the people had filed by like that, they didn't know what kind of people they were—neither the Indians nor the undersea people recognized them. They told about it and kept saying, "I wonder what they were?"

It remained that way for a long time. No one ever knew. It still remained the same. After a while they wanted to find out. When they did so, the [Russians] said, "How come you don't know that the people you are asking about are your kind of people." "No, we don't recognize those people," said the Indians of those people. "I wonder where they belong and where they come from." But they hadn't asked when they came through where they had come from or what people they were. They had just watched frightened—they only asked too late when no one knew.

It stayed that way. This that my grandmother told me, she also saw herself. She said that when they came by she was terribly frightened. The undersea people were afraid too, and gave them food even though they didn't ask for it. This is also true what happened there. This is the end.

Source: Farris 1992a.

CYRILLE PIERRE-THÉODORE LAPLACE'S VISIT
TO BODEGA BAY AND FORT ROSS (1839)

Cyrille Pierre-Théodore Laplace, captain of the French ship *Artémise,* visited California in 1839. Born at sea on November 7, 1793, Laplace's career in the navy began in 1809, during the Napoleonic Wars. He rose to the rank of captain in 1834 and was promoted to rear admiral in 1841, soon after he returned from his round-the-world voyage. Laplace died in the city of Brest in 1873 (Blue 1939: 326).

The *Artémise* anchored at Bodega Bay from August 11 to 20, 1839, and made a trip up to Fort Ross on horseback, a mode of transportation that he did not relish. His situation was very different from the visit of his countryman, Duhaut-Cilly, in that Alexander Rotchev, the manager of Fort Ross at this time, was fluent in French, as was his wife, and so Laplace derived far more information from his visit, as will be seen in the following account. Although Laplace was often given to lengthy digressions and sometimes bombastic prose, he did make a number of useful observations about the Russian settlements, not only of Fort Ross and Bodega Bay but also concerning three Russian farms or ranchos that were active at the time of his visit. His views on the native Californians that he met ranged from high admiration of a chief to rather degrading comments about most of the women. He was a man of his time and reflected the prejudices common in those days, not only in terms of gender but also in his political views of the value of "progress" to tame the wild redwood country to increase its agricultural usefulness.

I made use of the map drawn in 1792 by the famous English explorer, Vancouver, for I was following the same route as he did and in the same season. Also, we were encountering the same contrary winds against which he had struggled. And, like him as well, I entertained the same vivid concerns for the safety of the ship and its numerous crew that had been put in my care. The daylight finally came, but yet the sky and the horizon were obscured by fog which, pushed here and there by the wind, took a thousand fantastic forms which to my vision and my weary spirit sometimes took on an unquieting reality. Fortunately, the breeze had greatly softened and the sea was smoother. Also, it allowed me to approach the coast closer than two miles, permitting me to reconnoiter Fort Ross which I knew was situated at the summit of a cliff stuck out a little into the sea. Supposing, with reason, that we were north of it, due to the wind up to this point, I came about [into the wind] and my second in command, like me armed with a telescope, anxiously searched the rocks, the dunes and the meadows which passed in front of our eyes.

For two hours the frigate rapidly lost the distance which it had gained so painfully in tacking during the night and no sign of Fort Ross was to be seen. In vain I looked for it on the shore, among the rocks, either black or whitened by the droppings of the birds which covered them by the hundreds, or even at the summit of naked dunes to which the fog lent a thousand strange aspects. Nothing came to reassure us. Finally, I was going to give the order to resume the original route until the latitude taken at noon let me know for certain where we were. Just then my attention was fixed by a cliff that appeared to have a fort on it. I had a cannon fired, to which, after a short interval which seemed a century to me, the shore responded. We hove to and soon thereafter the frigate received on board two skin pirogues or baidarkas, which carried a Russian agent and some pilots who, at my request, earnestly directed the frigate toward Bodega.

It was truly Fort Ross that we had seen, and in this moment with the sun's rays already coming over the ridge of hills, the fog which until then had hidden it from view, disappeared little by little. I could judge better from its position, that we were very close, perhaps too much so, according to what the pilots told me; on this part of the coast the currents carry to the land strongly enough to cause the loss of a ship should it be becalmed.

Lighted by a brilliant sky, the Russian establishment offered a truly picturesque view. It was perched, so to say, at the summit of a high cliff jutting out in the sea like a peninsula and cut off on all sides except on the land side of which it was but a projection. The walls, above which appeared the roofs of the buildings and the chapel with its little bell tower, surmounted by a Greek [Orthodox] cross; and a windmill with white walls, whose large wings turned rapidly with the morning breeze. Below, at the edge of the shore, to the right and left of the cliff, were two ravines in which several boats [were] hauled up on the beach; all this formed the outline of a lovely tableau of which the base was embellished by pretty hills with gentle slopes, covered in greenery, and crowned with firs. But, the total picture seemed to me lacking in life and so imprinted itself as having an isolated appearance mirroring my feelings of the moment.

Artémise rapidly passed the various points [of land] which separated her from her new destination. The appearance of the coast did not change, everywhere the same uniformity and solitude met my view. I was soon tired of fruitless efforts at seeking out objects of interest, and profiting from the ability which the presence of practical matters allowed me to recover for several moments my role of observer, it was on these latter themselves that I directed my study.

[I have omitted a lengthy reverie by Laplace concerning the qualities of the Kodiak hunters.]

In any case, hardly diminished by troublesome suspicions, I had a good opinion of [ed: the Kodiak hunters] from the first instant in observing their morality, their calm and reflective air, and their steadiness in carrying out commands. Wholly about their business and showing excellent abilities at piloting, they occupy themselves solely with the conduct of the ship. And, without the kindness of their leader, who undertook to give me the nautical information of which I was so much in need, I would have found myself arriving at the anchorage as little informed on the navigation of these far-away places as the night before. His conversation was for me a source of distraction, as agreeable as it was useful. The details that he gave me on the crossing from land to shipboard amused me very much, and I easily understood that the idea of returning to the shore by the same route was not at all pleasant to him. I expressly promised him one of the two canoes to go back. This promise and the influence of the Bordeaux [wine] of which he accompanied a very good lunch, garnered for me his complete confidence, and made him, I believe, nearly forget the bad moments that, for my sake he had spent in a small boat that morning. He recounted to me in a piteous air how, stuck in the cockpit, which is often right in the middle of the baidarka for a passenger, and muffled up in a pea-jacket similar to that worn by his paddlers, he had believed twenty times that it was all over for him, at times when the least movement he made to maintain his equilibrium and when the sea, then a bit rough submerged him momentarily. In effect, to judge by the fickle stability, the lightness and the proportions characteristic of these singular craft, to see the confident manner in which the Kodiaks make them weather the strongest waves, the situation of a passenger on board must be very uncomfortable. In any case let us add that accidental wrecks are extremely rare due to the fact that the Aleutian mariners utilize much skill and intelligence in their manner of guiding them and foresee a long time in advance the bad weather that menaces them.

[Next Laplace describes their travel by sea down to Bodega Bay.]

In any case, there existed at the bottom of the bay and winding around the rocks and the sandbanks on which the surf broke almost constantly with violence, a channel that advanced into the interior to a small lagoon wherein ships of medium tonnage could sometimes find refuge, but today with the sand pushed up into the entrance by the heavy waves, only small sloops and coasting vessels could make it in. It was there that at the foot of high dunes of moving sand is situated what is called the establishment, that is to say, several structures serving as housing for the employees of the Company, and a vast storehouse full of provisions destined either for the colony or to the ships moored in the roads.

Continuing to look toward this part of the shore lying about a mile and half from the frigate, my eyes encountered on the left the islet and the chain of rocks of which I have spoken above as protecting the anchorage against the winds and the open sea; but when the sea is rendered furious by late season tempests, this protection disappears under the mountainous waves that, hurling themselves against the opposing bank and encountering the bubbling waters of the torrents coming from the high land creates a frightful chaos at the same place where the frigate was anchored.

Across the openings that these torrents made in the cliffs through which they ran, I perceived plains stripped of vegetation by a long drought and by the burning rays of the summer sun. The trees were rare here and only found grouped around little pools now nearly dry, but which would transform themselves three months later into vast lakes connecting with the ocean by these same openings of which I spoke above. Their banks are the meeting places at certain times of the year for a multitude of aquatic birds that the epicures would not disdain; of deer, buffaloes [sic] and bears as well as other wild animals which, when the soil is frozen [sic], the hunters often come to disturb their quiet abode. The rest of the time they travel these districts without fear of an enemy arrow or firearm, free from time immemorial to enjoy the most complete solitude.

On these frontiers not a vestige of habitation, not the least sound, the least movement announcing the presence of man; but from the day after the arrival of the frigate our young men had definitely changed this state of things and the noise of firearms, the shouts of the hunters, fishermen and lovers of natural history gave the indigenous creatures of these places a foretaste of the tribulations which would be visited again on them soon after our passage by the American settlers.

The sun set while I was making these observations. Then began one of the sweet, clear, star-filled nights such as one so often sees in our [French] southern provinces during this same season. The breeze had fallen with the day, so that everything indicating a prolonged calm, I went eagerly to enjoy some sleep that the recent hard work and that which I anticipated for the following morning both made necessary.

As expected, early next morning I met the governor at the establishment who, in planning the tour that he was about to give me, agreed to finish up by 5 p.m. in order to partake of my table to which I had also invited our visitor of the evening before and the captain of the transport anchored near us.

Mr. Rotchev appeared to justify all the praise which my acquaintances in the Sandwich Islands had heaped upon him. In his company I soon forgot the sad impressions that the view of the landscape had recently inspired in me.

I found a man still young,[16] of an agreeable physical appearance with distinguished manners, appearing to be well educated and speaking French perfectly, thus justifying by his good deportment and his spirit the high opinion that the Russian gentlemen who visit our country give us generally of their compatriots of an elevated rank.

And so our relations were soon all that I could have and ought to have desired, not less for my pleasure than for my instruction. It was decided that the next morning we would leave on horseback for Ross where he had told his gracious companion [Helena Rotcheva] of my coming, and for whom my visit, he assured me, would not fail to be a source of agreeable distraction. In the time before dinner we strolled through the various buildings of the port of Bodega which he himself in the two years that he had been governor, had considerably developed. We first entered a large wooden warehouse wherein lodged the company employees, be they white or mixed blood, they were housed together, I must say, not very properly with some indigenous or Kodiak women whose repulsive ugliness and filthiness gave me a sad image of the taste and habits of these residents. However, a part of the warehouse, a little better arranged than the rest, served as a lodging for the governor when, upon leaving Fort Ross, he came to oversee the loading of agricultural produce of the colony onto the ships that would carry them to New Archangel, or to ensure fresh goods for provisioning the crews of these same ships. This activity never failed to be tiring. The colony was founded in 1812 with the sole purpose of furnishing the Russian colonies of the Northwest with cereals, vegetables, all types of culinary articles and finally with dried meat. Since this purpose was accomplished, thanks to the intelligent activity of the top leadership, as we would see later, the maritime activity was very considerable at Bodega during the good weather.

I was able to get an idea of this activity when I accompanied my most amiable guide to visit the spacious storerooms where I saw the cargo for the ship moored in the roadstead fully prepared. It was composed of a multitude of sealed barrels, some containing a brine prepared right there in a sort of shed built for this purpose and where could be found several large heaps of white salt from San Blas. Others were filled with butter, eggs, cheese, as well as cabbages, carrots, turnips, and melons, carefully placed in the brine so that they would arrive safe and sound at their destination. Beside them were found piled up some sacks of flour, then some bundles of cattle hides or deerskins, tanned and destined to be made into shoes for the colonists. As quickly as these diverse items disappeared from the storehouse and were taken to the beach where the ship's boats awaited them, these latter disembarked numerous packages of smoked or salted salmon sent for the provisioning of the colony by the authorities of New Archangel where the soldiers as well as the white and native sailors lived on hardly anything else.

Also, the sailors of the transport, who had been limited to the same dietary regime for a long time, considered their presence at Bodega Bay as a time of feasting and of living well.

In effect, fresh meat and vegetables of all sorts were available to them in abundance, and the foreign visitors were not forgotten in these morning distributions. Our men benefited to their hearts' content from this precious bounty. In any case, they could hardly match their Russian comrades who, so it seemed, showed an insatiable appetite.

In addition, it must be said, the animals condemned to serve as food for so many famished stomachs were superb, large and fat, but unfortunately led from some distance away to the fatal pot and struggling with a furor until the moment when they fell under the knife, their meat had lost some of its natural savor. At least, that is how it appeared to me. In any case, as from my first excursion on land, I was witness to such sacrifice, it is possible that the distressing memory which remained with me has influenced my judgment.

Mr. Rotchev and I were talking, touching on the thousand curious subjects on which I successively directed the conversation, when I saw descend, or moreover roll from atop the nearby perpendicular cliff which rises behind the establishment, two guardians of the herd or "vaqueros" on horseback holding between them at a good distance at the end of their lassos looped around the horns, a furious bull that was putting all his effort toward throwing himself on one or the other of his two enemies. However, he found himself trapped by the vigor and intelligence with which each horse resisted the terrible shock that the lasso made when the animal threw himself in the opposite direction. This struggle lasted from the moment when the nearly wild animal had been chosen from a pasture several miles from there and was characterized by no less a rage on one side than with the strength and coolness of the other until the moment when the victim, worn out and having his hind legs fettered, fell panting in the dust. Then, one of the vaqueros got down from his horse and approached with his machete in hand and cut the bull's throat with both the dexterity and the indifference of a man habituated to daily practice of his cruel job.

However, the sun was already very high above the horizon and its rays, in these countries where the air is most often as pure as it is gentle in this season, being reflected by the surrounding white sand dunes burned our faces and hands. And so I returned by the path to the anchorage and my companion went to busy himself with his affairs or to take a rest until the time when he ought to come aboard.

The day ended for me as agreeably as it had begun, and the next morning starting at the crack of dawn, the governor, the senior surgeon[17] of the frigate and I started off on horseback, following the edge of the sea in the direction of Fort Ross where we were expected.

At first, with some difficulty, we crossed the sand dunes on foot, the same dunes on which I had seen such a terrible struggle between the bull and the two vaqueros the evening before. Then, after a very rapid descent, our mounts rode on a flat terrain, bordered by the ocean on one side while the land side offered a whitish and sterile appearance up to the foot of some rather far off hills covered in tall fir (or spruce) trees.

The view had nothing of the picturesque nor amusing. However, as the telescope had given me a foretaste of it the day before when the *Artémise* followed the coast very closely, I was not at all surprised not even of the view of two very skinny and miserable wolves[18] that had been hidden from our approach by the edge of the wood. They departed from a pile of wood of varying dimensions, thrown up by the sea on the beach during the storms of the previous winter, and that the next year the big waves would reclaim, no doubt to deposit them further away.

Often among these debris of forests, one finds some which had grown up on the coast of lands up by the Bering Strait, from where the currents had sent them toward the south and had carried them often as far as the Polynesian archipelago whose natives transformed them into canoes of such large size that they astonished the first navigators; whereas on the Aleutian Islands and on the coasts of Kamchatka the natives blessed the beneficial current which, flowing to the north, disposed annually on their shores a considerable quantity of enormous trees, extracted by the hurricanes of the tropic lands or of the equator and which they used to build their huts and to maintain their hearth fires during winter.

The magnificent trees that I saw lying here and there on the sand, denuded of their branches, serving as a sanctuary for all sort of marine insects, those which had once been (but no more) the pride of the earth which sustained them, caught my attention. The sight of them increased even more the sense of isolation which weighed on my spirit and which gave rise to a melancholy and solitary air, of the countryside that we were traversing.

I longed to see other places, woods, greenery, some verdure, some vestiges of civilization. In vain I looked far ahead of us as nothing came to distract me of the boredom of the route and of my own fatigue, since I was not a good rider, to the regret of our guide who was thus much slowed in his return home.

For several hours since we had left Bodega Bay the sun was hot and its rays reflected by the sand over which we traveled. This greatly inconvenienced the riders and their mounts. Finally we arrived at the mouth of the Slavianka [Russian River], now a small river flowing among obstacles which the opposing [ocean] waves made to its humble course, but in winter [it was] an impetuous torrent that carried in its deep waters debris from the mountains from whence it sprang, and of the plains through which it traveled. In the midst of this very image of a chaos of rocks and vegetation, one can easily imagine our satisfaction to find an excellent lunch prepared in advance on the orders of our amiable governor.

We were seated on the trunks of trees and had before us a tablecloth set on the sand. Behind and serving as shelter against the sun, was an enormous rock[19]; on the left the ocean and on the right the countryside wherein the waters that flowed at our feet had wound.

This countryside, although burnt by the heat of summer, had a less melancholy appearance than that of Bodega. To the degree that our view extended from the sandy beach, rocky from the sea, they encountered some small oases of greenery becoming less and less rare and indicating that a little bit farther in the interior, following the banks of the Slavianka, one would find lovely forests and plains covered with rich vegetation.

"In effect," Mr. Rotchev said to me seeing me worn out from an already long trail and seeking to revive my courage, "you would do our colony wrong if you judged it based on the sad sample that I have shown you since this morning. Perhaps your poor impressions would be justified if you traveled the shores of the ocean several leagues farther from Ross toward the north where begins a band of broad sterile lands that extend all the way to the mouth of the Columbia. But here, surrounding us at a short distance, are found excellent lands, considered to be among the best in California. This river which murmurs beside us has passed through superb regions covered by the most beautiful vegetation. Its waters have nurtured numerous herds of elk, cattle and even wild horses that our colonists in company with the natives will hunt to tame or to skin."

"These same places that you find with good reason so sad and arid are not always thus. For it is the same in these countries as in the southern provinces of your beautiful France that when the burning heat of summer that dries out the countryside, is followed by the rains of autumn, the land covers itself as if by magic with a magnificent vegetation. Favored by beautiful days that extend in these countries through the last months of the year, this vegetation only succumbs in January, under the frost and are reborn only two months later. Such it is that truly in California and in Southern Oregon the period that separates the two opposed seasons is considered with good reason by all the inhabitants as the most agreeable of the year. It is then that the northwest wind, this tyrant of our maritime regions, gives over to the breezes from the south bringing with them the welcome showers, which help the plants to be reborn in abundance everywhere. In the midst of winter, even, the temperature is ordinarily more humid than cold. And when the south winds have changed the atmosphere, some often very prolonged calms return it to its former serenity."

"And soon," added our obliging guide, "we will arrive on the plains that adjoin Ross. They are better cultivated than those on the shores of which is found the hamlet of Bodega which, lacking flowing water or only drinking water in spite of its port, has seen Fort Ross preferred as headquarters of the colony."

It was thus with a new infusion of courage that I re-mounted my horse to continue our route. And I had need of it because we continued to travel for two dreadful hours along the seaside where I would have been dead from the heat if not for the breeze which had arisen. Always there was this dismal scene of the coast bordered by dunes of sand or by steep cliffs extending a little into the sea where the surf sounded its monotone noise. Or even some small coves at the bottom of which were heaped up old tree trunks, playthings of tempests, on whose broken branches sat immobile, white-headed fishing eagles who doubtless gorged themselves on the carcass of some nearby dead cetacean. Little by little the landscape changed aspect. We passed near a farm[20] which, even though its fields were found partly lying fallow due to the state of exhaustion in which a prolonged use of cultivation had thrown them, they were no less carpeted by a luxuriant grass grazed on by a numerous herd of cattle scattered in the surrounding hillocks. These latter remained night and day despite many risks and entrusted nearly completely to the protection of their instinct and their courage emboldened them, as attacks of bears or wolves were very common in these isolated places. As for horses, they returned each evening to some sort of grassy fields where our servants, after they had herded them together in a large enough number chose those which would replace our worn out horses. The operation was promptly concluded: a lasso adroitly thrown to pull out an animal from the middle of the band and serve to bring the animal destined for the honor of carrying me to where we were. As he showed himself to be a spirited animal, they covered his eyes with a cape. He received the bit, the saddle and his rider then, finally returned to the light, he went at a gallop on the road to Ross, as did simultaneously the new mounts of my companions.

Seeing the ease with which Mr. Rotchev and his men rode their horses, I easily understood that this had become normal to them, habituated as they were to traveling very long journeys, catching nearly wild cattle or even to chase the often fearsome inhabitants of the interior forest. For them, being a pedestrian was no less disagreeable than being an equestrian was for me. Also, while they rather unconvincingly denied their impatience to be so held back on the trail by a poor rider, one or another of them often turned his eyes toward the horizon to seek the end of the already much prolonged journey. And already we had passed a great number of hillocks, one after another with a desolating continuity before us when after two long hours of travel having arrived at the summit of a very high hill, I made out in the distance Fort Ross with its buildings stretched out along the seaside.

This view and several minutes of rest taken in the shade of trees bordering the pretty road that we were following and perhaps a little pride in myself, rallied my diminished strength. I hastened the pace of my mount to the great satisfaction of our group leader and finally, after nine hours on the trail, we arrived well before sunset at our destination.

The mistress of the house, a young and gracious lady with a good figure and distinguished manners, speaking fluent French, gave us the nicest and most eager welcome. Dinner was ready and when we had refreshed ourselves in the lovely little rooms available to new guests, we sat down to table where, in spite of the fatigue of the trip, I found that the time passed all too swiftly. The spirited and informative conversation of Mr. Rotchev, who, as an author himself, was very familiar with the works of our distinguished writers. His comments were enhanced by the charm that his companion spread over our conversation by way of a spirit that was no less sound as colorful and by her genuine and affectionate tone; this all made the hours pass quickly. Poor exiles! We spoke of Europe, of our families, of our hopes of return, happy to enjoy a moment of abandon in which a happy mutual independence allowed us to indulge. Our new acquaintanceship soon became an old relationship. In the end, counting on a busy day on the morrow, I retired early and at dawn I took a walk in the fort and its environs.

As seen from the sea, the establishment grouped at the summit of a steep point of land seemed to me to be rather imposing. But now it lost almost entirely this image. The stockade walls were no more than a series of pointed posts about 4 meters high. The chapel, the houses and the warehouses, seemed to me merely wooden buildings without either style or permanence. But I must also add that it was all perfectly constructed and well-arranged and even had a military appearance enhanced by the field cannons, all ready for action, arranged in the middle of the little parade ground that was surrounded by the buildings of which I have just spoken. Moreover, at the two gates to the fort, some artillery pieces of large caliber aimed to fire outward through narrow embrasures,[21] announced clearly enough to strangers whether friend or foe, that no one should enter without the permission of the governor.

It is true that this defense would only be taken seriously by the natives, to whom the usage of firearms is practically unknown. In effect, these types of fortifications were raised to protect them from Indian attacks such as one in 1817 when the Indians showed themselves very hostile to the new arrivals.[22] In any case, placed as it is at the extremity of a jut of land flanked on three sides by the sea and by deep ravines, the well-defended fort could put up some serious resistance. For the most part, it was only a place of refuge for the colonists employed in cultivation, in case of invasion of the country by some sort of enemy. Also the dwellings of the artisans, their workshops, the warehouses in which the crops were stored, the grist mills and even the principle farm found themselves placed under the protection of the artillery and watched over day and night by the vigilant sentinels.

In consequence, to visit them up close I had to have recourse to the benevolent nature of my host who with the kindest enthusiasm gave me the honors of his government. Mrs. Rotchev, herself renouncing in my favor the stay-at-home habits that had restored a health very worn out by the dark climate of New Archangel where she had lived several years, agreed to leave her very clean and well furnished house at times to go for a walk with me to the neighboring farm where they prepared principally the shipments of butter, eggs, vegetables, cheese, a variety of grains and finally flour for the establishments of the NW coast for which this place could be considered as the farmyard and the kitchen garden.

I saw vast stables filled with superb cows whose milk, carried into a room carefully protected against the turbulent NW winds was there transformed into butter and cheese for the consumption of the households of the principal functionaries at New Archangel or Kamchatka.

I was suddenly on a European farm. I saw barns filled with grains and potatoes, yards filled with fat, healthy pigs, a sheepfold in which the animals seemed to me in good condition and justifying the hope that the governor had in soon deriving of their fleece a new branch of revenue. The hens scratched the pile of manure at the summit of which cocks strutted with an impudent air and with gaudy plumage whereas several paces from there were bands of geese and ducks, gathered around a pond making some deafening cries. Everything, even the momentary disorder caused by carts drawn by yoked cattle coming from the fields or even returning to them, reminded me of sweet recollections of country life, so different from that which I have led for so many months. However, something was lacking in the tableau to give it the life that I would wish for to complete my illusion. I saw men occupied actively in agricultural work as in our countryside: the noise, the movement was in no way missing, but the dairy maids and other maidservants who play such a great role in our lovely French farms were entirely lacking here and their absence, at least as I experienced it, lent a touch of sadness and monotony on the scenes that played out before my eyes.

At Ross, all the colonists were soldiers and vice-versa. They worked at agriculture as one would form a guard or a drill, with the manual at hand. Each hired man received a good salary, bed and board, for a certain number of years at the expiration of which, if he was a good worker and if he consented to contract again, he would be granted a considerable extent of land and of cattle thus obtaining the means to make money either in remaining a worker or an agriculturalist or in forming a small business. Otherwise, he must return to Europe, the Company wishing to have in its possessions only men subject to its authority.

Generally, these hired men stayed in the country and married native women. Russian women were extremely rare in the Russian colonies of the northwest, but they were replaced more and more each year and not without several advantages, I believe, for the community by the most interesting part of the mixed blood race, for nature seems to have treated them very favorably by the double advantage of intelligence and physical grace. I have seen several young girls and women who were very becoming, having agreeable traits of blue eyes, black hair, pretty teeth, small feet, pretty hands and European traits. But I must say that I was obliged to divine all that through a thin layer of slovenliness.

The [Creole] men appeared to me not less advantaged by nature. They are good workers, of a gentle and yet courageous character, dedicated when necessary. They were treated in the same manner as the whites, occupied the same occupations and enjoyed the same favor of the authorities.

Their number was already rather considerable and increased rapidly, but unfortunately, all the individuals of this new race carried in them a germ of phthisis[23] which prevents them from acquiring a great strength and generally leads to an early death, as it happens to many of the Kodiaks, in spite of the care exercised by both the administration and the doctors. It has been claimed that this illness derived not only from the severe climate but even more in the dietary regime in which the colonists in the establishments of the northwest are forcibly compelled to use fresh and salted fish according to the season since it is the only food easy to find. But as the same morbid phenomena are equally found among the mixed bloods born and raised at Ross, where the temperature is always moderate, animal and vegetable food abundant for all the subjects of the Company, one is disposed to search for another cause for this deadly disposition and to attribute it perhaps also to the disgusting uncleanliness in which the majority of them live. Moreover, I was able to confirm it when I strolled by the group of huts around the fort where the workers and the lower ranked government officers lived.

[Laplace digresses on subjects not pertinent to Fort Ross.]

However, the reader will perhaps find in my observations some trace of the influences that affected my point of view, the conversation so interesting and at the same time so instructive of my amiable hosts. But also how happy I was feeling, me a poor exile from a far-off land, constrained to live at sea in a profoundly isolated state, or even in the foreign colonies in the midst of people with whom I could have no intimate relation. So it was something of a gift from Heaven to find myself under an hospitable roof where I could enjoy the happiest moments of my long circumnavigation in the bosom of kind and gentle friends.

Also, I was able to put to use an enthusiasm which sometimes I would have thought approached indiscretion, if Mr. Rotchev had not actually encouraged me in it by his and his gracious companion's inexhaustible kindness. It was thus that with one or the other, or often with both, I visited successively all that Ross and its environs could offer of interest to my curiosity. And from each excursion, I came back loaded with a fine harvest of notes which, upon returning to my room, I put in order before going to bed.[24]

From time to time the strong heat of the sun chased us from the interior of the fort. This was on days when the breeze that usually cooled things failed to come. At such times we went to dine at a cottage situated in the wood near our residence,[25] in the middle of a clearing surrounded on all sides by magnificent conifers. In the shade of these ancient masters of the land, reigned a sweet obscurity and a delicious freshness, even during the worst heat of the day. The ground was not like the intertropical forests, covered with thick shrubs or parasitic plants that form such an impenetrable obstacle that only the Indian hunter and wild animals can enter. Rather it was like a well-kept park. We walked on veritable lawns of turf and our gaze penetrated deeply under the vaults of foliage. Around the house extended a kitchen garden where the preceding governor[26] had planted some of our European fruit trees and vegetables. Neither had prospered whether it was for lack of care or the soil of the forest. The fruits were small and badly formed and the exotic plants seemed to survive only with difficulty against the native plants that attempted to extinguish them.

Being used to finding myself all too often surrounded by wild plant life during my travels, I must say their splendors had greatly lost their attraction in my eyes. The imposing scenes that they presented with such abundance create in the spirit of the observer a grand image of the greatness of the Creator and the weakness of man, but do not speak to the heart and actually cause a sense of spiritual lassitude and boredom by their monotony.

Therefore I accepted with enthusiasm the proposition made by my host [Rotchev] to visit one afternoon before sunset an example of a hamlet that the natives and their families employed in agricultural work, had established in the vicinity of the fort.[27]

Its population was rather considerable and was composed of some several hundred individuals. During this visit and another that I made the next day, I was able to study these singular beings in more detail; although following the counsel of my guide [Rotchev], I only dared to wander among them in his company, so as not to raise their distrust, always dangerous for a stranger.

I understood this precaution in seeing the suspicious looks that followed my least movement, until the governor [Rotchev] having explained to my new hosts the motive of my visit, I distributed to the notables among them some glass trinkets, some little copper ornaments, and some cigars, to all of which both sexes seemed to attach a very high value. From this moment I could move freely in the huts and admit myself thus to the secrets of their interior.

This interior was hardly secluded, it is true, because the habitations of these poor people consisted without exception of miserable huts formed of branches through which the rain and wind passed without difficulty. It was there that all the family, father, mother, and children spent the nights lying pell-mell around the fire, some on cattle hides, the majority on the bare ground, and each one enveloped in a coverlet of wool that served him also as a mantle during the day when the weather was cold or wet.

Such was the costume of the men that all of them who surrounded me seemed to me nearly nude, except the chief and several young men who, only due to the presence of the governor for whom they showed profound respect, had decided to wear European shirt and pants. I was disappointed. I would have much preferred to see them in their native ceremonial costume, more picturesque, more in harmony with their martial spirit and their truly dignified air, which I was later able to verify when this same chief who welcomed me at his house came to visit me the next day.

Although taken by surprise by the visit, these men seemed to me handsome, tall, robust, and perfectly well-built. Their smouldering black eyes, an aquiline nose rising to a high forehead, rounded cheekbones, and strong lips showing white, well-spaced teeth, symmetrically traced tattooing on their copper skin, a vigorous neck supported by large shoulders; in all, an air at once intelligent and dignified, all reminded me perfectly of the descriptions made by [Captain James] Cook and our Lapérouse,[28] of the indigenous natives of the northwest coast of America, of which they were, if not the first, the most distinguished explorers.

In vain I sought to discover among the females some analogous advantages. I found all the women horribly ugly, having a stupid air, glum, their health broken by misery and hard work. If some young woman showed in her figure or in the features of her face some vestiges of the charms that in the bosom of civilized societies the women are so generously endowed by nature, they were so dirty, the hide or wool skirt that composed nearly their only garment was so filthy, their hair was so disheveled, that they could only inspire pity and disgust.

The majority were busy with the housekeeping, preparing meals for their husbands and children. Some were spreading out on the embers some pieces of beef given as rations, or shell-fish, or even fish which these unhappy creatures came to catch either at the nearby river [Fort Ross Creek?] or from the sea; while the others heated the [wheat] grain in a willow basket before grinding it between two stones. In the middle of this basket they shook constantly some live coals on which each grain passed rapidly by an ever more accelerated rotating movement until they were soon parched, without letting the inner side of the basket be burned by the fire. Some of these baskets [*paniers*], or more accurately, these deep baskets [*vases*] seemed to me true models of basketmaking, not only by their decoration but by the finishing touches of the work.[29] They are made of shoots of straw or compact gorse so solidly held together by the thread [sic, coiling] that the fabric was water resistant, as efficiently as baked clay and earthenware. But, more behind in material civilization than the Kaloches,[30] my savages [at Fort Ross] did not know how to construct wooden bowls in which the Indian housekeepers of the northwest came to boil liquids by immersing some stones red-hot from the fire.

Mr. Rotchev, noting my astonishment that contact with his compatriots had not modified more the ways and habits of the natives assured me that these people, just like their counterparts in New Archangel [Sitka], obstinately refused to exchange their customs for ours.

"However," he added, "thanks to a great deal of perseverance and enticements, I have succeeded somewhat in diminishing this adverse sentiment to whites among the natives of the tribes that frequent Bodega Bay; several chiefs and a good number of young people, encouraged by the bounty and generosity with which they were treated by the Russian agents, and finding, with reason, horribly miserable the life which they led during the winter in the woods where they had no other protection against the cold and the snow than the caves or the shelter of trees, and no other means of subsistence than the unreliable products of the hunt, remain near the fort during the bad season, working with our colonists and are nourished like them. So, one sees their tastes change more each day to the varied articles of adornment, dress and other things that are used to pay for the services that they provide to the colony. Thus one could hope that if the company retains this establishment (Note 2[31]) for long enough, the natives will be led little by little to submit to the yoke of civilization. Seeing their labors generously paid for, their freedom and religious beliefs, absurd as they are, respected; the most indulgent principle of justice exercised to the point that deportation to one of our other establishments is the most severe punishment that I may inflict on those among them who have committed the worst derelictions against our properties. Seeing, I say, the interest that the public functionaries take in their well-being, they return each spring in larger number than the year before, to cultivate our fields and attach themselves to us, to the degree that in their desire to remain always in good stead with the colonists, they are generally the first to denounce the troublemakers who, for vengeance or by love of disorder, kill the beasts in the fields or even destroy our crops.

"But," continued my helpful guide, "I have not yet been able to make these children of nature understand the value of foresight and the desirability of property. They are all, men and women alike, passionate for self-adornment. They seek with eagerness that which satisfies this taste and ask for it in preference to all else. Hardly have they obtained it, than they cover themselves with necklaces, pants, shirts, vests, and consider themselves in this ridiculous attire as being very attractive, the happiest people on earth. But the next day one encounters them as bereft of the ornaments and clothing as they were the day before. It is even common that the tribe to which they belong, and to which each member has been not less generously paid, are found, when they return to Ross toward the end of the bad season, as poor, as denuded of everything with which they were well provided a few months before."

What has become of this considerable quantity of varied merchandise which they had in their possession? We don't know yet. Were they sold, given to their compatriots who live in the forest all year? This is not likely. One is struck with the realization that giving in to the passion for games, which among these poor natives is pushed to a point unknown, perhaps, to the peoples of the Old World, they have seen their riches pass to the hands of players cleverer or more lucky than they. This supposition is even more admissible that, among themselves, people of the same tribe take advantage of one another. At every moment of the day, when they have something to lose, one sees them grouped four by four, squatting down on the ground, surrounded by numerous spectators awaiting impatiently the moment when it is their turn to take part. They play a sort of game which is hardly more complicated than "double or nothing," so common among our school children; but to which they have come to give a wholly greater importance by the singularly animated pantomimes to which the action is accompanied among them. In his hands, the playing partner holds two sticks, and while in the presence of his two adversaries whose carefully watching eyes follow with rapt attention his least movements, he separates the two sticks, or even rejoins them in one single hand; his associate, sitting beside him, seeks to distract the attention of his opponent by his cries, gambits, leaps, and contortions. If two times in three this person succeeds in saying, at a given moment, how many sticks the player has in the right hand, the stakes belong to him; in the contrary case, it is entirely lost.

So that this description would have some interest to the reader, it would be necessary for me to render all the vivid and lively [sudden] emotions which can be seen on the mobile features of these children of nature; the cries, the gesticulations, the laughter of those who won. Or, the cold impassive air of those who, losing often in a single stroke the fruit of many months of work, became again poorer than they had been before.

In every case they suffer the bad fortune with a philosophy, or to be more accurate, a dignified indifference worthy of the ancient stoics; and this native who came to the game bedecked with glass trinkets, or other ornaments, from head to foot, who had found means in order to make himself more attractive to cover himself with four or five shirts, as well as pants and vests superimposed one over the other, returned to his hut "gay as a finch and naked as a worm [happy as a lark]."

Such a carefree nature of character, inborn among those inhabitants of the northwest is necessary, one must admit, to let them endure the miseries without number, the cruel privations, unhappy consequences of their nomadic life, of perpetual wars among tribes, the frequent shortages to which they are often condemned by the absence of game, the destruction of roots by rains or by prolonged droughts, and, above all, the fatal consequences of epidemic maladies that since the beginning of the century have killed off half, at least, of the native populations of Russian-America and Oregon, as well as of the surrounding lands.

For intestinal or chest pains, caused by the variations of temperature, so sudden in these countries and so dangerous for the poor people who, condemned to wander in the forest in quest of their food have, for the most part, neither roof for shelter nor clothing to cover themselves, have come to be added since the arrival of the Europeans, other scourges of the same kind, which, just as in the civilized countries, terrify the people. I speak of smallpox, measles, and finally of the terrible cholera which, moving from east to west through the wilderness of the new world, has come to spread mourning among the native tribes of the northwest, taking away victims by the thousands. However, these fearsome enemies of the human species are perhaps not the cruelest illnesses to which the American Indians find themselves exposed because at least they only make their appearances in epochs often spread apart from one another; whereas the syphilis carries on. It spreads its ravages without respite in a shocking manner, to the heart of this primitive society where the laws of instinct are the only ones practiced as custom. So the majority of individuals of each sex, from puberty to old age, are affected by this horrible evil whose ravages are beyond their weak knowledge of medicine, decimate them cruelly and spread the sources of its generation among many of those who escaped death.

In order to survive they have recourse to their ordinary remedy, which with the use of several simple things gathered in the woods, composes all their means of curing. This remedy is the sweat bath of which the Red Skins in this part of America have made habitual use since time immemorial.

Down in a circular hole, dug into the soil, and being about five meters in diameter and a quarter of this measure in depth, is placed a roof of a flattened, conical form, constructed of branches covered with sod, such that the air could not pass through. In this type of sweating room, into the interior of which one can only enter by a very narrow opening, of which the entry is severely forbidden to women, are assembled, sitting on rocks ranged around an enormous hearth, the bathers, among whom the last arriving is careful to close with a flat rock or a plank, the single entrance so that in a moment the air rises to a very high temperature. The consequence of this excessive heat is, of course, an abundant perspiration among the patients, who after having been submitted to this ordeal during a fairly long space of time, according to their taste, return to the fresh air, scrape the body streaming with sweat with little wooden sticks, then go about their ordinary occupations as if nothing had happened.

Further to the northwest the natives also, in leaving these sweat houses, plunge in the freezing, often icy, water without suffering anything detrimental to their health. The women themselves, a little after they have become mothers, undergo similar immersions, always immediately preceded by abundant sweating, gained by means of the heat given off by a rock heated for this purpose on which the poor mother sits while being covered by thick furs.

What else happens in the obscurity of these foul bath houses from which women are excluded? There are some things it is said which recall the depraved tastes that still sully the memory of the brilliant Athenians. What a unique comparison, and even more similar, when I add that in each tribe of these savages no less ferocious, not less brutal than the wild beasts of their woods and obliged like them to wander ceaselessly in the plains or the forests to find their food and living under a hard climate, there were a certain number of young men serving for the pleasure of their fellow citizens who, considering them like the other sex, heap presents on them and take pleasure in adorning them. My guide [Rotchev], perfectly familiar with the habits of the men that we visited, pointed out to me several of these young people which I could have believed the most beautiful girls of the village if they had not been completely nude. They were then in the midst of the "squaws" with whom, moreover, they live constantly, sharing their work without these latter appearing to find it distasteful. Moreover, the gentle sex is not mistreated among the natives of Russian America or of the neighboring lands toward the south. The women even exercise, as they say, a notable influence in the community; young women, one seeks them for their charms; old women, one fears them as sorceresses. These abominable customs are found principally among the redskins who live in the high latitudes, in the vicinity of New Archangel [Sitka] and are considered by some noted travelers as truly superior, by all reports, to the natives of Oregon and California; to the point that one comes to believe that they are not of the same race.

[Laplace here goes on for several pages with comments about native peoples of Alaska and the Pacific Islands which add nothing to the present narrative.]

I had a number of reflections of this sort [e.g., thinking of Tlingit or Hawaiian chiefs] in contemplating the chief of the village whom I had seen the evening before and who had come to pay me a formal visit. I found him seated on a rock in the courtyard of the fort,[32] surrounded by several of his men, all warriors like him. Such was made sufficiently clear by the tattoos which ornamented their faces, also by irregular scars of various wounds, of which the healing had been abandoned, by all appearances, to the care of Nature.

I was really struck by the dignified air of my new acquaintance in his grand costume. A large mantle of tree bark decorated with brilliantly colored feathers, little shells or mother-of-pearl [abalone?] ingeniously interspersed, was draped majestically on his shoulders, and showed the bizarre but regular designs that covered his large chest and muscular arms. Around his neck were several necklaces of small glass red or black beads; and in his hair, done up and attached on the top of his head, were placed some carefully carved wooden pins, crowned by a cluster of black feathers similar to those which adorned his temples, and blended nicely with a mass of copper ear pendants, colored pebbles [magnesite?], and even of animal teeth. There was, in the commanding apprearance, the attitude of this chief, something noble and imposing. The large proportions of his body, one would have said a statue since he held himself immobile, his proud air, the impassive look of his physiognomy reminded me of the picturesque descriptions that [James Fenimore] Cooper gave his prairie Indians.

[A two-paragraph digression about the heroes of Homer is left out here.]

My new friend and his companions did not make a great production of conversation. They remained fully in their official role. However, when the presents appeared that I intended to give them, these faces, up till now so cold, so aloof, switched then and there; my tobacco, my glass trinkets, my copper baubles, produced a marvelous effect; and the ferocious warriors became true children, the less formidable since they were without arms in consequence of the wise measures taken by the governor, intending to avoid disorder. Otherwise, one encounters them rarely with their bows and arrows, unless they come from inland and even then they are anxious to carefully withdraw them from the view of whites as if they feared that an evil spell cast on them [the arrows] will render them useless in their hands.

This superstition is especially odd since they use these feathered darts [arrows] with a marvelous skill, and can hit the smallest four-footed animals at enormous distances. Skillful hunters, intrepid and indefatigable, they down the great black bear [grizzly?] this forest tyrant of the Oregon territory, so feared even among the natives, so strong and terrible is he, with hardly less ease than the timid reindeer and the deer in flight. They attack the ferocious animal when it has seized a cow or a horse and carries it in his forepaws across the marshes and cliffs; or even if chased, he would jump over some torrent on a fallen tree trunk across a stream. Often the bloody beast, wounded or pursued too close, runs at his enemy then the struggle becomes terrible and would finish in a fatal manner for the latter [man], if he was not almost always in a group.

To catch the timid creatures of the woods which, ever on the watch, flee with the speed of lightning at the least appearance of danger, these same hunters utilize a subterfuge which is nearly always successful.

One among them, disguised in the skin of a deer, horns on the head and the hide on his back, moves toward the poor beasts grazing peacefully on the plain, until he finds himself near enough to that which he wishes to make his first prey, to be able to shoot it with a killing arrow. A second is taken the same way, then a third, and the massacre continues thus here and there until the rest of the herd, finally taking alarm, disperses afar in the high grass or nearby woods. Such an endeavor is extremely tiring, often dangerous, still it is important to the survival of the Indians that they are so keen on it [hunting], because otherwise, inclined toward sloth as they are, they would often be seen to die of hunger due to lack of foresight or industry. It [i.e., death] only comes too soon for many of them.

Some among these savages, when hunger does not push them, spend entire days seated on a rock, head inclined on the chest, plunged in a sort of half-sleep, and they can endure a very limited diet over a long period. But as soon as he finds a good occasion to satisfy his appetite, just like a wolf and the majority of other carnivorous animals, he will gorge himself nearly to bursting with unbelievable quantities of meat.

I have heard it stated that these people had two stomach properties, both valuable, in the custom widespread among many of them of not only mixing their foods, but also of chewing without ceasing like they would tobacco, a species of seaweed that, dried in the sun or on the fire, developed a very pronounced salty taste, which is at the same time gently binding and extremely tonic, as necessary. However, this antidote against the effects of abstinence or gluttony does not combat the effects of drunkenness to which these natives are very inclined. Happily, the Russians save them from the consequences of their passion for rum by measures, as wise as they are severe, against the importation of strong liquors, because otherwise the tribes of Russian-America would have already disappeared, as has happened to those who, before the arrival of the Europeans, lived on the opposite shore [East Coast] of the New World.

For me who leads such a delightful and busy life according to my whims, the visit went very rapidly; and I could see with deep regret the moment approach when I must leave forever the hosts who had provided me with such happy moments. However, the day of departure for the *Artémise* that I had set so irrevocably had come. The topmast that had broken on our entry into Bodega Bay had been replaced without much expense by a superb tree that had been cut near the fort and carried to the ship aboard a large baidara.

The frigate was now completely ready to put back to sea and its crew was perfectly rested. It was necessary to leave. I therefore shut my ears and heart to the requests by Mme. Rotchev and her husband that I prolong my stay under their roof, and the 18th of August, at daybreak, after having received the goodbyes of the charming mistress of the house, we mounted our horses accompanied by her husband. He wished to show me himself the two principal agricultural settlements of the colony and to accompany me to our destination. The weather was fine with the freshness of the night before still upon us. We traveled rapidly and soon we had lost sight of the fort, the belfry of the chapel and the two windmills.[33] Several hours later we passed the Slavianka at the same spot where we had previously crossed. I saw again, neither more prompt nor less sleepy than the previous time, the Indian charged with steering the ferry. Lying totally nude in the shade of a rock near his rude hut, he got up without breathing a word, without even looking at us and took the caravan to the other side of the river and a moment later I saw him resume his former position. The diminution of hair that covered his head since our last encounter struck me; so much the more since his former enormous head of hair had been replaced by a sort of irregular tonsure similar to a dry turf over which fire had passed. Astonished by the remarkable change in the poor man's appearance that gave him an extraordinary look, I asked for an explanation from my traveling companion. I laughed heartily on learning that the Indian had followed his peoples' custom that when the vermin had become too numerous in his hair he took a burning stick and using all precautions to protect against burning himself, he rid himself of his mop and of the numerous creatures that had taken up residence therein.

At eleven o'clock, our worn out mounts were replaced at a rancho,[34] a name that the Spaniards give to farms solely devoted to keeping cattle and horses; and where, among the latter animals [horses] that are found here in the hundreds, our servants chose the best using the redoubtable lasso. As soon as the new arrivals had their harness removed and had been let free, they ran to rejoin their comrades in the nearby pasture.

These ranchos, usually situated at enormous distances from one another and belonging to individuals, are, for travelers, true way stations thanks to which they can travel great distances with a wonderful rapidity and they often make up to 40 leagues between sunrise and sunset, only stopping to change horses. A most notable thing occurred. These poor beasts that had just finished their grueling job, having only just been freed, went back on their own on the trail on which they had just galloped in, and in spite of their being weary in a few hours will have returned home to their own stable. Travelling nearly always freely by night as by day, these fine animals can take the weariness and privations with an extraordinary energy. They are generally of good size, very well proportioned and the beauty of their black eyes, the fine qualities of their legs and the elegance of their bodies attests to their Andalusian origins. Mounted on their backs, the vaqueros or guardians of the herds appear to be veritable centaurs; neither rocks nor rapid descents, nor the roughest terrain, nor even the deepest darkness stop them in their always speedy course; and even so, they seldom falter since their mounts show the greatest intelligence and vigor and are sure-footed. These men live, one could say, on horseback. For them, walking is unthinkable and they consider it to be at best a shameful necessity. So, they deeply disdain poor riders and except for my excuse (in their eyes) of being a sailor or even better the good example provided by the commandant [Rotchev], I truly believe that those who accompanied us would have mocked the captain of the *Artémise* when certain bruises forced him to travel slowly, and they would have gladly left him on the trail.

At this rancho we left the route that we had taken in coming [from Bodega to Fort Ross] and our guide directed us toward the interior of the country instead of following the seashore. At first we crossed a zone of waste-land strewn with pebbles and brambles, then some hills completely treeless and covered with a tall grass in tufts, but faded by the dry weather. Finally, we attained the shelter of the edge of the shady forest wherein I found it much more comfortable to ride, for the sun had burned me, in particular when we traveled through the valleys because at least when we traveled on the ridges the northwest breeze that blew strongly enough to concentrate the fog in the ravines, helped freshen the air.

We had only traveled a short while on a pretty trail that wound through the woods than we were treated to a delightful lunch served on the turf protected by beautiful trees, thanks to the care of the servants who had been instructed by our gracious hostess that morning. Nothing was left out and in the glow of this kind attention, I found myself after an hour of very agreeable rest ready to continue the journey. This time, the countryside through which we passed was truly charming. The route passed through massive stands of pines, oaks, and chestnuts[35] or even through lovely clear-ings of green turf cut through by little streams.

Charming vistas offered themselves to me at each step under the green vaults formed by thousands of giant pines [redwoods]. My helpful guide, even while pointing out to me the beauty of the Californian vegetation, explained to me the diverse characteristics of these magnificent trees. "These, said he in pointing out pines whose straight trunk was quite devoid of knots [i.e., lower branches] and seemed to come spontaneously from the earth to reach into the clouds, "furnish simultaneously excellent mast[36] and some seeds having the fine taste and high nutritive value of chestnuts,[37] are very much sought after by the natives. The others, which are admirable in their enormous proportions, however, are not so useful. They do not give fruit, their wood is too brittle and rots too easily to be useful for constructing ships or buildings. It is the same with the trees whose leaves are of a deep rich color and the knotty trunk reminds you of the oak and chestnut of France. However, they are only resemblances, for their fibers are spongy and offer no guarantee of strength nor endurance.

"The majority of this immense vegetation that appears to crush the soil with their weight, are abandoned," continued Mr. Rotchev, "for reasons analogous to those I have just given you, and with the exception of several wild gooseberry, strawberry or raspberry species, found here and there at the edges of this forest, we find hardly any edible indigenous fruits in these lands even though the climate is similar to that of Provence or of Italy and the soil shows itself to be fertile so that all the European fruit trees, cereals and vegetables can establish themselves here easily. So that the time is probably not far off," said my guide in finishing, "where the unlived-in places that we are now traveling through will be animated by the breath of civilization; where these forest giants will disappear by the effects of the axe and fire. One should remember then that it was the Russians who as the first ones here commenced the great work of the white race on this far shore of the North Pacific Ocean."

In truth, I had already noted the indications of the work of man in the cut-down trees, the great expanses of burnt grasslands and roads cut into the land. Soon thereafter, in the middle of a narrow plain that was protected by the heavily wooded hills from the northwest winds we saw the pretty little wooden houses surrounded by orchards and vegetable gardens in full growth. It was one of the farms[38] created two years before by Mr. Rotchev with the purpose of furnishing the fruit and vegetables of these temperate lands to his compatriots residing in New Archangel.

Until now, only these two latter products had succeeded there because the district was favorable for growing them in terms of its soil and, perhaps also due to the great efforts that had to be made to rid the land of the multitude of huge trees that cover it, and which I saw here and there on the land the extended skeletons lying in the middle of the plantations. One among them that the supervisor of this agricultural establishment[39] pointed out to me was four meters in diameter at the base and 60 meters high. So, although men had been working hard for more than a week to reduce it to planks and timbers it was hardly this type of red pine [redwood] which, as I have said before, splits so easily with an axe. The remains of this colossus of the northern forests served to complete the construction of several homes occupied by the director[40] and his ten Russian colonists employed as workers or gardeners on the farm. All of them, and especially that of the director, had a gracious appearance with their roofs of red tiles,[41] their exteriors painted gray so as to protect them from the destructive effects of the sun and rain, and windows trimmed with pretty green blinds [shutters?]. They are surrounded by thickets or beds of flowers. There, it is true, ends their resemblance to the pretty country houses that one sees grouped around our larger French cities. For the interior of this type of cottage is without exception void of comfortable furniture and ornaments. Of course, it is true to say that all furnishings are very costly, if not impossible to obtain at Bodega Bay where foreign merchant vessels never land.

In any case, on noticing several feminine faces that seemed, by modesty or coquetry, to try to avoid our looks, I had to say that even if the furniture was rare in the houses, the pretty faces were not lacking. I must say, in truth, the Indian women were not particularly seductive in their careless dress. However, the young lady that served us refreshments in the salon of the director, and for whose dress he had probably spent some money, did not seem too bad to me. Her hair was nicely done up and carefully pulled back behind the head. Her features seemed very pleasing to me. Her gaze and her physiognomy expressed gaiety and contentment. Let us also mention that her white blouse, tied at the waist and her perfectly clean cotton dress allowed me to guess at charms that hard work and misery had not yet tarnished. If I add to this image a gentle and lively look, pretty teeth, a svelte stature, small hands, a well turned leg and graceful feet and ankles, the reader will think as I did, I am convinced, that the native women of California and Oregon, when they have been cleaned up a bit, are not as worthy of disdain as is generally thought.

This oasis of agriculture, these fields where I recognized our European garden plants, our fruit trees in full growth, hidden, so to speak, in these ancient forests, had a certain picturesque quality that I could not quite define. These cherries, plums, and pears, so frail and delicate with their new leaves of a soft green seemed to beg the protection of these superb pines with their dark and severe foliage, against the intemperate harshness of a climate that was strange to them. This contrast of virgin nature, so imposing in its works, with the civilized nature of which all works are truly marked by not only the intelligence and industry of man, but also of his flaws and of the instability of his wishes, inspired in me a noble sense of the force of the spirit, of the courage of the first emigrants who had dared to begin the clearing in the midst of the great trees of the New World, where they found themselves battling simultaneously a very entrenched native vegetation, fierce Indians, and animals that were both dangerous and malevolent.

Happily, up to now Mr. Rotchev in his efforts to make his plantations prosper had encountered only the inconveniences inherent in the climate and localities. In summer there were frequent droughts, fogs and strong winds. In winter came tornadoes and heavy rains. Moreover, in all seasons there were the problems of a lack of flowing water necessary for irrigation as well as the forests whose thick foliage blocked the flow of air that purifies the atmosphere and promotes the growth of vegetation.

As noted above, thanks to the sage measures taken by the authorities, the indigenous people, rather than standing in the way of the development of raising crops, as had been feared, instead aided greatly to make them prosper. In effect, I saw a goodly number of workers who were resting in the shade of trees awaiting the hour to begin working again. The director greatly praised their gentleness as well as their aptitude to complete the tasks to which they were assigned and even the women and children pitched in happily to help accomplish the work. All of them lived in complete harmony with the Europeans who, for their part, in taking the native daughters as their companions, daily formed ever more amicable relations with them. So, year after year, the number of families who traditionally left the colony at the beginning of winter to return to the forests only in the following productive season, decreased.

The farms had not yet been much troubled by wild animals, these redoubtable enemies of the new plantations in America, although they were numerous in the plains and the surrounding woods where they probably found their nourishment very easily.

Bears, wolves, foxes, mountain lions and many other species of beasts of prey commonly found in the countryside, had not yet attacked the herds of domesticated animals, the sheepfolds, nor the poultry yards, and contented themselves with devouring the dead animals at the risk of being poisoned. The colonists are accustomed to leaving carrion around their houses after having completely tainted it with the sap of an herb deadly to carnivores and which comes from Mexico where they also use it greatly to this same end.

Elk and deer frequented the surroundings of the agricultural settlement that we visited, often in numerous bands. But such is the natural timidity and suspiciousness of these poor beasts whose tranquillity is so often disturbed by predators that, frightened no doubt by the hunters' rifles, they dared not yet to cross the barriers that surrounded the cleared lands. But if, by mishap, one among them, braver than the others, came to nibble the lettuces and peas, or some wolf, wildcat [chat-tigre?] or fox should taste some fowl or sheep destined for the banquet of the authorities in New Archangel, for sure the quietude that appears to be enjoyed in this peaceful coexistence by the director of the farm would be soon troubled nightly by the visits of his tasty neighbors.

Our visit ended, our observations made and having taken some refreshments, we remounted our horses to travel across the quiet grasslands and the woods, where the sound of our voices resonated afar. It was thus that we came at last, after several hours en route, to the second farm that we were to see, but not before we had stopped a moment by a little river on the banks of which my traveling companion pointed out to me the former habitations of beaver, probably destroyed by the Indians in order to catch the rich prize that lay within.

To accomplish this, Rotchev told me, they had to choose the moment when the river was covered with ice.[42] Then they barricaded the water a little above and below the lodge of the poor animals they sought to kill. The beavers were frightened by the noise made by the hunters striking the ice, not only to break it, but also to scare the animals and push them to the shore. The beaver came and went under the water so the bubbling at the openings of the holes betrayed their least movements, then finished by crouching at the end of their burrows. It was there that the hunters awaited them, they carefully closed up these entrances and set up women and children to demolish the homes of the poor animals which soon were dragged from their hiding place by a pitiless hand often armed with an iron hook, when they gave up both their fur and their meat to their torturers. At other times, the beaver were taken using steel traps, lured by the scent taken from the females and with which the voyageurs bait these devices that are furnished them by the foreign contractors.[43] Thus a huge quantity of these inoffensive quadrupeds have been destroyed since the beginning of the 19th century, above all during the epoch when the English and their American rivals invaded Oregon and California.[44] At this time 30 and even 40 thousand beaver skins were taken yearly for export. Today the Hudson's Bay and New York Companies barely catch a few thousand. It is a branch of commerce that has nearly died out.

The farm at which we arrived[45] did not resemble at all the one we had just left. There was no more woodland, no more picturesque irregularities of land, only vast fields of wheat where they had begun the harvest. There were no fruit trees, no flowers, nor were there any vegetable gardens. There were a few well-constructed wooden houses, but with a sad and isolated aspect. However, here also were found numbers of Russian colonists and of natives employed in agriculture. They were all away at the harvest and had taken with them the women and children, for I saw not a single person in the lodgings.

The sheaves that the carts carried to the granaries seemed to me to be rather meager. The grains were small, round, hard and many were found to be spoiled by rust which often seemed to attack the harvest and had diminished this one by a good third since they were unable to protect it. Beyond that, on seeing things up close it was easy to understand that the colonists were more gardeners than agriculturalists, even if they had worked in this capacity in their own country. But is it not always thus? My traveling companion assured me that the ground was too dry for this kind of production, they only got a 12 for 1 return on their plantings whereas further south in the center of California, they obtained three or four times more. The fact was that the soil seemed bleached out, chalky, and dried out by the sun.

I had been on horseback since morning. We had covered fourteen leagues [36 miles] over rather difficult trails. I had never in my life gone so far on horseback; so I could barely keep to my saddle. Thus since there was still a long road to Bodega Bay, I found myself very happy to exchange my mount for a type of *"tapecu"*[46] called in Russian "droschki," I believe, which deposited my body, bruised by the jolting over the rocks of the coast to the spot on the shore where my ship's boat awaited me. I said my good-byes to the kind and helpful Mr. Rotchev and soon after found myself, not without a deep pleasure, in the midst of my traveling companions and in a comfortable apartment.

The frigate was ready to put to sea. Its officers and crew, who had happily used the time at anchor to hunt, fish or to walk about the countryside, and for whom the good food was such an agreeable improvement, thanks both to the generosity of the governor [Rotchev] for both meat and vegetables, as well as to the nearby fish-filled lake. Everyone enjoyed good health and showed themselves perfectly disposed to pursue the course of our maritime peregrinations whose end was now in sight. So, the next day, August 20, at 11 a.m. when the morning calm gave way to the usual northwest afternoon breeze, the two Kodiak pilots that I had borrowed from Mr. Rotchev arrived, and we were under sail in an instant. I then directed the ship toward San Francisco which is only about 40 leagues from Bodega Bay.

This precaution against the risks of local navigation whose difficulties had shown themselves to me only a short time before, proved fortuitous. Hardly had we left the anchorage when a thick fog hid from us any view of the coast and continued thus in greater or lesser intensity. During this time we were the plaything of the rapid and changing currents. The second day, at noon, it cleared up, whereupon, thanks to our pilots and their amazing facility at seeing through the mist, we happily passed the rocky islands called the Farallones and entered finally into the magnificent bay [San Francisco] that we needed to visit next.

Source: Laplace 2006. Reprinted by permission of the Fort Ross Interpretive Association.

EUGENE DUFLOT DE MOFRAS'S TRAVELS
ON THE PACIFIC COAST (1841)

Eugene Duflot de Mofras was a French diplomat who had spent time in Mexico before traveling north to California. He came to California in 1841 aboard the *Nymph,* commanded by Henry Delano Fitch, and then traveled up to Monterey, where he arrived on May 6, 1841, after which he traveled farther north to visit Fort Ross. The word was out that the Russians were leaving California and were offering Fort Ross to various parties including the Hudson's Bay Company, the Mexican government, and John Sutter, and De Mofras considered trying to obtain the site for the French but due to that government's lack of interest was ultimately unable to arrange the purchase, which soon after went to Sutter. Like his compatriot Laplace, de Mofras was easily able to converse with Fort Ross's commander, Alexander Rotchev, who spoke French. In his visit to California, de Mofras was very much acting as an intelligence agent for France, attempting to collect background information on both people and events that might influence French diplomacy relative to the province of California. Like many other observers, he didn't always get all of his facts straight, and so the reader must be judicious in how much credence to give his commentary.

The following document hints at how Europeans, Americans, and Mexicans were all vying for influence during this period; the sale of Fort Ross provides an interesting view into this melee, although it's obvious from his writing that de Mofras is heavily biased and his words should be taken with a grain of salt. For further discussion of the sale of Fort Ross, especially from Russians' perspectives, see the next section of this collection.

De Mofras saw Fort Ross in its last months prior to the departure of Alexander Rotchev and the other employees of the Russian American Company from the fort down to the area of Bodega Bay to await their departure for Sitka/ New Archangel. In his book on travels on the Pacific coast, de Mofras includes some important maps of the territory between Bodega Bay and Fort Ross that detailed locations of the Russian ranchos and the trails that linked them. He also identifies several *"vigies,"* or lookouts, along the coast that presumably were used for sighting vessels and possibly for passing messages up and down the shore. His is the only mention I have come across that would shed light on how quickly word could get up to Fort Ross about the arrival of a ship at Bodega Bay.

In 1836[47] Admiral Baron de Wrangell, en route from Sitka, stopped for a time at Fort Ross before returning to Europe by way of Mexico. Apparently he was not fully aware of the many advantages to be derived by the Company and the Russian government from this settlement, for upon his arrival at St. Petersburg, he proposed to abandon it. Nevertheless, it was not until the end of 1840 that M. d'Etolin, ship's captain and acting governor-general, ordered M. de Rotchev to offer for sale to the Mexican government the livestock, farms, houses, and forts, in other words, the entire settlement and, in case of a refusal, to find another customer and abandon it after the transaction had been completed, burning whatever had not been included in the purchase.

The governor of Ross, M. de Rotchev, wrote officially on this subject to Don Juan Alvarado, governor of California at Monterey, and the latter transmitted the offer to sell to the central government at Mexico, which replied that their treasury had no funds and to take what the Russians should decide to leave. This reply was received at Monterey in March, 1841; I reached there on May 6, and after ascertaining the status of affairs went on to Bodega and Ross. The governor, M. de Rotchev and M. de Kostromitinov, intendant general of Russian-American colonies, who arrived soon after from Sitka, as well as all the Russian officers, received me in the most amicable manner and urged me to come to New Archangel aboard the sloop *Hélène,* promising to provide a steamer to take me to the English settlements along the Columbia River. These officers, it was said, had received word of a close alliance between France and Russia against England, and this undoubtedly contributed to the hearty welcome accorded me. They feared to see their establishments fall into the hands of the English concern, the Hudson's Bay Company, a dangerous rival of the Imperial Russian Company, for there was no other concern in California able to make so advantageous an offer.

M. de Rotchev asked me repeatedly to take over Ross on behalf of the French government, but I invariably replied that I had received no orders or instructions of any kind to this effect. M. de Kostromitinov added his pleas to those of M. de Rotchev, indicating that they preferred to see these establishments under the protection of the French flag rather than that of England or America. I believed it was my duty to point out to these gentlemen that it would be advantageous for Russia to retain a port on the Pacific Ocean, and to conceal from them my fear that their attitude might be censored at St. Petersburg. They yielded to my arguments and immediately dispatched the brig *Constantin* to Sitka to request further instructions from the governor-general M. d'Etolin. The latter sent the ship back with formal orders to abandon the port. Later I learned the true cause of this act: The Russian officers had confined themselves to saying that the company was losing ten thousand piasters annually in California and that new arrangements had been made with agents of the Hudson's Bay Company on the Columbia.

The only purchaser who appeared, but who failed to offer adequate guarantee, was Señor Vallejo, military commander of California who had become a neighbor of the Russians through pillaging Mission San Francisco Solano for his personal benefit. He had the support of his brother-in-law, a United States citizen, Mr. Leese, who was a merchant located at the anchorage of Yerba Buena at San Francisco. The Russians, furthermore, dislike dealing with Vallejo and so made some indirect overtures—which I urged them to continue—to Captain Sutter who was engaged at the time in founding the colony of New Helvetia on the left [right] bank of the Sacramento River about twenty-five leagues from the end of the Bay of San Francisco and thirty leagues east of the Russian farms. M. Sutter, although born in Switzerland, poses as a Frenchman inasmuch as he served for twelve years in our former royal guard. In fact, he always declared in California that he considered himself under the protection of France.[48] Reaching California in 1839, he received from Governor Alvarado a grant of eleven square leagues along the Sacramento and now owns an establishment that is increasing daily and gives promise of becoming extremely important.

Early in September I went to see M. Sutter in person and after spending several days with him and after he had asked my advice on the Russian proposal, I persuaded him to accept it. Furthermore, as I was going down the river [the Sacramento] on September 8, I met M. de Rotchev who was on his way to New Helvetia. These gentlemen went together to Ross where the purchase was concluded after a detailed inventory of all effects contained in these establishments had been completed. I shall give below a copy of this document and the terms of the sale.

When I reached Ross on May 23, the Russian establishments were flourishing. The number of colonists had increased to at least seven hundred persons [ed: this number is twice as large as any other recorded figure for the population of Fort Ross and is probably inaccurate], among whom were three hundred Europeans, the rest being Russian-Asiatics, Kodiaks, and half-breeds.

The Russians also employ a relatively large number of Californian Indians from tribes living along the coast and in the interior of the country. After the sale had been consummated, the sloop *Hélène* left [ed: for] Sitka carrying four hundred colonists. Mm. [ed: Messieurs] de Rotchev and Kostromitinov remained to complete delivery of the properties, finally sailing on December 30, 1841 [ed: other accounts say January 1, 1842], on the brig *Constantin* that carried the remainder of the colonists. The nineteenth of the same month M. Kostromitinov had written officially to Monterey to Governor Don Juan Alvarado apprising him of the sale made to M. Sutter, advising him at the same time of the text of Article IX of their contract, which read as follows:

"Since M. Sutter might be prevented from making payment in the event that death overtook him, and his heirs might be unwilling to acknowledge his debt, and since the extreme limit fixed for the entire payment is five years, it has been deemed advisable by mutual agreement to leave out as guarantee the two farms of Khliebnikov and Kostromitinov in their entirety, the Russians reserving the right to return and occupy them in case the contract should not be fully executed on the part of M. Sutter or his heirs."

For this reason the Russians upon their departure left an agent called Nicolai with a few men on the farms and two pilots at the port of Bodega.

[A version of the inventory of the buildings and equipment at Fort Ross prepared by Rotchev and Kostromitinov was entered here.]

All these animals were in prime condition and unquestionably the finest in California. M. Sutter moved them to his settlement on the Sacramento River where he had established his residence; however, he left several of his agents on the Russian farms which, by the way, are not more than thirty leagues from New Helvetia. It seems trite to observe that to understand the details of this section thoroughly it is indispensible to study the hydro-graphical and topographical map accompanying this volume.

After ordering Fort Ross demolished, M. Sutter transported by sea (to New Helvetia) by means of the sloop purchased from the Russians, the wooden houses that had been demolished and a few pieces of cast iron canon of small calibre as well as two bronze field pieces that had been pre-sented to him by M. de Rotchev. According to the terms of the contract one piece was left at the port of Bodega for signaling. The farms of Kostro-mitinov and Khliebnikov were allowed to remain intact.

The sale price of the property was 30,000 piasters (150,000 francs) pay-able as follows. For the first and second years M. Sutter agreed to remit to Russian ships sent to San Francisco for this purpose the amount of 5,000 piasters annually in produce of the country such as wheat, corn, beans, peas, concentrated wine, hides of cattle, beaver pelts, jerked meat, fat, butter, tallow, tobacco, etc. The third year he guaranteed to deliver produce to the value of 10,000 piasters; on the fourth he was to complete the payment of 30,000, the total amount of the sale by remitting to Russia 10,000 piasters

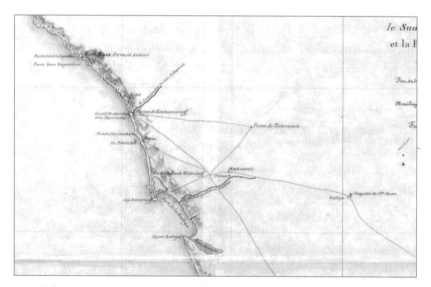

Detail of *Carte détaillée des Etablissements Russes dans la Haute Californie* by Eugene Duflot de Mofras, 1841. Courtesy of The Bancroft Library, University of California, Berkeley.

in silver. M. Sutter, moreover, has the right to pay in full either in products of the country or in specie, before the date stipulated. This privilege is as advantageous to him as the system of deferred payments.

The real reasons why the Russians abandoned their settlements are these: For some time the English concern, the Hudson's Bay Company, which was strongly supported by its government, had been planning to become mistress of all commerce and lands of the Northwest Coast of America and California. In the north she had succeeded in expelling United States vessels and, to facilitate expansion toward the south, had recently established a large commercial house in the Sandwich Islands, purchased another at the port of San Francisco and had received from Governor Alvarado under the name of one of her agents, MacKay, a large grant on the bank of the Sacramento southwest of M. Sutter. The only power now left to combat was the Russians, whose mercantile activities could not be compared with those of the English; and an unexpected coincidence materially furthered her designs.

Within the past few years two Russian agents, whom I cannot name, carried on their private affairs to the detriment of those of the Imperial Company. They derived lavish profits from the settlements in California and caused such disorder and turmoil by exploiting the sale of wheat to Spanish missions and private individuals that the company found itself facing a deficit.[49]

At the same time the colonies in the north, without wheat and flour, were forced to send down for it to Guaymas. It was at this time that Baron Wrangell reached Ross en route from his official post at New Archangel to St. Petersburg where in 1837 he proposed to abandon Bodega. Not until 1840, however, when the decision of the Company received the sanction of the Emperor, was the formal order given. Sir George Simpson, governor of the territory of the Hudson's Bay Company who went from London to St. Petersburg that same year met Baron Wrangell who had become one of the directors and imperial commissioners of the Russian-American Fur Company. M. de Wrangell, a distinguished engineer and hydrographer, was so impressed by the superior commercial knowledge of Sir George that a treaty was concluded between the two rival companies whereby that of St. Petersburg granted to the Hudson's Bay Company for ten years the exclusive right to settle, navigate, trade, hunt and fish along the Northwest Coast in the territories situated east of a line drawn from the summit of Mt. Fairweather in 59° 00' 42" n. lat., and 139° 57' 07" w. long., and 4552 meters above sea level, terminating at Cape Spencer in 58° 12' 30" n. lat., and 138° 24' 44" w. long., and from there drawn south to Point Wales at Cape Chacon.

Thus the Russians found themselves ejected from the sixtieth parallel, and retaining toward the south only the small island of Sitka. In exchange for this concession, the English company delivered annually to New Archangel two thousand pelts of fur seals with thick hides, with an estimated value of five or six piasters each. Furthermore, the Hudson's Bay Company guaranteed to furnish annually five thousand fanegas (2815 hectoliters) of wheat at the price of two piasters, delivered at Sitka. However, a clause was inserted by the Russians to the effect that if the English Company were delayed in delivering the grain they would charter a ship at their own expense to search for wheat in the ports of California, Guaymas, or Valparaiso. What advantages the English derived is obvious, since on the one hand they paid with furs, which are not used in England, and on the other, they received two piasters in silver for one fanega for which they paid the same price and even less in California, but in popular merchandise on which they made a large profit.

[Following is Appendix B of Wilbur's book (see source credit on page 280).]

The Russians, furthermore, in abandoning their establishments in California feared, as already indicated, to have them fall into the control of England. For this reason Governor Etolin failed to mention the sale of Ross to Sir George Simpson who happened to visit Sitka in September, 1841, and when the latter learned through me at Fort Vancouver on the Columbia River that M. Sutter had purchased the property in its entirety he appeared to be somewhat surprised that he had not been informed of this fact by the Russian officers.

I am of the belief that to possess the port of Bodega is of the utmost importance either to a European power, or the United States, for within a few years the settlement of the islands in the great ocean such as Otaheiti and especially the Sandwich Islands, the whaling industry, the scarcity of building wood in Norway, its high price in New France, and the wave of emigration from the United States and Canada which is pushing steadily toward the west, will focus extraordinary interest on the shores of the Pacific Ocean and above all on California. It would be comparatively simple to have a suitable agent purchase the remaining properties—M. Sutter, I believe, will give his consent—for approximately 15,000 piasters, or 75,000 francs.

Three highly intelligent Frenchmen who might prove useful in this undertaking reside in California; M. Deleissèques, a retired sea captain, M. Prudon, and especially M. Charles Baric, a merchant who is thoroughly familiar with this country and enjoys high standing. The latter might pretend to acquire the farms on his own behalf and devote his energies to exploiting the timber if, at the same time, he were furnished with carpenters who are extremely rare in California.

After this establishment has been formed, the agent might work cautiously to acquire five or six small farms located on the land that lies between the southern end of the port of Bodega and the northwest part of the Bay of San Francisco. Probably the acquisition of these homesteads with their livestock would not require more than 20,000 piasters, or 100,000 francs, and it would be a relatively simple matter to secure them under the name of other Frenchmen. A glance at the general map will indicate that the distance by land between these two ports is less than nine leagues.[50]

At this point it seems advisable to enumerate what advantages would be derived from possessing this port of San Francisco, one of the finest in the world and the key to all regions in the Pacific situated north of the equator. Certain conditions tend to make the northern shores superior to those of the south. The latter are sandy, arid, and without wood and water; the anchorage at Yerba Buena is exposed to sharp gusts of wind; and the sea is often so high and rough that weeks pass when ships are unable to make a landing. On the north side, on the other hand, there is a long narrow entrance where the shore is more rugged and higher than on the opposite coast and, when fortified, would command the channel. The soil, furthermore, is extremely fertile, and at the anchorage of Whalers Harbor [Sausalito] there is an ample supply of wood and water. The small farms belong to a Californian, Don Antonio Osio, administrator of customs at Monterey who is friendly toward the French, and a local resident called Rafael Garcia. These two holdings are located near Point Reyes. Another is held jointly by an American, Mr.

Thompson, and an Englishman, Captain Snook, and another by a Californian. The two most important, because of their location, belong to an Irishman, Read, and an Englishman, Richardson. The latter which is not, like the others, equipped merely with a dilapidated adobe house roofed with planks, is extremely important, for Richardson controls the small Bay of Sausalito where whalers and warships come to anchor. At the same time the small island of Los Angeles [Angel Island] should be purchased, because of its military importance, from Señor Osio. This commands the entrance to the port on its two divergent points and overlooks nearly all the points and anchorages in the harbor. The elevation of this island is 226 meters; it has wood, a good watering-place, and a cove where ships can be beached and careened. The entire wealth of these individuals consists in livestock which is used as legal tender in place of money and which serve to complete commercial transactions. I know all of these men personally and I am convinced that every one of them would be eager to sell.

Don Antonio Osio has recently lost his position and as he lives at Monterey, he cannot look after his animals. Thompson lives 150 leagues south of the mission of Santa Bárbara; Captain Snook is in command of a ship that makes long voyages; Rafael Garcia and the other Californian cannot resist the sight of piasters. Richardson is burdened with debt and Read has experienced such misfortune that his one desire is to leave the country. Yet, since his farm extends farther east that that of Richardson, its purchase would not be imperative. However, it lies along the shore and includes some extremely fine timber. Other good holdings lie farther east, especially the farms of the Englishmen, Murphy, Martin and McIntosh, and that of the American, Dawson. Yet their acquisition is of minor importance since they are all in the interior of the country with the single exception of Murphy's property which adjoins San Rafael Mission.

The fact should be stressed that the value of land in California has comparatively slight bearing on the purchase price of a farm, for only the livestock is purchased on a basis of five piasters a head, when the transaction is based on payment in merchandise, or four piasters, if in silver. In addition, beef on the hoof has a value of five piasters, yet fully this amount can be realized after slaughter, the hide alone being worth two piasters while three more can be realized from the fat, tallow, and dried meat. The number of cattle has diminished to such an extent and is still decreasing so rapidly because of the negligence and vice of the inhabitants that nothing would be lost by holding the animals. They could be sold with profit to strangers who are arriving daily and to the English, Canadians, and Americans of the Columbia River who come down year after year in search of them, the journey requiring less than forty days. Perhaps it would be advisable to reserve these animals for the colonists who might be induced to come out and replace the Russians. The latter will be deeply missed in California because of their generous nature and the protection they afforded all settlers living north of the Bay of San Francisco. In fact, these men, due to the vigilance of the Russian colonists, were banded together for military service, for they recognized the danger of raid by the Indians who were ravaging the country located farther south, stealing animals, and often killing settlers.

The Spaniards dislike the English, the difference in language, customs, and especially religion causing the English and Americans who are already posing as conquerors to be unpopular in California. On the other hand, the French, wherever known, are beloved; the departure of our two missionaries, MM. Bachelot and Short, was a matter of keen regret; memories of La Pérouse are still alive; and in later years, the visits of the sixty-gun frigates *Vénus* and *Artémise* have instilled a lofty idea of our navy in the midst of the inhabitants, who had seen only small English and American warships of eighteen and twenty-four guns. I do not hesitate to affirm that the first French settlement at Bodega would be warmly welcomed by all the Spaniards, and Governor Alvarado has definitely promised that he will give choice land to five hundred French colonists.

Less than twenty days from Bodega resides a sturdy, brave, and devoted population who would welcome with enthusiasm an opportunity to place themselves under the protection of the French flag. I refer to some two thousand French Canadians who have located on the banks of the Willamette, one of the tributaries of the Columbia River. The country where they reside is extremely unhealthful; I inspected it carefully, and found the population decimated by smallpox and fever resembling ague. The soil is not especially fertile, and livestock is expensive, beef being valued at fifty piasters. Although these Canadians are not in the employ of the English concern, the Hudson's Bay Company, yet they are forced to face many unpleasant acts on the part of its agents. So they would readily move south if they could find lands to cultivate. Those abandoned by the Russians might be distributed to them.

There is no reason to believe that the trip by sea from Europe to the Northwest Coast would be of long duration, for English ships have made the trip in four months by way of Cape Horn from London to the mouth of the Columbia River and American ships require the same time to travel from Boston to Monterey. It seems futile to add that by crossing the Isthmus of Panamá, the trip from Europe to California may be made in approximately sixty days, if connections are made at Panamá.

If a political pretext for occupying California seems essential, here is one that is extremely weak, but one which the English or Americans would not hesitate to advance. In September 1840, a Frenchman named Pierre Dubosc was robbed and assassinated on the farm of a Scotchman called McIntosh, by a baptized Indian known as José. The motives of his crime were as follows: McIntosh was occupying some excellent wheat land one league from Khliebnikov's farm where the Russians at one time had also planted crops. After this Scotchman, who was extremely courageous, had received permission from M. Rotchev to settle on this property—the Russians were about to leave the country—he had the land officially confirmed to him by a grant made by the Californian governor, Alvarado, at Monterey. These agricultural lands, situated on the banks of the tiny San Ignacio River, are unusually suitable for raising superb wheat. Señor Vallejo, military commandant, conceived the idea of preventing this move, but fearing to oppose him openly sent one of his proteges, James Dawson, an American adventurer, to erect a hut near that of McIntosh. The latter allowed him to construct a wooden shack, but informed Dawson that he was the legal owner of the land and that he would use his carabine on anyone found attempting to cultivate his soil. Pierre Dubosc was living at the time with McIntosh and working for him. I visited the property four times, saw Señor Vallejo, and Messrs. McIntosh and Dawson, and after investigating the case and acquiring information from the Russians it seemed evident that Vallejo and Dawson paid the Indian José to kill the Scotchman, but that the assassin erred, and in the darkness killed Pierre Dubosc. The Indian then passed by Mission San Solano [ed: formerly Mission San Francisco Solano de Sonoma] where Señor Vallejo resided, no effort was made to stop him, and finally he escaped with the stolen horses, personal belongings and guns to the vast plains of the Sacramento. Señor Vallejo, in an effort to cast the blame on M. McIntosh and prevent him from giving an account of the affair to the civil judge at Monterey, held him prisoner north of the bay with orders not to pass south under penalty of forfeiting of bail to the amount of four thousand piasters that had been put up for him by the English captain, Wilson.

When I met Señor Vallejo on the twentieth of last May, he failed to mention this affair, and did not even report the case to Governor Alvarado. Upon returning to Monterey I made an official complaint to Señor Alvarado, who replied that he had not received any report and that he would issue orders to apprehend the assassin. After M. Sutter was informed of the crime he sent several detachments of men out into the country with orders to trail the Indian and hand him over to the authorities; however, he was not captured. I do not know whether M. Sutter abandoned the attempt to punish the assassin. Pierre Dubosc left only some wearing apparel and a horse that McIntosh wished to give me, but which I requested him to keep.

At a time when England and the United States are making no effort to conceal their definite purpose of seizing California, which belongs to Mexico in name only, it appears probable that these two governments would welcome such a pretext to occupy this land—to protect, as they would say, their countrymen—by magnifying such an act, by exaggerating the insecurity of their citizens in a land where a supreme authority, [Vallejo] one from which there is no appeal, has men assassinated in order to seize their property. Had McIntosh or Dawson been killed instead of Pierre Dubosc, it is not difficult to imagine what would have happened and what deep significance the English and Americans would have attached to the death of an unimportant man.

[I have omitted a lengthy discussion by de Mofras of the politics of the Pacific Islands.]

In addition, two major factors favor the occupation of the port of Bodega and the Bay of San Francisco. According to the most reliable and detailed information, the population in the Sandwich Islands at the present day has decreased by 100,000 inhabitants, and is dropping so rapidly that within ten years only a few thousand will remain. Nor is it expedient to surmise whether these islands will fall to England, the United States, or

France, whose missionaries have succeeded in acquiring an amazing influence over the natives.

Thus, the occupation of at least one of these islands will be closely associated with the founding of a colony on the coast of California. A second and even more powerful consideration is to provide an outlet for the growth of our population, and to be able, within a few years, to draw to an important center a large part of the old French population that is now scattered throughout Western America and form a colony that will compensate for, without allowing us to forget, the disgraceful loss of Canada and the deplorable sale of Louisiana. The sons of our former colonists of Canada, Ohio, Illinois, and the headwaters of the Mississippi and Missouri dislike to mingle with the Anglo-American race that differs from them in language, customs, and faith. Without taking into consideration the immense line of island navigation that virtually links the two oceans, we can see that the Rocky Mountains are no longer a barrier to hardy adventurers, descendants of our trappers, especially since certain passes have been discovered that even permit four-wheeled wagons to cross the mountains. There seems, moreover, slight reason to doubt that these venerable sons of France would flock to place themselves under the protection of our flag, if they saw it raised on the shores of the Pacific Ocean.

Source: Wilbur 1937.

✿ 16 ✿

THE RUSSIANS LEAVE FORT ROSS

THE QUESTION OFTEN COMES UP in conversations with visitors to Fort Ross as to why the Russians sold out in 1841, considering what an idyllic location it appears to visitors today. One might compare the situation to the U.S. Army ceding the Presidio of San Francisco; why would they give up such an aesthetically beautiful location? The answer is that in both cases it came down to simple bottom-line decision making; the properties were simply too expensive to manage in comparison to their economic return. By the late 1830s, the California colony of the Russian American Company was a money-losing operation and, even worse, was not achieving its purpose as the most effective supplier of agricultural goods to the Alaskan colonies. In 1839, the RAC signed a contract with the Hudson's Bay Company to provide them with needed supplies, and with that the days of Fort Ross were numbered. Being situated right on the coast, the growing of crops provided only marginal returns compared to other suppliers, and although the Russians, starting in the latter half of the 1830s, made several last-ditch attempts to establish ranches and farms farther inland, even those were not sufficiently productive.

Meanwhile, the Californio authorities had maneuvered to block any real eastward expansion of the colony by establishing missions San Rafael and San Francisco Solano de Sonoma, as well as moving the presidial garrison from

San Francisco up to Sonoma under the command of Mariano Guadalupe Vallejo. In the period following the secularization of the California missions (1833–1834), there was simultaneously a decline in the agricultural production from the missions as well as a rapid expansion of land-grant ranchos that further acted to hem in the Russian settlement.

As a result, the Russians sought to sell Fort Ross. After sounding out several potential buyers—including the Hudson's Bay Company, the French government, and the governor of California—the moveable goods of the Russian colony were sold to John Sutter, a Swiss immigrant to California, who was setting up his own small empire in the Sacramento Valley. By July of 1841, the Russians had moved out of Fort Ross down to the area of Port Rumiantsev (Bodega Bay) and the Khlebnikov Rancho, near present-day Bodega Corners. On January 1, 1842, the manager of Fort Ross, Alexander Rotchev, along with his family and most of the remaining Russians and Alaskan natives from the settlement, embarked on the *Constantine,* headed for Sitka/New Archnagel.

In subsequent writings about his time in California, Rotchev wrote longingly of the beauty of Fort Ross and of how he had enjoyed his time there. Considering his position as the manager of the colony during its last three years, it is understandable that he would have looked back on it as a high point of his life. Following his return to Russia he and his wife, Helena, split up and she moved eventually to Irkutsk, the Siberian headquarters of the Russian American Company.

Later in this chapter we have a valuable description of Russian California as observed by French diplomat Eugene Duflot de Mofras in 1841 (pages 286–292). His version of the final inventory of sale document is important because he supplemented the basic inventory provided to Sutter (in French), augmenting it with some of his own observations about Russian California at the time. He also provided a drawing of a traditional house (*isba,* page 291) and created an excellent map of the area at the end of the Russian occupation. This map of the territory between Bodega Bay and Fort Ross includes the locations of the various farms and ranchos and the paths between them, and it also notes the positions of some of the lookout spots (*vigies*) that were used to send messages quickly between Fort Ross and Bodega Bay.

Although he is dealt with only briefly in this text, the enormous contributions of naturalist Il'ya Voznesenskii need to be mentioned. By all accounts his handwriting was not always easy to decipher, which is why so little of his written descriptions have been made available. However, his outstanding collections of the natural and cultural history of California (which he sent back to St. Petersburg) are extremely valuable, and his artistic ability provided us with the most remarkable image of Fort Ross, as well as several intriguing drawings of individuals encountered on his travels in the surrounding area (pages 293, 294, and 295).

A REPORT ON THE ECONOMICS OF FORT ROSS

AND THE DECISION TO SELL (1842)

The following short extract of the Accounts of the Directors of the Russian American Company was published in the *Journal de St. Pétersbourg* on October 31, 1842. It offers a stark, straight-forward explanation of the decision to sell the Russian American Company's California base to John Sutter, including specifics of the earnings and expenses associated with Fort Ross. One interesting comment notes that the political upheaval in Mexican California in 1837 (actually it had begun in 1836 with a series of revolving-door California governors) had made it necessary to augment the military force at Fort Ross by a considerable amount, a factor that in turn raised the annual expenses from 45,000 to 72,000 rubles. This addition to the number of military personnel may help explain the increase in the number of Europeans at Fort Ross in the last years of the colony, since neither the Alaskan natives nor the California Indians were employed as soldiers. The Russians were apparently concerned about repercussions of the political instability that occurred in California in the late 1830s, following the death of Governor Figueroa.

Subsequent to the comments about Fort Ross in this document is an interesting statement about the simultaneous construction that took place at Sitka/New Archangel, the implication being that eliminating the expense of maintaining the California establishment had made funds available for new development at home. In all, this short piece provides an interesting footnote to the history of Fort Ross and Russian America in general during this period of transition.

Among the most notable dispositions, executed in 1840 and 1841 in the Russian possessions in America, we cite first the abandonment of the Colony Ross, established in 1812 on the coast of New Albion. This establishment had been formed in the hope that the cultivation of fields in this part of America where the climate is less severe [than in Alaska], would offer an easy means to provision the other colonies situated more to the north on an arid coast. At first the sea otter were found in great numbers in the vicinity of [Fort]

Ross, so much so that the hunt and the commerce in pelts seemed to promise enormous economic returns.

However, it did not turn out that way. The fields and the prairies that the Company had been able to acquire were not extensive enough. Since they were situated at an elevation considerably above the stream banks, surrounded by rocks and precipices, these fields were too difficult to access, not to speak of the proximity of the ocean. The frequent fogs on this coast would often have disastrous results on the harvest. Soon the sea otter became rare in these places and the result was that the expenses to maintain this establishment rose to 45,000 rubles and for the period of 1825 to 1829 this became a considerable excess over the revenues that were returned to the Company which were barely 38,000 rubles annually by counting the value of the pelts as 29,000 rubles and the agricultural produce worth 9,000 rubles.

Later, in 1837, the political troubles that beset California, forced the Company to reinforce the Ross garrison so that the annual costs of this colony rose to 72,000 rubles, while the revenues dropped to 8,000 rubles, the value of the products of the land since the sea otter had become extremely rare on this part of the coast to the degree that the trade in pelts ceased entirely.

In these circumstances, the establishment and the surrounding fields were sold in 1840, with the authorization of the government, for a sum of 30,000 piastres to M. Sutter, a Swiss by birth, who had established himself in California.

Source: Farris 2005: 153–154.

INVENTORIES OF SALE FOR FORT ROSS,
BODEGA BAY, AND NEIGHBORING RANCHOS (1841)

Ultimately, with the sale of Fort Ross becoming a necessity, a prospective on the property was required for entering into an agreement of sale. Three versions of an inventory prepared by the Russian American Company have come down to us: the John Sutter version, the Duflot de Mofras version (both in French), and the Mariano Vallejo version (in Spanish) are clearly similar, however, there are some interesting variations. The Duflot de Mofras version lists details that are missing from the other two inventories. For instance, when discussing buildings down in the Fort Ross cove, the Sutter inventory speaks of "a forge and blacksmith shop, built of planks, 5⅓ fathoms long by 3⅔ *arshins* wide [an *arshin* was 28 inches wide, or ⅓ of a *sazhen*], with 4 partitions"; the Duflot de Mofras version describes it as "a forge, a shop for carpenters and locksmiths, and one for handling brass, copper and tin, built of wood 10 meters long and 6 meters wide." This latter description is important in that it is the only clear mention of tin-smithing being done in California prior to the gold rush. Following is the more detailed Duflot de Mofras version of the Fort Ross inventory.

REAL ESTATE

A. The farm or presidio of Ross.
B. Farm of Kostromitinov.
C. Farm of Khliebnikov or Vasili.
D. Farm of Chernik or Don Jorge.
E. Port of Bodega.

A. Fort Ross

A square fort constructed of wood measuring 80 meters on the sides and 4 meters high, with two turrets at opposite angles.

Within are:

1) The Commandant's house (an old structure) built of heavy timber covered with planks, 16 meters wide and 12 meters deep. This contains six rooms, a corridor, and a kitchen.

2) House of the Commandant (a new house) constructed of heavy timber, 16 meters wide and 8 meters deep enclosing six rooms and a corridor.

3) A new kitchen measuring 7 by 8 meters.

4) A building for food supplies, built of pieces of wood, 12 meters wide and 6 meters deep, which also includes a prison.

5) An old [ed: ware]house of two stories with an outside wooden balcony, 16 meters wide and 8 deep.

6) Employés' quarters, containing ten apartments and two corridors, 30 meters broad and 7 in depth.

7) Barracks with eight rooms and two corridors, with façade 22 meters and a depth of eight.

8) A chapel with a cupola and belfry, 12 meters deep by 8 in width.

9) A well 5 meters deep.

Outside the enclosure at the foot of the hill on the banks of the brook [ed: Fort Ross Creek]:

1) A forge, a shop for carpenters and locksmiths, and one for handling brass, copper and tin, built of wood 10 meters long and 6 meters wide.

2) A shop equipped with various machines for tanning, dressing, and preparing hides, 10 meters long and 6 deep.

3) A Russian bathhouse for troops and colonists, 5 by 6 meters.

4) A cooper's shop, 20 meters wide and 10 meters in depth.

In the vicinity are:

1) A barrack's [ed: sic], kitchen and bakery 6 by 10 meters.

2) Two wooden sheds for cattle, 40 meters by 7, with a wooden corral 6 by 40 meters.

3) A wooden pen for sheep, 40 meters by 5.

4) Shed for pigs, 40 meters square.

5) A milkhouse built of planks, 7 by 12 meters.

6) A wooden stable 12 by 7 meters.

7) A wooden house for trampling wheat 12 by 7 meters.

8) Threshing floor for wheat built of heavy timbers, 16 meters square with a board enclosure for the animals.

9) A new windmill with a single millstone, which has a daily capacity of 20 fanegas (11 hectoliters) containing another machine for crushing pine bark.

10) An old windmill with one millstone.

11) A windmill run by manpower, or animals, with one millstone; this has a capacity of 4 fanegas (2 hectoliters) a day; there is also a machine for crushing pine bark.

12) A cordage shop, and a machine for making rope.

13) A carpenters' shop, 14 by 6 meters.

14) A floor for threshing wheat, built of heavy planks measuring 13 by 10 meters.

15) A well 3 meters deep.

16) Four houses 10 by 5 meters.
Eight houses 9 by 5 meters.
Nine houses 7 by 4 meters.
Three houses 4 by 4 meters.
Each house has a small garden; the houses are covered with planks, their floors are of wood, and they have square windows.

17) Ten kitchens.

18) Eight Russian baths and eight wooden sheds.

19) Approximately 800 meters from the fort there is a wooden platform for threshing wheat, 20 meters square, with a loft 10 by 8 meters.

20) A fruit garden 110 by 50 meters surrounded by a wooden palisade enclosing 264 fruit trees, as follows:
207 apples
29 peaches
10 pears
10 quinces
8 cherries; also some [ed: grape] vines.

21) In the center of the garden stands a new house of four apartments covered with boards, having a façade of 9 and a depth of 8 meters; on one side is a kitchen 5 meters square.

22) Beyond the large garden is another small one 21 by 28 meters; this encloses more than 20 fruit trees and some vines.

23) A vegetable garden 140 by 40 meters surrounded by a palisade.

24) Fort Ross owns about 36 hectares of agricultural land which is adequate to raise 95 hectoliters of crops. These lands are surrounded by fences.

B. Farm of Kostromitinov

1) Barracks, containing three rooms and two covered corridors, 16 by 6 meters.
2) A store [ed: storehouse] 14 by 6 meters with lofts for storing grain and a wooden flume for sliding the grain to the brook that runs at the foot of the hill.
3) A house 6 by 4 meters.
4) Two wooden platforms for threshing wheat, one 20 meters, the other 8 meters square.
5) A wooden platform for winnowing the wheat, 24 meters square.
6) A wooden house for the Indians, 14 meters long by 5 meters wide.
7) A kitchen with two ovens.
8) A Russian bath 6 by 4 meters.
9) A large fenced enclosure for live stock.
10) A boat for traveling on the Slawinska [ed: Slavianka or Russian] River.
11) This farm contains approximately 40 hectares of agricultural land adequate to plant 140 hectoliters to wheat.

C. Farm of Khliebnikov or Vasili

1) House of brick (adobe) of three rooms, 7 by 5 meters, covered with shingles, with a kitchen and a sun dial. The house is surrounded by a staunch fence.
2) Barracks of three rooms, 20 by 7 meters, covered with planks.
3) A two-story house of planks, 15 by 7 meters.
4) A floor for threshing wheat built of planks 24 meters square.
5) A kitchen, bakery, and forge, 12 by 5 meters.
6) A Russian bath 7 by 4 meters.
7) Four structures of different sizes,
   One for storing food.
   Two for the Indians.
   One for drying and preparing tobacco.

8) A windmill [ed: sic, mill] run by hand or beasts of burden with a daily capacity of 4 fanegas or 2 hectoliters.

9) A wooden corral for animals.

10) A large vegetable garden.

11) There is also a large amount of agricultural land suitable for raising wheat, beans, or corn; tobacco also thrives.

D. Farm of Chernik or Don Jorge

1) A barracks of six rooms, 15 by 6 meters.

2) A kitchen 8 by 4 meters.

3) A Russian bath 6 by 4 meters.

4) A storeroom 14 by 6 meters.

5) A wooden platform for threshing wheat 36 meters square.

6) Two houses for storing supplies of food.

7) Two reservoirs for refuse [ed: in the Sutter document this is described as "two hothouses made of planks, each 8 *sazhens* (16 meters)"].

8) Vineyard with 2,000 plants and some fruit trees; the agricultural land is fenced and has 80 hectoliters of excellent soil for wheat, corn, vegetables, and cereals.

E. Port of Bodega

1) Warehouse 20 by 10 meters for storing provisions and ships' stores.

2) A house 6 meters wide with four rooms and a stove.

3) A Russian bath 8 by 4 meters.

4) A large pen for live stock.

5) A large canoe [ed: launch or *baidara*?].

6) A house with a stove.

7) A house and pen for live stock.

8) Another four-oar canoe.

9) A long covered boat of 20 tons suitable for navigating along the coast.

10) Other large boats of seal skin [ed: *baidaras*?].[1]

PERSONAL PROPERTY

Farm Machinery

1) Iron machine for cleaning wheat.
2) Twenty harrows with iron teeth.
3) Twenty harrows with wooden teeth.
4) Twenty-six plows for horses.
5) Twenty-one plows for oxen.
6) Twenty-five harnesses for horses.
7) Eighteen yokes for oxen.
8) Thirty-five bridles and halters.
9) Five four-wheel carts [ed: *droschki*[2]].
10) Ten two-wheel carts.

"Isba," or traditional Russian house, said to be like one seen in California by Eugene Duflot de Mofras, ca. 1841. Courtesy of the Fort Ross Interpretive Association.

Live Stock

Work Oxen	70
Steers for slaughter	174
Small steers	41
Cows, large	777
Cows, medium	409
Cows, small	159
Miscellaneous	70
	1700

Mules, large	55
Mules, medium	30
Mules, small	50
Mares, large	320
Mares, medium	70
Mares, small	90
Stallions	20
Mares	305
	940

Among this number are 100 work horses and 20 draft mules.

Sheep, large	100
Sheep, small	35
Ewes, large	540
Ewes, medium	217
Ewes, small	8
	900

Total, 3,570 head of live stock.

Source: Duflot de Mofras 1937: 250–255.

IL'YA GAVRILOVICH VOZNESENSKII,
RUSSIAN NATURALIST AND ETHNOGRAPHER (1840–1841)

Il'ya Gavrilovich Voznesenskii was a twenty-five-year-old naturalist when he came to California in July 1840, arriving at Port Rumiantsev aboard the *Elena* and traveling up to Fort Ross, which became the base for his collecting activities. He stayed on there until September 1841 (Shur and Gibson 1973: 55). His extensive collections of natural history and cultural specimens from California are extremely important, and the Indian artifacts he accumulated are presently housed in the Museum of Anthropology and Ethnology in St. Petersburg, Russia, forming the largest and best collection of pre–gold rush California Indian artifacts in existence. He was also a skilled artist and he drew several images during his time in California, including a panorama of Fort Ross as seen in its last year under Russian ownership.

In addition, Voznesenskii made several drawings of individuals, one of whom is identified as "the Ranchero, Don Garcia" (page 294). This almost certainly must be Rafael Garcia, owner of the Tamales y Baulenes Rancho, which was immediately south of the Bodega Bay and Khlebnikov Rancho holdings of the Russians. Since Garcia was granted this property in 1836, he would have been a close neighbor of the Russians for about five years before their departure.

Drawing of Fort Ross in 1841 by Il'ya Voznesenskii.
Courtesy of the Fort Ross Interpretive Association.

Drawing of neighboring
rancher Don Rafael Garcia
by Voznesenskii, ca. 1840.
Courtesy of the Fort Ross
Interpretive Association.

Indian arrows collected by Voznesenskii in California.
Courtesy of the Museum of Anthropology
and Ethnology, St. Petersburg, Russia.

Unfortunately, even though Voznesenskii did keep a journal of his time in California, historians who have seen the notebooks report that "the writing is small, very hurried and illegible. The text often alternates with lists of zoological and ethnographical collections and the like" (Shur and Gibson 1973: 56). One Russian biographer of Voznesenskii, K. K. Gilzen, has written an unpublished manuscript on his life and adventures, but up to this point no one has completed the monumental effort of organizing and translating Voznesenskii's original notes into English. From Shur and Gibson we know they contain tantalizing details: "During his stay at Ross from August to October of 1840 Voznesenskii made several excursions, such as northward to Cape Mendocino, where he spent

Chernykh Rancho by Voznesenskii. Courtesy of the Fort Ross Interpretive Association.

several days in the mountains 'among thick forests of gigantic pines—redwoods and majestic cedars'" (Shur and Gibson 1973: 55). He made additional excursions to San Francisco, where he stayed from October 20, 1840, to February 1841, and then he traveled to New Helvetia, in the Central Valley, from February to March 1841 (Shur and Gibson 1973: 55–56).

Leonid Shur, formerly a scholar at the Institute of Ethnography of the Soviet Academy of Sciences, stated, "I have established that in California [Voznesenskii] had a relatively wide circle of acquaintances. In San Francisco he lived at Yerba Buena with a French émigré, apparently Victor Prudhon....Voznesensky [sic] met the captain of the port of San Francisco, A. Richardson, the hotel owner J. J. Vioget, John Sutter, missionaries and others. Voznesensky's journal contains very interesting information about California's physical environment and the way of life of the population (not only the Indians) and includes descriptions of some ranchos and their Californian owners, as well as of settlers from other countries" (Shur and Gibson 1973: 57).

It would be a valuable contribution for someone to wend her or his way through these difficult writings and make them available for scholars and other interested readers.

SANDELS'S DESCRIPTION OF A VISIT TO
POST-RUSSIAN FORT ROSS (1843)

In April of 1843, a Swedish Finn by the name of Gustav Waseurtz af Sandels traveled up from the Smith Rancho at Bodega Corners to see the old Russian settlement at Fort Ross. Since Finland was at the time a part of the Russian empire, it is interesting to note comments by Sandels that he could speak to the local "Russian Indians" in Russian, and that he apparently knew a number of individuals who had been at Fort Ross in its last years and so was able to establish a certain rapport with these Indians. Sandels's drawing of the property at the time of its deconstruction (below) is also of great interest.

Sandels's personal background is somewhat murky, and he refers to himself in a manuscript in the possession of the Society of California Pioneers as "the King's Orphan." It was common at the time for the penurious sons of the aristocracy who had fallen on hard times to be educated at the expense of the monarch, however, we have no clear evidence of where his education took place. It appears that Sandels had been acquainted with various people who

Fort Ross in 1843 by G. M. Waseurtz af Sandels.
Courtesy of the Society of California Pioneers.

had been sent to Fort Ross, probably other Finns, who were found in somewhat greater numbers at Fort Ross in its terminal years, possibly due to the fact that the governor of Russian America from 1840 to 1845 was himself a Swedish Finn, by the name of Arvid Etholin.

🎋 🎋

Again I returned to San Francisco [ed: from San Jose] and had the pleasure of finding there my old friend [ed: Stephen] Smith who had settled all his business with the government about putting up his mill at Bodega. His family were all pretty well, except his mother-in-law, and after a few trips for pleasure about the farms on the other side, he persuaded me to visit them. Hinckley went with us as pilot and assistant to Smith, and after taking in more beef in Sausalito, we started for Bodega. Hinckley fell dangerously ill, and remained so for some days. Our passage was two days, and we anchored off the bird's rock outside of the little harbor of Bodega.

The storehouses that remained there since the Russians' time were completely hidden from view by the high bluff, and a small narrow channel led into the basin which could hardly hold more than two vessels at a time. Furthermore, vessels could not get in except at very high tide. The buildings were now in ruins.

I went next day on an excursion to find some flowers. Gentians. An Indian family lived near this port, and on their small farm raised fine green peas, potatoes, pumpkins, etc. I also went up to Smith's farm [ed: the former Klebnikov Rancho], which only a few years before was farmed by the Russians. I found the houses and some agricultural implements in tolerable condition.

Bodega was the principal port for the Russian establishment, but Ross was their farming center and it had been inhabited by some thousand people.[3] Only a hundred were Russians. The others were Kodiak and California Indians. The farming establishment and the hunters were to provide the northern stations with grain and beef. Ross was situated a snug day's ride from Bodega. If one rode through the mountainous and wooded part of the country from Basilii [ed: Khlebnikov] farm, it was shaded almost all the way. I did so.

An old Indian had engaged to guide me. It was most astonishing to see such affection as the Indians had for their former harsh and tyrannical masters, and how they took me in their good graces, fancying I was in some way related to them. There had been in this establishment a great many Finlanders, and as I was a true model of one, I suppose they reckoned I belonged to them. The old men and women came asking me in the Russian language after this or the other of my "gone countrymen," and, as I chanced to know something about them, I became quite a favorite. I took this favorable turn to attach them to my friend Capt. Smith's interests. He was very glad to hire their labor and to pay them well.

I passed in my road another Russian abandoned farm [ed: probably the Chernykh Rancho]. I do not remember its owner's name. It was a wilderness forest of oak and pine, sycamores and laurel. A small mountain brook wound through it. The soil did not in general compare with that in the neighborhood of San Francisco Bay, but the Russians were accustomed to poorer climate and soil and had been delighted with this country. After a day's ride we descended towards the sea. The stooping hills grooved by the heavy winter floods lay before us, and the coast of the Pacific in all its roughness was sown throughout with pieces of rock in forms of arcades and castles. It was very picturesque. Some were white as snow from the birds' excrement. Others were grown over with dark-colored weeds. All these plains and slopes had formerly been under cultivation by the Russians, and fences and farm buildings were yet standing in many places. They had been built substantially of logs and placed, generally, on some good and dry eminence. One we passed was situated on the high bank of a mountain brook, which, in winter must have been very powerful. There was also a small port for boats where farm products must have been rolled down to the landing place. [Ed: This sounds like the Kostromitinov Ranch, near the mouth of the Russian River; see the inventory document of Duflot de Mofras on page 286].

We travelled on over a high hill and descended towards the great Russian River. It had, through the immense forces of freshets, formed a very extensive bar of sand and broken timber at its mouth. We passed over this bar and on the other side I saw the largest tree trunk I had yet seen. Its diameter was eighteen and a half feet, and the length of what remained of the trunk was three hundred and twelve feet. It must have been magnificent when upright. It was a superior sort of redwood and although probably buried there in the sand for many years, it was still fresh, although many petrifactions were to be seen in this neighborhood, as well as various sorts of minerals which had been washed down from the mountains. The old Indian told us of many disasters which had happened to men fording the river when it was flooded.

Soon we entered on a new aspect of the country. High hills clothed with the most magnificent timber reached down amongst the deep ravines to the very edge of the sea where logs could be taken off on the beach and floated to the vessels for embarkation. We arrived finally at the edge of this woodland, and from the eminence, which formerly was a luxuriant wheat field and now was covered only with wild oats, we saw the majestic Pacific and the ruins of Fort Ross, an enclosed square turreted at each corner [ed: sic, there were turrets (or blockhouses) on only two corners, as is shown in Sandels's own drawing]. Solemnly the cupola of the Greek Church dominated the square, in the center of which was a large two-story blockhouse. All around were ruins of buildings that once belonged to a hundred quiet, industrious settlers. On the left, and calling for solemn thought, was a small enclosed field where rested the mortal remains of departed Russian souls. To the left and nearer the sea stood one of the windmills and the old beacon where the Russian flag once floated proudly. Even the flagstaff was now prostrate.

Riding down by the water's edge, I inspected the tanning vats and boat-houses where ornaments of the chapel and other furniture lay ready for shipping to Sutter's establishment. Finally we climbed through the ruins and found ourselves near the big gate of the deserted fort. It was locked. We knocked loudly. A hollow echo answered our call, and as the bell was gone, we had no other recourse than to scale the walls of the stockade. Just then some Indian squaws appeared and opened the gate near the sentry-box. I was very soon down in the Governor's house, the only one left intact and just as it stood the evening of the family's departure. The children's chairs were still around the fire place. A lady's work basket lay on the small round table. Some trunks of half burned wood were in the hearth. I thought about the variety and inconsistency of human affairs.

I visited next all the solitary and ruined establishments, and the orchard which was loaded with pears, and the little wheat plot. There was not more than three acres of wheat. A few disabled old horses came running almost up to the flagstaff in wonder to see a human being. Everything was solitary and gloomy. We slept there and the next morning put ourselves on the route again, to visit the so-called Russian Indians. They were a fine, healthy and active set of men, willing to work with foreigners though they denied their services to the Spaniards and Mexicans out of antipathy for former ill usage. They lived, as did the other Indian tribes, sometimes wandering about, sometimes settled. Their huts were round, well constructed and half underground. They seemed to retire more and more from the neighborhood of the white man.

After having ended this mission I returned by the road near the seashore, and who should I meet but my friends Captain Smith, Vioget, Hinckley and retinue surveying the land. I would have joined them willingly to see what boundaries belonged to the grant of Smith. But, as I was told the ladies aboard the *George Henry*[4] desired my advice about some indisposition [ed: Sandels was a doctor], I continued on my route and arrived in the afternoon only to find that Mr. Bell the ship surgeon, was expertly serving those who were unwell.

Source: Sandels 1945. Reprinted by permission of the Society of California Pioneers.

❧ 17 ❧

RUSSIAN REDISCOVERY OF FORT ROSS

RENEWED INTEREST IN FORT ROSS by the Russian community residing in California was especially pronounced among the Orthodox clergy, who were intrigued by the chapel and cemetery at the site. Nikolai Ziorov, the bishop of the San Francisco-based Orthodox Church for Alaska and the Aleutians, made a trip to Fort Ross early in 1897, accompanied by Hieromonk Sebastian Dabovich and lector Paul Grepachevsky. Following is an article published in the *Orthodox American Messenger* about their trip. It is clear that Bishop Nikolai was affected by his visit to the site of the old Russian community that had been sold to John Sutter some fifty-six years before. In particular, he was disturbed by the condition of the chapel, which was being used to house livestock. Their visit to the cemetery was also quite moving, as was learning that there were still Indians in the vicinity who spoke Russian, particularly a woman named Lukaria (see pages 197 and 229).

Bishop Nikolai was less than thrilled by his interaction with the owner of Fort Ross at the time, George Washington Call, who rebuffed his offer to acquire the chapel, cemetery, and a nearby house. It is interesting to note that four years earlier, in 1893, there was a plan afoot to highlight Fort Ross at the Mid-Winter Fair in San Francisco, which would have included constructing facsimiles of some of the buildings at the fort, in particular the chapel. The Orthodox bishop at the time was Vladimir, who went so far as to write to the tsar, suggesting that the property be acquired by the Russian government to preserve and restore the site. Apparently, Bishop Vladimir was recalled soon after, and whatever reply there might have been from the tsar is unknown. An article in the *San Francisco Evening Bulletin* from November 3, 1893, titled "Relics of Russians," stated that the plan was supported by George Washington Call, however, we don't know what happened in the intervening years to have made him so apparently antagonistic at the time of Bishop Nikolai's visit in 1897.

TRIP TO FORT ROSS BY BISHOP NIKOLAI

(MARCH 2/14, 1897)

Just now returned from the trip to Fort Ross, which at one time was a Russian Colony in California. For some time I wanted to visit there, look at the place of cultural exploit of our countrymen in this region and in due time to think of them in our prayer in the place of their repose. To travel there can be from San Francisco either by sea or land. By sea the travel is on the schooner of the present owner of the Fort Ross[1] and the cost of this trip is one dollar, also [the traveler] must spend ten hours of time for the trip; but by land the trip is from Sausalito through San Rafael by railroad to the station named "Russian River." Trip by this road will need almost as much time as by the sea with only difference that from the "Russian River" station one must travel by horse [carriage] and this pleasure is not less than $5.00 per person. We chose this mode of travel and later did not regret that we did that. Such air, such nature, an enchantment! Here are best views of Caucasus and best views of Crimea with addition to that of its own American [attraction], the redwood trees, California oak, larch, laurel, fir and eucalyptus. Same different types of the crawling vines—green everywhere. Flowers, hills and dales, murmuring brooks, noisy and frothy ocean, here is beauty that opened to our view constantly, selfsame whimsical variety of colors. Add to that a quiet sunny day, singing of larks and other birds and you will have a scene of the area where we traveled, which was once our Russian and of which to this time the name of the river [Slavianka] and the other place [Moscow] are reminders. From the station "Russian River" we traveled first along the shore of the Pacific Ocean, more accurately, along the steep side of the hills, crowded by the ocean and often above precipices then descending into a forest where each step opened views of wonder, either ocean on the left or dales and hills on the right, covered with green growth and flowers. Here I saw such places as I encountered between Kobulet and Batum in Caucasus between Livadia and Orianda in Crimea. After riding through the forest for a long time we started to descend and suddenly before us opened a view on Fort Ross. It stands on a hillock as if in the [palm] of the hand above the ocean. From afar this is purely Russian village with church and half-fallen buildings at one time painted white[2] but now faded from passing of time and action of the elements. Prior to entering the Fort we passed the Russian orchard which was in bloom. This orchard is from the time of the Russian occupancy. In it primarily were apple, pear, cherry and other fruit trees of Russian descent. Into the Fort we arrive through the gates which are usually built in the villages, of poles and boards. A similarity to the gates of the XIV century, they did not have. Such [gates] were used in our villages to lock almost any yard. The Fort has an elongated appearance of a square, with the half-demolished towers in the opposite diagonal ends. In the center of the Fort, a low rectangular building with a passage on posts, with flower beds nearby. Has an appearance of real middle class land owner's place. Rooms are not too large, with low ceilings and valanced doors. In these small but comfortable rooms were standing several pieces of Russian furniture. A piano-forte brought from Paris in 1820[3] and now an adornment of the furnishings, [when touched] gave out a beyond grave-like sounds. A pulpit from the church [one legged] painted blue color and several benches. Other furnishings there were of later American make. To the right of the house and perpendicular to it a large wing of a building, also painted white and with a double slanting roof.[4] Here resided official personnel of the Fort. To the left in a line with the house of the administrators large rectangular building,[5] all were probably storage buildings for bread, grain, and various types of the merchandise belonging to the Company. Opposite at a larger distance a long row of structures almost under one roof, which contained horse barns and other structures of rural daily home life. More to the left near the exit from the Fort, a "church" and further a small home with a vegetable garden and between all of this a wide street portioning off the yard of the administrator by a wide half-circle of a garden. Beyond the Fort, both sides have small homes of Russian and present day American construction. They are [now] rented to some Americans. It is said that there were more [of Russian construction] homes, but one American, an admirer of relics, has taken these small homes for himself in Sacramento.[6] Church is a small wooden building with a high roof and two towers of Georgian form, extended and sharp, now faded, peeling, dark and half-destroyed, with broken glass and frames. The belfry has saved a semblance of a cross but the cupola has only a pole [on top], the cross piece is missing. The door locks as we do in the Ukraine with a kliamka [hasp] and a piece of splinter. Upon entering a covered platform inside to the left is a ladder leading to the belfry, which is without bells; these bells were taken by the American lovers of antiques. Straight ahead large doors, open the doors and your eyes see a revolting sight. For the full length of the temple are stalls for the animals. The church cupola in the form of a sharp-topped tent is right above us. It is splintered and peeling to the utmost. Signs of [former] picture painting about which was written by one traveler at the beginning of the XIX century, who was in Fort Ross,[7] now not a sign is left. All the walls are criss-crossed by writings of the visitors of the church. Upon sight of this "abomination of desolation of a holy place" my heart ached from pity and involuntary tears came to my eyes. With a deep sadness we exited. From the church we went to the cemetery. It was on the other hill separated from the Fort by a deep ravine with growing trees and murmuring brook. To get there one must leave the Fort, descend the ravine, then ascend the hill and enter the field where can be seen the graves. The [field] ending with an abrupt steep grade above the ocean. Going through the ravine, involuntarily recalled the Martcob Monastery near Tiflis in which once I spent summer time. The illusion was complete even to the scent of the trees and flowers as well as murmuring of the brook. It was all the same as in Marcobi. At the cemetery we found only an insignificant remains of [exis-tence here of probable monuments]. One piece of sawn-lengthwise oak plank with a grape-vine branch around it, already half dry. A modern column [post] without any indication of writing on it, several over-grave rocks and wooden planks, but most of all small hills in regular squares, with wild grow-ing flowers. Here, before a wooden cross we read Paneheda, for our departed brothers. Service [was] by Father Sebastian while I, with lector Grenachevsky [ed: Grepachevsky], sang. It was a charming picture, to the right a noisy ocean, to the left a hill covered with trees, behind which later was found gold in porous sand and clay. Behind the ravine with a murmuring brook follow-ing church and Fort, in the front an open field covered with a motley rug of green and flowers. The setting sun with the slanted rays gilded the ocean, the Fort, forest, and us. Father Sebastian, from emotion, with difficulty pronounced requests of the prayer. We seconded him with our singing "The Sea of Life" in view of the noisy ocean, came out very touching. How many are here in repose, only God knows. But I think quite a few, since there are visible quite a few graves. Yes, and people who have lived here during 29 years [1812 to 1841], not less than one thousand,[8] indicating that there were a number whom to inter. About this, the graves are silent, keeping in mystery not only those in repose but the past as well. To them a Kingdom of Heaven! With quiet sadness and under the pressure of memories of the past and the present, we returned to the Fort. Here we met the present owner of the Fort [third by count[9]], Mr. Call. He is already an elderly and respected man, but obviously not too sociable. To my question why did he allow such a desolation in a church, he said something which none of us (three) could understand, then I asked could he possibly yield a part of the Fort, namely the Church, neighboring house with the garden and the cemetery, which I would bring all in shape and would occupy the small home during summer months. He replied in an enigmatic manner "of this we shall talk tomorrow morning." But when I met him the next day at the pier, he did not mention one word to us. It would have been very good for us to extract our Russian sanctuary from the hands of the Yankee and give it a proper appearance. The soul somehow involuntarily did cling to this location [which was] soaked in Russian sweat and Russian blood and consecrated by prayers of hundreds of people. But alas, the stubborn and covetous Yankee [was] unwilling to understand. In a grocery store we found something alike to a museum, with Russian antiques. Here are two Kazak sabers, a rusted razor, old large pad-lock with an over-size key [both from the church] the Americans considered this a wonderful rarity. A "Siberian coin,"[10] several of case-shot, a lamp for night use, a piece of cast iron, etc. As an outstanding item of these, the Yankee showed to us an old wooden candle-stick [used in the church] with this he tried to explain to us that in the hole of this, Russians placed wax candles. The evening and the night were amazingly pretty. The noise and the resounding of the surf, bluish light of the moon spreading and coloring all, thin scent of the flowers and grass, [brought] a whole cloud of memories of the past of this area. All of the foregoing pulled me from the room, to the outdoors, to the ocean. For a long long time, I and Grenachevsky wandered from one end to another of the Fort, examining its deadly pale of the past. [Later] we encountered one American who lived here for several years. In talking to us of several matters he, among other things, made an error in mentioning that six miles from the Fort lived an elderly Indian named "Lukeria"[11] who speaks

Russian and that "My father knows several more Indians who speak Russian." This information acutely pinched my heart so I started to ask him to let this "Lukeria" know about our being here, in order that she may come here to converse with us. But to our dismay he declined to accede to our request, saying that he does not have anyone that he can send and he is unable to absent himself. [I was] very distressed about not being able to see these living monuments of the Russian reign. We slept in the house of the administrator,[12] now named "Hotel Fort Ross." For a long time I could not fall asleep, it seemed to me that I will hear a sound of alarm from the tower, then a clang and tinkle of the arms, noise, bustle and then shots being fired, yell of command, then moans of the wounded and later the "Hoorah" of the victors. Finally the weariness has taken the upper hand and I fell asleep. The morning was more attractive that the previous evening. Before leaving, we once more went around the Fort and then, while sitting in the carriage, we looked back admiring the view of the Fort and its surroundings, which we tried to memorize indelibly in our memory. The feeling of unexplainable sadness filled my heart when I glanced for the last time on a "spread out" area, church, cemetery, and the Fort.

Source: Nikolai 1897.

18

THE ENDURING ROMANCE OF FORT ROSS

IN THE 1890s Gertrude Atherton was a popular writer known for publishing romantic stories drawn from pre–gold rush California. Although many of her tales were constructed around the Spanish Californios, she also became entranced with the Russians at Fort Ross, and in order to steep herself in the Fort Ross mystique, she would make the trip from San Francisco by train to Cazadero and thence by stagecoach to take accommodation at the Fort Ross Hotel. The hotel had formerly been the residence of Alexander Rotchev, his wife, Helena, and their children during the late 1830s, and so put Atherton in touch with the ghostly remembrances of those long-lost days.

While in the area, Atherton was fortunate enough to connect with some of the elderly Kashaya Indians who had first-hand memories of Russian California. In particular, she was able to interview Lukaria Yorgen Myers, a woman of many years' residence in the area who had been young during the Russian days and had many stories to tell. (See also Robert Oswalt's linguistic collections from Lukaria's grandson, Herman James, on pages 197 and 229.) Atherton drew on Lukaria's recollections to provide background for her own tales of Fort Ross, including stories about her character Natalie Ivanhoff, a young Russian aristocrat who had come to Fort Ross to work for Mrs. Rotchev and there ran into her old flame from Russia, the exiled Prince Alexis Mikhailof, who had come to California in reduced circumstances. In an attempt to meet secretly one night, Natalie went up to the old windmill, and in a tragic accident, the windmill starts to turn and Natalie's long hair is caught in the gears and she is killed. Lukaria told a similar story, though in more stark description, in which a young Kashaya woman fell victim to a similar fate at the mill (see page 200). I am convinced that Atherton transformed Lukaria's story and replaced the Kashaya woman with a beautiful young Russian, who would have been more appealing to her readers.

EXCERPT FROM "NATALIE IVANHOFF" (1902)

In this excerpt from the story "Natalie Ivanhoff," the countess Natalie, companion to Helena Rotchev, wife of the commander at Fort Ross, has discovered that her lover from Russia is at the settlement working as a common laborer. They make an appointment to meet at the old windmill around midnight.

The inmates of Fort Ross were always in bed by eleven o'clock. At that hour not a sound was to be heard but the roar of the ocean, the soft pacing of the sentry on the ramparts, the cry of the panther in the forest. On the evening in question, after the others had retired, Natalie, trembling with excitement, made a hasty toilet, changing her evening gown for a gray travelling frock. Her heavy hair came unbound, and her shaking hands refused to adjust the close coils. As it fell over her gray mantle it looked so lovely, enveloping her with the silver sheen of mist, that she smiled in sad vanity, remembering happier days, and decided to let her lover see her so. She could braid her hair at the mill.

A moment or two before twelve she raised the window and swung herself to the ground. The sentry was on the rampart opposite: she could not make her exit by that gate. She walked softly around the buildings, keeping in their shadow, and reached the gates facing the forest. They were not difficult to unbar and in a moment she stood without, free. She could not see the mountain; a heavy bank of white fog lay against it resting, after its long flight over the ocean, before it returned, or swept onward to ingulf the redwoods.

She went with noiseless step up the path, then turned and walked swiftly toward the mill. She was very nervous; mingling with the low voice of the ocean she imagined she heard the moans with which beheaded convicts were said to haunt the night. Once she thought she heard a footstep behind her, and paused, her heart beating audibly. But the sound ceased with her own soft footfalls, and the fog was so dense that she could see nothing. The ground was soft, and she was beyond the sentry's earshot; she ran at full speed across the field, down the gorge, and up the steep knoll. As she reached the

Star-crossed lovers Natalie Ivanhoff and Alexis Mikhailof at Fort Ross.
Illustration by Harrison Fisher.

top, she was taken into Mikhaïlof's arms. For a few moments she was too breathless to speak; then she told him her plans.

"Let me braid my hair," she said finally, "and we will go."

He drew her within the mill, then lit a lantern and held it above her head, his eyes dwelling passionately on her beauty, enhanced by the colour of excitement and rapid exercise.

"You look like the moon queen," he said. "I missed your hair, apart from yourself."

She lifted her chin with a movement of coquetry most graceful in spite of long disuse, and the answering fire sprang into her eyes. She looked very piquant and a trifle diabolical. He pressed his lips suddenly on hers. A moment later something tugged at the long locks his hand caressed, and at the same time he became conscious that the silence which had fallen between them was shaken by a loud whir. He glanced upward. Natalie was standing with her back to one of the band-wheels. It had begun to revolve; in the moment it increased its speed; and he saw a glittering web on its surface. With an exclamation of horror, he pulled her toward him; but he was too late. The wheel, spinning now with the velocity of midday, caught the whole silver cloud in its spokes, and Natalie was swept suddenly upward. Her feet hit the low rafters, and she was whirled round and round, screams of torture torn from her rather than uttered, her body describing a circular right angle to the shaft, the bones breaking as they struck the opposite one; then, in swift finality, she was sucked between belt and wheel. Mikhaïlof managed to get into the next room and reverse the lever. The machinery stopped as abruptly as it had started; but Natalie was out of her agony.

Source: Atherton 1902: 352–354.

19

STORY OF THE "KODIAK BELL"
AT MISSION SAN FERNANDO REY

THE PRESENCE OF a one-hundred-pound Russian bell, which came to be known as the "Kodiak Bell," in a mission far from the main points of Russian contact and a fair distance from the coast has puzzled and intrigued a number of people over the years. One of the earliest was a renowned researcher on the bells of the missions, Mrs. Alice Harriman, who in 1920 discovered at Rancho Camulos a bell that purportedly belonged to the Mission San Fernando Rey. She entered into a lengthy search on the history of the bell, from its original casting to how it arrived at Mission San Fernando Rey and then moved on to the Rancho Camulos, near the town of Piru, in Ventura County. The inscription on the bell stated that it had been cast on the island of Kodiak in 1796, and this early parameter led to suggestions that it may have been brought down to California as early as 1806 by Nikolai Rezanov, although several historians think this unlikely. Unfortunately, the bell disappeared sometime after it was finally restored to the San Fernando mission in 1948 (Pauley and Pauley 2005: 237).

Another historian, Marie T. Walsh Harrington, discovered that a second bell belonging to the same mission was reported as also being from Russia, but it lacked the detailed inscription to prove it (Pauley and Pauley 2005: 236–237). This seventy-five-pound bell can still be found at the mission, although it doesn't have the same level of dramatic effect that the first "Kodiak Bell" had presented. Monsignor Francis J. Weber of Mission San Fernando also weighed in on the story of the bells (Weber 1964; 1975: 94–95), but the full tale of how they made their way to a California mission remains a mystery to this day. Another discussion of the bells was laid out in a 2005 publication by the husband-and-wife team of historians Ken and Carol Pauley.

For my part, I can understand the likelihood of Rezanov bringing the bell down to California, since he was purchasing his supplies from the local missionaries. I can't see why the bell would have been brought by the local military commander, José Argüello, as Harriman suggests below; why would he cart it all the way down to Santa Barbara only to then pass it on to a mission? The whole story seems quite baffling.

One source that hasn't been discussed previously is Kirill Khlebnikov, the Russian American Company agent who had dealings with virtually all of the missions. He was known to have provided bells to Mission Santa Cruz (see letters from Fr. Luis Gil on page 90), and may well have done so for other missions farther south. Perhaps one day we will find the smoking document that clears up the mystery of the San Fernando Russian bells.

What follows is an excerpt from Fr. Zephyrin Engelhardt, author of a history of Mission San Fernando Rey de España in 1927.

A MYSTERIOUS BELL (1927)

From the inventory drawn up on March 12, 1849, it is clear that the belfry of Mission San Fernando then contained one large bell and two smaller bells. There was another in the early days, before the confiscation,[1] which had disappeared. It was not discovered till about the summer of 1920, by Mrs. Alice Harriman of Los Angeles.

This good lady, deprived by death of her husband soon after marriage, conceived an ardent desire for learning all about the bells in the twenty-one missions of California. Partly, too, as she acknowledged to the writer with a smile, she made this search her hobby to keep out of mischief. Mrs. Harriman, though not of the same faith with the Mission Fathers, at great expense and more hardship visited and searched every one of the missionary establishments and critically noted the number of bells, their names, their approximate weight, the dates of their arrival, the place of casting, and the names of the founder, along with any story connected with them, for she intended bringing out the facts in book form.

Often the persistent searcher would have to overcome great obstacles to reach the cherished objects so as to secure the inscriptions; but nothing deterred her, not even climbing up the interior of the church steeple at Mission San José, which the writer, also in search of the truth about local bells, at another time found it very difficult to ascend as there were no stairs, but a labyrinth of timbers. Sometimes Mrs. Harriman would hear of the existence of a one-time Mission bell in some out of the way locality. That clue was sufficient for her to risk a long and futile journey. It was in this way that the tireless bell-hunter learnt of the existence of the bell which with its interesting story we are about to describe. Mrs. Harriman related the discovery of this bell in an article published by the Los Angeles Times on July 8, 1923. She had found the bell three years previously in an orange grove of the Camúlos Rancho, now the Del Valle Ranch.

After long and minute investigations, Mrs. Harriman came to the conclusion that this bell was not of Spanish origin, which are usually nicely finished. Nor had it come to California from Mexico, Peru, Russia or Massachusetts. The inscription on the Camúlos bell, written in a forgotten language [ed: old Church Slavonic], at last betrayed the secret. It revealed the fact, briefly, that it had been cast at Kodiak, Alaska, in 1796; that it had been traded at San Francisco for food by the Russian Count Nicolai Reza-nov, and then it had until sixty years ago hung in the famed San Fernando Mission.

When Mrs. Harriman first saw the bell in the orange grove, the inscrip-tion could not be made out. The Del Valle family knew only that it had been removed from the Old Mission of San Fernando in order to save it from vandals sixty years ago, i.e., about 1860. Since then it had been exposed to the ravages of the weather on the Del Valle Ranch. A crude cross and the stenciled inscription *De Sn Ferno* hammered on the bronze surface showed that it had indeed once hung in the San Fernando Mission. Our energetic bell hunter appealed to the Rev. A. P. Kashereroff [ed: Kashevarov], curator of the Alaskan Historical Society. On studying the photograph of the bell, the curator deciphered portions of the inscription to read in English: "island of Kodiak—Alexander Baranoff—Month of January."

Two big gaps in the inscription could not be read from the photographs by Dr. Kashereroff [ed: Kashevarov]. The irrepressible Mrs. Harriman then sought the aid of Dr. Alexis Kall of Los Angeles, a student of the "forgot-ten" Slavonic language. The complete inscription was thus at last deciphered to read: "1796—In the Month of January this bell was cast on the Island of Kodiak through the generosity of Arichimandrite [ed: Archimandrite] Joasaphat and the Church Warden-elect Alexander Baranoff."

The question now arose, how did this bell come to California and reach San Fernando Mission? Baranoff in 1805 changed his headquarters from Kodiak to Sitka and most likely brought the bell along. When Count Reza-now [ed: sic] visited Sitka soon after and found the whole settlement in distress for lack of food, he had the ship *Juno* laden with all sorts of goods that would be welcome to the Spaniards in California. He knew that new Missions were being established there and that they would need bells. Hence the Kodiak bell most probably went along to be traded for grain. The *Juno* entered the harbor of San Francisco on April 8, 1806. Captain José Dario Argüello was then commander of the port. In 1806 José Argüello became commander of the presidio at Santa Barbara. The bell most probably went along with the effects of the family by sea. In 1815, having been made governor of Lower California, Argüello donated the bell to the new Mission of San Fernando. At all events, perhaps on the petition of the Fathers of San Fernando Mission, which stood under the military jursidiction of the commander of Santa Barbara, it must have reached the Mission between 1808 and 1815. Captain Argüello and his family were model Christians, one of the boys becoming the first priest produced by California, and one of the daughters, the celebrated Doña Concepción, being the first native Californian to enter a Sisterhood, may be taken as proof. The captain would hardly retain an article intended for religious purposes. Wherefore we may conclude that he donated the bell to San Fernando as soon as he arrived at Santa Barbara.

The material used in casting the bell also deserves a word or two. Baranoff informed Shellkoff, his superior in Russia, at whose instance the bell had been cast, that the copper Shellkoff sent had been received and that "that Englishman Vancouver" had sent him some tin. Baranoff, most fortunately, also noted that the name of the bell founder was Sapoknikoff. Mrs. Harriman acknowledges that most of her positive information was found in Tekmanieff's [ed: Tikhmenev's] History.

Mrs. Harriman completed her self-imposed task of gathering information about the California Mission bells, and had submitted the last chapter for the book which she intended to publish, to the writer for review in order to make sure that everything was historically correct, when she contracted a severe cold. This developed into pneumonia, and after only six days, carried her noble soul to her everlasting home the day before Christmas, 1925. R.I.P.

Source: Engelhardt 1927: 148–154.

20

FORT ROSS IN THE COLD WAR,
1950–1951

DURING THE COLD WAR between East and West following World War II, even the comic strips reflected the politics of the time. When the Korean War broke out in 1950, the level of antagonism and anxiety ratcheted up, and in the tenor of the times a twenty-three-year-old cartoonist named Warren Tufts developed a storyline called "Casey Ruggles: A Saga of the West," using Sutter's Fort, Fort Ross, and the Presidio of San Francisco as his scenic backgrounds. This series ran from November 20, 1950, to February 17, 1951, and surely titillated an untold number of readers at the time.

The main character, Casey Ruggles, is a handsome, blond ex–U.S. Army sergeant and later U.S. marshall who travels through the West in the early 1850s. In the course of a visit to Sutter's Fort, he is asked by John Sutter to dismantle and send back useful items from the old Russian fort on the coast, which he had bought nearly a decade before. Simultaneous to Casey's arrival at Fort Ross is the return of the (fictional) commandant and his wife as well as a hunting party who had left ten years earlier, gotten lost, and finally made it back. They find their fort abandoned and this strange American and his Indian sidekick, Kit Fox, busily removing the bell from the chapel and hauling away one of the cannons. The commandant, Ivan, is angered by this appropriation of his goods (since he had not been present during the sale of Fort Ross to Sutter and was at a loss as to what was going on). Of course, this commandant is nothing like the actual last commander of Fort Ross, the urbane Alexander Rotchev, but is rather a stereotypical coarse bully, somewhat henpecked by his buxom blonde wife, Sonja. Another character invented for the comic was the chief of the Pomos, named Valenila. Here Tufts had taken the name of the chief of the Bodega Miwok, changed his tribal affiliation, and fictionalized his personality. Using even more stereotypes, Valenila is shown wearing Western clothes and constantly seeking vodka, for which he is willing to agree with most anything Ivan wants, including directing an attack against the Presidio of San Francisco!

It appears to me that in this story Fort Ross may be seen as a stand-in for the territory (at that time) of Alaska, sold by the Russian tsar to the United States in 1867. There was fear in the states of the Soviet Russian bear return-ing to gobble up its former possession (the "domino theory" in full swing), and the Americans were gripped with paranoia that monolithic communism would absorb neighboring areas and eventually reach home soil, in particular the very sparsely settled territory of Alaska, which, being not even physically connected to the lower forty-eight states, seemed a likely victim for the "god-less Rooskies."

Ultimately, our hero Ruggles manages to escape to the Presidio of San Fran-cisco and marshall its military force to repel the Russo-Indian attack, after which Ivan and Sonja head back to their homeland defeated by the forces of good.

Although Tufts takes great liberty with the historical facts, it is interest-ing to note the homework he must have done to put together his story. I was especially impressed with his knowledge that Valenila was the name of an actual chief, even though it was not that of the Pomo chief, much less the Kashaya Pomo who lived near Fort Ross. Looking at the conceit of his story today, although we may be amused by the over-the-top Russian characters, we are also appalled at the image of the heroes, Casey and Kit Fox, wrecking the chapel in order to steal the bell. Likewise, the pejorative view of the benighted Indians is certainly unacceptable. However, as a window into the Cold War fears and attitudes, the characterizations are quite consistent with the times.

Source: Cartoon from Tufts 1979.

CASEY RUGGLES   By WARREN TUFTS

Casey Ruggles at Fort Ross, 1950–1951. "Casey Ruggles"
was drawn by Warren Tufts for United Features Syndicate.

EPILOGUE

IN THE EARLY TWENTIETH CENTURY Fort Ross came to the attention of the California Historical Landmarks League, a group initiated by Joseph R. Knowland, Sr., an Oakland newspaper publisher and state senator. This organization devoted itself to acquiring and protecting a number of places in California that were deemed important to the history of the state. In 1903 a man named J. J. Lerman, using three thousand dollars provided by the newspaper tycoon William Randolph Hearst, simultaneously purchased Mission San Francisco Solano de Sonoma and Fort Ross (specifically, the two-and-a-half-acre plot that encompassed the stockade area of Fort Ross). Three years later, these properties were gifted to the State of California. Fort Ross was the fifth such landmark acquired by the State.

Shortly after Fort Ross was transferred to the State, the Bay Area suffered a devastating earthquake, in April 1906. The effects of the quake hit the iconic Fort Ross chapel particularly hard, and it wasn't until 1916 that funds were obtained to reconstruct it. This was important to the history of the area, because most of the rest of the buildings had been renovated for use by a series of owners (the Benitz, James Dixon, and Call families) and had largely lost their distinctive Russian appearance; the chapel, meanwhile, had retained its original style.

Until 1972, the Coast Highway ran through the center of the Fort Ross stockade area, and it was a convenient stopping place for travelers but lacked the allure of being an enclosed fort. In 1970, an apparently accidental fire resulted in the destruction of the chapel, which was finally rebuilt in 1974 as part of a plan for reconstruction that grew to encompass a broader restoration of the buildings inside the fort, to bring the Ross settlement back into its original appearance. The project involved rerouting Highway 1 to allow the stockade walls to be rebuilt and additional structures inside the fort to be constructed.

The focus on the chapel was firmly supported by Russian emigrés to California following the revolution of 1917. Their Orthodox faith was a key element to their cultural survival, and so it was not surprising that priests from the Russian Orthodox church played a central part in organizing trips to visit this historic monument, which interpreted a piece of their history prior to the revolution.

At the same time, as strangers in a new land, Russian immigrants to the United States naturally gravitated toward the story of a time when their countrymen had had a foothold in California. Beginning in 1925, Fr. Vladimir Sakovich of the Russian Orthodox Church in San Francisco (Orthodox Church in America) began leading groups up to Fort Ross every July 4 to hold a service at the chapel. Later, another Russian Orthodox group that called itself the "Russian Orthodox Church in Exile" (and who was at odds with the San Francisco church led by Fr. Sakovich) also sought permission from California State Parks to hold services in the Fort Ross chapel. In order to maintain the peace, ranger/curator John McKenzie arranged with the latter group to hold their annual service on Memorial Day, at the end of May. This pattern continues to this day, supplemented by other special events over the course of the year, the principal one being Cultural Heritage Day, which occurs on the last Saturday of July.

Interest in the history of the Russians in California was strong among some Russian historians even during the Soviet era (1918–1989), a time when it would have seemed that any glorifying of the tsarist-era colonization activities would have been anathema. However, the romantic image of a time when Russia held a piece of the Golden State was just too compelling. When John McKenzie, the ranger/curator in charge of Fort Ross in the period just after World War II, made efforts to contact scholars who could help him better understand his park, one historian who emerged was Svetlana Fedorova. In the course of lengthy correspondence, McKenzie and Fedorova developed a close working relationship, and their efforts were augmented by the involvement of Professor Nicolas Rokitiansky of Foothill College, in the southern San Francisco Bay Area, who undertook a number of trips to Russia to seek more information and bring back useful data. Perhaps one of the most valuable items obtained in this collaboration was a detailed map of the Fort Ross area dated 1817, which was published in Fedorova's dissertation in 1972.

A number of other individuals have added to the scholarship of Fort Ross over the years. One who collaborated with the Russian scholars was Paul Schumacher of the National Park Service, who had been previously assigned to the site of the old capital of Russian America, Sitka, Alaska (New Archangel). I also have to mention the involvement of three grandchildren of the Call family—F. Kaye Tomlin, Mercedes Stafford, and Barbara Black—who likewise were active in promoting the history of Fort Ross, going beyond the Russian period to encompass the local Kashaya Indian history and the subsequent ranch eras. Another enthusiastic and far-flung group is the numerous descendants of the Benitz family, who periodically visit Fort Ross and have provided some invaluable information as well as the earliest photographs known of the buildings of Fort Ross, dating to the mid-1860s. Professor James R. Gibson of York University in Ontario, Canada, also contributed a number of important translations and pieces of research that have illuminated the Russian experience in California. When I came along in 1981 to work on the archaeological excavation of the fort's Old Warehouse site, I greatly benefited from the work done by all of these individuals, who very kindly included me in their band of aficionados of Fort Ross.

There has been a long, unofficial tradition of scholars using Fort Ross as the basis for their theses. Flora Faith Hatch (1922), Ynez Haase (1952), Mary Jean Kennedy (1955), and Janice Christina Smith (1974) were all relatively early contributors to the history of Fort Ross. (It is an interesting coincidence that during a time when men dominated the profession, female historians were the primary authorities on Fort Ross.) This research has continued in the guise of students of UC Berkeley guided by Professor Kent G. Lightfoot.

Fort Ross State Historic Park has acted as the tangible touchstone for those with an interest and tie to the site's history. This was especially true in the visit of an Alaskan man, Peter Kalifornsky, who in 1979 came to see the place where his forebearer, Nikolai Kalifornsky, a Tana'ina Indian from the Kenai Peninsula, had served under Ivan Kuskov as an otter hunter.

With the change of government in Russia in 1989, many of the difficulties of travel from Russia to America were minimized if not eliminated, and it soon became possible for Russian scholars to visit Fort Ross for themselves and to soak up the wondrous ambience of the place. Among the Russian historians who came to California to visit Fort Ross during this time were Nikolai Bolkhovitinov, Alexei Istomin, and Oleg Bychkov. A notable visit was made by Fr. Innocent Veniaminov, the great-great-grandson of the earlier Fr. Ivan Veniaminov, who, as a priest and later bishop in Alaska, had visited Fort Ross in 1836. The Russian consulate in San Francisco has also been an attentive guardian angel to the interests of Fort Ross, especially under recent consuls-general Yuri Popov and Nikolai Vinokurov.

Art conservator (and honorary Russian naval lieutenant) John Middleton-Tidwell was particularly active in utilizing his proficiency in spoken Russian to facilitate the travel of various other foreign scholars interested in Fort Ross. With his help, historical architects Igor Medvedev and Elena Klimkova, and architecture students Olga Zaitseva and Anna Semenova, applied their knowledge of traditional Russian architecture to produce drawings of how the original fort structures might have looked. Historical illustrator David Rickman also used his talents to create a number of historic scenes relative to life at Fort Ross.

Whereas it surprises many people even today that the Russians had this sort of semi-permanent presence in early California, the frequent and important Russian visits to Mission-era California are the greater story, and one that's enjoying increased exposure as the years go on. More and more documents from both the Russian side and the Spanish/Mexican archives have illuminated the interaction between Russians, Californios, and local Indians during the Fort Ross era. Thanks to a generous grant from the National Endowment for the Humanities (NEH), a project to mine the Russian naval archives was instigated by John Middleton and administered by Lyn Kalani and Sarah Sweedler. James Gibson has made available a number of documents from those naval archives as well as from other Russian archives, and Katherine Arndt, from the library of the University of Alaska, Fairbanks, contributed to this effort material available from Alaskan archives.

In addition to reconstruction of the Fort Ross chapel, another major project was the Rotchev House, the only building that remains from the original fort, and itself a registered National Historic Landmark. The importance of this structure has been long appreciated, and various attempts have been made to bring it back to its condition during the Russian era, it having since spent many years as a residence for the families that owned the ranch, as well as a quarter century as the Fort Ross Hotel. In more recent years, the Rotchev House was studied by architectural historian Richa Leann Wilson (1998), who prepared a Historic Structures Report that has made possible a plan to refurbish the old house and outfit it as a furnished house museum. The research on the building was orchestrated by Lyn Kalani, with assistance from a number of sources including the NEH, the Sonoma County Landmarks Commission, and California State Parks, among others. Most recently the Russian philanthropic organization Renova has provided funding for the repairs needed to eliminate the structural leaks that endanger the building and its contents.

As a historical archaeologist, I have endeavored to put my trowel to use in excavating some of the old sites at Fort Ross as well as to immerse myself in the archives—particularly those at the Bancroft Library, at the University of California, Berkeley—to further uncover source data concerning Russian presence in California in the first half of the nineteenth century. My introduction to Fort Ross came in 1981, when I was assigned by California State Parks to excavate the site of the Old Warehouse, which was to be added to the list of buildings that would be reconstructed inside the stockade. It is gratifying to see, some thirty years later, the building finally rising on the site.

As research into the historical documentary evidence has expanded over time, so has our appreciation of the broader connections between Russians and Californians in the early nineteenth century. On the one side, numerous documents from Russian archives have become available through translation by various scholars. In particular, James Gibson has a long record of important published translations and will soon release an impressive three-volume set of documents that he collected in collaboration with Alexei Istomin. Other key sources of Russian documents have been provided by Basil Dmytryshyn and E. A. P. Crownhart-Vaughan, whose work has been published by the Oregon Historical Society. California historian W. Michael Mathes also has produced a volume of Spanish-language documents related to Russians in California and, most recently, James Gibson is to publish a volume of additional documents related to the trading activities of the Russian American Company in California as well as the Russians' numerous naval visits to the province. For those interested in the early-nineteenth-century history of California, this is indeed an exciting time, and when all of these new sources are fully available, this particular era in the history of California will be vastly expanded, if not rewritten.

ACKNOWLEDGMENTS

THIS BOOK IS a long overdue compilation of material I have found interesting during my studies on Russians in early California. Despite having been intrigued by the subject for years, the impetus to produce this anthology grew out of a project intended to mine the Russian State Naval Archives (RSNA). Conceived by John Middleton-Tidwell, implemented by Lyn Kalani and Sarah Sweedler, and funded in large part by the National Endowment for the Humanities, this project brought together scholars from Russia, Alaska, Canada, and California to undertake a focused examination of the RSNA housed in St. Petersburg, with the hope of finding new material related to Russians in California. Participants included James R. Gibson of York University in Ontario, Canada; Katherine Arndt of the Elmer E. Rasmuson Library, University of Alaska, Fairbanks; Alexander Yur'evich Petrov of the Russian Academy of Sciences; Alexei Istomin of the Russian Academy of Sciences; and myself, of the Fort Ross Interpretive Association (FRIA). Vladimir Semenovich Sobolev was the director of the RSNA at the time of the study, ably assisted by research specialist Ludmila Ivanovna Spiridonova. High-quality electronic images of various maps and documents were made by Kiril Kriukov. Additional support for the project was generously provided by Sarah Sweedler, as FRIA president and NEH grant administrator; Sarjan Holt of FRIA; Natalia Gubina, in document transcription and translation; and Lyn Kalani, who spent endless hours organizing documents and images and creating an impressive edited version of this manuscript. James Gibson brought to the table a wealth of sources gleaned from various other archives throughout Russia, and he will be publishing a separate volume featuring a choice selection of these documents.

This volume stands on the shoulders of a number of intrepid scholars who have worked over the years to ferret out obscure documents, translate them, and publish them for the benefit of all. I am particularly grateful to Katherine Arndt, Glynn Barratt, Rose Marie Beebe, John Bisk, Lydia Black, E. A. P. Crownhart-Vaughan, Basil Dmytryshyn, Alton S. Donnelly, Svetlana Fedorova, James R. Gibson, Alexei A. Istomin, Herman James, John R. Johnson, W. Michael Mathes, Randall Milliken, Doyce Nunis, Jr., Adele Ogden, Sannie K. Osborn, Robert Oswalt, Kenneth N. Owens, Essie Parrish, Richard A. Pierce, Robert M. Senkewicz, Leonid Shur, Barbara Sweetland Smith, Oleg Terichow, F. Kaye Tomlin, Michael Tucker, and Stephen Watrous. All of these individuals have been instrumental in assembling the building blocks upon which future historical structures can be assembled.

Heyday was approached about this project, and its publisher, Malcolm Margolin, suggested an anthology utilizing items from the RSNA as well as other documentary material relevant to the Fort Ross era. I was designated by FRIA to piece it all together. Gayle Wattawa of Heyday acted as the developmental editor for the volume and provided many cogent suggestions and comments during our short production time, with the intent of having a finished book ready for the bicentenary of the construction of Fort Ross, to be celebrated in 2012. Lisa K. Marietta, copy editor at Heyday, provided an excellent sounding board and did wonders at tightening up and generally clarifying the language of the book.

NOTES

INTRODUCTION, PP. 1–6

1. Actually, this group included many other Alaskan native peoples, including Eskimo and Indian tribal groups other than ethnic Aleuts, but the Russians persisted in using the term "Aleut" as a generic catchall. It is therefore interesting that the Spanish called the same group "Codiacas," which was probably the term the people used for themselves as Kodiak Islanders.

2. The term "Creole" was used for people of mixed ethnic Russian and native ancestry (usually father and mother, respectively).

CHAPTER 2, PP. 11–16

1. In a number of publications, including Ogden (1941), this man was identified as Vasilii Petrovich Tarakanov, however, this was an invention of one of historian Hubert Howe Bancroft's researchers, a man named Ivan Petrov (Owens 1990: 25–29). In fact, the Tarakanov on this trip was Timofei Tarakanov, who was very important in the early sea mammal hunting expeditions along the Pacific coast.

2. Tarakanov was also in the area of San Francisco Bay in 1811 on another expedition, and was contacted by members of the Kuskov expedition, so it is conceivable that this event occurred at that time, instead of in 1807.

3. Account book of the *Mercury,* Mission Santa Barbara Archive-Library.

4. The intriguing story of the *Mercury* is told in a book by Robert Ryal Miller (2001).

5. *Artel* is the Russian term for a small cooperative work party, often used for groups assigned to killing and processing animals.

CHAPTER 3, PP. 17–44

1. Grigori Shelikhov was a co-owner of the Shelikhov-Golikhov Company, the precursor to the Russian American Company, which came into being four years after his death.

2. Ogden (1979) calls him Thomas Kilby and states that he was captured at San Juan Capistrano and taken to San Diego.

3. Passages from Langsdorff's narrative from the previous selection are repeated here to provide continuity.

CHAPTER 5, PP. 63–74

1. Kenneth Owens (2006) has provided a lengthy and compelling account of Tarakanov's activities.

2. See Owens and Donnelly (1985: 77–87) for a detailed account of Petrov's fraud.

3. It is not clear whether Golovnin is referring to the earlier arrangement by Tarakanov or to the "treaty" that Lieutenant Hagemeister had concluded with the Indians the previous year (1817), although the context of the statement does suggest an agreement dating back to or before the founding of Fort Ross.

4. Differences in how the chiefs' names appear leads one to wonder about their names' meanings in their own language. The name given to the chief of the village at Bodega Bay at the time of the purchase, Íollo, does not have a known meaning (Catherine Callaghan, personal communication, 1993), but it is tempting to suggest that it might be a corruption of *toion,* the word often used by the Russians for "chief" (and known to have been later used for the Kashaya Pomo chiefs). In contrast, the name Vallí:éla has been interpreted by Callaghan (personal communication, 1993) as being properly *"wállin ?éla,"* meaning roughly "Great Water Spirit." Isabel Kelly reports a shift in moieties from generation to generation among the Bodega Miwok; according to her main consultant, Tom Smith, a Bodega Miwok, "I am Land; [therefore] my boy gets a Water name" (Kelly 1991: 342). Kelly then goes on to point out a number of cases in which this model does not hold, but it may have been due to a breakdown in customs in the modern period. At any rate, it could be that if the name Vallí:éla derived from the water moiety, Íollo would probably be a land moiety name.

CHAPTER 6, PP. 75–86

1. This report of Moraga's trip was sent to Governor Arrillaga by José María Estudillo, which accounts for the use of the third person.

CHAPTER 7, PP. 87–96

1. In fact, these two figures are not equivalent if we accept the value of 1 pud as equal to 36 pounds and 1 arroba as equal to 25 pounds.

2. Probably José Bolcoff.

3. In addition to the November 12 date, Fr. Gil includes November 14. It is not clear why both dates appear on the document.

4. *Sayasaya nacar* is identified as Chinese silk of a pearl color in Perissinotto, 1998: 84–85.

5. It is interesting to note that the English brig *Fulham* (Henry Delano Fitch, master) that sailed from Monterey in early January 1828 carried a bell belonging to Santa Cruz Mission to be sent to Callao (Peru) for recasting (Ogden 1979). Whether or not this was the same bell is uncertain.

6. If he meant the captain of the *Kyakhta,* on which Khlebnikov was traveling at the time, this would have been Mikhail Prokofyev. According to Pierce (1990: 414), Prokofyev's wife was named Praskovya Petrovna.

7. Candida Castro was married to José Bolcoff in 1823.

8. Possibly Iakov Dorofeyevich Dorofeyev, a *prikachik* who accompanied Khlebnikov on various trips to California and who led a number of hunts for sea otters. He may have been skilled at navigation, which would have exposed him to the use and maintenance of chronometers.

9. Doña María Prudenciana Vallejo de Amesti was married to merchant José Amesti and lived at the Rancho los Corralitos near Santa Cruz.

10. Probably David Spence, a Scottish merchant in Monterey.

CHAPTER 8, PP. 97–102

1. Khlebnikov (1994: 17) stated that the brig *Ledi* [*Lydia*] and the brig *Atahualpa* were each valued at 20,000 rubles. The *Lydia* was purchased for 13,000 fur seal skins valued at 1.50 rubles each, and the *Atahualpa* was bought for 10,000 fur seal skins valued at 2 rubles each. In addition, the Russians purchased goods worth 55,512 rubles, 40 kopeks. The ships were noted as being sold with their armament.

2. A spurious account of the trip, attributed to a fictitious Vasilii Tarakanov (not to be confused with the genuine Timofei Tarakanov) has been frequently cited by distinguished scholars who were taken in by the fabricated "An Account of My Captivity," which was actually written by Ivan Petrov for Hubert Howe Bancroft's History Company.

CHAPTER 9, PP. 103–124

1. In 2000, Barbara Sweetland Smith created a marvelous traveling exhibit on the subject, titled "Science Under Sail: Russia's Great Voyages to America, 1728–1867."

2. Although Schabelski has entered dates based on the Gregorian calendar for the foreign audiences addressed in his book, he adds twelve days to the Russian dates as applied in Europe. However, in California, the date was only eleven days ahead, thus the Mexican documents record the arrival of the *Apollon* as occurring on November 25.

3. Agustín Iturbide proclaimed himself Emperor of Mexico, which had declared itself an independent monarchy in 1821. He was eventually deposed on April 8, 1823, and was executed by a firing squad in 1824, after which Mexico became a republic.

4. The Russian American Company port in California was generally referred to by the Russians as Port Rumiantsev.

5. The governor at the time was the newly elected Luis Antonio Argüello.

6. The Pious Fund supported the mission establishments.

7. This refers to the Napoleonic Wars and the ensuing turmoil in Spain.

8. Sangrado was a character in the novel *Gil Blas de Santillane* by Alain-René Lesage (1668–1747) who had only two remedies: hot water and blood-letting. The doctor referred to here was almost certainly Manuel Quijano, the post surgeon at the Presidio of Monterey, who served from 1807 until his death in August 1823.

9. The priests at Mission San José at this time were Fr. Narciso Durán and Fr. Buenaventura Fortuny.

10. British explorer George Vancouver, who visited California in 1792–1793.

11. François-René de Châteaubriand, a French writer (1768–1848) who had visited America in the late eighteenth century and, in the nineteenth century, was seen to have a considerable influence on the Romantic movement.

12. François, duc de La Rochefoucauld (1613–1680). His *Maxims* (1665) expressed his disgust of a world wherein the best sentiments are, in spite of appearances, dictated by self-interest. Alexander Pope, English poet and philosopher (1688–1744).

13. Fr. Juan Amorós, who wrote a letter dated March 8, 1823, in which he stated that he "had entertained some Russian officers at San Rafael but had prevented them from going to a place called Ros-Kosoff [sic] by enlarging upon the difficult terrain and other difficulties to be encountered in reaching it." This must have been another contingent of Russian ships' officers who were in California at the same time, considering Schabelski's comment on how helpful the priest was to him.

14. Presumably this was the Russian River.

15. At least two of these baidarkas must have been ones with three cockpits. These were commonly used to convey Russian officials who would ride in the middle cockpit.

16. Fr. Mariano Payeras gave a wonderful description of this bathhouse at Bodega Bay from his visit a few months previous to Schabelski's visit.

17. More commonly known as the Prince of Wales Archipelago.

18. A reference to Luis Antonio Argüello, who left the presidio for Monterey when he became governor in 1823.

CHAPTER 10, PP. 125–138

1. Annotation by Richard A. Pierce.

2. See the account of the Russian visitor to San Francisco, Dmitry Zavalishin, meeting Pomponio at the presidio in 1824, page 114.

3. The village location is known as archaeological site CA-Ker-33.

4. Senen was interrogated on June 1, 1824, at Santa Barbara. His testimony is found in the De La Guerra documents at the Mission Santa Barbara Archive-Library. It was published in Cook (1962: 153).

CHAPTER 11, PP. 139–144

1. The report is excerpted at greater length later in this collection (see page 156).

2. El Molino Rancho, in present-day Sonoma County, was given to John B. R. Cooper by Governor José Figueroa in 1833 and officially confirmed by Governor Nicolás Gutiérrez in 1836.

CHAPTER 12, PP. 145–152

1. Voznesenskii's contributions are dealt with at greater length later in this collection (see page 293).

2. More about Chernykh, especially his building of a Scottish thresher at Ross, is included later in this collection (see page 171).

3. Terry L. Erwin published this information on the species in the *Coleopterist's Bulletin* 19(1), 1965.

CHAPTER 13, PP. 153–182

1. Lieutenant V. Llvovich Illyasevich was also listed as captain of the *Baikal* during an earlier trip to California in 1830–1831, on which Kirill Khlebnikov was a passenger (Ogden 1979).

2. This soil is not, of course, true chernozem ("black earth"), which is confined to the temperate grasslands. Russians tended to classify any dark, tillable soil as chernozem.—JRG

3. The Russians adopted the word "Creole" from the French and Spanish to mean a person of mixed Russian and native parentage.

4. Vasilii Permitin, originally from Tomsk, arrived at Fort Ross in 1820 and was accompanied by his Creole wife, Paraskeva, as well as two sons and two daughters. He eventually had two more sons and two more daughters while at Fort Ross (Osborn 1997: 379). Permitin worked as a carpenter and was fairly prominent in the affairs of Fort Ross, particularly being noted for his shipbuilding skills (Khlebnikov 1990: 44, 97, 144).

5. In an entry dated Tuesday, March 26, 1833, in John Work's journal of his trip to California in 1832–1833, he stated that Michel Laframboise "arrived from the Russian Establishment which he left on Sunday....He was only able to obtain 10 lbs. of powder, 30 lbs. of lead, and 10 lbs. of tobacco" from the Russians at Bodega Bay. For this he was charged five beaver pelts for the powder and lead and another two for the tobacco (Maloney 1943: 340–341).

6. This is a reference to the Hudson's Bay Company trappers from Fort Vancouver on the Columbia River.

7. Since he dates the letter January 12, 1841, these prices must be for 1840.

CHAPTER 14, PP. 183–210

1. Archaeologist Kent Lightfoot has written more extensively about this subject (2005).

2. Tarweed (*Madia elegans*).

3. The artist Mikhail Tikhonovich Tikhanov illustrated this type of smoking in a painting done at Bodega Bay.

4. Oswalt (1964: 340–341) locates Forest Depths (*qhale sílil*) as being over the ridge from Fort Ross down in the valley of the Upper Gualala River.

5. Shohka was a village near the mouth of the Russian River, near present day Jenner.

6. Mention of the boys' bodies being taken to the church would mean that the event could not have happened before 1825, when the chapel was constructed.

CHAPTER 15, PP. 211–280

1. A calotte was a skullcap worn by priests at the time.

2. This is a remarkable statement. It is hard to imagine what hostile acts he could be referring to with regard to the Russians at this time. However, his comments were enough to make the new governor, Luis Argüello, sufficiently anxious to have commented on it in letters of his own, although once he met with the Russians aboard the *Apollon,* he was reassured of their peaceful intent.

3. Fernando VII, King of Spain, 1808–1833.

4. Fr. Mariano Payeras.

5. Various Russian deserters fled to civil settlements, San José, Branciforte, and Los Angeles prior to Mexican independence.

6. Osip Volkov. See below, and Pokriots 1997: 99.

7. Volkov and one Moliavin (Khlebnikov 1990: 120).

8. Stepan Kornilov, a deserter from Ross in 1822 (Khlebnikov 1990: 120–121).

9. The actual commandant was Karl Schmidt.

10. In 1810 the Pacific Fur Company of John Jacob Astor of New York established Astoria at the mouth of the Columbia River.

11. Frequently Fort Ross was referred to in Spanish and Mexican documents as Kuskov for its founder.

12. José Ignacio García Illueca (1780–1830) served under the Supreme Executive Power in 1823 as Minister of Justice (2 April–6 June), Internal and External Affairs (2–15 April), War and Navy (2 April–11 July), and Treasury (1–30 April).

13. Or Shabaicai, according to Otto von Kotzebue.

14. This name came from the Spanish, who termed the HBC camp the "Campo de los Franceses" due to the fact that the majority of the hunting parties were made up of French-speaking Canadian hunters who had been brought out to Fort Vancouver by the HBC.

15. I believe the word "Ayash" comes from the Chinook language, which was the lingua franca of the Hudson's Bay Company personnel at Fort Vancouver. There is a word in Chinook rendered as /hyas/ or /hy-as'/, meaning "big, great, or very."

16. Alexander Rotchev (1806–1872) was thirty-three years old at this time (Pierce 1990: 427–429).

17. The senior surgeon of the frigate was Mathieu Guilbert (Laplace 1841: xvii).

18. Laplace may have meant coyotes in this case.

19. This must have been Goat Rock, a major landmark on the south side of the mouth of the Russian River.

20. This may have been the short-lived farm established in early 1834 as "Los Tres Amigos" in the account of Governor Figueroa in 1834 (Vallejo 2000: viii).

21. This statement feeds into a long-standing debate as to whether there were gun ports piercing the stockade walls of Fort Ross. I am puzzled by the number of only two gates (*portes*), since Fort Ross seemed to have three gates. I have wondered if he actually meant the two blockhouses.

22. Laplace is probably confused on this point. What did occur in 1817 was a written agreement of mutual cooperation between the Russians and four chiefs of the local Indians (Dmytryshyn et al. 1989: 296–298).

23. A degeneration of the body, probably tuberculosis.

24. This comment makes me believe he was writing this from carefully kept journals and diaries, which would increase the likelihood of its accuracy, even though his account was not published until fifteen years after these events.

25. I believe this to have been the four-room house with adjoining kitchen mentioned in the 1841 inventories as being up by the Russian orchard (Dmytryshyn et al. 1989: 433).

26. A reference to Peter Kostromitinov, who was Rotchev's predecessor as commandant of Fort Ross (1830–1838).

27. Presumably this would have been the village of Métini, although where exactly it was located at that time is uncertain.

28. It is interesting that Laplace keeps harking back to explorers from the late eighteenth century rather than more recent explorers. Jean François Galaup de Lapérouse was another French visitor to California in 1786.

29. Of course, Pomo baskets are world renowned for their excellence.

30. The Russian term used for the natives of Alaska.

31. Note 2 in the text referred to a six-page endnote that is basically a statement of Laplace's later reflections on the decisions to abandon Fort Ross. It was left out of this work because it did not add any new direct observations about Laplace's time in California.

32. This mention of a large rock in the courtyard of the fort is confusing since the only large rock in the stockade is covered by the Kuskov House. Possibly his reference to "courtyard" (*la cour*) could be construed to mean the area out in front of the stockade.

33. This is an important comment because aside from the mention of two windmills in the 1841 inventory, there were no other sources to corroborate the presence of two windmills at Fort Ross. This would suggest that the second one had been constructed only a year or two before.

34. A reference to the Kostromitinov Rancho, a.k.a. the Munin Rancho, after Efim Munin, the overseer (Farris 1996).

35. In this case Laplace would be referring to redwoods (*Sequoia sempervirens*), probably tanbark oaks (*Lithocarpus densiflora*), and California chestnuts (*Aesculus Californica*).

36. Laplace uses the term *"mâtures"* or mast, meaning generally the "fruit" of forest trees.

37. This does not sound like chestnuts or redwoods but rather like a reference to pine nuts. The only pine that would fit this description would be the sugar pine (*Pinus lambertiana*), which normally grows at elevations above 1,200 feet. In fact, the local Kashaya Pomo people had traditions dealing with pine nuts (Farris 1982: 30;

Oswalt 1964: 135). On the other hand, it is possible that Laplace misconstrued what was being told to him.

38. This must have been the Chernykh Rancho, founded by agronomist Egor Chernykh and pictured in a drawing by Il'ya Voznesenskii, on page 295 of this collection.

39. Probably Egor Chernykh.

40. Another reference to Chernykh.

41. This remarkable comment is the only mention of any of the Russian wooden houses being roofed in tiles.

42. If this is true, the climatic regime of the area must have been far colder than it is today.

43. Indians trapping beaver directly at their lodges was commented on by Alexander Mcleod of the Hudson's Bay Company during his trip to California in 1829–1830: "A man would break a hole into a den, and, when the frightened animals bolted, they became entangled in a net. The Indians bartered their catch at Sonoma Mission for clothing and the red and white beans [sic, beads] that were so much to their taste" (Dillon 1975: 169–170).

44. The Hudson's Bay Company employed these steel traps in the areas south of their holdings in Oregon, intending to create a beaver-free zone in Upper California to dissuade the further advance of American fur traders coming north through California.

45. Apparently they had arrived at the Vasili Khlebnikov Ranch located near Bodega Corners.

46. *Tapecu* is a type of "bascule" or tip wagon, indicating that it was a two-wheeled cart rather than a four-wheeled wagon.

47. There is no corroboration that Wrangell visited Fort Ross on the occasion of his trip to Mexico from late 1835 to early 1836, only that he stopped briefly in Monterey, where he learned that Governor Figueroa had died a few months before. Wrangell's major visit to Fort Ross occurred in 1833.

48. De Mofras may have been putting his own spin on his interpretation of Sutter's background. Other biographies state that Sutter served in the Swiss guard, not in France.

49. It is difficult to substantiate these claims of intrigue and subterfuge as described by de Mofras.

50. In his role as a sort of spy for the French government, de Mofras evidently felt the need to put forth scenarios of possible French actions in the troubled province of California.

CHAPTER 16, PP. 281–300

1. Captain William Dane Phelps wrote of being ferried to Sutter's Fort from the embarcadero on the Sacramento River in a "bayardaka" [*baidara*] paddled by two Hawaiians during a visit in April 1842 (Phelps 1983: 278). This was almost certainly one of those purchased from the Russians at Fort Ross.

2. A *droschki* is a two- or four-wheeled wagon the Russians used to haul goods. In the original publication, Duflot de Mofras included a picture of a four-wheeled *droschki* adjacent to a "typical" Russian *isba* (peasant house), reprinted on p. 291 of this volume.

3. This number is far larger than any known figure of residents at Fort Ross during the Russian period. Actual population numbers for years in which we have censuses ranged from 236 to 335 (Osborn 1997: 196).

4. Also called the *George and Henry* or the *Jorge Enrique,* this ship was shown as being in the area of Monterey, San Francisco, and Bodega Bay in the period of June 12–25, 1843. It was owned by Sandels's friend Captain Smith (Ogden 1979).

CHAPTER 18, PP. 309–314

1. George Washington Call purchased Fort Ross in 1873 and took up residence there with his family.

2. There is no corroboration that the buildings at Fort Ross were ever painted white during the Russian occupation. The only color mentioned was blue. However, it is probable that William Benitz painted the buildings white during his tenure as owner (1843–1867).

3. It is highly unlikely that the piano-forte arrived in 1820, during the time of Ivan Kuskov; rather, it probably was brought in by the Rotchev family in the late 1830s.

4. This would have been the Officials' Quarters, which had been turned into a saloon at the time the Fort Ross Hotel was in existence.

5. This was the old warehouse or magazin, which was being used as a dance hall at this time.

6. This is presumably a reference to John Sutter, who had many of the Fort Ross structures dismantled and brought up to his new establishment in the Central Valley known as New Helvetia.

7. This may be a reference to the account left by Fr. Veniaminov, later Bishop Innokenti, in 1836.

8. This figure is double or triple the number given in various contemporary accounts of the population of Fort Ross.

9. Actually there had been four other owners since the Russian time and before George Washington Call: John Sutter, William Benitz, James Dixon, and Charles Fairfax.

10. This seems to refer to a classic large five- or ten-kopek piece from the time of Catherine the Great, in the late 1700s. One or two other examples have been found, and this has been the only type of Russian coin found at Fort Ross. These were probably keepsakes because the money used at Fort Ross was a type of company scrip stamped out on pieces of leather.

11. Lukeria or Lukaria Yorgen Myers was an elder among the Kashaya who was reputed to have been born before the arrival of the Russians and had close relations with them. Many of her stories were passed down through her grandson, Herman James (see pages 197 and 229), and she was also sought out by the author Gertrude Atherton as a source for stories of old Fort Ross (see page 309).

12. The Rotchev House, the only remaining building from the Russian era.

CHAPTER 19, PP. 315–320

1. This refers to the secularization of the missions, which the priests regarded as a form of confiscation of properties meant to go to the Indian neophytes.

GLOSSARY

ARROBA   Spanish measure equivalent to ¼ quintal or 25.36 pounds.

ARSHIN   Russian linear measure equal to 28 inches or ⅓ of a sazhen.

BAIDARA   Russian name for a large, open skin boat (*umiak*) used by the Alaskan natives to haul heavy loads (as much as 2,000 pounds). One *baidara* could be paddled by fifteen men.

BAIDARKA   Russian name for a sea kayak from the Aleutian Islands and Alaska peninsula. These skin boats usually had one, two, or three cockpits and were used for hunting and for transportation of Russian officials, who would ride in the middle cockpit.

CREOLE   In Russian America this referred to an individual with a Russian father and a mother of local native ancestry. These "mixed-blood" children were often trained in various professional skills useful to the Russian American Company.

FANEGA   Spanish measure for grain equal to about 1.5 bushels.

FUNT   Russian weight measure equal to .9 pounds or ¹⁄₄₀ of a pud.

HECTARE   2.47 acres.

HECTOLITER   2.84 bushels.

KOPEK   Russian coin valued at ¹⁄₁₀₀ of a ruble.

LEGUA   Spanish linear measure that was approximately 2.75 miles.

PUD   Russian weight measure equal to 36.11 pounds or 16.38 kilograms.

PIASTER   Word commonly used for the Spanish 8 real or peso coin from which the early American dollar was derived.

QUINTAL   Spanish measure equal to 4 arrobas or about 101 pounds.

REAL   Small silver coin equal to 1⅛ of a piaster, and the forerunner of the colloquial American term "bit" (as in two bits = a quarter).

RUBLE   Russian monetary unit; silver rubles were valued at about 50 cents and paper rubles were frequently valued at five to the dollar.

SAZHEN   Russian fathom that was actually equal to 7 feet and so differed from the Spanish, French, and English fathoms.

VARA   Spanish linear measurement equal to about 33 inches.

VEDRO   Russian liquid measurement that literally meant "pail" and amounted to 2.7 gallons; 12 vedros were approximately equal to 1 barrel.

VERSTA   Russian linear measure equal to .66 miles or about 1.06 kilometers.

REFERENCES CITED

Alekseev, A. I. 1987. *The Odyssey of a Russian Scientist: I. G. Voznesenskii in Alaska, California and Siberia, 1839–1849*. Translated by Wilma C. Follette, edited by Richard A. Pierce. Kingston, Ontario: The Limestone Press.

Archives of California. N.d. Departmental State Papers, Benicia. Tomo V, Vol. 39, Bancroft Library, University of California, Berkeley. C-A 39, pp. 384 ff.

———. N.d. Departmental Records I-III, CA-46. Bancroft Library, University of California, Berkeley.

Atherton, Gertrude. 1893. "The Romance of Fort Ross." In *The Californian Illustrated Magazine,* December 1893, pp. 57–62.

———. 1902. From "Natalie Ivanhoff: A Memory of Fort Ross." In *The Splendid Idle Forties: Stories of Old California.* Illustrations by Harrison Fisher. New York: Frederick A. Stokes Company.

Bancroft, Hubert Howe. 1886. "History of California," Vol. III, 1825–1840. In *The Works of Hubert Howe Bancroft,* Vol. XX. San Francisco: The History Company.

———. 1964. *California Pioneer Register and Index 1542–1800, and List of Pioneers.* Baltimore: Regional Publishing Company.

———. 1966. "History of California," Vols. II, III, and IV. In *The Works of Hubert Howe Bancroft,* Vols. XIX, XX, and XXI. Santa Barbara: Wallace Hebberd.

Baranov, Antipatr. 1815. Excerpt from the travel journal that was created on board the ship *Il'mena*, September 18–October 1 O.S. (September 29–October 12 N.S.). Translated by Irina V. Wender, edited for this collection by Susan Morris and Glenn J. Farris.

Bearne, Colin, transl. 1978. "The Russian Orthodox Religious Mission in America, 1794–1837, with Materials Concerning the Life and Works of the Monk German, and Ethnographic Notes by the Hieromonk Gedeon." Edited by Richard Pierce. In *Materials for the Study of Alaska History* 11. Kingston, Ontario: The Limestone Press.

Beck, Warren A., and Ynez D. Haase. 1974. *Historical Atlas of California*. Norman: University of Oklahoma Press.

Beebe, Rose Marie, and Robert M. Senkewicz. 1996. "The End of the 1824 Chumash Revolt in Alta California: Fr. Vicente Sarría's Account." In *The Americas LIII* (October 1996), pp. 273–283.

Belcher, Edward. 1843. *The Narrative of a Voyage Round the World, performed in Her Majesty's Ship* Sulphur, *during the years 1836–1842*. 2 volumes. London: H. Colburn.

Blackburn, Thomas. 1975. "The Chumash Revolt of 1824: A Native Account." In *The Journal of California Anthropology* 2(2): 223–227.

Blue, George Verne. 1939. "The Report of Captain Laplace on his Voyage to the Northwest Coast and California in 1839." In *California Historical Society Quarterly* 18(4): 315–328.

Brown, Alan K. 1975. "Pomponio's World." In the San Francisco Westerner's *Argonaut* 6.

Callaghan, Catherine A. 1970. "Bodega Miwok Dictionary." In *University of California, Publications in Linguistics* 60. Berkeley, CA.

Chamisso, Adelbert von. 1986. *A Voyage Around the World with the Romanzov Exploring Expedition in the Years 1815–1818 in the Brig* Rurik, *Captain Otto von Kotzebue*. Translated and edited by Henry Kratz. Honolulu: University of Hawaii Press.

Chernykh, E. L. 1967. "Agriculture in Upper California: A Long-Lost Account of Farming in California as Recorded by a Russian Observer at Fort Ross in 1841." Translated by James R. Gibson. In *The Pacific Historian* (winter): 10–28.

Cook, Sherburne F. 1962. "Expeditions to the Interior of California, Central Valley, 1820–1840." In *University of California Anthropological Records* 20(5): 151–213.

Coy, Owen C. 1925. *Pictorial History of California*. Extension Division, University of California, Berkeley.

Dana, Richard Henry, Jr. 1965. *Two Years before the Mast*. New York: Airmont Publishing Company.

Davis, William Heath. 1967. *Seventy-Five Years in California: Recollections and Remarks by One who Visited These Shores in 1831, and Again in 1833, and except when Absent on Business Was a Resident from 1838 until the End of a Long Life in 1909*. Edited by Harold A. Small. San Francisco: John Howell Books.

Dillon, Richard. 1975. *Siskiyou Trail*. New York: McGraw-Hill.

Dmytryshyn, Basil, E. A. P. Crownhart-Vaughan, and Thomas Vaughan. 1988. *Russian Penetration of the North Pacific Ocean*, Vol. 2, 1700–1797. Portland: Oregon Historical Society Press.

Dmytryshyn, Basil, E. A. P. Crownhart-Vaughan, and Thomas Vaughan. 1989. *The Russian American Colonies,* Vol. 3, 1798–1867. Portland: Oregon Historical Society Press.

Duflot de Mofras, Eugene. 1937. *Duflot de Mofras's Travels on the Pacific Coast.* Translated, edited, and annotated by Marguerite Eyer Wilbur. 2 volumes. Santa Ana: Fine Arts Press.

Duhaut-Cilly, Auguste Bernard. 1997. *A Voyage to California, the Sandwich Islands and Around the World in the Years 1826–1829.* Translated and edited by August Frugé and Neal Harlow. Berkeley: University of California Press.

Durán, Fr. Narciso. 1824. "Letter from Fr. Durán to Governor Luis Argüello Dated March 31, 1824." Document No. 2598, Mission Santa Barbara Archive-Library.

Eastwood, Alice. 1944. "The Botanical Collections of Chamisso and Eschscholtz in California." In *Leaflets of Western Botany* IV, pp. 17–32.

Engelhardt, Zephyrin. 1927. *San Fernando Rey: The Mission of the Valley.* Chicago: Franciscan Herald Press.

Farris, Glenn J. 1982. "Aboriginal Use of Pine Nuts in California: An Ethnological, Nutritional, and Archaeological Investigation into the Uses of Seeds of *Pinus lambertiana* Dougl. and *Pinus Sabiniana* Dougl. by the Indians of Northern California. Ph.D. diss. Anthropology Deptartment, University of California, Davis. University Microfilms, Ann Arbor, MI.

———. 1988. "A French Visitor's Description of the Fort Ross Rancheria in 1839." In *News from Native California* 2(3): 22–23.

———. 1989. "Recognizing Indian Folk History as Real History: A Fort Ross Example." In *American Indian Quarterly* 13(4): 471–480.

———. 1992a. "The Day of the Tall Strangers and Other Events at Fort Ross in 1833." In *The Californians* 9(6): 13–19.

———. 1992b. "Life at Fort Ross as the Indians Saw It: Stories from the Kashaya." Paper presented at the annual meeting of the Alaska Anthropological Association, Fairbanks, Alaska, March 28, 1992.

———. 1993a. "Visit of the Russian Warship *Apollo* to California in 1822–1823." Translated from the original French and annotated by Glenn J. Farris. In *Southern California Quarterly* 75(1): 1–13.

———. 1993b. "Talacani, the Man who Purchased Fort Ross." In *Fort Ross Interpretive Association Newsletter,* September/October 1993: unnumbered pages (7–9).

———. 1995. "Don Juan Maria Osuna (1785–1851), Native of San Vicente Ferrer and First Alcalde of the Pueblo of San Diego." In *Estudios Fronterizos: Revista del Instituto de Investigaciones Sociales* 35–36: 43–50.

————. 1996. "How the Muniz Rancho Got Its Name." In *Fort Ross Interpretive Association Newsletter,* July–August 1996: unnumbered pages (4).

————. 1998. "The Bodega Miwok as Seen by Mikhail Tikhonovich Tikhanov in 1818." In *Journal of California and Great Basin Anthropology* 20(1): 2–12.

————. 2001. "California's First Windmills: The Russian Windmills of Fort Ross." Manuscript on file, California Department of Parks and Recreation, Sacramento.

————. 2005. "Extract of the Accounts of the Directors of the Russian American Company for the Two Years Ending the 1st of January, 1842" (*"Extrait Du Compte Rendu de la Direction de la Compagnie Russe-Américaine, pour les deux années terminant le 1er janvier, 1842"*). In *Journal de St. Pétersbourg*, "Supplément d'Intérieur (October 31, 1842). Translated by Glenn J. Farris. In *Fort Ross–Salt Point Newsletter,* n.d. [2005].

————. 2006. *Visit of Cyrille Pierre-Théodore Laplace to Fort Ross and Bodega Bay in August 1839.* Translated and annotated by Glenn J. Farris. Jenner, CA: Fort Ross Interpretive Association.

————. 2007. "Otter Hunting by Alaskan Natives along the California Coast in the Early Nineteenth Century." In *Mains'l Haul: Journal of the Maritime Museum of San Diego* 43(3 and 4): 20–33.

Farris, Glenn J., and John R. Johnson. 1999. "Prominent Indian Families at Mission La Purísima Concepción as Identified in Baptismal, Marriage and Burial Records." California Mission Studies Association, Occasional Paper Number 3, December 1999.

Fedorova, Svetlana G. 1975. "Ethnic Processes in Russian America." Translated by Antoinette Shalkop. Anchorage Historical and Fine Arts Museum, Occasional Paper Number 1.

Flota, D. Ch. 1830. "О Молотильныхъ Машинахъ" ("About Threshing Machines"). In *Zemledelchesky Zhurnal* 29: 264–322.

Geiger, Fr. Maynard. 1969. *Franciscan Missionaries in Spanish California, 1769–1848: A Biographical Dictionary.* San Marino, CA: The Huntington Library.

————. 1970. "Fray Antonio Ripoll's Description of the Chumash Revolt at Santa Bárbara in 1824." Translated and edited by Fr. Maynard Geiger. In *Southern California Quarterly* 52(4): 345–364.

Gibson, James R. 1968. "Two New Chernykh Letters." 2 parts. In *The Pacific Historian* 12(3 and 4): 48–56 and 55–60.

————. 1969. "Russia in California, 1833: Report of Governor Wrangel." In *Pacific Northwest Quarterly* 60(4): 205–215.

————. 1992. *Otter Skins, Boston Ships and China Goods.* Seattle: University of Washington Press.

Golovnin, Vasilii M. 1979. *Around the World on the Kamchatka, 1817–1819*. Translated with an introduction and notes by Ella Lury Wiswell. Honolulu: The Hawaiian Historical Society and the University Press of Hawaii.

Haase, Ynez. 1952. "The Russian American Company in California." M.A. thesis, History Department, University of California, Berkeley.

Hansen, Harvey J., and Jeanne Thurlow Miller. 1962. *Wild Oats in Eden: Sonoma County in the 19th Century.* Santa Rosa, CA: Hooper Printing and Lithograph.

Hatch, Flora Faith. 1922. "The Russian Advance into California." M.A. thesis, History Department, University of California, Berkeley.

Howay, F. W. 1973. "A List of Trading Vessels in the Maritime Fur Trade, 1785–1825." In *Materials for the Study of Alaskan History* 2. Edited by Richard A. Pierce. Kingston, Ontario: The Limestone Press.

Hudson, D. Travis. 1980. "The Chumash Revolt of 1824: Another Native Account from the Notes of John P. Harrington." In *Journal of California and Great Basin Anthropology* 2(1): 123–126.

Istomin, Alexei. 1992. *The Indians at the Ross Settlement according to the Census by Kuskov in 1820 and 1821.* Jenner, CA: Fort Ross Interpretive Association.

Istomin, Alexei A., James R. Gibson, and Valery A. Tishkov. 2005. Россия в Калифорнии (*Russia in California: Russian Documents on Fort Ross and Russian-Californian Relations in 1803–1850*), Vol. 1. Moscow: Nauka.

Ivashintsov, N. A. 1980. *Russian Round-the-World Voyages, 1803–1849, with a Summary of Later Voyages to 1867.* Translated by Glynn R. Barratt, edited by Richard A. Pierce. Kingston, Ontario: The Limestone Press.

Jackson, Robert H. 1983. "Intermarriage at Fort Ross: Evidence from the San Rafael Mission Baptismal Register." In *Journal of California and Great Basin Anthropology* 5(1 and 2): 240 and 241.

Johnson, John R. 1984. "Indian History in the Santa Barbara Back Country." In *Los Padres Notes* 3: 1–24.

Kalani, Lyn, ed. 2011. *Imperial Russia Encounters Colonial California: Impressions and Interactions, 1806–1841.* Compiled and translated by James R. Gibson, and Katherine L. Arndt, Glenn J. Farris, Alexei Istomin, John Middleton, and Alexander Petrov. Unpublished manuscript. Jenner, CA: Fort Ross Interpretive Association.

Kalifornsky, Peter. 1991. *A Dena'ina Legacy, K'Tl'egh'i Sukdu: The Collected Writings of Peter Kalifornsky.* Alaska Native Language Center. Fairbanks: University of Alaska.

Kari, James. 1983. "Kalifornsky, the Californian from Cook Inlet." In *Alaska in Perspective* 5(1): 1–10.

Kelly, Isabel. 1991. *Interviews with Tom Smith and Maria Copa: Isabel Kelly's Ethnographic Notes on the Coast Miwok Indians of Marin and Southern Sonoma Counties, California.* Edited by Mary Collier and Sylvia Thalman. MAPOM Occasional Papers Number 6. San Rafael, CA: Miwok Archaeological Preserve of Marin.

Kennedy, Mary Jean (Aernie). 1955. "Culture Contact and Acculturation of the Southwestern Pomo." Ph.D. diss., Anthropology Department, University of California, Berkeley.

Khlebnikov, Kirill Timofeevich. 1990. *The Khlebnikov Archive: Unpublished Journal (1800–1837) and Travel Notes (1820, 1822 and 1824).* Edited with introduction and notes by Leonid Shur, translated by John Bisk. Anchorage: University of Alaska Press.

———. 1994. *Notes on Russian America: Part I, Novo-Arkhangel'sk.* Compiled with an introduction and commentaries by Svetlana G. Fedorova, translated by Serge LeComte and Richard Pierce, edited by Richard Pierce. Kingston, Ontario: The Limestone Press.

Kostromitinov, Peter. 1980 [1839]. "Observations on the Indians of Upper California." In *Russian America: Statistical and Ethnographic Information, by Rear Admiral Ferdinand Petrovich Wrangell with additional material by Karl-Ernst Baer.* Translated from the German edition of 1839 by Mary Sadouski, edited by Richard A. Pierce. Kingston, Ontario: The Limestone Press.

Kuskov, Ivan A. 1980. "Report to Alexander Baranov" [*"Raport I. A. Kuskova A. A. Baranovu"*]. In *Russia and the USA: The Establishment of Relations, 1765–1815* [*Rossiia i SShA: Stanovlenie otnoshenii, 1765–1815*], doc. no. 304, Moscow, 1980, pages 375–377. Edited by Nikolai Bolkhovitinov. Unpublished English translation by Stephen Watrous. Reprinted by permission of Stephen Watrous.

Langsdorff, Georg H. von. 1927 [1814]. *Langsdorff's Narrative of the Rezanov Voyage to Nueva California in 1806: An English Translation revised, with the Teutonisms of the original Hispaniolized, Russianized, or Anglicized, by Thomas C. Russell.* San Francisco: The Private Press of Thomas C. Russell.

Laplace, Cyrille Pierre-Théodore de. 1841. *Campagne de Circumnavigation de la Frégate l'Artémise pendant les années 1837, 1838, 1839, et 1840 sous le commandement de M. LaPlace, capitaine de vaisseau,* Vol. 1. Paris: Arthus Bertrand, Libraire de la Société de Géographie.

———. 2006. *Visit of Cyrille Pierre-Théodore Laplace to Fort Ross and Bodega Bay in August 1839.* Translated and annotated by Glenn J. Farris. Jenner, CA: Fort Ross Interpretive Association.

Leonard, Zenas. 1978. *Narrative of the Adventures of Zenas Leonard, Written by Himself.* Edited by Milton Quaife. Lincoln: University of Nebraska Press.

Lightfoot, Kent G. 2005. *Indians, Missionaries and Merchants: The Legacy of Colonial Encounters on the California Frontiers.* Berkeley: University of California Press.

Lightfoot, Kent G., Thomas A. Wake, and Ann M. Schiff. 1991. "The Archaeology and Ethnohistory of Fort Ross, California." In *Contributions of the University of California Archaeological Research Facility,* No. 49. Berkeley, CA.

Lütke, Fedor. 1989. "September 4–28, 1818" from "The Diary of Fedor P. Lütke during His Circumnavigation aboard the Sloop *Kamchatka,* 1817–1819: Observations on California." In *The Russian American Colonies: Three Centuries of Russian Eastward Expansion,* Vol. 3, 1798–1867. Edited and translated by Basil Dmytryshyn, E. A. P. Crownhart Vaughan, and Thomas Vaughan. Portland: Oregon Historical Society Press.

Maloney, Alice B. 1943. "Fur Brigade to the Bonaventura: John Work's California Expedition of 1832–33 for the Hudson's Bay Company," part II. In *California Historical Society Quarterly* 22(4): 323–348.

———. 1944. "Fur Brigade to the Bonaventura: John Work's California Expedition of 1832–33 for the Hudson's Bay Company," part III. In *California Historical Society Quarterly* 23(1): 19–40.

Mason, Jack. 1974. "The Solemn Land." In *Point Reyes Light,* July 4, 1974.

Mason, Jack, and Helen Van Cleave Park. 1971. *Early Marin.* Petaluma: House of Printing.

Mathes, W. Michael, ed. 2008. *The Russian-Mexican Frontier: Mexican Documents Regarding the Russian Establishments in California, 1808–1842.* Transcription, translation, and annotation by W. Michael Mathes, with the assistance of Glenn J. Farris. Jenner, CA: Fort Ross Interpretive Association.

Matiushkin, Fyodor F. 1971. "A Journal of a Round-the-World Voyage on the Sloop *Kamchatka,* under the command of Captain Golovinin." In *K beregam Novogo Sveta: Iz neopublikovanykh zapisok russkikh putesheshtvennikov nachala XIX veka ("To the Shores of the New World: From Unpublished Writings of Russian Travellers in the Early Nineteenth Century"),* pp. 66–80. Excerpt on visit to Bodega Bay translated by Stephen Watrous. Moscow: Nauka.

Miller, Robert Ryal. 2001. *A Yankee Smuggler on the Spanish California Coast: George Washington Eayrs and the Ship* Mercury. Santa Barbara: Santa Barbara Trust for Historic Preservation.

Milliken, Randall. 2009. "Ethnohistory and Ethnogeography of the Coast Miwok and Their Neighbors, 1783–1840." Technical paper presented to the National Park Service, Golden Gate National Recreation Area, June 2009.

Mission Santa Barbara Archive-Library. N.d. "Marriage Register of the Mission San Rafael Arcangel." On file at Mission Santa Barbara Archive-Library.

Nikolai Ziorov, Bishop. 1897. "Trip to Fort Ross." In *Orthodox Russian Messenger,* March 2/14, 1897. Translated by Waldemar Aktsinov. Manuscript on file at Fort Ross Visitors Center.

Northrup, Marie E. 1976. *Spanish-Mexican Families in Early California: 1769–1850,* Vol. 1. New Orleans: Polyanthos.

Ogden, Adele. 1941. *The California Sea Otter Trade: 1784–1848.* Berkeley: University of California Press.

———. 1979. *Trading Vessels on the California Coast, 1786–1848.* Typescript at the Bancroft Library, University of California, Berkeley.

Ord, Maria de las Angustias de la Guerra de. 1878. *Ocurrencias en California relatadas á Thomas Savage en Santa Bárbara por Mrs. Ord (D.a Angustias de la Guerra).* Republished in 1956 as *Occurrences in Hispanic California related to Thomas Savage in Santa Barbara by Mrs. Ord, 1878.* Translated and edited by Francis Price and William H. Ellison. Washington, D.C.: Academy of American Franciscan History.

Ordaz, Fr. Blas. 1824. "Letter from Fr. Blas Ordaz to Governor Luis Argüello, dated March 21, 1824." Document 2593, Mission Santa Barbara Archive-Library.

Osborn, Sannie Kenton. 1997. "Death in the Daily Life of the Ross Colony: Mortuary Behavior in Frontier Russian America." Ph.D. diss., Anthropology Department, University of Wisconsin, Milwaukee.

Osio, Antonio María. 1996. *The History of Alta California: A Memoir of Mexican California, by Antonio María Osio.* Translated, edited, and annotated by Rose Marie Beebe and Robert M. Senkewicz. Madison, WI: University of Wisconsin Press.

Oswalt, Robert. 1958. "Russian Loanwords in Southwestern Pomo." In *International Journal of American Linguistics* 24(3): 245–247.

———. 1964. "Kashaya Texts." In *University of California Publications in Linguistics* 36.

———. 1971. "The Case of the Broken Bottle." In *International Journal of American Linguistics* 37(1): 48–49.

———. 1988. "History through the Words Brought to California by the Fort Ross Colony." In *News from Native California* 2(3): 20–22.

Owens, Kenneth N. 1990. "Magnificent Fraud: Ivan Petrov's Docufiction on Russian Fur Hunters and California Missions." In *The Californians* (July/August 1990): 25–29.

———. 2006. "Frontiersman for the Tsar: Timofei Tarakanov and the Expansion of Russian America." In *Montana, the Magazine of Western History* 56(3): 3–21.

Owens, Kenneth N., and Alton S. Donnelly. 1985. *The Wreck of the Sv. Nikolai.* Portland: Western Imprints, the Press of the Oregon Historical Society.

Pauley, Kenneth E., and Carol M. Pauley. 2005. *San Fernando Rey de España: An Illustrated History.* Foreword by Doyce B. Nunis, Jr. Spokane, WA: Arthur H. Clark Company.

Payeras, Mariano. 1822. *Diario de su Caminata con el Comisario del Imperio, Noticias sobre Ross, 1822.* Manuscript at the Bancroft Library, University of California, Berkeley.

———. 1823. "Miscellaneous Notes by Fr. Payeras Regarding the Russians." Document 2350, Mission Santa Barbara Archive-Library.

———. 1995. *Writings of Mariano Payeras.* Translated and annotated by Donald Cutter. Santa Barbara: Bellerophon.

Perissinotto, Giorgio, ed. 1998. *Documenting Everyday Life in Early Spanish California: The Santa Barbara Presidio* Memorias y Facturas, *1779–1810.* Santa Barbara: Santa Barbara Trust for Historical Preservation.

Phelps, William Dane. 1983. *Alta California, 1840–1842.* Introduced and edited by Briton Cooper Busch. Glendale, CA: Arthur H. Clark Company.

Pierce, Richard A. 1990. *Russian America: A Biographical Dictionary.* Kingston, Ontario: The Limestone Press.

Pokriots, Marion D. 1997. "Don José Antonio Bolcoff: Branciforte's Russian Alcalde." In *Santa Cruz County History Journal,* Branciforte Issue: 96–107.

Pourade, Richard F. 1961. *Time of the Bells: The History of San Diego.* San Diego: Union-Tribune Publishing Company.

Quigley, Hugh. 1878. *The Irish Race in California, and on the Pacific Coast.* San Francisco: A. Roman and Co.

Russian American Company Correspondence (RACC). 1818–1867. Records of the Russian American Company, Correspondence of the Governors General, Correspondence Sent. Manuscripts on file, U.S. National Archives, Washington, D.C.

Sandels, G. M. Waseurtz af. 1945. *A Sojourn in California by The King's Orphan: The Travels and Sketches of G. M. Waseurtz af Sandels, a Swedish Gentleman who Visited California in 1842–1843.* Edited with an introduction by Helen Putnam Van Sicklen. San Francisco: Printed at the Grabhorn Press for The Book Club of California in arrangement with The Society of California Pioneers.

Sandos, James. 1987. "*Levantamiento!* The 1824 Chumash Uprising." In *The Californians* 5(1): 8–20.

Señán, José. 1962. *The Letters of José Señán, O.F.M., Mission San Buenaventura, 1796–1823.* Translated by Paul D. Nathan, edited by Lesley Byrd Simpson. San Francisco: John Howell—Books.

Shur, Leonid A., and James R. Gibson. 1973. "Russian Travel Notes and Journals as Sources for The History of California, 1800–1850." In *California Historical Society Quarterly* 52(1): 37–63.

Smith, Barbara Sweetland. 2000. *Science Under Sail: Russia's Great Voyages to America, 1728–1867.* Exhibition catalog. Anchorage: Anchorage Museum of History and Art.

Smith, Janice Christina. 1974. "Pomo and Promyshlenniki: Time and Trade Goods at Fort Ross." M.A. thesis, Anthropology Department, University of California, Los Angeles.

Stickel, E. Gary, and Adrienne E. Cooper. 1969. "The Chumash Revolt of 1824: A Case for an Archaeological Application of Feedback Theory." In *University of California Archaeological Survey Report* 11: 9–21.

Sutter papers (document collection). N.d. "Inventaire des Biens Meubles et Immeubles" ("Inventory of Movable and Fixed Goods Sold the Russian American Company to John Sutter in 1841"). Bancroft Library, University of California, Berkeley.

Tufts, Warren. 1979. *Casey Ruggles.* Nationally syndicated cartoon series, November 20, 1950–February 17, 1951. Reissued by Henry Yeo. Long Beach, CA: Western Wind Productions.

Vallejo, Mariano G. 2000. "Report of a Visit to Fort Ross and Bodega Bay in April 1833 by Mariano G. Vallejo." Translated by Glenn J. Farris and Rose Marie Beebe, and annotated by Glenn J. Farris. Occasional Paper Number 4, California Mission Studies Association.

Van Dorn, A. 1860. "Map of the County of Marin, compiled in 1860." San Rafael: Marin County Historical Society.

Watson, Douglas S., and Thomas Workman Temple II. 1934. *The Spanish Occupation of California: Plan for the Establishment of a Government.* Introduction by Douglas S. Watson. The "Plan" and "Junta" translated by Douglas S. Watson and Thomas Workman Temple II. The "Diario" of Miguel Costansó follows the translation of Frederick J. Teggart. San Francisco: The Grabhorn Press.

Weber, Francis J. 1964. "Historic Mission Bell: Mystery Shrouds Its Past." In *San Fernando Valley Times,* May 9, 1964.

———. 1975. *The Mission in the Valley: A Documentary History of San Fernando, Rey de Espana.* Los Angeles: University of Southern California Libraries.

Wilbur, Marguerite Eyer, trans., ed., and annot. 1937. *Duflot de Mofras's Travels on the Pacific Coast,* by Eugene Duflot de Mofras. 2 volumes. Foreword by Frederick Webb Hodge. Santa Ana: Fine Arts Press.

Wilson, Richa Leann. 1998. "The Rotchev House, Fort Ross, California: A Historic Structure Report." M.A. thesis, Historic Preservation Program, School of Architecture and Allied Arts, University of Oregon.

Wrangell, Ferdinand P. von. 1834. "Report of Governor Wrangell to Head Office, No. 197, dated April 28/May 9, 1834." Records of the Russian-American Company, microfilm roll 36, Washington, D.C. Typescript translation by Oleg Terichow.

———. 1839. *"Statische und etnographische Nachrichten über die Russischen Besitzungen an der Nordwestkuste von Amerika."* In *Beitrage zur Kenntniss des Russischen Reiches und der Angranzenden Lander Asiens.* Edited by K. E. von Baer and Gr. von Helmersen. St. Petersburg, Russia: Buchdruckerei der Kaiserlichen Akademie der Wiessenschaften [Royal Academy of Science Press].

———. 1980. *Russian America: Statistical and Ethnographic Information, by Rear Admiral Ferdinand Petrovich Wrangell with additional material by Karl-Ernst Baer.* Translated from the German edition of 1839 by Mary Sadouski, edited by Richard A. Pierce. Kingston, Ontario: The Limestone Press.

Zavalishin, Dmitry. 1973. "California in 1824." Translated and annotated by James R. Gibson. In *Southern California Quarterly* 55(4): 367–412.

INDEX

Abella, Fr. Ramón, 33

Aesculus Californica (California chestnut), 29

Agave Americana, Linn., 33

Agricultural Journal, 122

Alaskan Historical Society, 318

Alexander I, Czar, 74, 90, 93, 104, 130

Alvarado, Juan Bautista, 269–271, 273, 277–279

Amador, Maria Antonia, 127

Amesti, José, 335

Amorós, Fr. Juan, 336

Angel Island, 276

Argüello, Gervasio, 83, 211

Argüello, José Dario, 17, 26, 31, 318

Argüello, Luis Antonio, 20, 120, 136, 214, 336, 337

Argüello, María Concepción (Concha), 18, 25, 26

Argüello, María Ygnacia Moraga, 26, 31, 32

Arkin, Alan, 1

Arrillaga, José Joaquin de, 17, 18, 20, 23, 46, 61, 82, 334

Astor, John Jacob, 339

Astoria, 339

Atherton, Gertrude, 202, 309, 343

Avacha River (Estero Americano), 167

Ayash Expedition, 229, 231, 233, 339

Babin, Yakov, 15, 16

baidaras (umiaks), 15, 101, 130, 259, 290, 342, 345

baidarkas (kayaks), 12–15, 22, 56, 59, 67, 68, 97, 112, 129, 132, 140, 158, 200, 209, 220–222, 230, 236, 239, 336

barabara, 188, 190, 191

Baranov, Alexander, 4, 10, 13–15, 22, 45, 46, 48, 57, 58, 63, 67, 74, 76, 99, 352

Baranov, Antipatr Alexandrovich, 99, 126, 127

Barber, Henry, 22

Baric, Charles, 275

bathhouse (banya), 77, 158, 287, 337

beaver, 169, 226, 227, 265, 266, 272, 338, 341

Beechey, William, 103

Belcher, Edward, 171

Bell, Mr., 300

bells, 36, 91, 92, 94, 96, 108, 236, 299, 315–319, 321, 322, 335

Benitz, William, 208, 230, 325, 327, 342, 343

Bennett, James, 99

Benzeman, Khristofor Martynovich, 76, 129

Black, Barbara, 327

Blas de Santillanes, Gil, 336

Bodega Corners, 282, 296, 341

Bodega Miwok and Bodegin, 4, 14, 63, 65, 67–69, 72, 183, 184, 322, 334

Bolcoff, José Antonio (a.k.a. Osip Volkov), 90, 92–95, 100, 125, 127, 128, 215, 334, 335

Bolcoff, Terencio, 128, 135

Bonetes Point (see Point Bonita)

"Boston Men," 12

Botta, Paul-Emile, 145, 219, 221, 225

brickmaking and brickworks, 153

Brown, Thomas, 45, 97, 98

Buena Vista Lake, 133, 134

Bulygin, Nikolai, 45, 50–52, 58

CA-Ker-33, 337

Cabo San Pedro, 130, 132

Caigane (Kaigani), 98, 113

California Historic Landmarks League, 325

Call, George Washington, 301, 302, 306, 325, 342, 343

Callao, Peru, 335

Camilo Ynitia, 175

Canton, China, 12, 50, 97

Cape Chacon, 274

Cape Mendocino, 2, 59, 294

Casey Ruggles, 321, 323

Castro, Candida, 125, 127, 335

Castro, José Joaquin, 127

Catalina Island (a.k.a. Ekaterina Island), 130, 132

Catherine II, Empress of Russia, 103

Chamisso, Adelbert von, 4, 145–147, 150–152, 348, 349

chapel at Fort Ross, 154, 158, 166, 200, 219, 223, 236, 246, 259, 287, 299, 301, 321, 322, 325, 326, 329, 338

Charles III, King of Spain, 2, 7

Chavano, Rodivon, 135

Chernykh, Egor (Georgi) Leontievich, 145, 152, 157, 168, 171, 175, 178, 182, 202, 337, 341

Chernykh Ranch, 182, 295, 298, 341

Chinook, 339

Chumash Revolt of 1824, 125, 135, 348

Chunagnak (St. Peter the Aleut), 125, 128, 131, 132

Chwachamaju, 186

clothing and footwear

    boots, 30, 85

    jackets, 62, 85, 187

    overcoats, 85

    shoes, 85, 240

    trousers, 65, 66, 68, 85, 187

    vests, 85, 253, 254

coaks, 172, 174

Coal, Elijah, 126

Cook, James, 251

Cooper, Juan B. R., 169, 226, 333

copper ornaments, 250

Coronado, Francisco Vásquez de, 1

Costansó, Miguel, 9, 10

cradle boards, 230

Creoles, 4, 163, 183

Crespí, Fr. Juan, 3

Croix, Carlos Francisco de, 2, 9

Cruz, José de la, 119

Dabovich, Sebastian, 301

Dana, Richard Henry, Jr., 123

Davidov, Gavriil Ivanovich, 30, 31, 33

Davis, William Heath, Sr., 14

Dawson, James, 276, 278, 279

d'Castro, John Elliot, 99

Decembrist Revolt, 105, 115

Del Valle Ranch, 317, 318

Destruction Island, 45

Dixon, James, 325, 343

Dorofeev, Iakov Dorofeyevich, 214

Drake, Francis, 1, 112

Drake's Bay, 53, 67

droschki, 266, 342

Drushinin, Petr, 126

Dubosc, Pierre, 278, 279

Duflot de Mofras, Eugene, 272, 282, 286, 291, 292, 298, 342,

Duhaut-Cilly, Auguste Bernard, 154, 211, 218, 219, 22, 235

Duncan's Point, 184

Durán, Fr. Narciso, 133, 135, 336, 349

D'Wolf, John, 22

Eastwood, Alice, 145, 146

Eayrs, George Washington, 14, 56

Echeandia, José María, 105, 124

Egorov (Yegorov, Llegoroff), Prokhor, 125, 128, 133–137, 215

Engelhardt, Fr. Zephyrin, 317

Eschscholtz, Johan Friedrich von, 4, 145, 146, 148, 150

Eschscholtzia Californica (California poppy), 146

Estudillo, José Joaquin, 214

Estudillo, José María, 334

Etolin, Arvid, 157, 169, 297

Fabeau de Quesadas, Antonio, 9, 10

Fairfax, Charles, 343

falconets, 23

Farallon Islands (a.k.a. Farallones), 15, 67, 99, 224, 267

Fedorova, Svetlana G., 25, 183, 327, 332

Fernández de San Vicente, Agustín, 65, 12, 155, 213, 214, 217

Fernando VII, King, 339

Figueroa, José, 155, 284, 337, 339, 341

Fitch, Henry Delano, 258, 335

Flat, Mr., 172

flora and fauna named for Russian explorers, 152

Forest Depths (*qhale silil*), 198

Fort Ross State Historic Park, 327

Fort Vancouver, 168, 226, 227, 274, 338, 339

Fortuny, Fr. Buenaventura, 336

Fox Islanders, 59

French Camp (*Campo de los Franceses*), 227

fur seals, 3, 15, 46, 56, 59, 162, 166, 167, 274

Gálvez, Joseph de, 2, 9, 10

Garcia, Rafael, 276, 293, 294

Gibson, James R., 12, 327, 328, 329, 331, 332

Gil y Taboada, Fr. Luís Gonzaga, 90, 99, 127

Gilzen, K. K., 294

Goat Rock, 339

goats, wild (i.e., mule deer), 69, 143, 187, 188

Golovnin, Vasilii, 45, 68–71, 178, 211, 334

Gray's Harbor, Washington, 45, 51, 58

Grepachevsky, Paul, 301, 305

Grimaldi, Marqués de, 9

Grudinin, Vasilii, 214

Gualala River, 338

Gualinela (see Valli:éla)

Guilbert, Mathieu, 339

Gutenop brothers, 173

Gutiérrez, Nicolás, 337

Haase, Ynez, 327

Hagemeister, Leontii, 74, 132, 334

Harriman, Alice, 315–319

Harrington, Marie T. Walsh, 315

Hartnell, William Edward Petty, 89, 92, 154, 169, 226

Hatch, Flora Faith, 327

Hawaii, 67, 98, 100, 154, 219

Hearst, William Randolph, 325

Herman, Fr., 132

Hudson's Bay Company, 182, 226, 230, 268–270, 273, 274, 278, 281, 282, 338, 339, 341

Huymenes, 46, 61

Illueca, José Ignacio Garcia, 217, 339

Illyashevich, V. Llvovich, 157, 337

Il'men Island (Santa Rosa Island), 99, 129

Imperial Moscow Agricultural Society, 160

Institute of Ethnography, Russian Academy of Sciences, 295

Ióllo, Chief, 65, 68, 69, 72, 334

Irkutsk, 282

isba, 282, 291, 342

Iturbide, Agustín, 104, 106, 127, 213, 336

Ivanhoff, Natalie, 309, 311, 312

Jaime, 136

James, Herman, 197, 198, 200, 202, 204, 205, 208, 229, 230, 233, 309, 332, 343,

Joasaphat, Archimandrite, 318

Johnson, John, 138

José, 278

Kaigani, 98

Kainama, 186

Kajatschin, 192

Kalifornsky, Nikolai, 184, 328

Kalifornsky, Peter, 184, 328

Kall, Alexis, 318

Kamchatka, 31, 42, 43, 78, 104, 126, 142, 171, 242, 247

Kanakas, 123

Kashevarov, A. P., 318

Kegli (Kyglai, Kykhlai), 125, 128, 129

Kenai Peninsula, Alaska, 183, 328

Kern River, 137

Khlebnikov, Kirill Timofeevich, 4, 73, 88–92, 96, 101, 123, 128, 133, 135, 153, 213–215, 316, 335, 337

Khvostov, Nikolai Aleksandrovich, 18, 31, 33

Kilvain (Kilby), Thomas, 23

Kimball, Oliver, 13, 14, 23, 48, 52, 54, 66, 68

Kit Fox, 321, 322

Klimovskii, Afanasii, 126

Knowland, Joseph R., Sr., 325

Kolosh, 162, 170, 190

Korean War, 321

Kornilov, Stepan, 339

Kostromitinov, Peter, 143, 154, 157, 167, 168, 183, 184, 186, 226, 227, 269–271, 340

Kostromitinov Ranch, 141, 272, 286, 289, 298

Kotzebue, Otto von, 100, 132, 145, 146, 148, 153, 154, 211, 339

Krusenstern, Ivan Fedorovich, 30

Kuskov, Ivan Aleksandrovich, 4, 15, 16, 45, 46, 48, 49, 58, 60, 61, 63, 66–68, 75, 76, 78–84, 101, 129, 154, 183, 213, 216, 328, 333, 339, 340, 342

Laframboise, Michel, 226–228, 338

Landaeta, Fr. Martín, 32, 33, 38

Langsdorff, Georg Heinrich von, 17, 18, 25, 26, 28, 29, 39, 334

La Pérouse, Jean François Galaup de, 277

Laplace, Cyrille Theodore, 103, 184, 187, 188, 202, 211, 212, 235, 237, 238, 249, 256, 268, 339–341

La Push, Washington, 45

Latuk, 189

Lazarev, Mikhail Petrovich, 115, 119

Leese, Jacob, 270

Leonard, Zenas, 138

Lerman, J. J., 325

Lesage, Alain-René, 336

Lisiansky, Yuri Fedorovich, 30

Lithocarpus densiflora (tanbark oak), 340

"Lone Woman of San Nicolas Island," 16

Loreto, Baja California, 3

Los Angeles, 13, 15, 276, 317, 318, 339

Lukaria (Lukaria Yorgen Myers, a.k.a. Lucaria, Lukeria, Caria), 185, 197, 200, 202, 229, 301, 306, 307, 309, 310, 343

Lütke, Fedor, 70, 185

Lutkovsky, Feopempt, 118

Lyman, George, 98

Lyman, Theodore, 97, 98

MacKay, Alexander, 273

Macorio, Ana, 126

Makamov, 192

Malaspina, Alessandro, 103

Manila galleons, 1, 2

Mannerheim, Carl Gustav von, 152

Marin Miwok, 63

Mark West Creek, 141

Martcob Monastery, 305

Martin, John, 276

Matiushkin, Fyodor F., 71, 72

McIntosh, Edward, 276, 278, 279

McKenzie, John C., 326, 327

McLeod, Alexander, 341

Mendocino, Cape, 2, 59, 294

Métini, 68, 197–200, 202, 208, 230–233, 340

Mexican Revolution, 18, 134

Mid-Winter Fair, San Francisco, 301

Mikhailof, Alexis, 309, 312, 313

missions

    Carmel (San Carlos Borromeo), 91

    La Purísima Concepción, 91, 99, 126, 128, 133–136

    Rosario (Baja California), 13

    San Buenaventura, 41

    San Fernando Rey de España, 315, 316

    San Francisco de Asís, 18, 32, 115, 116

    San Francisco Solano de Sonoma, 169, 270, 278, 325

    San Gabriel, 130

    San José, 18, 28, 30, 35, 61, 110, 125, 136, 137, 215, 297, 317, 336, 339

    San Luis Obispo, 14, 90, 95

    San Rafael, 14, 63, 65, 66, 69, 73, 91, 111, 148, 276, 281, 303, 336

    Santa Clara de Asís, 34, 35, 106, 109, 148

    Santa Cruz, 90, 91, 93, 95, 96, 119, 125, 128, 316, 335

    Santo Domingo (Baja California), 13

    Soledad, 127

Mitochea (Pelican Island), 137

Moliavin, 339

Molino, El, 141, 337

Monroe Doctrine, 104

Monterey, 2, 3, 8, 17, 19, 20, 30, 32, 34, 42, 43, 82, 93, 99, 100, 106, 107, 109, 121, 125–128, 131, 170, 213–21, 225, 226, 268, 269, 271, 275, 276, 278, 279, 335, 337, 341, 342

Moraga, Gabriel, 78, 82, 83, 211, 334

Moscow Agricultural School, 160, 171

Mt. Fairweather, 274

Muniz Ranch, 5

Muravyov, Matvei, 135

Museum of Anthropology and Ethnology (Kunstkamera), 293

National Endowment for the Humanities, 328, 331

New Archangel (Sitka), 2, 4, 15, 16, 46, 48, 58, 67, 68, 74, 84, 97, 99, 101, 104, 127, 128, 134, 168, 217, 240, 247, 252, 256, 262, 265, 268, 269, 273, 274, 284, 327

New Helvetia (Sutter's Fort), 171, 182, 270–272, 295, 342

New York Company, 266

Nikolai, Bishop, 301, 302

Nova Albion, 1

Nueva Galicia, Kingdom of, 9

Oahu Coffee House, 123

oats, wild, 159, 189, 299

obsidian, 39

O'Cain, Joseph, 12, 13, 22, 50

Ogden, Adele, 332

Okhotsk, 42, 50, 142

Olamentke, 186

"Olfama" (see also José María Ortega), 126

Onalaska, 62, 78

Ordaz, Fr. Blas, 134, 136

organ, 84, 85, 94

Oriolus phoenicearis (oriole), 40

Ortega, José María, 99, 126

Orthodox American Messenger, 301

Osio, Antonio María, 88, 275, 276

Osuna, Juan María, 13

Oswalt, Robert, 184, 185, 229, 230, 309, 332, 338

Otaheiti (Tahiti), 274

otter skins, 12–15, 39, 226

ovens, bread, 104, 289

Owens, Kenneth N., 332, 334

Pacific Fur Company, 339

Pánac:úccux, 65, 68

Paneheda, 305

Paraskeva, 338

Parrish, Essie, 197, 207, 229, 230, 231, 332

Parrish, Otis, 207

partridge, California (*Tetraonis cristati*), 40

Payeras, Fr. Mariano, 14, 63, 65, 66, 68, 126–128, 133–136, 212–214, 337, 339

Perkins Brothers (James and Thomas Handasyd), 98

Permitin, Vasilii, 164, 165, 338

Petropavlovsk, Kamchatka, 126

Petrov, Ivan, 63, 333, 335

Petrovna, Praskovya, 335

Phelps, William Dane, 342

phthisis, 248

piano-forte, 304

Pierce, Richard A., 332, 337

pinole, 201

Pinus lambertiana (sugar pine), 340

plants near the Presidio of San Francisco, 149, 151

Point Arena, 101, 127

Point Bonita, 46, 62

Point Conception, 126

Point Reyes, 62, 112, 148, 275

Point Wales, 274

Pomo, 4, 68, 74, 183, 322, 334, 340

Pomponio, 115, 118, 119, 137, 337

Pope, Alexander, 110, 336

poppy, California (*Eschscholtzia californica*), 4, 145, 150

Port Jackson, Sydney, Australia, 104

Port Rumiantsev (Bodega Bay), 65, 69, 282, 293, 336

Port San Luis, 14

Portolá, Gaspar de, 3

Presidio of Monterey, 34, 133, 336

Presidio of San Diego, 12, 34

Presidio of San Francisco, 3, 34, 46, 59, 104, 115, 120, 145, 154, 213, 281, 321, 322

Presidio of Santa Bárbara, 34, 99, 318, 319

Prokofyev, Mikhail, 335

Prudon (Prudhon), Victor, 275

Quijano, Manuel, 336

Rancho Camulos, 315

Rancho Los Tres Amigos, 339

Rancho Nuestra Señora del Refugio, 99, 126

Rancho Olompali, 175

Rancho San Emigdio, 133, 136

Rancho Tamales y Baulenes, 293

Revillagigedo, Conde de, 11

Rezanov, Nikolai, 3, 17–20, 23–28, 30–33, 41, 42, 55, 57, 61, 217, 315, 316, 318

Richardson, William, 276, 295

Richardson Bay, 46, 61

Rio Vista, 148

Rivera (Ribero) Cordero, Manuel, 8

Rochefoucauld, François duc de la, 110, 336

Rodriguez, Corporal, 128

Rokitiansky, Nicolas, 327

Rosanov, Lieutenant, 3

Rotchev, Alexander, 168, 202, 211, 235, 239–241, 243, 245, 246, 249, 250, 252, 256, 260–262, 264–272, 278, 282, 309, 322, 329, 339, 340, 342, 343

Rotchev, Helena Gagarina, 247, 259, 309, 311

Rufino, 65, 69

Ruiz, José Manuel, 12

Rumiantsev, Nikolai Petrovich, 18, 20, 24, 42

Russian Orthodox Church, 326

Russian River (a.k.a. Slavianka, Sacabaya River, Shabaicai), 5, 75, 76, 140, 141, 157, 167, 169, 183, 186, 192, 221, 222, 227, 230, 243, 259, 289, 298, 303, 336

Russian State Naval Archives, 338, 339

rye, wild, 189

Sagimomatsse, Andres, 136

Sakovich, Fr. Vladimir, 326

salt, 37, 87, 108, 142, 161, 164, 240, 248, 268

Sanak, 50

San Blas, 2, 7–10, 23, 34, 213, 240

San Clemente Island, 100

San Diego: bay, 3, 34, 43, 105, 123, 127, 175; pueblo, 12, 23, 334

San Fernando, College of (Mexico), 41

San Ignacio River, 278

San Joaquin, El Fuerte de (San Francisco), 29

San Juan Francisco Regis, Estero de, 65

San Nicolas Island, 129

San Pedro, 13, 99, 100, 125, 128–132

San Quintin Bay, 12, 13

Sandels, Gustav Waseurtz af, 296, 299, 300, 342

Santa Rosa Island, 100

Sapoknikoff, 319

Sarría, Fr. Vicente, 91, 127

Schabelski, Achille, 104, 106, 211, 336, 337

Schlechtendal, D. F. L. von, 147

Schmidt, Karl, 65, 153, 154, 213, 214, 216

Scottish thresher, 172, 173, 202, 337

sea lions, 15, 80, 152, 201, 217

Sebastopol, California, 5

Señan, Fr. José, 18, 41

Senen, 137, 337

Sequoia sempervirens (coast redwood), 340

Serra, Fr. Junípero, 3, 7

Severnovskie, 186

Shelekhov, Paul (Pavel Ivanovich), 154, 219–222, 224, 225

Shelikov, Grigori, 17

shipbuilding, 153, 338

ships

  Aleksandr, 50

  Apollon, 3, 104, 105, 114, 117, 335, 338

  Aréthuse, 218

Artémise, 235, 237, 242, 259, 260, 277

Atahualpa, 99, 335

Baikal, 123, 157, 337

Blagonamerenny, 103, 121

Chirikov, 15, 66, 68, 75, 76

Constantin, 270, 271, 282

Derby, 99

Enterprise (a.k.a. *Predpriatie*), 103, 145, 148

Fulham, 335

George Henry (a.k.a. *George and Henry, Jorge Enrique*), 300, 342

Golovnin, 135

Hamilton, 98

Hélène, 269, 271

Héros, 218

Il'mena (formerly the *Lydia*), 15, 99–101, 126, 127

Isabella, 67

Juno, 3, 17, 18, 20, 31, 318

Kadiak, 15, 45

Kamchatka, 70–72, 103

Kreiser, 103–105, 114, 115, 117

Kutusov, 103

Kyakhta, 335

Ladoga, 103, 104, 114, 117

Lydia (renamed the *Il'mena*), 15, 97–99, 335

Mercury, 14, 15, 333

Mirt Kadiak (*Myrtle-Kodiak*) 49, 51, 52

Nadeschda, 30

Neva, 30, 50

Nymph, 268

O'Cain, 3, 13

Okhotsk, 123

Otkrytie, 103

Peacock (ship), 13, 23, 45 58, 68

Predpriatie (see *Enterprise*)

Rurik (Ryurik), 100, 103, 145–147, 150

St. Nikolai, 45, 67, 98

Sulphur, 171

Urup, 169

Vénus, 277

Shohka, 205, 206, 338

Short, Fr. Patrick, 277

Shur, Leonid, 294, 295, 332

Shushkov, Dmitrii, 126

Shvetsov, Afanasii, 12, 13, 55, 56

Simpson, George, 273, 274

Sitka (see New Archangel)

Slobodchikov, Sysoi, 13, 45, 51, 52, 54, 59, 76

Smith, Jedediah, 226

Smith, Stephen, 297

Snook, Joseph, 276

soap plant, 142

Society of California Pioneers, 296

Sokolov, Fedor, 126

Sola, Pablo Vicente de, 100, 125, 127, 128, 151

Stafford, Mercedes Call, 327

Starkovskii, Vasilii, 214

Stewart's Point, 184

Stroganov, Grigori, 42

Sutter, John, 268, 270–275, 279, 282, 284–286, 290, 295, 299, 301, 321, 341–343

Svin'in, Fedor, 214

syphilis, 195, 255

Tamkan, 38

Tana'ina, 183, 184, 328

tarweed (*Madia elegans,* a.k.a. *Latuk*), 189, 338

Tarakanov, Timofei, 12–14, 45, 46, 48, 50, 52–54, 63, 66–68, 98, 333–335

Tarakanov, Vasilii Petrovich, 63

Tarasov, Boris, 99, 128–131

Thompson, Alpheus, 48, 72, 276

threshers: Chaplygin and Makhov, 160; Scottish, 172, 173, 202, 337

Tikhanov, Mikhail Tikhonovich, 338

Tiutuye, 73

Tlingits, 162, 170, 256

Tomlin, F. Kaye, 152

Tomsk, 338

Toribio, 73

trade goods and supplies

  barley, 38, 87, 159, 160, 164, 181

  beaver, 81, 169, 226, 227, 265, 266, 272, 338, 341

  beef, 142, 161

  beeswax, 91, 92, 94

  blankets: wool, 108; flannel, 164

  braid, 94

  broadcloth, 142, 165

  brocade, 92, 94, 96

  buckwheat, 159

  calico, 164

  candles, 96, 164, 306

  candlesticks, 96

  cannons, 75, 80, 84, 109, 121, 158, 216, 321

  cheese, 92

  chocolate, 33, 34, 37, 117

  chimney flues, 85

  coffee pot, 92

  door accessories, 85

  flags, 86

  flax, 159

  garbanzo beans, 179

  gingham, 165

  glassware, 85

  goats, 42, 161

  grapeshot, 84

  hats, 86

  hazel nuts, 94

  hides, 15, 37, 87, 153, 240, 250, 272, 275, 287

  icons, church, 86, 129

  irons, 95

  iron-heaters, 85

lanterns, 96

lard, 41, 136, 164, 181

linen, 34, 85, 164

locks, 84, 85, 95, 304

maize, 38, 178, 179, 181

mirrors, 84, 85, 195

molasses, 57

nails, 85, 96

needles, 93

padlocks, 96

pears, 94, 180, 263, 288, 300

peas, 36–38, 179, 181, 265, 272, 297

pewterware, 84, 85

pigs, 161, 247, 287

pipes (smoking), 92, 95, 189

pistols, 84, 111, 116

plates, 84, 85

powder cartridges, 84

rifles, 77, 84, 265

rope, 142, 288

rye, 87, 159

sabers, 80, 84, 131, 306

sailcloth, 93

sayasaya nacar, 92, 335

scissors, 96

sheep, 32, 36, 42, 161, 265, 287, 292

sheepskins, 164

shoes, 85, 99, 240

sickles, 85, 172, 176

snuff box, 90, 92, 93

spears, 84, 192

spoons (iron and pewter), 85, 108

still (for distilling spirits), 93

stockings (silk, worsted, cotton), 86, 99, 164

sugar, 34, 66, 92, 94, 164

swords, 84

taffeta, 92

tallow, 37, 41, 87, 136, 161, 164, 272, 276

tea, 37, 95, 164

teapots, 84, 85

ticking, 164

tobacco, 95, 164, 189, 257, 258, 272, 289, 290, 338

tongue (beef), 92, 94

treacle, 164

trousers, 65, 66, 68, 85, 187

velvet, 96

wagon parts, 90

wheat, 18, 38, 55, 87, 88, 95, 108, 136, 143, 144, 158–160, 163, 164, 172–174, 177–181, 200, 223, 224, 230, 251, 266, 272–274, 278, 287–291, 299, 300

wheels, 144, 162, 172, 176

wicks, 84

travois, 231

tribes near Port Bodega (Estero, Tuiban and Tabin), 38

Trinidad Bay, 15, 45, 51, 54, 58, 59, 170

Tscholban, 38

Tufts, Warren, 321–323

Tuliatelivy Bay, 58, 59

Ukase of 1821, 104

Unalaska, 15, 22, 61, 62, 78

"undersea people," 200, 201, 206–209, 230, 233, 234

Uria, Fr. Antonio, 30, 32, 33

Valli:éla (a.k.a. Valenila, Wallin-éla, Vallinela, Vallenoela, Gualinela), 69, 73, 322

Valle, Antonio del, 213, 214

Vallejo, Mariano Guadalupe, 73, 154, 155, 184, 212, 270, 278, 279, 282, 286

Vallejo de Amestí, María Prudenciana, 335

Valparaiso, Chile, 274

Vancouver, Fort, 168, 226, 227, 274, 338, 339

Vancouver, George, 51, 103, 110, 235, 319, 336

Veniaminov, Fr. Innocent, 328

Veniaminov, Fr. Vladímir (later Bishop Innocent), 155, 211,328, 342

Vera Cruz, Mexico, 27, 34, 127

Vicente, 65

Vila, Vicente, 9, 10

Villa de Branciforte, 128

Viñals, Fr. José, 41

Vioget, J. J., 295, 300

Virgin of Guadalupe, 33

Vizcaíno, Sebastian de, 1, 2

Vladimir, Bishop, 301, 302

Volkov, Osip (see José Antonio Bolcoff)

Volkov, Fr. Yakov, 126

Wadsworth, William (Vozdvit), 99, 126

Walker, Joseph, 138, 226

Whaler's Harbor, 275

Willamette River, 277

windmill, 154, 158, 171, 202, 236, 259, 288, 290, 299, 310, 311, 340

Winship, Jonathan, 13

Work, John, 154, 168, 226, 227, 231, 338

Wrangell, Baron Ferdinand Petrovich von, 141, 154, 156, 157, 168, 170, 184, 186, 211, 269, 273

Yanovskii (Ianovskii), Semen Ivanovich, 101

Yakutat Bay, 53

Yerba Buena (San Francisco), 270, 275, 295

Young, Ewing, 154, 169, 226

Zavalishin, Dmitry Irinarkhovich, 105, 114, 115, 120, 337

Ziorov, Nikolai, 301

ABOUT THE AUTHOR

GLENN J. FARRIS was born into an army family during World War II and spent his early childhood moving every two to three years, which included a stint in France, where he learned the language. Following graduation from Georgetown University he spent three years as an officer in the army, mostly in East Asia. Following his last assignment, in Vietnam, Farris traveled back home over the course of two and a half years, slowly circumnavigating the globe, and taking the opportunity to do archaeology work in Israel and Norway.

After a decent interval of visiting family in Florida, Farris then forsook his East Coast roots to come West, living in San Francisco, Berkeley, and finally Davis, where he entered graduate studies in anthropology (archaeology) and received his Ph.D. in 1982. In the meantime, he began working for the California Department of Parks and Recreation as an archaeologist in 1978, eventually reaching the level of Senior State Archaeologist. His archaeological fieldwork extended the length and breadth of the state, but his special interests were Fort Ross and Spanish/Mexican mission sites. As a historical archaeologist, Farris developed a deep interest in the documentary record and has spent many happy hours in repositories such as the Bancroft Library, the California State Library, the Mission Santa Barbara Archive-Library, the Huntington Library, and the San Diego Historical Society Archives, seeking out new sources of information to better understand the archaeological finds of whatever project he is engaged in. Whenever possible, Farris develops his findings into articles or books for broader distribution.

Having retired from California State Parks in 2008, Farris currently works as a consultant. He was elected as a board member for the Fort Ross Interpretive Association, and his broad general background in the history of Russians in California led to his being asked to prepare this current anthology. Farris enjoys life in the university town of Davis with his wife, India, and two teenage daughters, Ariane and Mariah.

A California Legacy Book

Santa Clara University and Heyday are pleased to publish the California Legacy series, vibrant and relevant writings drawn from California's past and present.

Santa Clara University—founded in 1851 on the site of the eighth of California's original twenty-one missions—is the oldest institution of higher learning in the state. A Jesuit institution, it is particularly aware of its contribution to California's cultural heritage and its responsibility to preserve and celebrate that heritage.

Heyday, founded in 1974, specializes in critically acclaimed books on California literature, history, natural history, and ethnic studies.

Books in the California Legacy series appear as anthologies, single author collections, reprints of important books, and original works. Taken together, these volumes bring readers a new perspective on California's cultural life, a perspective that honors diversity and finds great pleasure in the eloquence of human expression.

Series editor: Terry Beers

Publisher: Malcolm Margolin

Advisory committee: Stephen Becker, William Deverell, Charles Faulhaber, David Fine, Steven Gilbar, Ron Hansen, Gerald Haslam, Robert Hass, Jack Hicks, Timothy Hodson, Jeanne Wakatsuki Houston, Maxine Hong Kingston, Frank LaPena, Ursula K. Le Guin, Jeff Lustig, Ishmael Reed, Alan Rosenus, Robert Senkewicz, Gary Snyder, Kevin Starr, Richard Walker, Alice Waters, Jennifer Watts, Al Young.

Thanks to the English Department at Santa Clara University and to Regis McKenna for their support of the California Legacy series.

For more on California Legacy titles, events, or other information,
please visit www.californialegacy.org.

Other California Legacy Books

The Anza Trail and the Settling of California
Vladimir Guerrero

Black California: A Literary Anthology
Edited by Aparajita Nanda, Foreword by Ula Y. Taylor

Death Valley in '49
William Lewis Manly

Eldorado: Adventures in the Path of Empire
Bayard Taylor

Gunfight at Mussel Slough: Evolution of a Western Myth
Edited by Terry Beers

Lands of Promise and Despair: Chronicles of Early California, 1535-1846
Edited by Rose Marie Beebe and Robert M. Senkewicz

Life in a California Mission: Monterey in 1786
Jean François de la Pérouse, Introduction by Malcolm Margolin

The Marine Mammals of the Northwestern Coast of North America
Charles Melville Scammon, Foreword by Dick Russell

No Place for a Puritan: The Literature of California's Deserts
Edited by Ruth Nolan

A Yankee in Mexican California
Richard Henry Dana Jr., Foreword by John Seibert Farnsworth

HEYDAY
into California

About Heyday

Heyday is an independent, nonprofit publisher and unique cultural institution. We promote widespread awareness and celebration of California's many cultures, landscapes, and boundary-breaking ideas. Through our well-crafted books, public events, and innovative outreach programs we are building a vibrant community of readers, writers, and thinkers.

Thank You

It takes the collective effort of many to create a thriving literary culture. We are thankful to all the thoughtful people we have the privilege to engage with. Cheers to our writers, artists, editors, storytellers, designers, printers, bookstores, critics, cultural organizations, readers, and book lovers everywhere!

We are especially grateful for the generous funding we've received for our publications and programs during the past year from foundations and hundreds of individual donors. Major supporters include:

Acorn Naturalists; Alliance for California Traditional Artists; Anonymous; James J. Baechle; Bay Tree Fund; S. D. Bechtel Jr., Foundation; Barbara Jean and Fred Berensmeier; Joan Berman; Buena Vista Rancheria; Lewis and Sheana Butler; California Civil Liberties Public Education Program, California State Library; California Council for the Humanities; The Keith Campbell Foundation; Center for California Studies; Jon Christensen; The Christensen Fund; Berkeley Civic Arts Program and Civic Arts Commission; Compton Foundation; Lawrence Crooks; Nik Dehejia; Frances Dinkelspiel and Gary Wayne; Troy Duster; Euclid Fund at the East Bay Community Foundation; Mark and Tracy Ferron; Judith Flanders; Karyn and Geoffrey Flynn; Furthur Foundation; The Fred Gellert Family Foundation; Wallace Alexander Gerbode Foundation; Nicola W. Gordon; Wanda Lee Graves and Stephen Duscha; Alice Guild; Walter & Elise Haas Fund; Coke and James Hallowell; Hawaii Sons, Inc.; Sandra and Charles Hobson; G. Scott Hong Charitable Trust; Humboldt Area Foundation; The James Irvine Foundation; Kendeda Fund; Marty and Pamela Krasney; Kathy Kwan and Robert Eustace; Guy Lampard and Suzanne Badenhoop; LEF Foundation; Judith and Brad Lowry-Croul; Kermit Lynch Wine Merchant; Michael McCone; Michael Mitrani; Michael J. Moratto, in memory of Ernest L. Cassel; National Wildlife Federation; Steven Nightingale; Pacific Legacy, Inc.; Patagonia, Inc.; John and Frances Raeside; Redwoods Abbey; Robin Ridder; Alan Rosenus; The San Francisco Foundation; San Manuel Band of Mission Indians; Sonoma Land Trust; Martha Stanley; Roselyne Chroman Swig; Thendara Foundation; Sedge Thomson and Sylvia Brownrigg; Tides Foundation; TomKat Charitable Trust; The Roger J. and Madeleine Traynor Foundation; Marion Weber; White Pine Press; John Wiley & Sons, Inc.; The Dean Witter Foundation; Lisa Van Cleef and Mark Gunson; Bobby Winston; and Yocha Dehe Wintun Nation.

Board of Directors

Getting Involved

To learn more about our publications, events, membership club, and other ways you can participate, please visit www.heydaybooks.com.